Citizens of the Whole World

Anti-Zionism and the Cultures
of the American Jewish Left

Benjamin Balthaser

VERSO
London • New York

First published by Verso 2025
© Benjamin Balthaser 2025

The manufacturer's authorized representative in the EU for product safety (GPSR) is LOGOS EUROPE, 9 rue Nicolas Poussin, 17000, La Rochelle, France
contact@logoseurope.eu

All rights reserved

The moral rights of the author have been asserted

1 3 5 7 9 10 8 6 4 2

Verso
UK: 6 Meard Street, London W1F 0EG
US: 207 East 32nd Street, New York, NY 10016
versobooks.com

Verso is the imprint of New Left Books

ISBN-13: 978-1-80429-137-5
ISBN-13: 978-1-80429-138-2 (UK EBK)
ISBN-13: 978-1-80429-139-9 (US EBK)

British Library Cataloguing in Publication Data
A catalogue record for this book is available from the British Library

Library of Congress Cataloging-in-Publication Data

Names: Balthaser, Benjamin author
Title: Citizens of the whole world : anti-Zionism and the cultures of the American Jewish left / Benjamin Balthaser.
Description: New York : Verso, 2025. | Includes bibliographical references and index.
Identifiers: LCCN 2025007323 (print) | LCCN 2025007324 (ebook) | ISBN 9781804291375 hardback | ISBN 9781804291399 ebook
Subjects: LCSH: Jews, American—Cultural assimilation | Jews—United States—Attitudes toward Israel | Radicalism—United States—History | Social justice—Religious aspects—Judaism | Left-wing extremists—United States | Progressivism (United States politics)—History | Zionism—United States—History
Classification: LCC E184.35 .B35 2025 (print) | LCC E184.35 (ebook) | DDC 305.892/4073—dc23/eng/20250326
LC record available at https://lccn.loc.gov/2025007323
LC ebook record available at https://lccn.loc.gov/2025007324

Typeset in Minion by Hewer Text UK Ltd, Edinburgh
Printed and bound by CPI Group (UK) Ltd, Croydon CR0 4YY

Contents

Introduction: The American Jewish Left in the Shadow of Zion   1

1 When Anti-Zionism Was Jewish: Jewish Racial Subjectivity and the Anti-imperialist Literary Left from the Great Depression to the Cold War   50

2 Not Your Good Germans: Holocaust Memory, Red Scare Anti-fascism, and the Anti-Zionism of the Jewish New Left   71

3 Exceptional Whites, Bad Jews: Class, Whiteness, and the Racial Politics of the Anti-Zionist Jewish New Left   125

4 A Kesher with the Left: Jewish Identity Politics and the Remaking of a Diasporic Left, 1970–1980   157

5 The Antinomies of Jewish Liberalism: Socialist Memory and the (Re)Emergence of Jewish Anti-Zionism   219

Acknowledgments   273
Notes   277
Index   307

Introduction: The American Jewish Left in the Shadow of Zion

You're an alien in Israel because you are a citizen of the whole damn world.

—Robert Gessner, "The Volunteer"[1]

What is there to SAY about Jews in progressive movements? That there were a lot of them? That now there are less?
I say this to Vivian in my fantasy, and in my fantasy she looks at me, eye to eye, and says, Them, Fran? a lot of them?

—Melanie Kaye/Kantrowitz, "Some Pieces of Jewish Left: 1987"[2]

The sight of thousands of Jewish protesters descending on Grand Central Terminal to drop a banner reading "Never Again for Anyone" during Israel's 2023 invasion of Gaza for many seemed to have exploded out of nowhere. In an era marked by what neoconservative editor Norman Podhoretz described as the "mass conversion of Jews to Zionism" such apostasy taking place in public—and countless similar protests in train stations, Israeli embassies, the Capitol Rotunda, and on college campuses—suggested that the heretics had taken over the temple.[3] Jews who participate in such protests must be led astray by a "scam" or the "woke mob" according to one right-wing Jewish newspaper.[4] Will Alden, taking a more positive spin in the *Nation*, also seemed struck by the protests' novelty, arguing, "A new Jewishness is being born before our eyes."[5] Yet for others, the sight of Jewish protesters holding a Passover seder at Columbia University in protest—shortly before a violent police crackdown—seemed a kind of déjà vu, history repeating itself in uncanny ways. After all, the Students for a Democratic Society (SDS) chapter that co-led the student takeover of Columbia in 1968 was, in the words of Mark Rudd, "as much a Jewish fraternity as Sammie." As student encampments against a genocide echoed the 1968 occupations, they also formed a striking parallel with an even earlier moment in left-wing history. The 1936 American Student Union strike "against war and fascism" also prominently featured Jewish students, especially at CUNY and the UC systems, who keenly felt that fascism at home and abroad called them forth. From this perspective, then, what we are witnessing is less a break than a continuity.

Of course, differences are hard to miss. The student protesters at the 1968 Columbia sit-in did not hold a seder in public. While the lack of Jewish identification in the New Left of the 1960s has been overstated—Abbie Hoffman recounts winking at Rudd while both were in jail as "a member in good standing of the International Jewish Conspiracy"—Jewish cultural identity was not a public display.[6] When Rudd, the SDS campus leader, cooked matzo ball soup for his comrades, he did this in his small apartment, not in public. And as my own grandfather related to me, in his Philadelphia chapter of the Communist Party, they nominated the only gentile member to be chapter leader, so as not to appear *too* Jewish to the larger public. And while the Jewish left of the early to mid-twentieth century certainly organized within Jewish groups such as the Jewish People's Fraternal Order (JPFO) and the United Hebrew Trades, the religiosity is quite new, or at least its public mobilization is new. In a recent interview, one of the Palestine solidarity protesters expressed that her own sense of historical continuity traced back to Arthur Waskow's 1969 Freedom Seder rather than the Jewish leadership of SDS at her own university: radical rabbis, not Communists, seemed closer to her own remembered past.[7] Of course, much of this has to do with the ways in which the hegemony of Zionism has overtaken not only Jewish institutions but the entire US political establishment. While the anti-Zionism of the Jewish left may not be new, the need to dress it metaphorically and literally in kippot may be: Jewish Voice for Peace, IfNotNow (INN), and *Jewish Currents* are simultaneously more observant, less Marxist, and more intensely focused on Zionism than any previous generation of the Jewish left.

Several years prior, another less reported on yet equally seismic shift took place, the reemergence of "socialism" both into the public discourse and on the organizational left. In late 2016, the Democratic Socialists of America (DSA) went from being just another small socialist organization on the margins of America to surging with tens of thousands of new members and electing high-profile candidates to local and national office. And rather than emerging out of the shadows a more cautious organization, it immediately took on the question of Palestine solidarity. Previously, DSA had been the only significant Marxist organization in the US to not support the Boycott, Divestment, Sanctions (BDS) call against the state of Israel; it had reputedly been the one party on the left in which Zionists could feel more or less at home. That DSA's entrance into the political mainstage of American politics should seek to change this might have seemed to veterans of an earlier era to be a form of organizational suicide—yet the vote to pass the BDS resolution at DSA's biannual convention in Chicago in August 2017 was nearly unanimous. It passed so overwhelmingly from the floor that no official tally was even required. The crowd of over 700 socialists broke into applause and then chants of "free, free Palestine" as the organizers of the resolution high-fived and embraced. Anti-Zionism, it would seem, was no longer a divisive issue on the US left—it was rather, much like opposition to the Vietnam War two generations earlier, a point of left unity.

Yet given the coverage of the vote in DSA, one might be surprised to learn that DSA had and continues to have a sizeable Jewish membership.[8] Then and now, reporting about DSA's support for Palestine tends to focus on high-profile resignations from DSA, with Ronald Radosh and Maurice Isserman publishing their resignations in the *Daily Beast* and the *Nation* respectively, and the right-wing Jewish magazine *Tablet* fulminating that DSA had become an antisemitic organization.[9] The one historian to write about the 2017 vote in the longer history of the US anti-imperialist left chose to focus on the resignation of a single Jewish member, giving the distinct impression that the vote was controversial among Jewish members of DSA.[10] Not only did the vote *not* lead to a mass exodus of Jews from the DSA, it coincided with the foundation of a Jewish caucus, which stated clearly in its opening manifesto that it was committed to the politics of anti-Zionism. Indeed, the platform of the Jewish Solidarity Caucus (JSC) noted that it is precisely because of the members' Jewish identity that they are "uniquely positioned to challenge the nationalism that appears in our community as Zionism."[11] So settled were the anti-Zionist politics within the JSC, the major debate within the caucus did not concern Zionism at all but instead the relationship of the caucus to the broader left: should the JSC be a religious caucus, an ethno-cultural caucus, or an aligned social group; and do Jews in DSA even need a separate organization at all, given how welcomed Jews felt within it?

As the US socialist left firmly realigns around anti-Zionism, the crisis of Israeli settler colonialism has become global in ways that are unprecedented: the International Criminal Court has issued arrest warrants for Israel's prime minister, and the International Court of Justice has warned that Israel may be guilty of committing a genocide against the Palestinian people; most legacy human rights organizations, such as Amnesty International and Human Rights Watch, have declared a genocide well underway. In the face of this, history seems to be moving faster than the pen can write. All the same, Jewish left-wing history is often history written in the shadows of dark times: as Walter Benjamin reminds us, it is dark times that make subversive history suddenly visible. This book then will ask what this rupture with history can tell us about the past of the Jewish left: what are the continuities and the discontinuities between us and generations previous? What unbroken line can offer a path through a labyrinth, or warn where such paths are dangerous and lines dim? And most importantly, how did we get here, so that Jews on the left understand their relationship to Jewishness as having something to say to questions of nationalism and imperialism from the 1930s to the present? And the often posed but never satisfactorily answered question: Why is there an American Jewish left, when other "(mostly white) ethnic" lefts have ceased to exist? In some ways, the answers the book provides are simpler than the questions it raises: First, that there has always been an anti-Zionist Jewish left; indeed, it is the emergence of a Zionist consensus, post 1967, that has been the historical oddity. And second, that in moments of left-wing upsurge, there has (re-)emerged a distinctively Jewish left that has held a remarkably consistent critique of Zionism: Zionism was formed out of a violent ethnic cleansing of the land and a continued apartheid control over Palestinians, and Jews on the left have both a particular opportunity and duty to ally with Palestinians and Israelis who wish to dismantle this state project.

What Is the Left? What Was Jewish Liberalism?

As historian Karen Brodkin tells it, socialism was "hegemonic" in American Jewish life before the Cold War. Not in the sense that every American Jew was a socialist, but rather that a "working class" and "anti-capitalist outlook" was a familiar, even dominant political position of American Jews between the first waves of mass Jewish immigration in the 1880s and the Red Scare of the late 1940s.[12] The shape such political commitments took were in broad-based community organizations, labor unions, socialist publications, and leftist parties built in Jewish communities or in non-Jewish organizations with large-scale Jewish participation. The International Ladies' Garment Workers' Union (ILGWU) and the Amalgamated Clothing Workers of America (ACWA) not only formed with an overwhelming majority of Jewish workers, but formed through militant strikes and built a culture far beyond the workplace in dancehalls, housing cooperatives, and left-wing Yiddish publications. The Socialist Party had almost unparalleled support among Jewish workers, with Eugene Debs receiving nearly 40 percent of the Jewish vote in 1920, compared to less than 4 percent of the vote from the general population.[13] Victor Berger, Debs's running mate and one of the most popular socialist politicians in the US, was Jewish, as was Meyer London, an outspoken Socialist congressperson.

One of the great misconceptions about the sizeable Jewish left of the early to mid-twentieth century (an error repeated by Brodkin among others) is that American Jewish socialism was an import from Eastern Europe. Brodkin's quite reasonable claim, and indeed what I think is common sense among American Jews and historians of the left, is that Jewish socialism was born out of the crucible of tsarist antisemitism and a late-arriving Haskalah, fueled by an overeducated if underemployed working class. While this may be true for the arrival of the Bund in the early twentieth century, for the emergence of the late nineteenth-century American Jewish left, according to historian Tony Michels, there was little Jewish socialism to import. As Michels argues, the Jewish labor and socialist movement precedes the Eastern European labor and socialist movements by two decades; "the Jew had not always been a radical; the Jew had become a radical in New York and in other American cities."[14] In part, Michels suggests, this has to do with Jewish contact with radical German American workers, who brought with them texts from the

Oyfkerlung of German socialism, including Marx, Engels, Lassalle, and Liebknecht.[15] Michels's historical observation functions as a critique of a far more pervasive assumption, that Jewish socialism is a single-generational affair and that, upon assimilation, socialist Jews quieted down into electoral liberals. Little could be further from the truth—indeed, the movement of Jewish socialism from the 1880s to the 1940s suggests an increasing radicalization *the more assimilated* Jews became in the US, and the more comfortable in their environs.

Indeed, the Communist movement of the 1930s and 1940s was, as Michael Denning observed, a movement of largely second- and third-generation "ethnic American" immigrants rather than more recent arrivals.[16] The Communist movement was also the high point in many ways of the Jewish left in the United States, with the Communist Party averaging nearly 100,000 members at this time, over half of whom were Jewish—and given the party's high turnover, it would mean hundreds of thousands of American Jews passed in and out of the ranks of the organization. Yet the range and scope of the CPUSA went far beyond its membership rolls, to the many affiliated unions, civil rights organizations, anti-imperialist and anti-war organizations, and cultural organizations in the party's orbit. The left wing of the Congress of Industrial Organizations (CIO), the National Negro Congress, American League against War and Fascism, Civil Rights Congress, Jewish People's Fraternal Order, and others meant that millions of Americans were fellow travelers with the CPUSA or active members in CPUSA-aligned organizations. This both followed and helped produce the greatest realignment of American mass politics in history—a coalition of white liberals, labor, civil rights organizations, people of color, and American Jews. The alliance is such a bedrock of modern American life, it causes confusion if it begins to unravel. The high point of the American Jewish left, in other words, also coincided with and helped produce the common sense of left-wing American politics.

And while the Communist movement of the 1930s promoted its Popular Front slogan, "Communism Is Twentieth-Century Americanism," it has been noted by wide swath of both historians of Communism and Jewish history that the movement of the 1930s and '40s was anything but assimilationist. As Brodkin writes, "Jewish workers did not accept the notion that a Jewish identity was peripheral to their working class interests" as late nineteenth- and twentieth-century

Jewish socialists.[17] Describing the same phenomenon a decade after the period Brodkin describes, Hoffman and Srebrnik argue that "Jewish Communism" in the United States "was a combination of socialism and secular Jewish nationalism."[18] Indeed, reading through the left press of the 1930s, "assimilation" was understood to be anathema to socialism; not only something a socialist Jew would not want to do, but very much a project conceived to counter socialism and undermine it. As one of the major Communist Party editors and theorists of the late 1930s and 1940s, Alexander Bittelman, writes,

> everybody knows that the non-democratic forces in American Jewish life are either assimilationist ... or reactionary-nationalistic. The assimilationists are altogether opposed to the building of a Jewish life in America or they seek to reduce the American Jewish community to a religious group, which is tantamount to a denial of Jewish life. And on this point, the reactionary nationalists, who deny the possibility of building a Jewish life in the diaspora (the Goluth), take the same position as the assimilationists. Namely: they either oppose altogether the building of a Jewish life in America or—which is virtually the same thing—they want to confine it to a religious community.[19]

For Bittelman, the alternative to "assimilationism" and "reactionary nationalism" (that is, Zionism) is "progressive Jewish values." Much like "tikkun olam" a generation later, "progressive Jewish values" in the lexicon of the 1930s and 1940s Jewish left refers to a secular culture of social democracy, anti-racism, and cultural diversity, expressed through Jewish tradition. As the scholar Yuri Slezkine articulated it, of the three Jewish answers to antisemitism in the twentieth century—immigration to the Americas, emigration to Israel, and the Bolshevik Revolution (that is, assimilation, nationalism, or socialism)—socialism remained by far the most popular solution to the "Jewish question" in the early to mid-twentieth century.[20] As a solution then, Communism was not a form of assimilation, but rather an alternative to it.

Of course, this raises the question, what was it about the United States that allowed for the flowering of Jewish socialism? While that may be an overdetermined question, it is clear that Jewish socialists expressed their political commitments through a language of ethnic identification *and* racial solidarity; indeed, these tended to be inseparable. As Amelia

Glaser writes in her comprehensive history of left-wing Yiddishkeit poetry in the US, part of Jewish leftists' acculturation to the United States was through the language of racial solidarity and racial identification. American poets writing in Yiddish would often transpose language of pogroms onto stories of lynchings and would compare the sufferings of African Americans with the sufferings of Jews in the Pale of Settlement.[21] Yiddish-speaking poets would even translate Black idiom and Black poetic styles into their writing. While such forms of borrowing and identification could be seen as a kind of left-wing minstrelsy, it expressed a critique of the Al Jolson modality of shedding Jewish tears through blackface. Rather than expressing Jewish grief through transposition, such poems were a way of communicating the oppression of African Americans to other Jews in an idiom they could understand. In an analogous move, the mid-century novelist and editor Mike Gold's 1930 *Jews without Money* features a dark-skinned, curly-haired Jew—nicknamed the N-word by the community—as his hero. Rather than see this as appropriation, I would argue Gold features this character to reject a "teleology of assimilation" and embrace solidarity with other marginalized Americans.[22] While there are many other reasons for Jewish socialism to have thrived in the US, including a greater atmosphere of freedom than in tsarist Russia (albeit often circumscribed), I would suggest it was rather that the American left lent itself to an expression of ethnic politics as a politics of socialist liberation. In the US, unlike Europe, racial solidarity was an expression of radicalism.

Bittelman, as a Communist Party theorist, attempted to schematize Ashkenazi Jewish identity and its relationship with non-Jewish people of color throughout the world within a Marxian and intersectional framework after World War II.[23] Bittelman first conceives of Ashkenazi Jewish life in the US as existing within a "bourgeois nationalist" framework that seeks to incorporate the "Jewish bourgeoisie" into aims of US-dominated global capitalism and offer a form of subordinate "assimilation" to the Jewish masses.[24] Bittelman then goes on to say that race in the US is not simply an epiphenomenon of class; rather, there "exists in the United States a peculiar system of oppression of peoples, usually spoken of as minorities, which is a system of persecution of peoples and discrimination against them." In other words, the US is not only a capitalist country existing through the exploitation of labor, but the inheritor of the British Empire externally, and the product of settlement and slavery internally. While eschewing a strict hierarchy of oppression, Bittelman nonetheless describes the oppression of African Americans as akin to colonization, framing it as a "national oppression" analogous to the colonization of the Philippines and Puerto Rico within the "Black Belt of the South," and a regime of oppression and discrimination throughout the rest of the United States. Bittelman describes a system of racial oppression that ultimately serves the interests of capitalism while placing "Anglo-Saxons" as the dominant group and subjecting white ethnics such as "Poles, Russians, Italians, Jews and others" to various forms of exclusion. Bittelman goes on to suggest that Jews stand apart from this general framework insofar as "anti-Semitism itself" is a form of "national oppression and discrimination" that is less systemic than the oppression faced by Black people, yet both sharper and more important to the forces of "imperialist reaction" than the general forms of social exclusion faced by non-"Anglo-Saxons." In this framework, it is in the interests of American Jews to ally with the "Negro people" who are fighting for their "national liberation" within the Black Belt and are a "vanguard force against the whole imperialist system of national discrimination and oppression in the United States."

It should also be remembered that "race" for the socialist lefts of the 1930s and 1940s was understood as a transnational term, linking slavery, colonialism, Jim Crow, and capitalism into a single frame of analysis.[25] The Council on African Affairs and the Communist Party frequently sponsored meetings between civil rights leaders in the US and independence figures from Africa and Latin America, raised money for and awareness of the colonized world within the US, and sponsored labor union and community members to travel abroad. Likewise, both organizations recruited and were composed of members that participated in Garveyite movements and transnational Negritude movements that preceded the Popular Front, but also formed an important component of it.[26] Equally, the Communist Party's rhetoric of "self-determination for minority peoples" implicitly connected nationalist claims in overseas colonies with African, Mexican, and Native American struggles in the US.[27] In part, this was due to the influence of the Soviet Union and its own policy on "minority peoples" within its borders, but as critics such as Anthony Dawahare and Robin D. G. Kelley have argued, it was also a response to grassroots pressure within the party to develop a coherent policy on race, capitalism, and imperialism, and to respond to members' articulations of the centrality of race and empire to the development of capitalism.[28] The connection between racism and imperialism implies that these scholars and activists understood Black Americans as an "internally colonized" population and perceived that there was more than a relation by analogy between the regime of South Africa and the southern United States.

Scholar Santiago Slabodsky traces out the genealogy of a longer theoretical foundation of Jewish anti-colonial thinking, rooted in the ontology of European Jewish-Marxist thought. Colonialism relies on a "Manichean divide" between colonizer and colonized, with the presumption that the colonized is a primitive "savage" and the colonizer is a bearer of "civilization."[29] Slabodsky notes how common it was for Jewish Marxists—including Marx himself—to invert this binary, invoking "for Marx barbarism is a characteristic of the West and not of the victims it exploits."[30] Marx finds the seeds of Western barbarism lie not only in the foundations of capitalism, with its rapacious looting of India and the Americas, but in the Christian state itself, with its nominal veneer of formal equality and implicit hierarchy of racial and religious forms of citizenship. "On the Jewish Question," while often castigated for its rejection of Judaism, is also a seething critique of Western state and civil society, with its assumption that rights are only granted to the extent that one conforms in public to a singular civilizational and religious stricture. Walter Benjamin takes this analysis a step further in his famous "Theses on the Philosophy of History," in which the very foundations of the Western ideal of "progress" contain within them the threat of annihilation and genocide. Progress for Benjamin "empathizes . . . with the victors," meaning that in a very material sense, those who are slaughtered in its march forward—workers, colonized subjects—are deserving of their fates. "There is no document of civilization that is not at the same time a document of barbarism" is not just a statement about Western complicity with fascism, but an indictment of capitalist modernity, its imperial coordinates.[31] Theodor Adorno and Max Horkheimer come to a similar conclusion after the war in *Dialectic of Enlightenment*, noting that the very "instrumental reason" of Enlightenment rationality contains within it the kernel of domination, even annihilation, of the Holocaust.[32] There is "no coincidence," Slabodsky suggests, that this inversion of terms—a barbaric Europe, the un-civilized civilization—emerges out of the real experience of

Jews as Europe's internal "other," the noncitizen or half-citizen subject of capitalist, imperial states.[33]

It makes sense, then, that in his analysis of the role of Jewish socialists in the United States, a critique of Zionism emerges out the Jewish left's general worldview. Thus for Bittelman, American Jewish identity is linked primarily to its conditions in the US and its lived solidarities with other "oppressed nationalities," especially African Americans and people in the colonized world. Bittelman's theorizing an American Jewish relationship to Zionism follows from his general theorization of race and capitalism as transnational formations, linked through circuits of military and economic form. If Zionism is a form of imperialism, it is not only directly antagonistic for the Palestinians, it is also against the direct self-interest of working-class Jews. Bittelman grants that Jews form a "national group" in the Yishuv, the pre-state Jewish settlement in mandate Palestine. But their national character, language, territory, and national culture does not then grant Jews in Palestine the right to form a Jewish-only state. As Bittelman writes,

> the Zionist solution of the Palestine question, being anti-democratic and reactionary and oriented on collaboration with imperialism against the Arab people, endangers the security of the Yishuv and tends to turn the Jewish people into accomplices and partners in imperialist oppression and exploitation.[34]

Bittelman was hardly alone in seeing Zionism as a form of imperialism in the 1930s and 1940s; indeed, that was the commonsense understanding on the left. Not only would Zionism, as Hannah Arendt accurately predicted, displace hundreds of thousands of Palestinians and set a minority of Jews against an entire subcontinent of Arab neighbors, it would be aligned with British and US imperialism and the bourgeois interests of the Jewish ruling class.[35] Bittelman spoke for most American Jewish leftists including luminaries such as Mike Gold, Albert Einstein, Leon Trotsky, Muriel Rukeyser, and many others, when he wrote that Zionism was anathema to "progressive Jewish values." Anti-Zionism seemed to swim well within the mainstream of American Jewish life. As Robert Gessner succinctly put it, in the US "about one percent of Jews are Zionist."[36]

To quote Stuart Hall on Gramsci, ideas are "*never* only concerned with the philosophical core" of their existence; for their "organic" presence in movements and communities, "they must touch practical, everyday commonsense."[37] It's important to point out that American Jewish anti-Zionism emerged *organically*, in the Gramscian sense, from the already-existing socialist commitments of Jews in the US. While the US Jewish left was briefly "converted" to Zionism, it was not by Israeli military prowess, but rather the Soviet Union's support for Partition in the UN. Yet this was short-lived for both the Soviet Union and the American Jewish left. When Israel again emerged in the spotlight in 1967, the New Left response was remarkably consistent with the response of Jewish leftists a generation earlier. While the Trotskyist Socialist Workers Party (SWP) remained consistent on Palestine throughout the nadir of the 1950s, for many in the leadership of SDS, there was a process of relearning. When the Student Nonviolent Coordinating Committee (SNCC) came out in support of the nascent Palestinian Liberation Organization (PLO) in 1968, leaders in SDS felt that they should be supported. Susan Eanet-Klonsky, who was in SDS leadership and worked out of the national office in Chicago, said she received a stack of pamphlets and books "on the Palestine question" from older comrades and took up a study of the issue for the first time.[38] Writing several articles for SDS's newspaper, *New Left Notes*, Eanet-Klonsky framed Israel-Palestine much like Communists of the 1930s had, as an imperialist conquest "analogous to the flight of early colonists in America ... to a land already occupied by Indian people."[39] When, fifty years later, Jewish Voice for Peace unveiled the "deadly exchange" campaign to highlight the racism of both the US police state and the Israeli apartheid state, they were articulating a hundred-year tradition of linking Zionism to racial violence and imperialism. While in each case the conditions and context may have been new, the left-wing transnational conception of race has remained a constant. Such a conceptualization of race is not a new phenomenon, but rather emerges from solidarities and articulations of a much longer tradition of an American Jewish left.

This is not to say there is no difference, political or otherwise, between the Jewish left of the 1930s Communist Party and Jewish Voice for Peace. In the radical anti-Zionist literature of earlier generations, authors frequently described Zionism as a particular class project of the Jewish elite and petit bourgeoisie. In Bittelman's 1946 "Study Guide for the Jewish Question," he suggests among the divisions between American Jews, from the Zionists to the "Bundists of the Second International,"

Introduction: The American Jewish Left in the Shadow of Zion 13

the greatest weight is wielded less between different ideological factions, and more in the outsized role "the Jewish bourgeoise plays in national group life."[40] Calling out the American Jewish Committee in particular, Bittelman describes their outlook as "assimilationist" and "Zionist," as they enforce their will through philanthropy, social services, and political lobbying. For Bittelman, assimilation into the structure of "imperialist nationalism" and into dominant ideologies of whiteness are one and the same: bourgeois nationalism, that is, nationalism aligned with capitalism and imperialism, is the ruling ideology of the bourgeoisie. Working- and middle-class Jews who become Zionists are then not only complicit in the discrimination against Palestinians, they are aligning with forces inimical to their class interests. The 1970s socialist Chutzpah Collective continued in this tradition, not only noting the working-class roots of its own members, but arguing that the failure of early Middle East "peace groups" in the US such as Breira lay in their bourgeois, professionalized outlook and composition.[41] Chutzpah further argued that, when opposing the rise of domestic fascism in the US, bourgeois-oriented organizations such as ADL frowned on direct-action tactics and taking to the streets.[42] With the emergence of the Jewish Solidarity Caucus of the DSA, a similar critique was offered: that Jewish life is not only dominated by Zionism, but the domination by Zionism is inseparable from the domination of US Jewish life by wealthy bourgeois organizations such as the AJC and ADL. "We seek to create the conditions under which barriers to being Jewish no longer exist," the JSC manifesto reads, first and foremost "a society abolished of class" where "synagogue membership" is not exorbitant and where "funding" does not "emphasize Zionism."[43]

At core of the emphasis on the class nature of the Jewish left is a larger, often unposed question: In whose name and interests should a Jewish left act? Central to the belief system of socialism is that the working class, broadly conceived, is the agent of its own interests and liberation. To pose American Jews as both majority working class and under the thumb of bourgeois institutions not only suggests that their class interests ally with Palestinians (albeit far more brutally) under oppression of the Israeli and Jewish American ruling classes, but that they have no interests in common with the Jewish bourgeoisie, any more than they have a life-world in common with the ruling class more generally. Jewish Voice for Peace, as an ally organization to the Palestine liberation movement, sees their role far differently, less in terms of working-class Jewish self-interest than Jewish allyship with Palestinians and Palestinian-led organizations declaring the general terms of the discourse and the struggle. And indeed, the class nature of the Jewish community has changed, with the Jewish college-graduation rate twice that of the general US population, a rate that increases if one concentrates on more secular, left-wing Jews. Yet as many socialists have pointed out, a college degree, even a white-collar job, does not mean that one has left the working class; they've simply joined a different layer of it.[44] In their "Port Authority Statement," one can see three Jewish members of SDS, David Gilbert, Robert Gottlieb, and Gerry Tenney, attempt to answer the question of class self-interest by invoking an emerging educated middle class—a class into which Jews have just entered in large numbers. "This new group," the Port Authority Statement declares, may "enjoy greater benefits" if they still "remain in a position of class exploitation (non-control over production and the quality of their lives)."[45]

In addition to the changing class nature of the Jewish left, there has also been a changing racial nature in the Jewish left in the last few decades. Given the makeup of older Jewish lefts, this has meant that my project largely, though not entirely, tells the story of Ashkenazi Jewish radicals. This is not to say that the question of whiteness remains unaddressed: indeed, "whiteness theory" was largely an invention of Jewish New Left radicals, many of whom felt especially keenly the changing racial dynamics of European-descended Jewry in the US. Yet a critique of whiteness does not change it; with some exceptions, the Jewish left from 1880s to the 1990s, especially the leadership, remained largely Ashkenazi, of eastern European descent. While Daniel Bensaïd comments that the French Jewish left of the 1960s was likewise largely Ashkenazi and Yiddish-speaking, he found that studying the intersection of his own Algerian Sephardic roots with Yiddishkeit was productive and provocative, using the term "Marranism" over Deutscher's formation of "non-Jewish Jew," even while stressing that in many ways they meant the same thing. And, with the formation of the Jews of Color/Sephardic/Mizrahi Caucus of Jewish Voice for Peace, and Jews for Racial and Economic Justice's Jews of Color and Sephardi and Mizrahi Caucuses, much-needed dialogues about the Ashkenormative history of the American Jewish left have finally begun. Works by Melanie

Kaye/Kantrowitz, the Jews of Color Initiative, Devin Naar, and others have done much to address these gaps in the historical narrative about the presence of Sephardic and Mizrahi Jews in the United States. While there is much to mourn in the passing of earlier generations of Jewish leftists, the relative diversity of JVP, JFREJ, INN, and other Jewish left spaces and their attention to the Ashkenormative nature of the earlier Jewish left formations is a marked improvement. While one cannot collapse the term "Jews of color" with "Sephardi/Mizrahi"—many Jews of color are Ashkenazi, and many Sephardi and Mizrahi Jews are white or white-identified—I found it compelling enough to conclude my final chapter with a discussion of the two most important Jewish left poets writing today, Martín Espada and Aurora Levins Morales, both Jews of Puerto Rican and Ashkenazi descent who have written movingly of the connections between Caribbean anti-colonialism and the labor and anti-racist struggles of earlier generations of the Jewish left. While many cleavages remain, such imaginative ventures can look forward to a moment when histories of the Jewish left and anti-colonial struggles of the Global South are seen not as antagonistic but as complimentary.

Thus one can return to the moment remembered in the Columbia encampments: Which Jewish left are we to recall in this current moment? The Jewish left of SDS taking over President Kirk's office in the name of student power against the Vietnam War? Or the Jewish left of Waskow's Freedom Seder, articulating a Jewishness as a cultural practice in solidarity with the African American freedom struggle? I would suggest both are currents within the contemporary Jewish left at this moment, even if they have their own teleologies and theories about subject formation. Yet perhaps one can point to far more continuities than breaks: on the question of Zionism and solidarity with other oppressed ethnic groups and religious minorities, there is a straight line from the Communist Party to SDS, to the Chutzpah Collective, to New Jewish Agenda (NJA), to Jewish Voice for Peace. Indeed, one can even trace such lineages through singular individuals and families. Jewish Voice for Peace, JFREJ, and DSA are intergenerational organizations, and many of the founders and activists hail from multigenerational left-wing families themselves, including Melanie Kaye/Kantrowitz, whose career spans from NJA to JFREJ; to David Duhalde, a Jewish socialist in DSA whose parents are exiles from Chile; and Molly Crabapple, who is the great-granddaughter of a well-known Bundist. In this sense I would suggest that the Jewish left(s) are not peripheral to Jewish identity, but rather integral to understanding the ongoing cleavages and oppositions within the Jewish community, as well as the continued presence of self-identified Jews and Jewish organizations on the streets in protest over Israel's latest war.

These questions are far from academic. As now right-wing Jewish institutions, from the AJC to the ADL and Hillel International, attempt to quash debate among the American public on Zionism and the continuing displacement of Palestinians from their land, not only is a living memory of the Jewish left a resource for American Jews, it can point to ways forward for those who wish to challenge such institutions on their own cultural grounds. As opposed to theories of the Jewish left's "vanishing" or interest in the American Jewish left as a form of "nostalgia," it should be remembered that Jewish leftists were not merely brave individuals, but representatives of rooted communities and class perspectives, part of a longer story of class struggle, anti-imperialism, and assimilation into dominant modes of whiteness and power. As much as this is a cultural history of "the Jewish left," Jewish lefts are inseparable from the longer history of the American radical left, of which Jewish lefts have been an active and influential part. Of course, this is not to say that the (Jewish) American left has been infallible (indeed, blind adherence to the foreign policy of the Soviet Union was a disaster for Palestine and for the credibility of American Communism): its defeats are primarily the result of the uneven terrain of class struggle, not internal contradictions. The two Red Scares, COINTELPRO, and the alignment of liberal Jewish institutions with the inquisitions of the right have played outsized roles in establishing the dominance of Zionism over Jewish and American politics. But it should be remembered that past struggles emerged and were fought out over terrain not wholly different from what we face now: an imperialist superpower against the interests of the global majority. My intervention is not the idea that Jewish leftists were exceptional, farsighted, or cosmically visionary—rather that such lefts emerged out of the quotidian interests and struggles of ordinary people in a grotesquely unjust world. As such, earlier Jewish leftists built a Jewish left—and a critique of Zionism—out of the terrain that was autochthonous to the United States: one in which racial oppression, a rapacious bourgeoisie, a bloated military budget, and precarious living standards even for the educated are the norm rather than the exception.

American Jews, like all other members of the 99 percent, have grounds to fight such formations in their own language, in a common language, in one's own language in common with others.

Diasporism, or Twenty-First-Century Communism?

Many years before I thought to write about the American Jewish left and anti-Zionism, I had a long conversation with former Students for a Democratic Society (SDS) member and Chutzpah Collective co-founder Myron Perlman about our childhood impressions of Zionism. We were just getting to know each other; we had spent the day handing out fliers for a pre-Bernie socialist candidate on Chicago's quickly gentrifying Southwest Side. Looking back on the conversation, we were probably trying to figure out what kind of socialist and what kind of Jew the other might be. Myron recalled growing up in the working-class North Chicago Jewish neighborhood of Rogers Park and how he came to hear the word "Israel" for the first time. "I was in grade school," he explained, and another Jewish classmate was trying to explain to him "why Israel was my home." He said he was confused: Why would he want to go live in another country half a world away, that spoke another language? "Because it's for Jews," the girl said, as if that settled it.[46]

Myron often recounted that this was how he explained the concept of *ideology* in Marxist terms: the appreciation of something distant over something close, the abstraction of life over its direct material apprehension. What further struck me about Myron's early memory was that he did not express the political problems of Israel—its occupation of Palestinian land and displacement of Palestinians, its militaristic culture, its hostile and aggressive relationships with neighboring countries—but simply, its *foreignness*. Israel is so often treated by Jews—and to be honest, many Americans—as the fifty-first US state, that to hear it discussed as just another country was sort of shocking. Israel for Myron was over there, something alien and far away; his own life, Jewish, working-class, Chicagoan, was right in front of him. In short, Myron was my first contact with the idea of *diasporism* as a secular, working-class Jewish politics.

In recent years, "diasporism" has come to be the keyword, the touchstone for the contemporary Jewish left and its anti-Zionist politics.[47]

From Molly Crabapple's retrospective on the Jewish Bund and its working-class de-territorialized politics, to the Diaspora Alliance's call for a pluralistic, multiracial democratic society, to theorists such as Judith Butler and Daniel Boyarin who name diasporism as the core of Jewish ethics and cultural vitality, to claims by Jewish activist-authors such as Melanie Kaye/Kantrowitz who hail "diasporism as a deliberate counter to Zionism," the term has come to be the way many different tendencies on the Jewish left signal a specifically Jewish anti-Zionism.[48] In one sense, the meaning of diasporism is simple: in an era when mainstream Jewish institutions from Hillel International to the American Jewish Committee claim Zionism is at the center of the meaning of Jewish identity, diasporism is a modality to reject this particular definition of Jewish nationalism and still claim a Jewish identity.

Key to diasporism's assertion—especially in the language of Boyarin and Butler—is that it is perhaps a more authentic form of Jewish practice than nationalism, especially the form of nationalism that emerged as Zionism. Butler argues that diasporism is the "ethical substance" of Jewish life. Daniel Boyarin describes a tradition in the Babylonian Talmud that defines Jewish practice as located in exile, a cultural resource, even a treasure, born of the "lack" and "absence" of a center, or a homeland.[49] Jacob Plitman, former publisher of *Jewish Currents*, suggests diasporism is an emergent movement, yet, as Butler and Boyarin argue, it is one that hearkens back to a Jewish practice far older than Zionism. Daniel Boyarin argues that "diasporism" is indeed the name for a Jewish-centric cultural nationalism dispersed across the globe, in solidarity with other cultural and political minorities. Scholar Atalia Omer argues in an era of Palestinian displacement, a Jewish diasporism that can "decenter Jewishness" is the core of Jewish solidarity.[50] While the nuances and valences of the term differ in ways I will get into later, it is clear diasporism is the negation of Zionism's negation of exile.

It should come then as little surprise that the organization Myron help found, the Chutzpah Collective—and its newspaper *Chutzpah*—was one of the early left-wing Jewish organizations of the 1970s to conceive of diasporism as both its political and Jewish form of praxis, or perhaps its political form of Jewishness. As Chutzpah lays out in its 1977 Statement of Principles, "Jews" whether "in the Soviet Union, Chile, the United States, Ethiopia or Argentina . . . have the right to live whatever way they choose to define their Jewishness." The statement articulates a Jewish home wherever Jews happen to be and asserts that Jews' beliefs also must be a product of their immediate needs, not a Zionist state. The statement furthers the same principle to Israel: "what constitutes a nation is fluid and controversial," and even if Chutzpah affirmed the possibility of a Jewish state in the last instance, their caveat specified that it must be in the democratic interests of both Jews and Palestinians who live in that land.[51] Over its roughly ten-year span, Chutzpah dedicated itself to the survival and recovery of Jewish diasporic culture, from multiple histories of the Bund and interviews with surviving Bundists (long before that was cool), to reprinting anti-fascist partisan songs and Yiddish poetry (translated by members), advocating for left-wing Jewish organizations to combat US white nationalists, and, perhaps most provocatively, meeting with both Palestinian and Jewish leftists in Israel and the Occupied Territories, even when the PLO was still considered an official sponsor of terror by the US government.

I mention Chutzpah and its re-foundation of diasporic politics paradoxically because the word "diaspora" rarely emerges in their writings, except as a neutral description of Jews who do not live in Israel. Jewish internationalists, from the ranks of SDS or the SWP, defined their internationalism as one of anti-colonial liberation. Chutzpah's internationalism—in Myron's words, its *kesher*, or bond, "with the left"—appeared as the modality through which their Jewishness was expressed. They showed up in Jewish organizations such as Breira and New Jewish Agenda as radicals, ready to push such organizations left and address missing questions of class conflict, Israel/Palestine, imperialism, antisemitism, racism, queer rights, and so on. They were Jews on the left, and as importantly, leftists among Jews.

That is, if one might call Chutzpah a "diasporist" organization, it is only in hindsight. Unlike the late 1960s and early 1970s, during which "revolution," "internationalism," or "anti-imperialism" were key terms, in our own moment "diaspora" has emerged as the descriptive slogan for Jewish radicals. In 2018, Jacob Plitman, then the new publisher of a rebooted *Jewish Currents*, penned a manifesto of sorts, declaring "a new diasporism" the hallmark of radicalized, Trump-era Jewish organizing.[52] The editorial names protests against Trump's Muslim ban spearheaded by longstanding Jewish progressive organizations such as

Jews for Racial and Economic Justice (JFREJ) and Bend the Arc (BtA), the Jewish presence in the then-rapidly growing Democratic Socialists of American (DSA), newly organized Sephardi/Mizrahi and Jews of color caucuses, as well as other newly launched progressive Jewish publications such as *Protocols*. Framing his own narrative as not merely personal but a collective story for Jewish millennials, Plitman begins the call for a new "diasporism" with a story of his immersion in Zionist orthodoxy, from Jewish summer camps and synagogue trips to tzedakah boxes for the Jewish state, constructing a Jewish world both removed entirely from the left and insularly built around supporting expansive Jewish nationalism in Israel. What awakens Plitman to the reactionary limits of such a world, according to his telling, is not politics immediately available in the United States, but within the discursive and political formation of Zionism itself: "what the symbols and experiences of Jewish nationalism meant and still mean to millions of Palestinians living under occupation."

In other words, what makes "diaspora" a meaningful term for Plitman and *Jewish Currents* is what it is not: it is an explicit rejection not only of Zionism as the center of American Jewish life, but of the Israeli state's near-century-long displacement of and violence enacted against Palestinians. In some ways, "diasporism" is not a term that could have existed as a signifying slogan on the old or new Jewish left, for the simple reason that it's only since the 1970s that there has been a consensus around Israel as the primary meaning of being a Jew in the US. This is not to say anti-Zionism is new; indeed most of the history of the Jewish left has been in opposition to or at least ambivalent about Zionism. Historically speaking, not only is the expectation a Jewish leftist would automatically be a Zionist a recent phenomenon, the entire infrastructure of Jewish cultural support for Israel, from birthright trips to pro-Israel summer camps, is to a large degree the product of the last forty years. When *Jewish Currents* editor-at-large Peter Beinart penned his 2020 break-up letter with Zionism, titled in the *New York Times* "I No Longer Believe in a Jewish State," he opened his longer version in *Jewish Currents* with the question "What makes a Jew"?[53] The implication in Beinart's essay is that, as it stands, it is Zionism that makes American Jews Jews; yet this would be a question that would make little sense in a critique of Zionism a half century earlier. This is not to say earlier leftists were not diasporists—they certainly were, and they described their attachment to a transnational, de-territorialized Jewish peoplehood as connected to their anti-imperialism and internationalism. Yet there was no need to *name* the politics as such: for the most part, they simply existed. In Philip Roth's 1993 *Operation Shylock*, Moishe Pipik's diasporism is seen as both idiosyncratic and also a little ridiculous— Roth seems to be at great pains over the fact that such a name now, because of Israel, needs to exist. If Israel has remade Jewish life, it has also remade the meaning of the diaspora, from a fact of Jewish life to a source of opposition.

Yet there remains a question, beyond opposition: What does it mean to embrace the diaspora? In one sense, there is a kind of liberal, common-sense diasporism of American Jewish life. We can hear echoes of it in Seth Rogan's "No, I am not going to live in Israel" and Larry David's defense of a Palestinian American restaurant defiantly opening next door to a Jewish deli as an affirmation of American multiculturalism: "This is America; people can open a restaurant wherever they want." Both are statements less of solidarity with Palestinians or grand visions of internationalism and more of a liberal-American common sense of personal freedom.

Philip Roth is perhaps this liberal version of diasporism's most articulate champion, satirizing West Bank settlers, Sabra kibbutzim, and neo-fascist Israeli politicians as either humorless automatons or messianic if violent fools. In his 1986 novel, *The Counterlife*, Roth mocks a middle-aged Jewish man who makes aliyah to an ultra-orthodox West Bank settlement after he loses his virility. If Israel is a prosthetic erection for the overly civilized American Jewish man, Israel's victory in the Six-Day War is psychic compensation for the mediocre beer-drenched afternoons of the narrator's father's Florida retirement. Menachem Begin's far-right nationalism is portrayed as the fascism of the humiliated Jewish grocer, the store clerk who now has an army of his own. Israel is a fantasy-other for American Jews, whether still nursing historical slights or trying to find fulfillment in a reified, capitalist life: Israel is the Jewish Disneyland, the fabled Main Street of a Jewish life that never existed. Israel is thus a kind of tenant-lieu, a placeholder for a feeling of emptiness, a stand-in for a Jewish life lived anxiously if all too well in the US. Yet it is hard to say what exactly exists on the other side of Roth's critique of militarized, colonial Jewish nationalism: certainly not a robust defense of a multicultural, democratic state shared among Jews and Palestinians. The end of *The Counterlife* renders Jewishness a kind of vacant space in history, an object "like a glass or apple," an "I" without a "we."[54] Refusing to stand for "Hatikvah" after receiving an honorary degree from the Jewish Theological Seminary in 2014, Roth's *non serviam*, in the words of one critic, was a "refusal to take sides" and to be a patriot, rather than an alignment with the Palestinian cause, or even an articulated view of Jewishness.[55]

Jacobin writer Ben Burgis evoked the idea of diasporism-as-cosmopolitanism in his critique of Naomi Klein's *Doppelganger*. While applauding her rejection of the blood-and-soil nationalism of a Jewish supremacist state in the Levant, Burgis takes her to task for suggesting that as a white Canadian, she is but a "guest" in the northern republic, a settler in a settler-colonial state. For Burgis, the diasporist idea of *doikayt*—hereness—suggests that Jews *belong* wherever they live; there are no real indigenous people, just as there are no real nations. Suggesting that diasporism is synonymous with universal humanism, Burgis argues that "cosmopolitan, egalitarian universalism," and not relational identity, has "historically formed the normative bedrock of the socialist Left."[56] Much like Roth's invocation of Jewish diaspora, for Burgis, to be a Jew is little different from, or perhaps just another way of articulating, a deracinated, modern subject who belongs nowhere and thus belongs everywhere. While Klein I believe would argue that it is *precisely* the idea of doikayt to critically analyze the structures of power within the political and economic system in which one lives, Burgis's reading of diasporism as just another name for cosmopolitan universalism begs the question of what, if anything, diasporism means beyond a rejection of Zionism. In Burgis's framing, diasporism rejects Zionism, but then is a modality to erase settler histories elsewhere: to not belong in Tel Aviv is another way of naturalizing belonging in Toronto or New York City.

There have been recent attempts to theorize Plitman's "new diaspora" with both religious and political significance beyond simply positing Jews as naturalized citizens or unmarked bodies within citizenry. Shaul Magid's collection of essays *The Necessity of Exile* endeavors to frame Zionism itself as a departure from millennia of Jewish tradition, in which the formation of the Jewish state is seen not simply as a political development, but "the negation of exile."[57] Exile, or *galut*, was framed by early Zionists as a metaphysical condition, the cause of Jewish "weakness" and "parasitism." Many early Zionists, as others to this day, substantiated antisemitic frameworks of the Jew in exile, with Benjamin Netanyahu referring to Holocaust victims as "weak" and Likud referring to Israeli peace activists as sickly remnants of Jewish diasporic life.[58] Zionism, as Daniel Boyarin observed, did not counter antisemitic ideas about Jews, but rather "absorbed" them and offered a solution on their terms: a "normalizing" nation-state that would adopt the racial and gendered hierarchies of the European state.[59] Rather than adopting the Zionist framework of Jewish dispersion, Magid offers an embrace of galut, suggesting that according to Jewish religious and ethical tradition, "home" is not a condition one can experience short of the return of the *mashiach*, the messiah. In other words, Magid replaces the question of a place with a question of time: to be a diasporist Jew is to yearn for not a homeland in the Levant, but rather a homeland in the world to come. Whether that be a secular socialist utopia or the religiously perfected world brought by the redeemed, Magid leaves for the reader. Magid quotes Eugene Borowitz, who observed that "exile results because our universal Jewish ideal is unrealized anywhere," even "in Jerusalem."[60] Departing from Roth and David, Magid argues, "diasporists reject the idea of exile for normative life in the diaspora," suggesting that a life of plenty in the United States may not be Zionist, but it is not a break with Zionism's hegemony over Jewish life: it is at best a kind of compromise with the Israeli state, and the American one.

Judith Butler, in their seminal 2012 *Parting Ways: Jewishness and the Critique of Zionism*, like Magid, sought to find something immanent within Jewish tradition that would offer an ontological grounding for a diasporic Jewishness. Butler's formula is one rooted, or perhaps routed, through pluralistic praxis; they state on the first page that the "cohabitation with the non-Jew is the ethical substance of diasporic Jewishness." Butler extends from this, however, beyond simply the commandment to love one's neighbor and accept the stranger among us, to suggest that diasporic Jewishness is unique precisely for its constitutive *lack* of stable, essential nature. Citing Edward Said's provocative reading of Sigmund Freud's portrait of Moses, they posit that the founder of the Jewish religion and, perhaps, what we could call a concept of the Jewish people, is essentially non-Jewish and non-European. As Said writes, "Moses was an Egyptian, and therefore always outside the identity inside which so many have stood."[61] Undermining the "reschematization of races" into settler and native that the Zionist project undertakes, Freud's location of Moses as a non-Jew and an Arab was understood as his attempt to challenge the construction of a homogenous racial or even cultural identity at the center of the Jewish tradition. For Butler, Freud's insistence on difference at the origins of Jewish peoplehood signifies "ineradicable alterity" at the "center of what it means to be a Jew."[62] To be a Jew is not only to live with the other, but to be other to oneself. As Butler themself is fond of quoting, Franz Kafka's rebuttal to Zionism, "What have I in common with the Jews? I have scarcely anything in common with myself" is not a rejection of Jewishness, but an articulation of it. Dispersion is not merely a fact of existence, but what constitutes it. The Jewish sense of otherness is thus constitutively anti-nationalist, as Jewishness is formulated by its own tradition as relational, dialogic, and incapable of forming a unified basis for separation.

Daniel Boyarin's 2023 *No-State Solution* is an attempt, contra Magid and Butler, to recover diasporism less through religious reinscription or secular ethics than through his own reimagined vision of the "diaspora nation." In a way, Boyarin's manifesto is far more existential than Magid's and Butler's works on the need to examine even the concept of "Jewishness" after renouncing Zionism as a "racist, fascist" nation.[63] Boyarin begins his book with a stark provocation: both right-wing Zionists and anti-Zionists agree that the only recourse from the perils of the Israeli state is to define Jewishness through religion. Taking on Shlomo Sand in particular, in part due to the popularity of his *Invention of the Jewish People*, Boyarin suggests that his attempt to "knock down" Zionism by insisting on the recent "invention" of a Jewish nation and singular origin fails less in its descriptions than its definitions. Boyarin does not object to Sand's claim regarding the hybridity of Jews as much as the unchallenged idea that Jews primarily defined themselves in the ancient world through what we would understand today as *a religion*. Religion, for Boyarin, as a "system of beliefs" or "proscribed values" is indeed what is modern, owing to the Protestant Enlightenment and the secularism of modern religious value: religion is merely a set of ideas or a "faith" rather than a whole way of life with customs, a history, a collectivity, a shared space in common.[64] For Boyarin, the "cosmopolitanism" of what we understand as religious belief now would be quite foreign to Jewish ancients who created "Jewish colonies," or mini-nations, rather than dispersed communities of Torah-reading believers.[65] While this debate may seem arcane, for Boyarin to have to surrender a collective

Jewish sense of peoplehood to the disaster of Zionism would be an equal catastrophe, destroying much that is positive about Jewish history, folklore, diversity, and uniqueness in the process. For Boyarin, this is the "new Jewish question"—less how will Jews survive European antisemitism (which was answered by the Holocaust), more "what is the Jews" once we leave Zionism behind? *Is*, Boyarin asserts in the singular, as one must posit a Jewish collective subject, a positive entity, or the project becomes meaningless.

Boyarin asserts that prior to the foundation of Israel and even after in the diaspora, "Jews manifest many of the characteristics usually assigned to nations, such as shared narratives of origins and trials and tribulations, shared practices . . . shared languages, and other cultural forms."[66] For Boyarin, it is not a question of idealism; it is a question of whether "Jews . . . simply disappear as a collective," which, after both the loss of Jewish languages in the United States and the moral and political revulsion many, especially younger Jews, feel toward Israel, seems to Boyarin a distinct possibility. Boyarin proposes, instead of Zionism, a "diaspora nation," one constituted with "dual loyalties and doubled culture," an "ardent transterritorial collective solidarity" both to other Jews and with "proximate others," especially "the oppressed." While it's clear Boyarin is winking with the line about "dual loyalties," an antisemitic charge leveled against early Zionists, he means the line seriously: to be Jewish is to belong to two nations simultaneously, one in which one lives, and the "diasporic nation" of the Jewish people. For Boyarin, the Jewish nation is not a community "imagined in space, but in time."[67] This is different from the messianic time of Magid's spiritual galut and in some ways quite literal, even "carnal," to use a word Boyarin likes: the time of Jewish generations. In other words, Jews are linked to one another not through space but via *memory* and *history*. For Boyarin, there is nothing wrong with ethics of cohabitation or movements for a better world; yet there is very little that is *Jewish* about them. Solidarity for Boyarin is constructed through the concrete terms of historical memory, Yiddishkeit, or doikayt, specific Jewish histories of solidarity with the oppressed, and solidarity offered to them in moments of oppression. Solidarity in that sense is not an individual undertaking, but a collective one.

In some ways, Boyarin's interlocutors are not in Jewish studies so much as with writers in the tradition of Black diaspora studies. As Brent Hayes Edwards describes of the radical diasporic thinking in the 1920s and 1930s, "diaspora is a term that marks the ways that internationalism is pursued by translation."[68] Diaspora for Edwards cannot be located outside of a political project: if they are given any charge beyond mere description (which he argues the word inherently has, thanks in part to the historically Jewish inflection of the term), then diasporas are inherently internationalisms, beyond nation-states, and often against them. Perhaps one way to think of Boyarin's framework of diasporic thinking is not alongside radical internationalists, but rather through them. To the extent that Black writers have deployed the term to mean circuits of radical culture beyond and between European colonialisms, so too Boyarin, to save something worthwhile in a Jewish memory tradition, would need to reach for similar cultural resources. Interestingly, Stuart Hall remarks in passing that diasporic studies, at least among Black radicals in the UK, were "modeled on Jews post Holocaust."[69] While Hall may just be referring to the temporal development of a field of thought, one could also say the Holocaust represented Jewish exile from even the potential as a normative subject in the West: exceptional now, for better and for worse. Rather than deploying Holocaust imaginaries to demand inclusion as full colonial Europeans, as the Israelis are, Hall seems to be inviting an analogy in some ways with the historical ruptures of the Black Atlantic: to be finally sutured from Western origins, what Richard Wright refers to as being "in but not of Western Civilization."[70]

If we consider diasporism as less something uniquely Jewish and more in dialogue with the longer history of colonial and socialist conceptions of the term, it seems clear that "diasporism" is another name for internationalism, in this case, with Jewish characteristics. Indeed, African American and anti-colonial intellectuals borrowed a great deal from their own understandings of both Jewish Marxism and the Jewish diasporic tradition. Said's "Reflections on Exile" works the trope of a homeless modernity back on itself by posing that "Palestinians and Jews have certain patterns to them . . . a particular ethos remains alive in exile."[71] Taking exemplary Jewish modernists such as Georg Lukács and Theodor Adorno who, in Lukács's words, see modern culture as an expression of the "transcendental homelessness" of the subject under capitalism (revised as "reification" in his later work), Said suggests that their capacity to reflect productively on this condition and suggest an alternative is not reducible to "ethnicity" but is not removed from it either. In other words, to render one's homelessness without nostalgia or despair, one must have a way to collectively locate oneself, if not in space, in time or history. Stuart Hall and Brent Hayes Edwards also cite Walter Benjamin in their construction of the dialectics of diaspora, between the empirical fact of one's existence in place and time, and the imaginary of a global subject. The "secular relics" of the collector, Hall observes, are also the markers of a new, portable culture.[72] Paul Gilroy, the scholar who perhaps did the most to theorize a diasporic Black "counter-culture of modernity" also makes wide use of Benjamin's writings, noting that Benjamin's "history from the point of view of victims" is also history as Gilroy wants to tell it, from the point of view of the slaves.[73] The questions of "homelessness" in Benjamin's writings contain a political question that inverts the location of the so-called "savage" and "civilized worlds." As Santiago Slabodsky notes, it was Benjamin's inversion of these terms, noting that every work of civilization is also a world of barbarism, that locates the colony in the metropole and the factory in the museum. The West for Benjamin is, in some ways, a floating slave ship, with its majestic figurehead at the prow and its sweltering prison holds below.

This is not to suggest that diasporas are all made equal—there are some scholars of African diaspora studies who reject metaphors entirely and insist the essence of Blackness is precisely its "incommensurability," its inability to be recognized and addressed.[74] Yet as Hall reminds us, diaspora is a space of unsettling, "aesthetic creolization" of meanings that elude fixity and produce new terms. In his theoretical intervention on diasporas, Hall locates dancehall music as precisely a form that came out of a fusion of the multiethnic, multinational, and multicultural Caribbean communities in postwar London.[75] Diaspora is not that which yearns for a return but produces new forms out of its dislocations, its neither-here-nor-thereness. Amelia Glaser notes the same sense of metaphorical dislocation and transformation in her work on Yiddish poets writing in the United States. Many of the poets, upon arriving in the United States, substituted writing about pogroms for writing about the lynching of African Americans. Referring to this as the "translocation of culture," Glaser shows that such a move doubly includes non-Jews in poetic diction formerly reserved for Jews while weaving Jewish experiences with pogroms and mass violence into an American narrative.[76] One might simply call such translocation an act of literary translation for the word "solidarity," and to be sure, "solidarity" is likely closer to the language such poets would have used than "translocation," or even "diaspora." Yet it is important to point out that solidarity includes as much as it leaves out. The poems Glaser unearths are acts of solidarity, the joining of the oppression of Jews in the Pale of Settlement with the oppression of African Americans under Jim Crow, yet they are acts of translation, to use Edwards's term: not only from a European context to an American, but of one form of life to another. One way to put this: the poems are situated in context, one specific location to another, without giving up on the subjectivity or positionality of either.

In this sense, "diasporism" may serve then as more than simply a depoliticized way of saying "internationalism" or "anti-Zionism." It is a politics simultaneously of Jewish presence and also disavowal, locating Jewishness in the process of egocentrism and relationality. One can feel Isaac Deutscher in his essay "What Is a Jew" wrestle with the contradictions of this formulation. As a "classic Marxist," in his own words, holding that class struggle and therefore sociologically observable classes are the engines of history, Deutscher is skeptical something as dispersed and culturally vague as "Jewishness" can be a vehicle for social transformation.[77] Yet he is also forced to acknowledge in hindsight, "We tried theoretically to deny that the Jewish labour movement had an identity of its own; but it had it all the same"; we had to admit Jewishness was "its driving force." The essay is marked by this back-and-forth movement, in which Jewish left culture is "meaningless" and lacking in "identity of its own" yet at crucial junctures a socially vital force, an important counter-memory: both sides of this debate fill the often painful and dialectical negation of the text. Deutscher claims that after the Holocaust, Yiddish is a spent literary force and antisemitism is all that defines the state of Israel, yet he acknowledges that both antisemitism globally and a Jewish left, at least in the United States, continue. The essay wobbles, dialectically, personally, historically, claiming and denying the historical importance of Jewish identity and Jewish culture before Deutscher finally decries both in what is perhaps his most famous paragraph:

> Religion? I am an atheist. Jewish nationalism? I am an internationalist. In neither sense am I therefore a Jew. I am, however, a Jew by force of my unconditional solidarity with the persecuted and exterminated.

I am a Jew because I feel the pulse of Jewish history; because I should like to do all I can to assure the real, not spurious, security and self-respect of the Jews.

Deutscher is not a Jew, and he is a Jew; he is not a nationalist yet wants to assure the "real, not spurious, security and self-respect of the Jews"; he defines Jewishness as religion and then declares his own fidelity to the secular memory project of Jewish history. While Deutscher resolves his contradictions through the "force" of his solidarity as a question of personal commitment and affective bond, this dialectic of non-nationalist solidarity with the persecuted and connection to Jewish history for many post–New Left Jews would be less a negation and more a positive articulation of their diasporism.

As a Polish Jew who escaped the Holocaust and as a Trotskyist who evaded Stalin's purges, Deutscher can perhaps be forgiven for framing his own Jewishness as less an ongoing tradition than as barely surviving revenant of a vanished tribe. But his dialectical articulation is in many ways parallel to Boyarin's embrace of a de-territorialized diasporic nationalism, one held together less by religion or territory—even language—and more by a shared "pulse of history" and "force" of solidarity. Mike Gold's 1930 anti-Zionist novel of working-class New York, *Jews without Money*, refers to this "de-territorialized diasporism" as a "broken Jewish nation," one that "reveres its writers" and people "of thought."[78] Gold's sense of Jewish identification, like Deutscher's, is one that eschews religion or race (there are "no racial types" among Jews, Gold states quite emphatically) and lives in the interstices of solidarity and borrowed, liminal identifications. It is a book about racial displacement, its hero a dark, petty gangster who wears his neighborhood nickname, the N-word, as a badge of honor. In one sense "brokenness" in the text refers to the dispersion of Jews as global refugees in the decades leading up to World War II, and the fragmented and jagged Jewish life crammed into one of the most densely populated tracts of land on the planet, the Lower East Side. Yet the "brokenness" can be said to be an embrace of difference, mobility, non-wholeness, incompletion, the ragged, brutal, but also poetic and vital Lower Manhattan of Gold's childhood. That the most Jewish figure in the text, the first Jew among Jews without money, is frequently taken for an African American and celebrates rather than disavows this, seems to be the point of the novel, not a deviation from its thesis on Jewishness. The book's sole Jewish enemy, Baruch Goldfarb, is a "Zionist dry goods merchant" and in his own domestic version of Zionism, schemes to move Jews into the all-white then-suburban outer boroughs of Brooklyn. Diasporism to *Jews with Money* seems to be in this doubleness, this articulation on one side of a prescriptive guidebook to Jewish life, and on the other side, non-essentialism, otherness, polysemy.

Deutscher's younger comrade Daniel Bensaïd, the French Jewish Algerian (Sephardic) member of the Fourth International, framed his own sense of mobile, transnational doubleness/duality in less teleological terms. For Bensaïd, the experience of what he calls "Marrano Judaism" offers a far longer tradition of diasporic identity than Deutscher's framework of the "non-Jewish Jew," an experience Deutscher locates in the generational experience of post- Haskalah modernity. The "split identity" of Marranism traces back at least metaphorically to the Sephardic Spanish and Portuguese "conversos" of the fifteenth century, who nonetheless held on to a Jewish subjectivity and memory despite the need to conceal their names and/or adopt new names and identities.[79] As the philosopher Donatella Di Cesare articulates, the Marrano condition is marked by an ellipsis, neither one thing nor another, a "movement between two poles without a strong center."[80] As Bensaïd describes in his own memoir, *An Impatient Life*, his father, an Algerian Jew of Sephardic descent, was neither religious nor active in the Jewish community of Southern France, yet wore a Magen David when Nazis came to power in Europe.[81]

Referring to his father as a "Jew of defiance," so too Bensaïd first experienced his own reckoning with Jewish identity and Jewish community when Israel invaded Lebanon in 1982. Signing on to a letter by French Jews opposed to the invasion, "En tant que juifs," Bensaïd found his way to "Jewish collectivity" through defiance, not of Nazis and the Vichy state but of Israeli mobilization and deployment of "Jewishness" in the name of colonialism and state violence.[82] Bensaïd described himself primarily as an "internationalist," and it is precisely through his internationalism that he found his way back to identity. This is not to say Bensaïd was shy about his own Jewish identity—and indeed, Bensaïd notes the overwhelming number of French Jews in the radical Marxist organization that he helped found. (They joked that the meetings could have been held in Yiddish if it wasn't for Bensaïd's Sephardic background.) Yet it was the totalizing pull of colonial Jewish nationalism that paradoxically prompted Bensaïd to reconsider—and remember—his father's Jewish "defiance" and to speculate on ways the Holocaust prompted French Jewish youth to join the radical left. Speculating about whether "Jewish identity can be defined," Bensaïd responds with the double negation so common to diasporic thinking: Jewishness is a "spectral presence," a "hauntology," that lives in the ongoing practices of memory and resistance, even, or especially, among those whose Jewish community is defined primarily through international Marxist commitments on the left.[83]

Alberto Moreau (born Alberto Moise), an émigré to the US from a Sephardic community in then-Ottoman Salonika, framed his own diasporic perspective as a Jewish internationalism among and between competing nationalisms, imperial American, Israeli ethno-nationalism, and the ethno-nationalism of pan-Arabism. Writing for the Communist Party's *Political Affairs* shortly after the 1967 Israeli-Arab War, Moreau is quick to point out that "anti-Arab racism" is a central reason for the lack of "understanding the basic causes of the war" between Israel and its neighbors.[84] Quickly dismissing the analysis of *Morgen Freiheit*, which declared that Israel acted in "self defense," Moreau describes *Freiheit*'s position as "caught in an avalanche of imperialist propaganda." Describing the Arab states, whether headed by secular nationalists such as Gamal Abdel Nasser or the more reactionary leaders of Saudi Arabia, he suggests that "Marxist internationalism" requires that one acknowledge that they are part of the "historical direction" of the "Arab world" toward "political and economic independence from imperialism." Further, Israel, Moreau argues, acts at the behest of "American imperialism," the interests of which are to prevent the Middle East from achieving postcolonial independence. As clear as the binary Moreau describes may be, with an imperialist West arming an increasingly aggressive and ethnically chauvinist Israel, a kind of interstitial suspicion of all nationalisms seeps through Moreau's rather classic geopolitics. Describing the US perspective as tinged with "anti-Arab racism" that cannot see legitimate claims of sovereignty and independence as valid, Moreau also warns against the "reactionary tendencies" of "Arab nationalism" that expresses itself in its own form of ethnically exclusive nationalism and apocalyptic calls to "destroy Israel." Israel itself, Moreau notes, is not only at war with its predominantly Arab neighbors, "within Israel" the "Arabs also suffer oppression" that "extends also to Sephardic Jews."

While Moreau defends his critique of nationalist orthodoxy as "Leninism," it is also clear that nationalism itself as a complex formation, one that often—even in the cause of anti-imperialism—can be at the expense of racial and religious minorities, particularly Jews. It is not a coincidence, I should think, that Moreau's article is one of the few in *Political Affairs* and other Communist Party publications to note the fate of the Sephardim in Israel, to say nothing of the twin racisms of Western and Middle Eastern nationalisms.

However occluded the Sephardic roots of Moreau may be in his "objective" analysis of imperialism and nationalism, the relationship between internationalism and specifically Jewish culture emerged formally in the heady years of the post–World War II Jewish left, the brief Indian summer between the aftermath of the Holocaust and the foundation of the state of Israel. Such debate also coincided with the heyday of the Soviet Jewish Anti-Fascist Committee (JAC), which granted a gravitas to questions of Jewish identity and culture within the global left.[85] The story that touched off several months of discussion was Howard Fast's "Epitaph for Sidney," appearing on the pages of the Communist-aligned *Jewish Life* in January 1947.[86] "Sidney" is a retrospective on the life of a young Jewish Communist, told as an elegy by a friend and comrade hearing about his death under a hail of German bullets in Italy in 1943. As *Jewish Life* editor Morris Schappes wrote, Sidney was "type," someone "I know; you know;" he is one of their "friends and comrades who died fighting fascism."[87] Sidney Greenspan's life spanned the American Jewish Communist left, from an impoverished upbringing on the Lower East Side, to the student movement at CCNY, to Spain in the International Brigades, to a fascist jail cell, to organizing with Southern sharecroppers in Alabama, to finally volunteering for the US medical corps and dying a heroic death saving a wounded comrade under fire, only to posthumously have his medal of honor application withdrawn when the US military investigated his political background and discovered he was a Communist. The elegy itself is told as a debate—between the long, discursive life story his friend wants to narrate, and the single sentence they include in his coffin: "To the memory of Sidney Greenspan, anti-fascist, who fell in the people's struggle—from his comrades."

In some ways, the debate the narrator has with himself is analogous to the debate that erupted in the pages of *Jewish Life*: How do we define

Sidney Greenspan? That it touched off such a debate was no accident. The story's publication was headlined with a short introduction by the journal's editors, posing the question of what "Progressive American Jewish Culture" might be, and how the magazine could help facilitate its growth.[88] While all respondents praised the fictionalized Sidney Greenspan, some headed by Morris Schappes (who was clearly in the minority) felt that there was nothing particularly *Jewish* about Sidney. For Schappes, because Sidney did not also take up the struggle against "bourgeois assimilation and bourgeois nationalism," his story is that of a heroic socialist, but not one of a *Jewish* socialist. While Schappes acknowledges that Greenspan is a Jew fighting fascism, for Schappes this is not enough. In the face of assimilation and Jewish nationalism, simply fighting against fascism does not provide the cultural coordinates to maintain Jewish life. For Schappes, if the only alternative to Zionism is the deracinated class struggle, then the Zionists have won the cultural argument, and perhaps will win Jews to their aggressive nationalist project.

Milton Blau and Moise Katz did not see it this way. While Blau agreed with Schappes in spirit, he felt that Schappes was too hard on our poor Sidney, and that we must take Jews, especially working-class Jews, where they are: if Sidney is a type, then perhaps it is too much to ask that they also fight for a culture and an anti-Zionist cause that is not their first calling.[89] Katz made a more robust defense of Sidney's Jewishness, stating, "We accept that he did not completely understand—with every sense, at every step, that he was a Jew, and that his Jewishness was something for which the society he lived in made him suffer." In other words, Sidney's fight against fascism was inseparable from his Jewishness, whether or not Sidney articulated it that way to himself. Indeed, perhaps because of the relative paucity of information about Sidney's inner life—and Sidney's own refusal to answer for his motives—both Schappes and Katz engaged in a kind of odd speculation about whether or not Sidney reflected on his Jewishness while being tortured in a Nazi prison camp, as if to imagine that clearly torture would bring the hidden suffering Jew out.

Strangely, all commentators took Fast's narrator at face value, when it is clear the narrator signals one shouldn't: in the first paragraph the narrator says he decided to sum up Sidney "in a single line," and then spends the next several thousand words detailing Sidney's life from boyhood to his death in battle in his midtwenties. The narrator begins with describing Sidney as the child of "poor Jews," whose poverty and traumatization from poverty and antisemitism shadow their entire world. Sidney's body is described several times by the narrator as "thin" and "spindly," without "muscular efficiency," and Sydney experienced "myopia early" from excessive reading.[90] Sidney is also described as having both "affective and gentle" eyes and a "prominent nose," and his Jewish features are often offered in connection to his gentle personality, his "sensitivity" and "mildness," as someone who "hated and mistrusted guns." The narrator tips his hand when he says, "Sidney Greenspan was not the stuff of which heroes are made, at least in the conception of heroes which is most popular in America today," suggesting that Sidney's model of masculinity is not the Anglo-American ideal yet that there may be other places, or models of masculinity, in which Sidney would be considered heroic. The repetition of Sidney's "sensitivity," effeminacy, and physical slightness calls to mind Daniel Boyarin's observation that for Ashkenazi Jewish men, bookishness and gender nonconformity were not simply permitted but held as positive social values, along with nonviolence and a distaste for martial vigor.[91] To be a "sissy" Jewish hero is not a contradiction in terms, but a highly cherished ideal before the foundation of Israel. In other words, despite the final summary line—"antifascist"—the story invites the reader to think of Sidney's whole being summarized by the first sentence about him, rather than the last: "poor Jew." Or perhaps another way of saying it would be this: the first sentence about Sidney and the final sentence about him are in a dialectical tension.

Sidney seems to say as much, or rather Howard Fast seems to say as much through Sidney. When asked directly about why Sidney is a committed anti-fascist—a cause for which he gives his life—his answer is both elliptical but also revealing. "Why does a man do anything?" Sidney asks rhetorically, concluding: "The factors in him add up. They make a sum total, and he adds to that out of his understanding." The sum total of Sidney for the narrator is inseparable, it would seem, from his Jewishness. Yet, Sidney's public face disavows such ethnic or cultural identification, at least in the final single line offered by his friends. Is that assimilationism? Is that the fear of "Jew baiting" that Sidney suffered his entire life? The closing paragraph gestures toward this duality as much as it leaves it unresolved: the narrator says Sidney was buried in "Italian soil" and that there is no "place he wouldn't have been at home, fully and completely at home." What better statement of internationalism than Sidney's homelessness, "fully at home" anywhere there is a battle against fascism? Yet in the next sentence, the narrator remarks on the "heavy black lines to bind" his left-wing newspapers, much like a socialist form of tefillin, binding his news of the day in a kind davening prayer.

One could say that this form of diasporism revives the old Leninist dictum, "national in form, socialist in content," in which socialist internationalism is spoken in its regional dialect or cultural specificity. Yet the politics of Jewish diasporism are more complicated, slippery, and far more charged than a formula—however flexible—can accommodate. Returning to the Chutzpah Collective of the 1970s, the relatively small but culturally and politically influential organization was riven on numerous questions that vex the Jewish left today. When should a Jewish left take the lead? When should Jews work in the background in solidarity? What if, as it often happens, political events do not conform to neat dictums and political paradigms? For local Chicago movement politics, Chutzpah took the position that when it came to opposing the far right, the Warsaw Ghetto Uprising Coalition, of which Chutzpah was the convening member, should take the lead, on the grounds that neo-fascists are virulently antisemitic and were also, in this case, targeting a Jewish neighborhood. Yet when the neo-fascists marched through a predominantly African American neighborhood, it was thought more appropriate for Chutzpah to be one member in a broader coalition headed by African American community organizations and labor unions. As complicated as these conversations were—many in the Warsaw Ghetto Uprising Coalition felt that Jews should not center themselves and that the name was inappropriate—Chutzpah's perspective became even more complicated when related to the politics of Zionism.

For Chutzpah, Zionism was denaturalized as the logical or teleological end point of Jewish life. It is not the "negation of exile" but rather another place in which Jews must understand how to cohabit with non-Jews. If the millions of Jews living in Israel are an important part of Jewish life, Israel remains something foreign that bears little relationship to Myron or his collective's particularist "life here." The territorial boundaries of Jewish life are negated entirely—Israel is no more an "end to alienation that has lasted 1,000 years" than the US is; alienation or lack of fixity is the ontological condition of the term "Jew."[92] Israel may be a place where Jews live, but it offers no telos of security or answer for global Jewish existence. As one Chutzpah writer explained it, "self determination embodied in a state does not automatically imply support for the particular state of Israel."[93] And while Chutzpah aligned itself with the Israeli anti-war left and the New Left "New Outlook" movement—which argued for full rights for Palestinian citizens of Israel, demilitarization of Israel, and peace negotiations with the PLO and neighboring states—*Chutzpah* and its Israeli partners also wrote about and made contact with far more radical organizations in Palestine, most notably the Israeli Black Panther Party and Palestinian Communist leaders, and even printed extended interviews with armed Palestinian guerrillas in Lebanon. *Chutzpah*'s politics regarding Palestine were complicated, dialectical, and in motion, never fully fitting in with a Zionist or anti-Zionist left. One could call their politics "non-Zionist," yet that fails to capture the contradictions of their positions, or their capacity to change with historical conditions.

Yet Chutzpah's position leaves unanswered questions. What to make of armed struggle by Palestinians? The killing of Israeli civilians? What to make of calls for Israel's dismantling? In the US such ambiguities open questions about whom to ally with and who should form coalitions. If Chutzpah disavowed Palestinian groups that it deemed too militant or antisemitic, should they form coalitions with groups in the US that support them? As Chutzpah member Maralee Gordon framed it, "It made sense for the Black Panther Party to support Palestine in the same way it made sense for Chutzpah to support the Israeli left. And because we live in the US, it also made sense for Chutzpah to support the Panthers."[94] While this makes perfect diasporic and dialectical sense, it also opens such groups to accusations that such diasporists are opportunistic or incoherent. Today, such dilemmas face Jewish-centric diasporic groups like Jewish Voice for Peace and IfNotNow (INN). Even though both organizations officially denounce the attacks of October 7, they have allied with organizations such as Students for Justice in Palestine that support the attacks, and are often in protests with other groups such as Within Our Lifetime and International Jewish Anti-Zionist Network that have taken positions against many JVP shibboleths of nonviolence and productive alliances with progressive politicians. This has opened JVP and INN to criticism from both

Zionists and anti-Zionists. Yet one could argue there is a fidelity at work, perhaps an inner core of Jewish identity and non-identity, the call to be both oneself and against oneself in any act of solidarity. While one could say the structure of "Epitaph for Sidney" leaves the story as simply an unresolved contradiction, I would argue that a state of unresolved contradiction, of being two things at once and neither, is perhaps the "non-identity" of actual politics, actual struggle, and what the Jewish left can offer the world. In this vision of the diaspora, we hear an echo of Adorno's famous maxim, "It is part of morality not to be at home in one's home," to be ironically a partisan of one's politics and outside it.[95] One can also think of Terry Eagleton's edict that he trusts no revolutionary who does not want to do themselves out of existence: a true Marxist must be an ironist, organizing around the very class marker they want to abolish.[96] Thus Jewish diasporism, much like the diasporism of the Black Atlantic, is a flexible modality of political life, eschewing the narrow politics of essentialist identity formation and class-based universalism.

It should also be noted diasporism is a kind of end run around the "end of Jewish history" or at least a diffusion of its gravitational Götterdämmerung. One of the more ironic features of our age of Zionist crisis is that both American Zionists and anti-Zionists seem to agree that the history of the Jewish left has reached a terminus. Franklin Foer in his 2024 essay for the *Atlantic* states the position forcefully: the "Golden Age of American Jews Is Ending."[97] For Foer, the hundred-year ascendency of Jewish liberals and even leftists into the American cultural spotlight— from iconoclasts such as Susan Sontag and Lenny Bruce to elder statesmen such as Richard Hofstadter and Eric Foner—has come to a crashing end with the rejection of Jews as, on the left, Zionists and, on the right, Jewish liberals. The sight of kaffiyeh-clad protesters for Foer is not different from the sight of tiki-torch neo-Nazis, except perhaps that the kaffiyeh-clad protesters have academic cachet in some quarters. And while this Zionist hand-wringing is easily dismissible as centrist schwarmerei, it does in some ways bear a kind of echoing similarity, a structural homology, to many on the left who feel that secular Jewish social democracy, even Communism, has led us down the path of nationalism with its focus on Jewish trauma, memory, and history. As Dorothy Zellner opines on the pages of *Jewish Currents*, it was the Jewish left, seduced by the Soviet Union in 1947, that sanitized Zionism for a generation of left-wing Jews.[98] The title, "What We Did," summarizes the takeaway of the article: it was

Jews' self-absorption and racism that betrayed Palestine (even if this Communist heyday for Israel lasted only a few short years). Shaul Magid comes to a similar conclusion regarding the ascension of Meir Kahane's politics both in the US and in Israel. While his own political career may have ended in infamy, Magid suggests there is a kind of parallel to his "Jews first" politics echoed in the slogan of Arthur Waskow: "From Jewish radicals to radical Jews."[99] These groups, focused on Jewish particularity, Jewish history, Jewish Renewal, were all part of the Jewish-centric world that spawned Jewish nationalism.

Diasporism then is a counter to this idea of Jewish terminus, a kind of anti-teleology, a refusal to accept either Zionism or assimilation as the telos of Jewish history. In a sense, the kind of nostalgia performed by Foer is predicated on a feeling that Jews and Jewish history are determined to point to justice. In the same way Foer believes Jews are unfairly singled out, so too those who feel Jewish left history is to blame seem to suggest that tautologically, if Jews are liberal, then mustn't Jewish liberalism, even Jewish leftism, be to blame for the hellscape of modern Israel? Both reach back into the myth of American Jewish life, as if history, to quote Fredric Jameson on nostalgia, could be outside of the social forces and class struggle that produced it. Perhaps then a Benjaminian idea of memory is inherently diasporist in its conception. Refusing a telos of history—indeed, suggesting a telos of history is at best a bourgeois fetish—opens history up to the multiple directions, courses, and struggles our current crisis demands. In the way a diasporist history is relational, not one thing and not another, an identity of non-identity, so then the practice of counter-memory can be a disruptive force, entering political discourse in a moment of danger to suggest the reemergence of lost futures. As many Jewish activists and scholars are now unearthing histories of Jewish anarchists, socialists, Communists, and anti-Zionists, they do so not to preserve a Jewish status quo, but rather to chart new paths through a fragmenting present. Indeed, every generation of Jewish radicals invents its own past to break with what Benjamin refers to as the "social conformism of progress," what Foer would describe as the seamless march to the future of (Jewish) America. Whether Molly Crabapple's histories of Bundist anti-Zionist socialism, Chutzpah's evocation of radical partisans and garment workers, Amelia Glaser's recovery of radical Yiddish poetry, Alan Wald's literary biographies of Jewish Communists such as Abraham Polonsky and Mike Gold, or Butler and Boyarin's reclamation of "diaspora," such histories are specters in Marx's phrasing, to haunt the present and present, by way of the past, a different path forward. One can think perhaps as well of Anna Elena Torres's evocation of early twentieth-century Jewish anarchists, for whom "anarchist diasporism" is a kind prefigural formation, as much a political projection as an empirical or sociological description of Jewish polities.[100] While diasporism is a lived experience for many Jews, one has to consider it at this point well beyond the facts of Jewish life to be an active position of relationality and resistance, both inside and outside Jewish communal life.

Jewish Left-Wing Memory and Forgetting: An Absent-Presence

However central the socialist left has been in both shaping Jewish American life and American life writ large, lived memory of the Jewish left remains contradictory and refracted, both forgotten and mythologized at the same time. Such left-wing memory and forgetting is what one author refers to as an "absent-presence," or what Althusser refers to as the "absent-cause" of history, structuring experience without social or allegorical reference points consciously referenced.[101] Indeed the memory of the Jewish left in contemporary American Jewish life is often citational, rather than deeply historical: there is an intimate reference that Jewish artists, intellectuals, and politics will cite—perhaps even unconsciously—without narrative or teleological coherence. Such references often appear in what one literary critic referred to as a "dissociated metaphor," the repetition of a trope without a full development of its meaning. The archetype of this form of citation might be the Coen brothers' films: there is passing reference to a largely Jewish Trotskyite sect in *Inside Llewyn Davis*; the Dude in *The Big Lebowski* was a founding member of SDS; and *Barton Fink* is both an homage to and a satire of Clifford Odets, Arthur Miller, and Melvin Levy, well-known Jewish Marxist playwrights of the 1930s who wrote with varying success for Hollywood.[102] Yet one can also find the presence of Communists and Jewish radicals in *Seinfeld*, Philip Roth, and Aaron Sorkin's films, often without explanation or extended commentary. And while *Seinfeld* plays off its Communists for laughs, and Roth involves them in bedroom drama, the citational presence of the Jewish left within Jewish progressive culture—from liberals such as the Coen brothers and Larry David—speaks to if not exactly an active historical memory of the Jewish left, then an intimacy with the history that lives on to shape both Jewish liberals and the Jewish left in ways that are sometimes conscious, often refracted. While I would argue for the explicit memory of the Jewish left, this citational presence is important as it speaks to the many continuities and ruptures between what is sometimes referred to by shorthand as "Jewish liberalism" and "the Jewish left," with the dividing lines often quite obscured between the two.

Indeed, the title of this book, *Citizens of the Whole World*, derives from a line in an unpublished novel by the Jewish film critic and fellow traveler Robert Gessner, one of the many ghosts in the Jewish memory machine. Gessner was one of the few left-wing writers in the 1930s to explicitly make connections among indigenous genocide in the Americas, Zionist settler-colonialism, and fascism. In his best-known essay, "The Brown Shirts of Zion," in the influential left-wing arts and culture magazine *New Masses*, Gessner not only describes the Revisionist Vladimir Jabotinsky as a "Jewish Hitler" and refers to the kibbutzim as the "Socialist Nationalists of Zionist Movement"; he adds there is also a colonial character to Zionism, citing the Balfour Declaration and noting that the Palestinians are to be "disposed ... as so many American Indians."[103]

In Gessner's unpublished novel "The Volunteer," he poses an extended dialogue between young Jewish socialists from the US and hardened members of the right-wing Jewish paramilitaries, the Irgun. The American Jewish socialists are quickly disillusioned and finally attempt to flee the country, only to die in the crossfire between Palestinian and Jewish militias. In his final internal dialogue, Jacob, the American narrator, notes that the "socialist dream" of the kibbutz "sleeps in Marinette County," not in Israel, and that "socialism" is but a "footnote" to the messianic Christian-like fervor of Zionism. The whole "country is a second Sermon on the Mount." Jacob finally concludes, "You're an alien in Israel because of you are a citizen of the whole damn stupid world."[104]

Crucial to the conclusion of Gessner's manuscript is the idea that the Jewish socialism dreamed of by Jacob is one born out of his particularly American life as a left-wing activist organizing in a multiethnic milieu. To be a citizen of the whole world—an internationalist—is irreconcilable with Zionism: indeed, Zionism kills him. And perhaps the most controversial thought he expresses is that Israel is a "second Sermon on the Mount," suggesting that Zionism has more in common with Christian prophecy and politics than Jewishness. All three objections to Zionism comprise what I would argue is an American Jewish left common sense about Zionism, that it violates strongly held beliefs about internationalism. Zionism is incompatible with the multiethnic democratic culture of the US left, and Zionism is a violation of Jewish ethics of diasporic mobility and an ethic of cohabitation. American Jewish messianism is an ethic, not a place.

It's also important to note that this is an unpublished novel; written in 1948, it may have run afoul of FBI sensibilities if not censors. And this is perhaps the most important intervention this book would like to make. Far too much Jewish historiography relies on major Jewish institutions such as the Anti-Defamation League, the American Jewish Committee, the American Council for Judaism, and so on. While these histories may be necessary, they recall a statement by Jewish historian Bernard Lazare, that Jewish history tends to be told "by the bourgeoisie, for the bourgeoisie," and rarely centers either on Jewish radicals or Jewish popular classes.[105] Yet it is impossible to tell the story of Jewish anti-Zionism as merely a history of ideas or even a history of institutions. The unconscious of Jewish life and the long history of Jewish anti-Zionism owe as much to the history of the Jewish left as they do to the official history of Jewish institutions or Jewish religious practice. This is not to discount the role of religious liberals and leftists who have come to prominence especially since the 1970s with Waskow's Freedom Seder and the emergence of "Jewish Renewal," but rather to say the set of associations we understand as Jewish progressive politics were set long before a broad mass secular realignment of American politics. And this history of the Jewish radical left is often buried, archived, and banned, so that radical leftists are known more by the long afterglow they cast over Jewish life, and less by their recorded presence.

It is something of a truism to suggest that the Jewish left has "vanished" or that attempts to recall its living history engage in "nostalgia."[106] In Irving Howe's epic of Yiddish New York, he tells a story of coherence and dispersion, from a pure Yiddish socialism to first a breakup over the Soviet Union and finally a slow assimilation into mainstream American culture.[107] As historian Cheryl Greenberg suggests, Jews are seen as America's "quintessential liberals," and like many other Jewish historians, she focuses her study on such organizations as the AJC and ADL.[108] Such a view implicitly marginalizes the cultural force of the Jewish left and often overplays the cultural importance of mainstream Jewish organizations, mistaking radicals' gains for theirs. In a review essay on Howe's *World of Our Fathers* collectively written by members of a 1970s Jewish socialist collective the year of its publication, the authors responded with outrage at Howe's suggestion that the Jewish left is over. "Our mistrust of Howe," they wrote, "increased when he ignored the highly significant contributions of our generation—the antiwar movement and campus radicalism," and they proceeded to list a number of prominent Jewish activists such as Jerry Rubin, Jane Alpert, and Mark Rudd.[109] They went on to offer a compelling critique of a linear Jewish American historiography:

> [Howe] seems to have a strong desire to have the complexity of Jewish life as he expressed it so skillfully in early chapters, reducible only to those patterns and choices he deemed representative of the Jewish American typified by himself: the Jew who lives a fully Americanized and secularized life, but who remembers and commemorates the past: the Jew who feels "our travels are over," that our forebears emigrated to find material and political freedom, paid the price of their heritage, but gave us an abiding and equally valuable legacy—American success.

It is not, of course, that members of the socialist, Chicago-based Chutzpah Collective saw no difference in the American Jewish world from the 1920s to the 1970s; rather their project was to carry on with Jewish left-wing, even revolutionary, traditions, yet to do so within a contemporary context, even while honoring the past. As former SDS founding member turned sociology professor Dick Flacks wrote, based on extensive research with New Left activists, the young, often Jewish, people in groups such as SDS tended to come from progressive families, and often saw their activism less as a break with earlier generations than as a continuation of it in a new form.[110] The fact that this is not often as obvious as it should be goes a long way to suggest, again, the left's absent-presence in Jewish life: lived but not historicized.

The reasons for this presence and erasure are complex and without a single narrative source: forces of suburbanization, assimilation, class advancement, and mass education all play roles. Yet I would suggest that, to paraphrase Michael Rogin's classic *Ronald Reagan, the Movie*, counterrevolution is a regime of forgetting.[111] The Red Scare not only wiped out the Communist Party and its many affiliated unions and organizations—driving them into dissolution and in many cases causing their leaders to be arrested and deported—it also wiped out the memory of the Old Left. While the Reagan counterrevolution was nowhere near the scope of what Ellen Schrecker described as "the most widespread, longest lasting wave of political repression in American history," its impact was analogous if not as total.[112] Cultural memory in the US reshaped the anti-imperialist and anti-racist mass movement of the 1960s New Left into a story of hippies and anti-war protesters, substituting the Jewish liberal break with the New Left for Jewish radical support of it. For all the breathless coverage of the "conversion of American Jews to Zionism" in 1967, it is little remembered that the most publicly visible Jews of the late 1960s were hardly Zionists: Abbie Hoffman, Judy Gumbo, Jerry Rubin, Philip Roth, Grace Paley, Noam Chomsky, and so on.

Yosef Yerushalmi makes the argument in his influential book on Jewish memory and history, *Zakhor*, that history runs in some ways counter to memory. That Jewish memory, embodied in the commandment *zakhor*, is an essentially conservative force, marking Jewish life as the repetition of cyclical phenomena, the same story told over and over, perhaps with new embellishments.[113] This book wrestles with a contrary phenomenon, the insistence that contemporary Jewish life has formed a total rupture with what has come before *and* that Jewish life has not changed at all. In some ways, left politics are the folkways of American Jews, in ways that both record and problematically mythologize the past. While, of course, my goal is not to erase American Jewish complicity in whiteness, assimilation, classism, and settler-colonialism, neither is it to suggest that left-wing politics are an authentic Jewish identity. Rather, I take the view that the "folk-memory" of the Jewish left continues to play a role in shaping American Jewish life and that there is nothing particularly exceptional about the Jews who are its vanguard: the explosion of left-Jewish activism over Israeli genocide is just the latest chapter in this story. The absent-presence of the left in American Jewish life is both a reservoir of left memory and an accommodation to anti-Communism and whiteness. As sociologist Laurence Kotler-Berkowitz points out, "liberal politics" is actually a form of cultural adhesion or a "structural basis of cohesion" for American Jews, particularly those Jews for whom daily religious observance is not the form of communal life.[114] In other words, liberal politics is not just something American Jews engage in to advance material interests but rather an expression of Jewish communal life and belonging. Memory and forgetting, citing left-wing history while also keeping one's distance from it, are a particularly Jewish modality of American life. Perhaps with the explosion of Zionism into the public arena and obligation forced upon Jews to take sides, this quiet accommodation can no longer be sufficient. Or, as one conservative writer dismissively put it, it is liberalism and not necessarily Zionism that is the "civic religion" of American Jews.[115] While the rise of Zionism would seem to place such claims of civic religion in question, perhaps another way to put it might be: the reemergence of anti-Zionism suggests perhaps American Jewish "religion" has changed less than we think and is now praying out in the open.

Methodology

This book is not an attempt to offer a comprehensive history of the American Jewish left, or Jewish anti-Zionism. In one sense my choices follow from my thesis: that Jewish anti-Zionism emerges, much like Zionism, not solely within the Jewish community as an autochthonous formation, but rather in dialogic relation to the non-Jewish world. Thus in many ways, this book is a snapshot of four moments of left-wing upsurge as much as they are particular moments of Jewish history: the Old Left, the New Left, the "identitarian" left of the 1970s, and finally, the new socialist and anti-racist movements of the Trump era. While I attempt to construct an implicit genealogy from the Communist Party to SDS and the SWP, to the Chutzpah Collective and the Jewish Solidarity Caucus and Jewish Voice for Peace, there are many organizations and individuals I leave out or do not address fully, which could have been part of this book. This book is not then an encyclopedia of the Jewish left, but rather four snapshots in time, brushing as they are against the grain of the present. The book does however follow two narrative arcs, from the Marxist internationals and domestic anti-racist coalitional politics of the Popular Front era and the New Left, to the declension of that particular combinatory structure of feeling in the present to a new Jewish left.[116] And it is the narrative of memory, asking what are the stakes of the stories from the past that emerge, through the smoke of the present to the dark fields of the past?

As historian Michel-Rolph Trouillot reminds us, what is remembered in a historical narrative is largely a function of power. Exercise of power dictates not only what narratives will or will not remain within the public sphere, but what accumulates as "fact": archives, let alone histories, are produced at multiple points into which lasting and even permanent silences may be introduced.[117] Silence in this sense is not merely a negation; it is also generative. The silences in the historical record do not confront us like hidden treasures that merely need to be recovered; rather, silences accumulate to render such objects unintelligible to future scholars or activists. For instance, the assertion that the remembrance of the Holocaust was initially deployed against US imperialism and Zionism is a statement greeted like a single raindrop in a clear sky—simply negligible, evaporating as soon as it touches ground. The struggle then is not to prove the Jewish left existed, but that its existence was unexceptional, ordinary, currents of common sense that must be recognized as such. The task is not to show curios or oddities in vanished documents, but to show them as hidden pathways to the present. That "Never Again for Anyone" banner dropped in Grand Central Station after the invasion of Gaza is both an interruption into the present and an invitation to reread silences from the past.

While I have been keen to include canonical texts from twentieth- and twenty-first-century American Jewish culture such as Philip Roth's *Portnoy's Complaint*, Hannah Arendt's *Eichmann in Jerusalem*, Tony Kushner's *Angels in America*, and Mike Gold's *Jews without Money*, my sources were primarily archives, memoirs, and interviews. I interviewed over three dozen activists. Two-thirds of my interviewees were members of New Left–era movement organizations, ranging from SDS and SWP to the Chutzpah Collective, the Communist Party, International Socialists, Revolutionary Union, and the Revolutionary Communist Party. During these interviews I wanted to simply get the subjects—some of whom I had known as a friends and comrades and some who were complete strangers—to start talking. Many spoke through a tradition they were not aware of, even as they embodied it. Others taught me of traditions I thought I knew backward and forward; for most, it was some of both. Through the gestalt I assumed patterns would emerge—which of course, they did: the importance of the Red Scare, Holocaust memory, antisemitism, anti-racism—in the interviewees' relationship to the left and to the state of Israel. While some foregrounded their Jewishness, for some it was far more submerged; for everyone, being raised *Jewish* informed part of their subjectivity and perspective in ways that seemed inextricable from who they were, as if an element of their height or retinas. Among the second group of interviewees, people who came of political age in the second decade of the new millennium, it was surprising to see in many ways how similar their perspective was. For some, their Jewishness was the point of view from which they understood their world, but for most, they were Jews, leftists, queers, anti-Zionists in a relationship that could not be reduced to a sum of their parts. Yet also, many of the same themes emerged, from Holocaust memory to antisemitism, anti-racism, and a general sense that there was a Jewish left in the past that had been gifted and stolen from them simultaneously.

It may go without saying, but the interviews were the most vital part of the project. They were not oral histories, for the most part, but conversations across generations about left history and Jewish history, Jewish subjectivities and de-colonial Jewish thought. While there are some well-known subjects I interviewed or whose memoirs I included, for the most part the histories I recorded and engaged with were from activists who had not consciously thought of themselves as making history as they made it, either left-wing or Jewish. This is, of course, the second rather straightforward thesis of the book: most Jewish history is working- and middle-class history, carried about by activists who are not in Jewish organizations, who are not intellectuals in universities. Not only is such history often not written down, to many Jewish studies scholars the history of the SWP or Revolutionary Union is not even Jewish history. While it is debatable perhaps *what kind* of Jewish history it is, that more Jews participated in the Communist Party, SDS, and the SWP than organizations such as AJC or ADL suggests perhaps such histories are excluded not for their marginality, but for their politics. Just as examples, the best Jewish histories I came across—of secularism, antisemitism, and racism—were written as pamphlets by Jewish socialists without advanced degrees, and in most cases, no college degree at all.

Perhaps to the disappointment of those for whom history should be always in the service of immediacy, I do need to warn readers that this is *not* a history, nor am I a historian: it's a cultural studies project and relies as much on literature, feelings, and affect as it does on causal narratives of how, say, the CPUSA crumbled and SDS rose, briefly, in its ashes, or how the ascendency of Zionism happened and so on. My reliance on fiction and to a lesser extent poetry and film is because literature is a form of non-instrumentalizable world-making; it is not the opposite of politics, but perhaps the other to politics: it says, or at least can say, what is between the lines of slogans. I believe also fiction can function as a counternarrative, never fully capturable by ideology and thus, paradoxically, the best vehicle for ideology's need for both structure and incoherence. Ideology can only function after modernity, to quote Slavoj Žižek, when there is a gap between the stated belief and the practice: there must be room for the ironic self.[118] Fiction can provide this cultural complexity; pamphlets are designed not to.

A return to the complexities of fiction is also a function of historical uncertainty. Stuart Hall makes the point that cultural studies emerged only in the 1950s, in a moment of historical rupture, when empirically known quantities such as "class" and "capitalism" became far more complex than the easily divided binaries.[119] Hall invokes Raymond Williams's observation that culture is not just a question of ideas, but a "whole way of life," suggesting that simple binaries—base/superstructure, working-class/ruling-class—are not so much meaningless but caught in a complex matrix of propositions not always separable from one another. Another way to put it might be that cultural studies emerges in a moment of defeat and reflection, in which the German masses offered the world fascism, and the Soviet Union replaced class struggle with its own version of a managed, Keynesian state of working- and ruling-class collaboration and harmony. In this sense *cultural studies* in this book—a look at the sprawling, spawning world of novels and literature, slogans and pamphlets—fits a subject in which the narrative arc, its own "whole way of life," is in conflict, and there is an increasing separation of signs and signifiers. What does it mean to be an American Jew? A leftist? An anti-Zionist? If one has clear, unambiguous answers to these questions that do not also include their opposites I will believe this person either a genius or a fool.

As a matter of memory and dialogue, no other work of fiction poses the question of the Jewish left and the work of cultural memory quite like Melanie Kaye/Kantrowitz's "Some Pieces of Jewish Left," published in the first issue of Jewish feminist magazine *Bridges*, in 1987.[120] The story imagines monologues by and between four Jewish women, all of whom have different relationships to Jewishness, the left, and the women's movement. The story begins tellingly with a silence: the first narrator, an estranged red diaper baby, says her family was "CP" but "didn't talk about it." Indeed, the story is constructed through a series of silences, the parents of Rosa and their own membership in the Communist Party, the New Left that happened before one narrator is born, the recitation of names of famous leftists, during which their Jewishness is not mentioned, the silence between a mother and daughter about the daughter's antisemitism.

The story concludes with the final narrator, Vivian, who is "preoccupied" with being Jewish while also being the farthest from any Jewish community. Vivian suggests her preoccupation is precisely the result of her distance from Jewishness and, in that sense, the condition of all Jews in the United States, produced by the "chasm," created by "immigration, the Holocaust, assimilation," between what she should be able to take "for granted" and the vast sea of her estrangement. The Red Scare is suggested as yet another chasm, a rupture in memory and even space as few of the Jews in the story still live in the Communist parents' Brooklyn neighborhood. Israel, while barely mentioned, is rendered as yet another rupture, as Chava spends her single trip feeling alienated by the confident, unalienated, muscular Jewishness she encounters there. The story further refuses any closure: it is four women narrating their own relationship to Jewishness, and often challenging one another, interrupting one another, erasing and also revising one another's experiences. This chasm, the story concludes, is what we will later call "history"—an ending that echoes Walter Benjamin's theory of progress, the entrance of silence into what should be the lives of the oppressed spoken at full volume.

The story, written in the late 1980s, came at a moment in which the Jewish left itself was fraying, as with the left writ large (a social rupture much like the one Hall observes before the birth of cultural studies in the 1950s). Of course, this is not to say the Jewish left was over—shortly after this story was published, Kaye/Kantrowitz would help to found JFREJ, and Jewish Voice for Peace would be founded in the Bay Area not long after. But the waning of the New Left, like the ending of "actually existing socialism," created a crisis of narrative, and a crisis of identity. The story itself seems uncertain what narrative of the left it is trying to tell: on the one hand, the Communist parents are described as narrow-minded, shrill, and racially insensitive; on the other hand, the story is more than just a nostalgic window into the Old Left: with its freedom seders decades before Waskow's Freedom Seder, with its "civil rights before civil rights," with its unbending uprightness for justice and comfortability with being Jewish, it makes its narrator, Rosa, seem like she is less in control of her own narrative than the historical moment she is trying to evoke in all its shortcomings. Fran sees her own disavowals about Jewishness harden into a kind of quiet antisemitism in her daughter and is shocked into a reevaluation of her own Jewishness as a result. The story seems to understand that both the left and the Jewish left will continue so long as the conversation, the dialogue, continues: it is a dialectic and not an end point. In this sense this book is not written to be the final word on the Jewish left or anti-Zionism, but rather to meet an open space of history with voices, some of which will be quite familiar, some new, even to themselves. As Kaye/Kantrowitz says, "crossing the perilous chasm which only later gets called history."

1
When Anti-Zionism Was Jewish: Jewish Racial Subjectivity and the Anti-imperialist Literary Left from the Great Depression to the Cold War

There is a scene in Mike Gold's 1930 novel *Jews without Money* that links the many strands of left-wing Jewish identity formation to political Zionism at mid-century. Mikey, the novel's narrator and proletarian icon for the "red decade" of the 1930s, travels with his father, Herman, to the outer suburbs of Brooklyn to buy what his father hopes will be a suburban dream house. Herman, a Romanian Jewish house painter, has been offered the house through his associations with the "Zionist leader" and "big dry goods merchant" Baruch Goldfarb—a man Herman believes will rescue him from a life of poverty.[1] Herman joins a gaudy Jewish lodge, full of ritual and costume, and pays substantial dues to Goldfarb's burial association, even when Goldfarb ignores Herman's repeated requests for a loan to restart his tailoring shop. Believing that his association with wealthy Jews is his ticket to success, Herman becomes friendly with an associate of Goldfarb's, a real estate agent, and agrees to move his family to the suburbs where he imagines he will no longer be an "East Side beggar."

While this scene is *Jews without Money*'s lone comment on Zionism, it's worth pausing to consider what Gold's sly intervention on the topic suggests about his view of Jewish colonialism in mandate Palestine. Goldfarb is introduced as "a Zionist leader" who not only cheats Herman out of his money through his burial association, but also inducts Herman into the reactionary political formation of his lodge: organizing vote rigging, labor spies, and the alignment of Jewish workers with the interests of the Jewish bourgeoisie. That Zionism is further associated with Herman's desire to move out to the suburbs is also telling: Mikey's class-conscious mother wants to remain on the multiethnic Chrystie Street rather than move to the isolated and assimilationist suburbs. "God's country" of the suburbs—a not-so-subtle dig at God's country of Zion—is associated not only with bourgeois con men, but also with whiteness, assimilationism, and class betrayal.

Ultimately, Herman's acts as a labor spy for Goldfarb's associate, Mr. Cohen, can be read as a tragic just deserts, as Herman pitches to his near death from a faulty catwalk at Mr. Cohen's worksite that might have been fixed had a union been allowed to organize. It should be noted that Herman's dreams of middle-class success in an isolated Jewish enclave away from the racially mixed, transnational pressures and pleasures of urban life are also what finally kill him. Does Zionism kill Herman? No, but the racial and economic formation out of which Zionism arises does.

From a contemporary perspective, what is most remarkable about Gold's anti-Zionist subplot is not the prominence of the author, but that Gold assumed it did not need explanation. Mike Gold, born Itzok "Irwin" Granich, was perhaps the foremost practitioner and promoter of the proletarian literary movement in the US. As a founding editor of the leading left-wing arts journal during the Popular Front, the *New Masses*, Gold became the cultural arbiter of literary taste for the Communist Party USA (CPUSA), pugnaciously denouncing both high modernism and middlebrow literature alike. And to say Gold was merely a novelist is something of an understatement: as Alan Wald and others have noted, "creative literary practice" took precedence over other forms of cultural output for those in the Communist orbit.[2] For Gold to denounce Zionism in such terms, as both the editor of the most prestigious socialist arts journal of the era and the most popular Jewish literary figure of the Popular Front era, suggests that it is more than just the idle opinion of a lone eccentric.[3] For Gold's Jewish readers, the idea that a "Zionist leader" is a petty bourgeois scammer who ensnares gullible working-class house painters into his utopian schemes would be immediately recognizable, part of the left-wing common sense of the era.

Criticism of Zionism was common on the Jewish left in the 1930s and 1940s, so common that a historian of Zionist cultural literature could find only one left-wing Jewish author, Meyer Levin, who took up pro-Zionist themes (and his novels were widely panned).[4] As Yuri Slezkine writes, of the three Jewish "Promised Lands" of the twentieth century, citizenship in the United States, emigration to Israel, and the Bolshevik Revolution (that is, assimilation, nationalism, or Communism), Communism remained by far the most popular solution to the "Jewish question" in the decades between the wars.[5] Or as writer and Communist Party critic Robert Gessner put it bluntly in *New Masses*, "In America, about one percent of America's Jews are Zionist."[6] Derided as nationalists, imperialists, and the petty bourgeoisie, Zionists were a small and often-mocked minority within the Jewish socialist left, so much so a recently revived Yiddish song ridicules Zionists as "little" and "foolish," out of touch with "the workers' reality."[7] While there has never *not* been an anti-Zionist Jewish left, that Zionists could be referred to as small-minded idiots, relegated to the ash heap of history, is clearly a sentiment one must regard in our current conjuncture with wonder.

The erasure of this left-wing, working-class, anti-Zionist common sense can not only be laid at the feet of Israel and its defenders. Or rather, its erasure is complex and, as with Mike Gold's prescient trip to the suburbs, part of a larger ideological and material project that included an incomplete but nonetheless wide incorporation of immigrant Jewish life into dominant American ideas of race, politics, and identity.[8] As Bernard Lazare observed, Jewish history has been written by bourgeois historians for a bourgeois readership—radical Jews, especially working-class radical Jews, rarely figure much in historiography that locates Jewish life in religious institutions and well-funded advocacy agencies such as B'nai B'rith or the Anti-Defamation League (ADL).[9] The Communist Party and other smaller socialist and Trotskyist organizations have been underexamined as major sites of Jewish identity formation. It is, for instance, seldom appreciated that the Communist Party witnessed more Jews move through its ranks in the 1930s than the liberal American Jewish Committee (AJC) or more explicitly anti-Zionist Reform movement's American Council for Judaism (ACJ), let alone organizations such as the ADL.

Indeed, throughout the 1930s, it is estimated that half of the CPUSA membership was Jewish, nearly all of eastern European, or Ashkenazi, descent, and given the rapid turnover of members, it may have amounted to as many as a few hundred thousand Jewish members over the decade, or perhaps as much as 5 to 10 percent of the entire Jewish population.[10] That is to say, Communism should not only be considered something many Jews participated in, but as a subjective site in which Ashkenazi Jews made and remade their identities as often first- and second-generation Americans. But rather than examine Jewish anti-Zionism through a lens of Jewish exceptionalism, I would suggest that Jews in the Communist Party orbit, like other non-Anglo-Saxon "oppressed nationalities" in Alexander Bittelman's framing of the time, strove to adopt a racialized framework of otherness that identified a Jewish subjectivity in solidarity with oppressed people of color, whether in the US or under colonial rule. As Michael Denning, Robin Kelley, and Bill Mullen have argued, ethnic identification became the language of international class solidarity, rather than its antithesis, during the period of the radical midcentury left.[11] In Michael Denning's articulation of Stuart Hall's famous phrase, "Ethnicity and race had become the modality through which working class peoples experienced their lives and mapped their communities."[12]

"Throughout the era of the British mandate in Palestine, the international communist movement regarded Zionism as a settler-colonial movement expropriating the rights of the indigenous population in alliance with British imperialism," writes historian Joel Beinin. For the most part, local Communist Parties followed the Soviet Union, which up until it supported Partition in 1947, either sided with Palestinian anti-colonial revolts or at least was ambiguous enough so that local and national Communist Parties often went their own way.[13] Until 1947, the CPUSA and other radical left-wing groups in the US opposed Zionism as an imperialist project, chartered by the Balfour Declaration, directly or indirectly requiring the support of the British Empire.[14] "Palestine is a colony of British imperialism," CPUSA General Secretary Earl Browder said in an address on Zionism in the New York Hippodrome in 1936, "and no matter how deplorable present attacks on the Jews in Palestine are . . . there is a rising revolutionary movement of the oppressed people fighting for its national independence."[15] Browder was clear to separate pogroms against Jews in Poland and other parts of Europe from Arab attacks on Jewish settlers—the former he compared to the "Ku Klux Klan and the now infamous 'Black Legion'" in the United States, while the latter he offered was resistance to "British imperialism by the Arab masses."[16] In other words, while Jews may have been an "oppressed nationality" in Europe, in Palestine, the recent immigrants were part of an imperial project. The Communist Party also made clear that Zionism would require the "forcible expropriation of almost a quarter of a million Arabs." While prescient, the statement was a drastic undercount.[17] And as most other left-wing parties throughout the world, Communists also opposed Zionism on the grounds that it was right-wing nationalism, an abandonment of both the class struggle inside Europe as well as joint Jewish and Arab struggles against imperialism in the Middle East.[18] Zionists, as Gessner wrote in a 1935 essay, "The Brown Shirts of Zion," were "Nazis": an imperialist ethno-nationalism.[19]

It would be tempting to suggest that left-wing Jewish anti-Zionism in this period was just an extension of Communist Party policy on the question of Palestine and that Jews in the CPUSA's orbit just fell into line. Jewish anti-Zionism at mid-century, while perhaps "common sense," was far more complex a formation. Liberal critics of Zionism in the ACJ such as Reform rabbi Elmer Berger often expressed their attacks on Zionism from an assimilationist perspective, worrying that Zionism would imply "dual loyalty" among US Jews and cut Jews off from mainstream American life.[20] Berger and others in the ACJ circle also expressed a profound unease with the politics of ethnic belonging they felt were particular to secular Zionism, expressing that Jews were not "a nation" and had no common cultural or collective identity beyond a shared religious faith.[21] For the largest left-wing Jewish organization in prewar Europe, the Bund, or the General Jewish Labor Union of Eastern Europe, dual loyalty was not the issue: Zionism's "separatist, chauvinist, clerical, and conservative" culture was understood as the "polar opposite" of the radical Yiddish-speaking organizations of Europe that were progressive, secular, and internationalist.[22] Even Trotsky, who was no fan of the Bund's cultural separatism, lauded the union insofar as it "demanded full rights for the Jews where they lived and worked and fiercely opposed Zionism as a utopian, reactionary scheme, a form of self-expulsion, preached by Jewish bourgeois nationalists who played into the hands of anti-Semites and further divided the working class."[23]

Despite differences with the Bund, Jewish Communists and socialists in the US constructed an ethnic particularism that echoed some of the Bund's own cultural politics. As one historian suggests, Jewish socialists articulated their own politics of "nonassimilation" through, rather than despite, their attachment to the left. For US Jewish radicals, the culture of the left became a way to separate themselves from what they understood to be a bourgeois, Anglo-Saxon, Christian-dominated American culture, while also avoiding the right-wing nationalism of Zionism.[24] "The most radical Jews [in the Communist Party] tended to be the most insular," a historian offered, and they created an ethnically separate Jewish world inside the party, through radical Jewish journals and party organizations.[25] *Morgen Freiheit*, the CPUSA-affiliated Yiddish-language newspaper, along with other Communist-affiliated publications and organizations such as Yidburo and the Organization for Jewish Colonization in Russia (known by its transliterated acronym ICOR) formed a kind of subculture on the left, devoted to Communism and articulating a particular modality of secular, socialist Jewish existence, of which Mike Gold was very much a part.[26] For Jewish socialists, Communism was the opposite of Browder's slogan regarding the Popular Front: Communism was not twentieth-century Americanism so much as it was twentieth-century Judaism.

Perhaps one of the leading, if now unknown, theorists of Jewish life in the Communist Party was Alexander Bittelman, editor of the Communist Party's theoretical journal, the *Communist*, and on the editorial board of the Communist-affiliated magazine *Jewish Life*. Bittelman wrote extensively about Jewish identity formation in a series of treatises distributed by the Communist Party, as well as in editorials and articles for *Jewish Life* and other left-wing Jewish publications. Bittelman was a Russian immigrant who arrived in the US in the 1920s, worked for a time in the mid-1930s in Moscow writing anti-colonial party literature, and often mixed Jewish identity with Marxism in surprising ways, including his attempt to merge the cultural nationalism of the Bund with the CPUSA's analysis of colonial nationalism, or writing, for instance, that his journey through the Suez Canal to the Soviet Union was "reliving the story of exodus." [27]

Bittelman's position on Jewish identity should be placed in contrast not only to the liberal ACJ's formulation that Judaism is just another religion, but also to the secular notion of "peoplehood" as articulated by Jewish studies scholar Noam Pianko. Pianko offers that Jews assimilated into the fabric of American life under the "ethnicity paradigm"—that all ethnic and racial groups could express cultural differences under a formal regime of legal equality.[28] Bittelman, however, approached the question of race and Jewish identity from a Marxian perspective of colonialism and national self-determination. Unlike Pianko, whose "ethnicity paradigm" tended to flatten differences in power between disempowered racialized groups,

Bittelman offered an intersectional, Marxian framework to understand the ways in which capitalism structures race both nationally and globally.

Bittelman begins by offering a portrait of global capitalism and the ways it produces not only immiseration by class, but also "oppressed nations" such as "Porto Rico" (*sic*) and "the Philippines" as well as "geographical colonialism" by "economic and political pressure and intimidation."[29] These external colonies are reproduced internally as a "system of national discrimination" in the United States, a "peculiar system of oppression of peoples usually spoken of as minorities."[30] It's clear that Bittelman is trying to move the reader away from normative democratic explanations of racism—through either an "ethnicity paradigm" or questions of personal intolerance. Rather, Bittelman argues "the white ruling classes have established a regime of naked and brutal oppression in the so-called 'Black Belt,'" where African Americans form "a nation" and suffer "national discrimination" throughout the rest of the country. He continues that "Mexicans and Porto Ricans . . . occupy a special position in the American system of national discrimination" due to their countries' colonial relationship to the United States. And finally he places Jews with "other various national groups such as Poles, Russians, Ukrainians" which are not "separate nationalities" but still face discrimination in terms of their class and from the "so-called superior Anglo-Saxon race." What, for Bittelman, all these groups have in common is that they face exploitation by a racialized form of capitalism, "imperialism . . . the most reactionary circles of finance capital."[31]

Jewish Americans, for Bittelman, are not an "oppressed nation," even if unlike other European "national groups" they share a "community . . . large numbers have a common language, Yiddish, and . . . the struggle against anti-Semitism."[32] As Jewish oppression is not "colonial," Bittelman refused to see the Yishuv as a national liberation project. Bittelman observes, "Our people is made up of various communities with differing forms of national existence," and he lists the Soviet Yiddish-speaking oblast of Birobidzhan, Soviet citizens of different republics, the Yishuv, and the United States. "This does not negate the existence of a Jewish people with common national characteristics and tasks but . . . each Jewish community has its own special problems and tasks determined by the conditions of the country in which it lives."[33] Calling this diasporic, non-national character of an ethnically defined people "progressive Jewish culture," Bittelman concludes that it is only

When Anti-Zionism Was Jewish

through socialism—not nationalism—that Jews may finally live in their home countries in peace.

Bittelman's anti-imperialist framework adopted the position of the Palestine Communist Party, leading him to accept the Yishuv as one site of Jewish community, while at the same time denouncing Zionism, by which he meant the "programmatic demand to turn Palestine into a Jewish state."[34] While Bittelman tried to split the difference between the Yishuv and his anti-imperialist commitments, other Jewish writers were far less nuanced in their critiques of Zionism. A pamphlet issued at the end of the war by Jewish members of the Trotskyist Socialist Workers Party (SWP) was forcefully blunt, describing Palestine as "not our homeland" but "just one of many . . . colonies of Great Britain."[35] They went on to say that while they did not support the arming of the Jewish population in the Yishuv, they did support "the arming of colonial peoples" and that the central struggle after the war would not be for a "Jewish homeland" but between the "capitalist ruling class" and "workers, imperialism and the colonial peoples."[36] In other words, if Jews had any role to play in Palestine, it would be to free Palestinians from colonial rule, no more or less.

Perhaps the best-known critique of Zionism from the time period, Hannah Arendt's "Zionism Reconsidered," first appeared in 1944 in *Menorah Journal*, a liberal intellectual magazine of Jewish culture that featured both anti-Zionist voices such as Salo Baron and Herbert Solow and those sympathetic to Zionism such as Elias Ginsburg. Despite Arendt's distance from the left, and her own quasi-Zionist commitments at least in theory, her position echoes many of the claims and concerns of the socialists and Communists. Zionism would be "bad enough" as a form of nationalism, but "certainly worse" insofar as it would "depend upon the force of a foreign nation" for its survival.[37] She warned that Jews would become "tools" of foreign powers by adopting such a position, and would, ironically, place themselves in the same position they had been historically, caught between big powers and the angry masses of the Middle East, who would single Jews out as the proxy for greater— and often untouchable—interests. And in a statement that could only be seen as prophetic, Arendt notes that Zionism was a project of elite brokerage between a small group of Zionists and the great powers of Europe and later the United States—and would "pass over" the "genuine national revolutionary movement which sprang from the Jewish masses." Zionism for Arendt is not only a collaborationist project with European imperialism, it is also an elitist one, in line with the most reactionary governments of the world.

What is most remarkable about the writings of Arendt, the SWP, and Bittelman is not only what they say but also when they say it. These tracts were all published toward the close or at the very end of World War II, after the full breadth of the Holocaust began to become widely known. Perhaps the single most pervasive narrative about Zionism, even among scholars and writers who acknowledge its marginal status before the war, is that the Holocaust changed Jewish opinion and convinced Jews of its necessity. While certainly it is unlikely that Israel would have been founded without the Holocaust—if only for the simple fact that nearly a million Jews were forced to emigrate from Europe and likely would not have otherwise done so—from these tracts it does not seem the Holocaust had much of an impact on their analysis of Zionism as an ideology or as an actual practice. While some such as Bittelman and others in the *Morgen Freiheit* group felt that Holocaust survivors in displaced persons camps should have been allowed to emigrate to Palestine as their entry was barred from the United States, their analysis of imperialism could not allow them to see a Jewish-only state as legitimate. In language that seems quite prescient for our current moment, the Communist Party labeled Jewish-only settlements as "Jim Crowism," a charge that could not help but stick with the anti-racist sentiments of its Jewish members.[38]

Jewish Whiteness and Its Discontents: The Radical Racial Politics of Anti-assimilation

Bittelman's writings on race and Zionism were not just idle theorizations: the racial assignment of Ashkenazi and other European-descended Jews underwent a seismic transformation during years just preceding and after World War II. "The history of Jews in the United States is a history of racial change," Karen Brodkin writes, as European-descended Jews moved in and out of racially marked geographies, occupations, and cultural formations from the colonial period to the present.[39] European-descended Jews experienced a sharp change in "racial assignment" in the late nineteenth century to the dawn of the Cold War, as Ashkenazi

Jews and their second-generation descendants not only formed a major part of the low-wage industrial labor force on the eastern seaboard after the 1880s, but also came to be seen as the paradigmatic biopolitical threat to an Anglo, Christian nation. This racial panic culminated in the 1924 enacting of "national origin" quotas intended to reduce immigration from southern and eastern Europe to almost zero. The rise of the anti-immigrant Klan hardened racial lines in the 1920s, shifting national discourse from "melting pot" assimilation to an ideology of biological racial difference, often equating African Americans and southern/eastern Europeans as not only culturally inferior, but genetically inferior.[40] Jews in particular were singled out as "abnormally twisted" and "unassimilable," and linked phenotypically with African Americans and Asians.[41] Dividing the globe into East and West, the Johnson-Reed Act differentiated European immigrants by geographical proximity to Asia and Africa.[42] Jews received their own racialized term, "Hebrew," on the census form from 1899 to 1943, marking the period during which they were seen as most racially alien and thus barred from entry, which trapped them in Europe as the machinery of Nazi Judeocide started in earnest by the late 1930s.[43]

Yet, as Michael Omi and Howard Winant articulate in their groundbreaking *Racial Formation in the United States*, the racial paradigm in the United States began to change dramatically in the 1930s from a "biologist" view of essential racial difference to an "ethnicity" paradigm of assimilation and cultural pluralism.[44] This major cultural and political shift shaped and was shaped by realignments in liberal institutions such as the northern Democratic Party, labor unions, and liberal civil rights organizations, as government agencies adopted "liberal anti-racism" as their public language.[45] As much as the "immigration quotas" act could in part be attributed to the rise of the second Klan, so the racial realignment away from biologism to "ethnicity" can be at least in part attributed to the rise, for the first time since the Reconstruction, of a multiracial left that centered racial justice as part of its political articulation. Grassroots organizations such as the American Committee for the Protection of the Foreign Born, the Civil Rights Congress, Council on African Affairs, and the National Congress of American Indians often moved among positions including nationalism, separatism, cultural pluralism, and anti-racism as the situation demanded and members' moods shifted. Such new racial militancy, flexible if also transformative, suggests that "liberal anti-racism" of the post–New Deal era was a strategy of containment against more militant demands as well as an accommodation to real social and political pressure.

Ashkenazi and other European-descended Jews, as perhaps the most racialized among "off-white" Americans, benefitted tremendously from the new "ethnicity" paradigm, as the state and corporate elite opened suburban housing tracts, Ivy League schools, and government, educational, and civil service positions to white ethnics in large numbers. As Pianko argues, "Jewish peoplehood" was "invented" to fit with the changing racial paradigms by offering Jewishness as just another ethnicity, one of many inside the vast mosaic of US democracy. Other putatively liberal postwar Jewish authors, however, had different explanations for Jewish success. Nathan Glazer openly adopted anti-Black racism to highlight Jewish postwar assimilation: in his opinion, it was Jewish cultures of hard work, educational attainment, and in-group solidarity that enabled Jews to thrive in the years following World War II, unlike African Americans who were mired in what Daniel Patrick Moynihan referred to as "cultures of poverty."[46] Pianko's formulation, that Jews naturally fit with the postwar liberal order of "ethnicity," and Glazer's neoconservative arguments about Jewish "pre-figurative whiteness" were both attempts to explain the changing racial assignment of Jews after the war that fit with either liberal or conservative mainstream opinion.[47]

It's important to note that Bittelman, Paul Novick, Morris Schappes, and others in the *Morgen Freiheit* circle also deployed "peoplehood" to denote a non-territorial diasporic Jewish culture. Yet their analysis of Jewish identity broke with both the ethnicity paradigm of Pianko and the neoconservatism of Glazer in crucial ways. Rather than imagining that different ethnic groups would advocate for their interests within a legal framework of individual rights, or that Jews are culturally predisposed to educational or economic success over and above other racialized Americans, these Jewish authors advocated for alliances with African American and working-class organizations to overthrow capitalism. For Bittelman and others on the Jewish left, articulating solidarity with African Americans was more than just strategic politics: it was a way to challenge Ashkenazi Jewish conscription into the political and geographical formations of whiteness. In Bittelman's formulation, while Jews may have a distinct cultural formation and may experience antisemitism, they are not "colonized" in the same way Puerto Ricans may be, nor do they form an "oppressed nation" in the same way African Americans do. Yet, according to Bittelman, their long-term material interests lie with those racially oppressed, not with the oppressors.

While many scholars have pointed out Jewish fascination with and appropriation of blackness as a mode of whiteness and/or assimilation, what is remarkable for these authors is that their articulation of Jewish liminality—between whiteness and blackness—performed the exact opposite: solidarity with African Americans against racism reinforced their own feelings of Jewishness.[48] As an Abraham Lincoln Brigade veteran expressed to *Jewish Life* in a letter to the editor, he experienced antisemitism all his life, and was ridiculed by classmates in school and physically assaulted by "Coughlinites on 14th St" as a young man in the 1930s.[49] Yet it wasn't until he "saw the Negro people were victims of similar persecutions as the Jews—in many instances far worse" that he began to understand "there was a common enemy" faced by Jews and African Americans: "the capitalist system." Rather than abandon his Jewish identity to fight capitalism, the author expressed that his quite literal fight against capitalism as a Spanish Civil War veteran "helped the enrichment of progressive Jewish culture."

This rhetorical and political stance of left anti-assimilationism was quite common among articles, letters, pamphlets, and novels written by Jewish authors in the red decades of the 1930s and 1940s: that the only way to retain a distinctly Jewish identity was to reject the racial conscription of capitalism. In the opening mission statement of *Jewish Life* in November 1946, the editors eschew "bourgeois ideologies, nationalism and assimilationism," affirming Jewish solidarity with "allies among the non-Jewish sections of the American people, particularly the Negro people," repeating again in the same paragraph a desire for solidarity with "the Negro people and all other oppressed groups, for a common struggle against anti-Semitism, discrimination, lynching, and Jim Crow."[50] In the same issue, a story ran on the "American SS," describing the postwar rise of the Klan by linking them to Nazi death squads. And *Jewish Life* also ran a longer piece by Samuel Barron on the postwar rise of antisemitism in the US that noted, "Other minorities only need look at the fate of the Negro to see their own future."[51]

Bittelman and others did not perceive a postwar order of expanding US democracy: they looked at the coming Red Scare and expanding security state as omens of a nascent fascism. As liberal Jewish organizations such as the AJC and ADL celebrated the persecution of Jewish Communists during the height of the Red Scare, Bittelman's and others' warnings of assimilation came to be all too prophetic: in exchange for safe assimilation of Jews into their new racial assignment, the Jews who did not fit the mold would be happily sacrificed to the House Un-American Activities Committee.[52] Anti-Zionism informed a larger global racial imaginary, in which a "white Protestant American supremacy" was the foundation of a refashioned postwar imperialism.[53] While they would not use this language, for Bittelman and others, one could say that Zionism was a form of whiteness.

Of course, one does not want to romanticize African American and Jewish relations in the twentieth century. There is a small cottage industry troubling the contours of this relationship, in which most scholars acknowledge that outside radical political parties such as the CPUSA and strategic alliances between liberal Jewish and African American organizations such as ACJ and NAACP, African Americans and Jews in the US more often than not related to each other along the unequal legal, economic, and social binary of white and black. European-descended Jews' white privilege, while still circumscribed in the mid-twentieth century, allowed them class and social mobility not granted to most African Americans.[54]

Yet it is also true that the African American and Jewish political alliances on the left emerged at a time when the left experienced a major realignment on the question of race and imperialism. In the words of Hakim Adi, the Communist Party became the "era's sole international white-led movement . . . formally dedicated to a revolutionary transformation of the global political *and* racial order."[55] A half century before, it would have been nearly unheard of for the labor movement and the socialists in its orbit to place race or imperialism at the very center of their analysis of capitalism, a shift that was owed to the Communist Party's embrace of anti-racist anti-imperialism in the late 1920s, as well as to the growing militancy of both labor and civil rights organizations at the time.[56] For first- and second-generation Jews who were part of the working-class Popular Front of the red decade, orientation to the classed and raced projects of the United States became part of their socialization as both Americans and Jews. One could argue that for this generation of left-wing Jewish Americans, the Communist Party and its affiliated unions, organizations, and cultural journals became a way to center their revolutionary commitments around a very American language of race. This relationship was most lastingly concretized on the left in shape of the most successful Communist-affiliated anti-racist organization during the modern era, the Civil Rights Congress, which was not only staffed largely by African American and Jewish activists, but often deployed the intersectional language of anti-fascism to protect the lives of African American lynching victims as well as the Rosenbergs.[57] Such gestures of solidarity made it abundantly clear that Jewish nationalism was merely the flip side of Jewish assimilation: a literally fatal embrace of whiteness.

The most remarkable radical expression of Jewish identification with blackness is in some ways hidden in plain sight—the book that arguably defined working-class literature in the US for a generation, Gold's *Jews without Money*.[58] As the ur-text of US proletarian literature, it became a template for a generation of proletarian writers, launching Gold into national prominence as the most widely known Jewish leftist of the era. Yet for a working-class manifesto, *Jews* is an odd book: though Gold calls for literature on topics of "strike, boycott, mass-meeting, imprisonment, sacrifice, agitation, martyrdom, organization," his novel has none of these things—its call for revolution seems almost an afterthought.[59] Rather, the arc of the novel is explicitly racial; its dramatic turn depends on how the narrator comes to define his Jewishness. As Michael Denning writes in *The Cultural Front*, the impact the novel had on American culture was to place the urban, ethnic, immigrant landscape at the heart of the working-class imaginary.[60] Another way to put it might be: *Jews without Money* is one of few prominent Jewish novels published in the US in the late 1920s/early '30s to not only resist assimilation entirely, but to also embrace Jews' liminal racial status as a positive *class* marker of resistance.

The hero of the novel is not the narrator who converts to socialism, however, as much as the narrator's best friend, the black-haired, swarthy, broad-nosed, impoverished Jewish adolescent described as a "gypsy" and nicknamed the N-word by the community. Yet Mikey's dark friend was far from an outcast for Gold: "He was ready to die for justice," Mikey says of his adolescent friend, proudly boasting that he "hit a teacher on the nose" after the teacher called Mikey a "little Kike." Mikey's dark-skinned friend defied the racist and antisemitic authority against which

Mikey and his friends fought on the street against rival Irish and Italian, "Christian" gangs, as well as the official authority of the state manifested in the school system and the police (often dodging the latter as he was frequently arrested for illegal card games).[61]

One could say Gold's novel responds to increasing pressures to assimilate in the 1920s by substituting a teleology of assimilation with a teleology of revolution. As a fictional narrative, the novel's tension lies in the narrator's decision to join with the appropriately labeled "dark proletarian instinct" of his mother, rather than the dreams of whiteness imagined by his father. While the Jewish messiah whom Mikey waits for is secularized into a call for "workers' Revolution" in the final page of the novel, what is clear in the text is that Mikey's path does not lead toward the white suburbs of his father's dreams. The "darkness" of his proletarian instinct has distinct racial cast, as the call to revolution was resolved through the narrator's decision to align himself *racially* with members of his own class, rather than abandon them for bourgeois utopias or a flight of middle-class fancy. Thus we can read Gold's anti-Zionism in a long chain of solidarities starting with an imaginary of working-class blackness.[62] As the rise of the anti-immigrant Klan hardened racial lines in the 1920s, shifting national discourse from "melting pot" assimilation to an ideology of biological racial difference, Gold turns this logic on its head by asserting blackness as a site of cultural and ethical value.[63] As Gold replaces one teleology with another based on Jewish-Black identification, it should be noted that his revolution does not rely on a universal, unmarked subject. Rather, it is through Gold's identification with a racially marked Jewishness that he comes to his political awakening.

Howard Fast was, in addition to Gold, one of best-known radical Jewish novelists of the "red decade." He, like Gold, explored Jewish identity in the context of race and imperialism and, also like Gold, stuck with the Communist Party throughout the bulk of the Red Scare, even winning the Stalin Peace Prize in 1953. He had a reputation, perhaps well-deserved, of being a rather orthodox Communist, despite or perhaps because he joined later than many of his comrades, in the middle of World War II. His best-selling historical novel of an interracial political community during Reconstruction, *Freedom Road* (1944), takes the metaphor of "Jewish blackness" quite literally: he introduces us to the historical figure of Francis Cardozo, a politician of Sephardic descent who became the first African American elected to statewide office, exploring metonymically Cardozo's Jewishness as a mark of both his radicalism and his distance from the oppression of the newly emancipated slaves.

This difficult, affective relationship with solidarity and identity is further explored in a short story Fast published in *Jewish Life* in 1948 during the first Arab-Israeli War, a war that culminated in Israel's state-foundation and the expulsion of some nearly 700,000 Palestinians from their homes. The story chronicles the life of a Jewish fur trader and his son who "dwelt and traded" among "the Mingoes ... Delawares, Wyandottes" as well as several other tribal nations, and as the story's title, "Where Are Your Guns," suggests, it focuses on the Orthodox man's refusal to carry a weapon while he trades with numerous tribes.[64] The British, upon seeing the narrator's father easily navigate among the first nations with no weapons (while also calling him an antisemitic slur), hang the narrator's father as a traitor and subject the adolescent son to thirty lashes. The son's final statement is that he will buy a gun and fight with the Mingoes, to be "against any man in a uniform." While Fast's politics on Zionism remained ambiguous and shifted throughout his life (often with the Communist Party line), it is hard not to read the story as a commentary on Jewish settler-colonialism and European imperialism in Palestine.[65]

The CPUSA position in Palestine after World War II—as with *Jewish Life*—was that Jews and Arabs should create multiethnic coalitions to oust the British, and live together in a bicultural, binational state. Historians of the Communist Party of Palestine have chronicled how difficult this was to achieve on the ground, especially given the segregated nature of Jewish settlement. For an American Jewish activist it was, however, a utopian way for the Jewish left to imagine Jews in Palestine within an anti-colonial framework.[66] The concept of solidarity has always embedded within it a potential for bad universality—a tendency to flatten differences among disparate groups—yet such calls for solidarity also create the framework for dominant groups to break with hegemonic forms of identity construction and to question legitimated forms of violence, privilege, and exclusion.[67] In practical terms, an imaginary of global solidarity, however utopian, created a framework for which Zionism was politically impossible to support. Even if, in hindsight, the story could be read as a fantasy of Jewish settler belonging, the "sabra" myth, the story nonetheless posits the diasporic sensibility of Jewishness as a kind of anti-colonialism, equally at home and not at home anywhere in the world, adhering to a portable Jewish "law" of supporting the weak against the strong, the powerless against the powerful. As Bittelman wrote in an editorial for the April 1947 issue of *Jewish Life*, Zionists align with the reactionary forces of the national state wherein they reside, while "democratic forces of Jewish life" are "links in a chain . . . that binds the Jewish communities of all countries into a people."[68]

Fast's most clear articulation of this global, anti-imperialist diasporic spirit emerges in his short story "An Epitaph for Sidney," which first appeared in *Jewish Life* in January 1947. Fast's story centers on a working-class Jewish Communist who serves first as a volunteer for the Abraham Lincoln Brigade in Spain, then organizes Black sharecroppers in the Deep South, before finally falling to Wehrmacht bullets in the Anzio campaign in southern Italy. Alan Wald mentions how the story serves to produce a kind of collective memory of the 1930s in a time when the movement was under threat, soon to be crushed by the Red Scare.[69]

Yet the fictionalized life of Sidney does more than simply tell the collective story of the left. The story touched off months of debate in the journal about whether it was an example of "progressive Jewish culture," or if the story only happened to be about a Jewish character whose fight for justice was universal. While Morris Schappes felt the story was only "Jewish" in relationship to the antisemitism experience by Sidney, most editors came firmly down on the side of the story's Jewishness and its centrality in articulating "progressive Jewish cultural" values.[70] The story closely adheres to the formula of *Jewish Life*'s opening editorial by merging Sidney's story of fighting fascism with fighting Jim Crow in the South: left-wing Jewish identity is defined by both a racially specific struggle against fascism, and a solidarity with African Americans. In the closing lines, as Sidney's friends and comrades gather to write an elegy, the narrator draws a portrait of Sidney's worldview:

> They buried Sidney Greenspan in Italian soil, good soil, and the soil of Spain is good, too, and the soil of America, and the soil of the Soviet Union, and of China—and if he had his choice, I don't think there is any place he wouldn't have been at home, fully and completely at home . . .

In the personal columns of the paper he read and loved, there were many boxes with heavy black lines to bind them in, and whatever the name, there was a reference to the struggle against fascism ... So we gathered it into a word and wrote: "To the memory of Sidney Greenspan, anti-fascist, who fell in the people's struggle, from his comrades."[71]

It is impossible to miss that Sidney's elegy reads as an elegant rendering of the meaning of diaspora. Sydney was a de-territorialized subject, someone who could be "at home" anywhere, the US, the Soviet Union, China. The focus on soil, and on Sidney as someone who exists within nations but across nations, roots him in the earth at the same time as it links him to peoples across the globe. And, it needs to be stressed, Sidney's diaspora never mentions Palestine. Rather, it is a global radicalism stitched together through anti-fascist struggle, against both racism in the US and Nazism abroad. While not explicitly anti-Zionist, the story is against the fundamental principles of Zionist nationalism and ethnic exclusion, insofar as it links the radical struggle for racial justice with a diasporic sense of Jewish identity. Opposing the dominant Zionist narrative—in which the diaspora is something to return from and gather into a single nation-state—the diaspora itself is portrayed as the primary ontological expression of Jewish identity: a non-place define by gestures of solidarity. Tellingly, Sydney's socialist newspapers, "with heavy black lines to bind them," are reminiscent of tefillin, suggesting Sydney's secular socialist identity is a kind of observant Judaism. As Judith Butler articulates in their intellectual history of anti-Zionism, "Jewish values of cohabitation with the non-Jew ... are part of the very ethical substance of diasporic Jewishness."[72]

The Unpublished Dissent: The Cold War and the (Brief) End of Diasporic Radicalism

From the left-wing Jewish press, it would seem the endorsement of Partition at the United Nations by the Soviet ambassador, Andrei Gromyko, decided for many Jewish socialists what their position on Palestine should be.[73] *Jewish Life* went overnight from advocating a binational, democratic state to supporting a single Jewish state with, of course, some obligatory language about democracy and friendly relations with

Arab neighbors.[74] As Wald and Yuri Slezkine note, the Soviet Union was, for many Jewish Communists, their utopian Jewish homeland, where antisemitism had been abolished and the working class was in power: defending its line, however it may seem counterintuitive, took precedent over all else.[75] While such a shift was tragic and regrettable, it should also be noted that it had little to do with the standard Zionist narrative of the Holocaust: it was over three years after the end of the war that left-wing Jewish magazines backed Partition. While there were Jews on the left, notably members of the Socialist Workers Party, who continued to vocally oppose Zionism, it is not much of a comfort for those afflicted by decades of displacement and state violence to know that Jews whose internationalism should have led them to ally with an anti-colonial cause were led astray by a Soviet Zion, if not an Israeli one. Slezkine's trio of solutions to the "Jewish question," liberal assimilationism, Zionism, and socialism, were suddenly in a rare accordance on the question of the establishment of a Jewish state, aided by the Red Scare's climate of repression and paranoia. Perhaps only now, with the Cold War over and the Jews who associated Zionism with the left having passed on or recanted, an anti-Zionist Jewish left has space to reemerge, with organizations such as Jewish Voice for Peace and the Jewish Solidarity Caucus of the Democratic Socialists of America articulating many of the same arguments: Zionism is right-wing nationalism and imperialism.

In this context, I was surprised and rather moved to find that Mike Gold's single literary contribution immediately after the foundation of the state of Israel was an unpublished play, "Warsaw Ghetto," about the 1943 Jewish uprising. Going through the pages of *New Masses*, for which Gold still regularly wrote columns though no longer editor, I noticed that he—a man not known for withholding his opinions—was strangely quiet on the question of Palestine. It's hard to know what to make of Gold's silence, though it is possible it may have hidden more discomfort with the Soviet line than he could publicly admit. Or perhaps, like *Jewish Life* and *Menorah Journal*, the rising threat of McCarthyism, the plight of Jews in displaced persons camps, and the general sense that the postwar order was going to be marked by a backlash against the left, took up most of his attention.

The play imagines dialogue between Jews in the United States and the presumed dead militants who took part in the uprising.[76] The American laments that he did not see the threat of fascism soon enough or understand its awful destructive power. Yet rather than allowing this conclusion to lead him to a narrow nationalism, he fears that the Nazis are "back in power" in Germany and are coming to the United States. His counterpart, perhaps imagined, perhaps a ghost, perhaps real, describes a Communist Poland "for the people," in which Jews "can hold their heads up high" for having fought the Nazis. The only mention of Zionism or Palestine comes from the Nazi ghetto guards, who reassured the death-bound Jews they were being sent to Palestine. "We didn't want to believe," one woman says, "we wanted to go on hoping and dreaming."

This passage suggests Zionism is a tool deployed by Nazis to keep Jews quiet, and echoes Jewish Marxist critic Abram Leon's observation that Zionism is a bourgeois utopian dream, opposed to present needs of anti-fascist resistance in Europe.[77] The symbol of the Warsaw Ghetto Uprising, the last gasp of the diasporic Jewish Bund before it was liquidated in the camps, becomes thus a way to continue the marker of a diasporic anti-fascism in the light of what many saw as a rising fascist movement in the US, and ethno-nationalism in Israel. The conclusion—Jews returning to Poland—is celebrated as the rightful end to the war, not emigration to Palestine. It's hard not to see Gold's unpublished play as a kind of tragic elegy for what could have been: the voices haunt the narrator, chastising him for his lack of vision, his moral cowardice, and his sense of personal safety. America, in the play, is not bound to a new life of prosperity or multiethnic inclusion, but a place in which Nazis are welcomed after the war.

Despite or because of Gold's warnings, this pre-1948 Jewish anti-Zionism can still provide readers with an intellectual and cultural resource as, yet again, the US Jewish left is parting ways with the Zionist project. The political implications should be clear at our current conjuncture: observing the widespread opposition of working-class and left-wing US Jews to Zionism during the 1930s and most of the 1940s undermines, of course, the central claim that Zionism represents the unified interests or will of "the Jewish people." Zionism was seen not only as a "sinister deviation from the true path" of Jewish liberation in Europe; it was understood as part of a larger reactionary project of white racism, or "chauvinism" in the language of the day, aligned with elite interests, and inimical to the interests of the Jewish working class and, of equal importance, to their working-class and colonial allies. The erasure of this history often gives the impression that Jewish opposition to

Zionism in the US among secular Jews is marginal and, more importantly, new: a reaction to the rise of the right-wing Likud Party, to the increased violence of the post-'67 occupation of the West Bank or now genocidal siege of Gaza. While recent events do mark an intensification of Israel's settler-colonial project, they are neither a rupture with the past nor a break with dominant Zionist ideology, and it would be wrong to interpret much recent Jewish opposition to Zionism on the socialist left as merely a wish to return to a mythic and harmonious liberal past. Judith Butler and others demonstrated the long ethical tradition of Jewish diasporic thought, that living with—and not excluding—the stranger is a cornerstone of Jewish epistemology.[78] Yet it is important to also place such thought within a US context of socialist, anti-imperialist movements that rejected both whiteness and Zionism as a concrete *political* project, as national and international expressions of the same formation. Zionism was first challenged by a global, transnational left; the same global coalition will be necessary to help achieve democracy west of the Jordan River.

2

Not Your Good Germans: Holocaust Memory, Red Scare Anti-fascism, and the Anti-Zionism of the Jewish New Left

There's a scene in Students for a Democratic Society (SDS) organizer turned Weatherman Mark Rudd's autobiography that articulates both the ruptures and continuities of a Jewish left in the 1960s from what came before.[1] After organizing the Columbia student strike with the Society of Afro-American Students, SDS members barged into the empty offices of Columbia president Grayson Kirk, intending to occupy them. Rather than go directly to Kirk's files to establish his connection to the Institute for Defense Analysis, as Rudd's comrades did, the young Rudd was more interested in the presidential suite itself. As he writes, he saw the suite not as an activist occupying the halls of power, but as a "Jewish kid from New Jersey" finally ascending into the inner sanctum of "Them," the "goyim."[2] Kirk's crimes for Rudd (Anglicized from Rudnitsky) were momentarily less fascinating than the half-million-dollar Rembrandt painting on the wall, the Chinese Ming Dynasty vases, the liquor cabinet and crystal sherry glasses, and most of all the books. Describing himself early on as a thoughtful, well-read young man who resented the idea of "play," he notes none of the texts on the expansive shelves had been read, even opened. "This guy's a phony," Rudd thought. Rudd begins calling Kirk "the shithead" in public, as if to confirm the reduction in stature of the Protestant cultural elite, inverting the associations of gentile probity and sanctity with a fusion of fecal matter and gray matter. "What outraged me and my comrades so much about Columbia," Rudd writes in a later essay, "along with its hypocrisy, was the air of genteel civility. Or should I say gentile?"[3]

For a Jewish readership, more significant perhaps than Rudd's surprise at the goyim's pretentions, is the moment when young Rudd sits down in the president's "executive armchair" and "magnificent mahogany desk" and immediately, "without thinking," calls his parents. "We've taken a building," Mark says to his father, and his father replies without missing a beat, "Well, give it back."[4] His mother tells him to be careful, that she does not want him to "get in trouble." Rudd muses on why he called his parents, and comes up with three possibilities, all of which seem true, though all are contradictory: he imagines that he is bragging to his parents, that he has grown beyond the Jewish neighborhood of suburban Maplewood, New Jersey, and that he's "made it in America," willing to challenge even the president of Columbia University. Yet without seeming to notice that he's changed the topic, he finishes his boast by saying he's "become a Jewish defender of the weak," in what we might call the "prophetic tradition" of Jewish culture, one Isaac Deutscher secularized in his famous 1960s essay "The Non-Jewish Jew." Rudd finishes by saying simply that Jewish boys "call home, that's deeply ingrained."[5] Taking Rudd's "call home" as metonymic, we can think of the ways the Columbia takeover is not a rupture with Jewish left history, but rather a conversation with it, if perhaps on new terrain and through someone else's phone. As importantly, with his call home, Rudd signifies that Jewish life itself is as much a story of generational continuities as it is generational rebellions.

This might seem an odd place to begin a narrative about New Left Jewish anti-Zionism, but Rudd's narrative importantly complicates much of the received wisdom of the 1960s, without which it's impossible to understand both the significance of Jewish criticism of Israel and its underreported presence. It is often assumed that, with some exceptions, both the Jewish left and right joined the general American jubilance over the Israeli victory in the 1967 war. As Norm Finkelstein writes, "American Jewish elites suddenly discovered Israel" after the Six-Day War, while Norm Podhoretz takes this a step farther to suggest "nothing less than the mass conversion of the American Jews to Zionism."[6] Amy Kaplan, Marc Dollinger, and Melani McAlister also document how the US press and much of the Jewish and non-Jewish institutional world deeply identified with Israeli's lightning victory over Arab states, contrasting Israeli missiles blowing up Soviet jets before soaring over Africa to free hostages with "with images of Americans fleeing in helicopters from rooftops in Saigon."[7] Many Americans, Jewish and non-Jewish alike, identified on a personal level with the Israeli victories, as if they were their own. For many scholars of Jewish life, the sudden identification of the United States with Israel, combined with Jewish class ascendency after World War II, marks the end of Jewish otherness in the United States: internationally and domestically, Jews had entered the mainstream of American life. Rudd's narrative, it would seem, asks us to question that assumption.

On the level of large Jewish institutions, this narrative of Jewish "conversion to Zionism" and the sense of belonging it implies would seem to bear itself out. Historian Matt Berkman notes how such jubilation followed the money: he tracks how after the 1967 war, a massive institutional shift developed in communication strategies, donor accounts, and political priorities toward supporting Israel—even among mainstream Jewish institutions such as the American Committee for Judaism (ACJ) that had up to this point remain non-Zionist.[8] Prior to the late 1960s, Berkman comments, large Jewish institutions mostly focused on the plight of Jews in the US, including refugees and Holocaust survivors.[9] This shift in funding not only suggests a turn to Zionism as definitional for American Jewish life, it also suggests that large Jewish institutions felt Jews were no longer, in the main, a special case needing extensive extra-governmental support. And more than this, for many Jewish liberals who were turning away from what they understood as the excesses of the radical left, Israel seemed to be like America, only better—"there were no draft dodgers in Israel," historian Michael Fischbach writes of the new pro-Israel consensus, and no Vietnam War, no burning ghettos, no drug addicts, no crime.[10] This merger between liberals and conservatives on Israel was perfected by Otto Preminger and Dalton Trumbo's 1960 film *Exodus*, based on Leon Uris's novel of the same name. As Kaplan notes, it frames Uris's narrative of Israel's founding as violent retribution for the Holocaust, while also maintaining concern with international legitimacy, the United Nations, and world peace after World War II.[11] The new support for Israel seemed to be a progressive war of liberation by a persecuted people, while also magically defeating America's enemies supported by the Soviet Union. Jews were America's best story.

For center-right and even liberal commentators such as Nathan Glazer and Irving Howe, supporting Israel took on a "mystical" importance, cementing Israel for the first time as not only a center, but *the* center of Jewish American life.[12] For social democrats such as Howe and liberals turned neocons such as Glazer, Jews who were outspoken in their antagonism against Israel or support for Palestinians ceased to be Jews. As troubling as Howe and Glazer's conclusions are for their gatekeeping of Jewish identity, there are a number of radical historians who ironically uphold Glazer and Howe's thesis. As Keith Feldman argues in his study on the role of Palestine in the formation of American empire, "both the Jewish left and the Jewish right felt threatened by the Black Power movement," especially Black Power activists' critique of Israel after the 1967 Arab-Israeli War.[13] For the right, the Black left was dangerous because of their attention to Jewish practices of economic exploitation and their rising class status. Jews, Glazer felt, were singled out as the enemy of Black Power. While for Feldman, the Jewish left does not descend into such racist rhetoric, Black Power organizations' increasingly hostile stance toward Israel and ouster of Jewish activists from the Student Nonviolent Coordinating Committee (SNCC) meant for them the historic and often quite material alliance was over. In titling his chapter "Jewish Conversions," Feldman documents the rightward drift of former Jewish leftists, as their support for Zionism and multiethnic democracy isolated them from the radicalizing currents of the antiimperialist left.

Historian Michael Staub has tried to push back on the idea of a New Left turn to the right by chronicling a left-wing Jewish revival in the 1960s, with Arthur Waskow's famous Freedom Seder and the rise of radical Jewish groups such as Jews for Urban Justice (JUJ). Like other left-wing Jewish collectives such as Chutzpah in Chicago and the Brooklyn Bridge Collective in New York, such groups rejected the binary laid out by Glazer and found ways to celebrate both a renewed interest in Jewish culture and explicit left-wing politics. As Eric Goldstein suggests, the Jewish Renewal Movement, as it is sometimes called, borrowed language from the Black Panthers and other Black Power movements, celebrating Jewish features, hair, and non-assimilated modes of dress and cuisine.[14] In an essay by Myron Perlman of the Chutzpah Collective, he celebrates his Jewish nose and curly hair, echoing the "black is beautiful" rhetoric of the Black Arts Movement.[15] Yet these groups and movements rejected both the hard anti-Zionism of Black Power movements by and large and the racially separated modes of organizing. Ironically, the one organization to openly model themselves on Black Power was the Jewish Defense League, paraphrasing Shirley Chisholm's slogan that "black problems come first for blacks" to say "Jewish problems come first for Jews."[16] Yet it was an organization so reactionary it protested outside of a Black Panther Party office and supported the Vietnam War. Even for groups such as JUJ and Chutzpah that remained on the left, their small size, inward-facing programs, and continued if highly circumscribed and critical support for Zionism limited their ability to engage with the Black Panther Party or other elements of the radical anti-imperialist left. Marc Dollinger documents how the rise of Black nationalism encouraged progressive Jews to support Jewish nationalism, seeing Jewish nationalism as complimentary, not contradictory, to Black Power. In many ways, the Jewish radicals of Staub's world fault the Jewish community for not being Zionist *enough*.

As whiteness scholars such as Karen Brodkin, Marc Dollinger, George Lipsitz, and Eric Goldstein document, Jews experienced a racial "reassignment" in the years following World War II, as they moved in large numbers, including Rudd's family, from industrial cities to inner suburbs, especially after the 1948 Supreme Court case that ended the widespread practice of restrictive covenants.[17] This rise in class status and entrance into the post-urban geographies of whiteness complimented Jews' entrance into elite colleges such as Columbia for the first time in large numbers, as restrictive quotas were lifted. Yet there is an assumption that follows from this well-documented historical trajectory that Jews then experienced the 1960s like other middle-class white people, as allies of the civil rights movement, and later in opposition to more militant forms of Black Power. The "white skin privilege" theory forwarded by 1960s radical scholar Noel Ignatiev did more than just describe Jewish class status in a settler-colony, it ended an identity crisis. Rudd's narrative does not deny his own whiteness—and indeed, when the campus occupation broke into two groups, one for white students and one for Black students, Rudd joins the white students and argues forcefully for their role in solidarity with African American students, even as African American students declared their autonomy. Rather, Rudd articulates a particular Jewish perspective with its own narrative and perspective on class and race. Rudd, like many other Jewish members of SDS, understood the Black Power movement as a positive revolutionary development. Not only that, following the Panthers and even laying down their lives with and for them became an almost central focus of SDS and later the Weather Underground.

Rudd's story, however, does not fit comfortably with the narrative laid down by Glazer, Feldman, or really even Goldstein and Dollinger: SDS referred to itself as the "northern arm of SNCC" and continued to back SNCC after it transformed into a Black Power organization. SDS also published a number of articles and pamphlets critical of Zionism and the 1967 war, authored by Jews. And perhaps most importantly, as Rudd and others observed, SDS was, as he referred to it, a "Jewish fraternity," as was much of the white socialist and Marxist left at the time.[18] SDS was estimated to have been, like the Communist Party (CPUSA) during the "red decades" of the 1930s and mid-1940s, roughly half Jewish at its outset, and retained a high Jewish membership. As Paul Berman notes in his history of SDS, *Tale of Two Utopias*, the Jewishness of the New Left could be felt in other organizations as well.[19] The white participants of SNCC organized the Freedom Rides that were overwhelmingly Jewish; three of four Kent State students gunned down by the National Guard were Jewish, despite only comprising 5 percent of the student population. At SUNY Buffalo, fully two-thirds of SDS was Jewish. The Socialist Workers Party (SWP) and then-diminished CPUSA also had sizable Jewish membership, from one-third in the former and nearly still half of the latter. When the young Mark Rudd is calling home, he is in a sense being a good Jewish boy, signifying on a longer tradition of Jewish radicalism, while also noting its rupture with this past. As Rudd's anecdote of the Columbia strike reveals, this racial reassignment was perhaps materially undeniable yet more subjectively complicated than histories of the Jewish ascension in middle-class whiteness suggest: "The world consisted of two kinds of people: Us and Them, the Jews and the goyim," Rudd recalls thinking as he scrutinized the president's office— and by goyim he meant Anglo-Saxon white Protestants, presumably with money and power.[20]

Unlike left-wing Jews in the Jewish Renewal Movement, Rudd and others in SDS did not openly identify as Jews or organize primarily as

Jews. Indeed, as early SDS activist and the child of Communist Party activists Dick Flacks commented, he and his other New York City comrades were delighted that the group was *less* Jewish than other small radical groups in the early 1960s.[21] Yet it is clear that for Rudd, Flacks, and others, their Jewishness was an integral part of their outlook, subjectivity, and radicalism. As Joyce Antler articulates regarding Jewish radical feminists of the late 1960s and 1970s, "currents of ethnic identity," specifically Jewish ethnic identity, "ran deep, even when submerged."[22] This sense of being both Jewish and non-Jewish, organizing as socialists but also seeing the world as Jews, was summarized in Isaac Deutscher's seminal postwar essay, "The Non-Jewish Jew"—an essay that captured the zeitgeist of the Jewish New Left. As Marxist critic George Novack pointed out in a 1967 review, the title itself was an intentional contradiction, one is both not a Jew and a Jew.[23] And reading it, one never quite knows where to place the emphasis: Is one a *non-Jewish* Jew or a non-Jewish *Jew*? Or is it simply a new portmanteau, the creation of an entirely new identity—a *non-Jewish-Jew*? The contradiction is, of course, the pinnacle of Deutscher's dialectical style—a subjectivity that is particular and universal simultaneously, a unity of opposites, a tense material rootedness in history that is also transcendent. Like Du Bois's theory of "double consciousness" it is a particular view of the world, a unique way of seeing. In the way that Dick Flacks related seeing gentiles at the 1962 Port Huron meeting as a positive experience, he also related that he wanted to express this insight to other Jews on the left, as if to say, "You know that we are as Jews and non-Jews simultaneously and it is only the gentiles who are not aware of this fact."[24]

Jewish radicals in the 1960s and early 1970s would reject both right-wing whiteness and multicultural liberalism, yet it is important to remember that, for Jewish leftists, radicalism is not a break with Jewish tradition but rather part of a continuum of Jewish responses to life in a global diaspora. Marking the anti-Zionism of Jews in SDS and the SWP as a particular formation of Jewish left-wing common sense is not to challenge Staub's account of the Jewish Renewal Movement, or Brodkin and Goldstein's scholarship on the changing relationship of Jews to whiteness, or the reorganization of postwar capitalism. As Jewish studies scholar David Verbeeten suggests, Jewish assimilation into whiteness has not been so unitary as to erase either cultural memories of antisemitism or more working-class, radical political formations. Jewish assimilation into whiteness, Verbeeten maintains, has often looked quite different from other European-descended ethnic groups'. American Jews, Verbeeten argues, refashioned notions of Americanness to mean a kind of multicultural liberalism, rather than more aggressive forms of right-wing backlash.[25] Citing the Irish American anti-busing protests and the Italian American assault on Martin Luther King Jr., one can think of Jewish liberalism as its own form of whiteness, stressing fairness, meritocracy, secularism, and a welfare state as modalities of Jewish class ascension. Unlike other white ethnic groups that have been recruited en masse into right-wing backlash politics, the overwhelming majority of Jews have retained a kind of loyalty to a normative liberalism and to its institutional forms in education, social work, and the Democratic Party. That so many Jews of the New Left rejected normative forms of Jewish liberalism and Jewish whiteness suggests paradoxically that such avenues were perhaps more widely available to the Rudds, Klonskys, and Gilberts than for other formations of ethnic America.

That is to say, "whiteness" for the roughly two-thirds of Jews who consider themselves liberals or on the left, is expressed as a contradiction, through economic success and geographical segregation, and on the other hand through a multicultural liberal framework. Joining the New Left was both an expression of assimilation as well as a resistance to a politics of bland, whitened identity. It is this contradiction that constituted the gestalt of the 1960s Jewish left. We can think of Rudd's phone call to his parents—and his inability to exactly explain his phone call—as an expression of that contradiction: at once signaling a break with his parents' middle-class whiteness and at the same time signaling his ongoing connection to them and continuity with their lives. David Gilbert's story traces a similar trajectory, acknowledging the liberalism of his parents' anti-racism, while also acknowledging that the very conditions that allowed his parents to succeed are racist. Many of the Jewish activists who got their start in the 1960s expressed similar relationships to their parents and extended family, acknowledging that their parents taught them racism is wrong, while also rejecting the upward class ascent of their family. Dick Flacks, himself a Jewish member of New Left, documents that Jewish New Left activists tended to come from liberal to left-wing homes and, despite the generational divide, were "fulfilling values that their parents had inculcated."[26] One can say that on the Jewish radical left, there is a continuity between the 1930s and the 1960s, not only in the centrality of Black and "third-world" liberation, but also in understanding that Zionism was not compatible with a revolutionary project of human emancipation. Much as Yuri Slezkine says in his reading of Sholem Aleichem's *Tevye's Daughters*, when Holder's elopement with her revolutionary lover receives Tevye's blessing—radicalism may be frowned upon, but it is still part of the Jewish lineage.[27]

Israel Didn't Seem Kosher to Me: Anti-imperialism and the Jewish Left

When former Freedom Rider and SWP activist Phil Passen was invited in 1967, along with well-known anti-war activist Jerry Gordon, to a local radio show in Michigan to discuss recent developments in the anti-war movement and upcoming protests, he knew the right-wing host would try to trap them. Both Passen and Gordon were members of the Student Mobilization Committee or "Student Mobe," and later the "New Mobe," a multi-tendency coalition that included Trotskyists, Communists, SDS members, unaffiliated radicals, and liberal Democrats. As SWP leader Peter Camejo describes in his memoir, achieving unity in such a coalition was always difficult at best. At various points Communists and other Marxist groups on the left, such as the Progressive Labor Party (PL), attempted to take over leadership and turn it into a front for their own organizations, going so far in the case of the PL as to actually assault New Mobe activists on stage and take over the speakers' platforms.[28] And even without such pressure, such a coalition was under intense strain internally over competing agendas, from liberal Democrats who wanted to turn the coalition toward electoral politics, to "ultra leftists" who wanted the coalition to declare unconditional support for the National Liberation Front, the guerrilla army fighting the US occupation of Vietnam, even when such a position might fragment the coalition whose members all agreed the war needed to end. So when the radio host asked what their position was on the recent 1967 Arab-Israeli War, Passen knew what his answer was supposed to be: we are a single-issue organization, to end the war in Vietnam, and we do not have a position on the conflict between Israel and other nations in the Middle East, even if many of our members do. Not only did Passen know that he was to stick to the line as part of his role in the SWP, he was also aware that the radio host asked precisely because he knew the fragility of the coalition: the 1967 war was just such an issue that could splinter the movement into a dozen different factions.

In an interview with me, Passen related that, just as Gordon was set to answer, he grabbed the mic and spoke his mind: Passen reaffirmed that the coalition was a single-issue movement to stop the war, but then added, "I support the Palestinian struggle, the Palestinian people, and the Arabs in their struggle against Israel."

Passen told me, "Jerry Gordon kicked me so hard under the table. I thought he broke my leg." Passen said he knew "what the host wanted to do, but I fell for it and wanted to fall for it." When I asked Passen about why he broke ranks on this issue in a follow-up conversation, he replied,

> Of all the different political positions [one could have] in the antiwar movement, the pro-Israeli/anti-Palestinian position angered me the most because it was so contrary to support for an oppressed people and anti-imperialism. And I really was (and still am) angry at pro-Israeli Jews in the anti-war movement who I felt should know better and of whom I expected better.[29]

In other words, for Passen, that the New Mobe should not have a position meant not only that it was too narrow in its focus, but also that it was hypocritical: if the coalition was opposed to imperialism in Vietnam, then it should be equally opposed to it in Palestine. But Passen also felt such commitment personally—it was "pro-Israeli Jews" in the anti-war movement whom he "expected better" of—in other words, he felt they were betraying what it meant to be a Jew, or at least a Jewish leftist. Passen also expressed elsewhere in the interview, "I reacted very strongly against this whole use of the Holocaust by the Zionists"—suggesting that Jews had hijacked the memory of Jewish oppression and were deploying it to keep the anti-war movement from mentioning Israel, and, in the process, silencing Passen as well.

Passen was actually somewhat surprised when I asked him if Gordon, who was also Jewish, kicked him because he disagreed. "Of course Gordon agreed with me," Passen said. "He just felt we needed to stay on topic and was more disciplined than I was." Passen's surprise, as well as the radio host's knowing question, was perhaps the quiet part of this story that is really the most thunderous. Both Passen and the host assumed that any Jewish radical in the late 1960s would be critical of Israel. It's often taken as a given that the American Jewish world fell in line behind Israel after 1967 in a swell of pride at the military prowess of the Israel Defense Forces (IDF). conforming to the growing elite consensus that Israel would be a reliable ally to US imperial interests in the Middle East. That Black Power militants increasingly criticized Israel for its territorial aggression also underscored the growing consensus around Israel, so the story goes, either as a rejection of Black Power's perceived antisemitism, or, as Marc Dollinger argues, an ironic embrace of its identity politics.[30] While it is undeniable that key Jewish institutions such as the AJC, ADL, and ACJ embraced Zionism financially and politically in ways that a decade earlier would have been unthinkable, that the Jewish left supported Israel would have been news to Jewish leftists and Jewish liberals alike. "Black Power made Jews more Zionist" only works as a formulation if Jewish leftists such as Passen, Eanet-Klonsky, and Rudd are not included in the narrative.[31]

Indeed, if anything, the Jewish mood by the late 1960s was quite the opposite: from the overheated rhetoric of the Jewish Defense League to the more dulcet tones of Jewish professors and the Jewish press, the assumption was that Zionism was in crisis on the left, even and perhaps especially because of the left's Jewish constitution. If one reads Jewish right-wing radicals and liberal intellectuals, the feeling among both seemed to be that Jewish youth sided far more with SDS than with the IDF, let alone the JDL. The mood was so dire that in 1970 a conference was convened by the American Histadrut Cultural Exchange Institute in New York's Arden House, gathering over a dozen leading liberal to leftist Jewish intellectuals to discuss the crisis. The lineup included sociologist Nathan Glazer, socialist historian Irving Howe, distinguished Hebrew professor Robert Alter, Mordecai Chertoff, Harvard professor Seymour Lipset, and journalist Leonard Fein, and with the exception of Noam Chomsky there was broad consensus that the Jewish left had turned against Zionism and thus, in their reading, the Jewish people. Jewish activist Fein summed up the mood of the New Left, saying, "Considerable intellectual support the left once had for Israel is gone."[32]

One fact that perhaps also would puzzle a contemporary readership was how *Jewish* these dignitaries of liberal Jewish life also assumed the left to be. Irving Howe lamented, "Jewish boys and girls, children of the generation that saw Auschwitz, hate democratic Israel and celebrate as revolutionary the Egyptian dictatorship . . . A few go so far as to collect money for Al-Fatah."[33] Buried in Howe's lament is not only the grief over Jewish youths' rejection of Zionism, but grief that in their revolutionary fervor they were "indifferent to the antisemitism of the Black Panthers," suggesting that Black Power and Jewish nationalism were diametrically opposed.[34] Seymour Lipset also noted accurately that the New Left was "disproportionately Jewish" and concluded that the New Left Jewish youth had joined a tendency "opposed to the Jewish people as a people."[35] For Lipset and many others on the panel, the post-Bolshevik left had long opposed Jewish nationalism and Jewish culture, and the opposition to the state of Israel was not about American empire, but rather the long war of the left to destroy Judaism in the name of universalism and advocacy for the most marginalized. For some others, such as Walter Laqueur and Chertoff, this was explicable as a Jewish rebellion against one's liberal Zionist parents, and attributable the wider youth movement.[36] And for others such as Lipset, joining the left blended with the desire to "assimilate" and to use the left as a vehicle to become fully American. Yet for most there was a broad recognition that the new Jewish left, like the old Jewish left, was hostile to Jewish nationalism, or "particularism," especially as it manifested in the Israeli state. For Glazer, this was all about race, as he cogently and perhaps aptly summed up the many alliances and solidarities of the left by saying bluntly: "The New Left supports the Arabs because the blacks do"—which for Rudd and Eanet-Klonsky would be a point of pride; for Glazer it was an act of "sycophancy."[37] For nearly all the authors, Chomsky excepted, "there [were] Jewish interests and it [was] the thrust of the New Left to oppose them."[38] Or as SWP leader Gus Horowitz dryly summarized in 1971, "The Zionist forces are . . . on the defensive. They are much less confident of public sympathy than they used to be."[39]

This combination of anti-Communism and Jewish nationalism is expressed perhaps in its most distilled form by the Brooklyn rabbi turned right-wing radical Meir Kahane. Like the roundtable of nominally liberal Jewish intellectuals gathered by the Histadrut Cultural Exchange Institute, Kahane assumed that most young American Jews not only were assimilated, but supported the New Left's anti-Zionism. "Not only is he"—the Jewish youth—"not emotionally involved with Israel but he marches, instead, for all sorts of strange causes named Vietnam and Laos and Angola and Mozambique . . . allowing that El Fatah and other such cutthroats and Jew-haters are a proper national liberation group . . . The number of Jews who have lost their children, in this manner, is staggering."[40] Kahane, who organized the Jewish Defense League (JDL) to contrast with both the "nice Irvings" of the liberal Jewish establishment and the "Uncle Jakes" of the New Left, felt only a militant, even military nationalism could stem the tide of anti-Zionism.[41] For Kahane, the issue went much deeper than the 1967 war and, as he understood it, began with the longer tradition of the left and its desire to erase Jewish history and identity. The Soviet Union was not, for Kahane, the opposite of fascism, but rather the most developed form of state-led antisemitism. Like the Holocaust for Kahane, he felt opposing the "Marxist-Leninist dedication to internationalism" was an existential question of equal weight: "the left is a deadly enemy of Jewish survival."[42] Jews who joined groups like SDS were trying to assimilate, to erase their Jewishness in a global proletariat: "What better way to do away with anti-Jewishness than to have no Jews to be anti-."[43]

Kahane, I would argue, understood Jewish anti-Zionism better than most liberal Jews insofar as he knew that Zionism was directly opposed to left-wing projects of decolonization. Israel to the left, Kahane understood, was "that cat's paw of neo-colonialism; puppet of Western imperialism . . . successor to Saigon as the major target of 'progressive' forces . . . the Zionist enemy whose overthrow and elimination would be one more giant stride in the creation of a brave new socialist world."[44] Far from anti-Zionism being fringe on the left, Kahane saw it as central— and as soon as the Vietnam War wound down, the anti-imperialist left would target Israel next. For Kahane, opposing the Jewish left was an existential issue, and not one that he was certain would go away. His often-exaggerated sense of victimhood had a rational core: for a Jewish nationalist, the forces of global anti-imperialism did pose a threat not only to the state of Israel, but to Jewish youth for whom the memory of a global left might inspire a feeling of anti-fascist solidarity. When the JDL arrived at Brooklyn's Temple Emanu-El with baseball bats to chase off Black Panther Party member James Forman, who intended to a make speech, it was not the threat that Forman posed that Kahane wanted to signal, but rather that Rabbi Eisendrath's *sympathy for* Forman was the threat.

What makes the New Left's anti-Zionism legible beyond just the opinions of individual activists and appear as an existential threat to Zionists and the Jewish right is that "anti-imperialism" had become perhaps the central slogan, the ideological anchor, of New Left movements by the late 1960s. Left common sense increasingly understood the US invasion of Vietnam as less a policy mistake than an expression of US imperialism, or even a crime, and one episode in a global fight between the Third World and the West. As Martin Luther King Jr. reframed the war in his famous "Beyond Vietnam," the US was no longer being called to fulfill its own principles of democracy, but rather to grasp that it was on the "wrong side of a worldwide revolution," a phrase that would be understood commonly in the 1960s to mean the anti-colonial uprisings from Vietnam to Cuba to Algeria to Ghana to South Africa. King's shift in this moment was not only surprising to many because he "broke the silence," but also because he signaled his support for the New Left and their analysis of the war and the role of America in the world. This connection between Black liberation and the struggle against imperialism was the core focus of the Black Panther Party, and came to be the dominant frame of radical analysis for the leadership and much of the membership of SDS.[45] As David Gilbert summarized Eldridge Cleaver, "You're either part of the solution or part of the problem; either on the side of the people of the world or of imperialism."[46] The Jewish intellectuals gathered by the Center for Cultural Exchange understood very well what this broad global analysis would mean for Jewish nationalism—and indeed, the 1967 war seemed to cement Israel in the minds of much of the New Left as yet another imperial power. "Our job," as SDS activist Gilbert wrote, "was to win large numbers of white people to solidarity with people of the world."[47]

SDS's theoretical commitment to anti-imperialism overlapped with their political commitment to challenging racial structures of power, in solidarity with first SNCC and then later the Black Panther Party. Many of the intellectuals in SDS understood the war in Vietnam, along with the revolution in Cuba and the anti-colonial struggle in Africa, as a new phase in the struggle against global capitalism. In a series of pamphlets and articles in *New Left Notes*, a group within SDS including David Gilbert, Mark Rudd, Robert Gottlieb, Bernardine Dohrn, David Loud, and others attempted to articulate a theory of US imperialism connected to the praxis of a global revolutionary subject. In a widely circulated and reprinted 1967 pamphlet entitled *US Imperialism*, Gilbert and Loud connected the military expenditures on the war in Vietnam with the global capitalist empire in Latin America and the Middle East. Suggesting that it was the high "fixed costs" of US capital-intensive production that required secure markets and low-cost labor and resources abroad, simple economics explained coups from Guatemala to the Dominican Republic to Iran.[48] Yet beyond questions of markets, labor, and resources, the military had become a "binding power of this entire complex," absorbing surplus production, as well as preventing parts of the globe from exiting the circulation of US capital. Gilbert, Gottlieb, and Gerry Tenney expanded on this insight in what is sometimes affectionately and pointedly called the "Port Authority Statement," a document designed to replace the Port Huron Statement with a clearer Marxist analysis of both capitalism and the role of SDS in a sharpening struggle. In this statement they related that it is absolutely necessary for American capitalism to maintain an empire in order to secure orderly reproduction and circulation of capital, while also connecting the vast surplus returned to the United States in the expansion of high-tech forms of communication, control, and a large salaried class of managers. This means not only is the struggle against a global empire, but that a significant portion of the white working and middle classes have been "bought off" with the surplus capital, and have been shaped into a "mass individual," an atomized yet homogenized consumer, capable of no independent critical thought.[49]

While high-profile left-wing Jewish writers and activists such as I. F. Stone, Isaac Deutscher, Irwin Silber of the *National Guardian*, and Noam Chomsky were publicly critical of Israel after the 1967 war, what obscures the Jewish left critique of Zionism in hindsight (even if it was quite clear in the 1960s), is that the liberation of Palestine was understood by members of SDS and the SWP as part of a larger anti-imperialist struggle against Western capitalism. Rather than summarize the conflict as between competing religions or ethnic groups, SDS, the SWP and their allies tended to frame Palestine, much as they did the struggle in Vietnam and Cuba, as within a wider global conflict between the Third World and the capitalist West. As Richard Saks, a member of SDS and later the Revolutionary Communist Party, framed it: insofar as "imperialism was at the center of our analysis of American capitalism," they also understood that "Israel was an outpost of American empire."[50] As Rudd summarized, support for Palestinians "distinguished the true anti-imperialists from the liberals" and he wanted to be on the side of anti-imperialism.[51] It was an issue that marked the New Left's rupture with the liberal 1960s consensus, clarifying that the US failure in Vietnam or the unpopularity of the draft were not particular issues to be solved, but systemic crises in a world system they meant to overthrow. In 1968 the SDS leadership decided to explain its position on Palestine in a series of articles by Susan Eanet-Klonsky, a staff writer for *New Left Notes* and founder of the SDS faction Revolutionary Youth Movement (RYM) and later the new Communist October League. Eanet-Klonsky also expressed in an interview that it would be strategic for the articles on Palestine to be authored by someone who was known not only to be Jewish, but the daughter of the founder of a major synagogue in Washington, DC.[52]

Despite or perhaps because of Eanet-Klonsky's background, her articles do not frame the conflict in the Middle East as a Jewish and Arab issue; rather, in an editorial note describing the series, the editor argues, "Outside of Vietnam . . . movement against imperialism in the Arab countries . . . may be the leading struggle against US imperialism in the world today."[53] Turning the New Right thesis that Israel is like America, but better, Eanet-Klonsky describes a country like the United States, only perhaps worse—as the dispossession of Palestinians from their land and Israel's expansive agenda is far from complete, and the Israeli working class saturated with racism. Eanet-Klonsky remarks in the beginning of the article that the "situation in Palestine [is] analogous to the flight of early colonists in America . . . to a land already occupied by Indian people." Noting that it was the racism of early Jewish colonists that prevented them from joining with the Arabs against the British, Eanet-Klonsky also argues that it was Jewish racism that informed the kibbutzim labor policy of hiring only Jews, not socialism. Divesting Palestinians from their land and "means of production" in the cities was just a start. "Zionism was an ever expanding policy," Eanet-Klonsky writes, and given the "metaphysical concept of a 'homeland' and 'chosen people,'" the Israelis will "expand as they can militarily." With the rise of Al-Fatah and its "support of the Arab masses" one should see not only the analogy to Vietnam, but the analogy to the United States: one can stop an Indian War before it is over. This analogy was furthered by a second SDS pamphlet, by Larry Hochman, who argued, "[The] fundamental ... central issue in Southwest Asia is the fact that a Jewish state has been established in the Arab midst without the invitation or consent of the indigenous population at the aegis of Western imperial rule."[54]

Eanet-Klonsky's final article in the series goes further than a critique of Zionism, to explicitly support the guerrilla war waged by Al-Fatah against the Israeli state. Contextualizing the idea of "holy war" against the Israeli state, Eanet-Klonsky suggests that Al-Fatah is not only fighting against Zionism, but also working to educate and lead the Arab masses in a progressive direction, away from "feudal monarchies" and toward a broader war against imperialism. In downplaying and contextualizing the military struggle over Palestine, Eanet-Klonsky not only opposes the narrative that Al-Fatah members are terrorists or reactionaries, but also connects Al-Fatah's struggle with guerrilla struggle in Vietnam. As many have pointed out, Régis Debray's book *The Revolution in the Revolution* (1967) was highly influential within the SDS and among sections of the New Left; it posited that small bands of armed guerrillas would succeed where the statist forms in the Soviet Union and its satellites have failed. "Many of the activists at Columbia were taken by Debray," Gilbert remembers, especially for the idea that "action" and spontaneity are part of vanguard revolutionary struggle; one did not need to wait to win elections or build mass movements.[55] By connecting Al-Fatah to Latin American *foquismo* or the "foco theory," Eanet-Klonsky was doing more than explaining Al-Fatah strategy, she was knowingly linking the Palestinian struggle in demand, ideology, and practice to the broader struggle against imperialism. The Palestinians, not the militaristic Israelis, were more like the Jewish student revolutionaries than Jews who ran the Israeli state.

This point was driven home in Eanet-Klonsky's second article for *New Left Notes*, in the special International Women's Day issue, which noted how "Arab women guerillas and masses of Arab women and young girls have been leading fighters in the Palestinian liberation movement."[56] The article, entitled "Arab Women Fight," is placed alongside an article noting the role of women in revolutionary movements from Vietnam and China to the United States. Next to the famous image of Leila Khaled wearing a kaffiyeh and carrying a Kalashnikov rifle, Eanet-Klonsky's piece again suggests that the Palestinian liberation movement has more in common with the feminist revolutionary struggle waged in the United States by SDS and other left-wing groups. The article closes with an image of schoolgirls in Gaza rioting after their classmates were seized by Israeli security forces, challenging the police with stones and clay torn from the walls of their school. This image, like the Days of Rage and the 1968 protests against the Democratic Convention, recalls the global student movement as much as a specific national struggle.

Perhaps no other publication touched off more debate on the left in the late 1960s than SNCC's insert into their June–July 1967 newsletter titled "The Palestine Problem," framed as thirty-two rhetorical questions critical of Israel and Zionism. Describing it as "Black power's first major shot in its battle to include support for the Palestinians," historian Michael Fischbach notes that support for Palestine also signaled SNCC's transformation from a primarily US-focused civil rights organization to a Black Power organization that understood white supremacy and Black oppression as a global phenomenon.[57] As Fischbach notes, the decision to publish the piece came after a great deal of deliberation, precisely because it would send a shock wave through the liberal pro–civil rights world. And indeed, the piece pulls no punches when it comes to Zionism or the foundation of Israel. Much like SDS and SWP analyses, the "questions" begin with the forcible removal of Palestinians from their land, the support Zionism received from imperial powers, including the US and Great Britain, and the apartheid between Jews and Palestinians, as well as Jews of color and European Jews. While the piece ends on an antisemitic note, "THE ROTHSCHILDS ALSO CONTROL MUCH OF AFRICA'S MINERAL WEALTH," the real work of the piece can be summed up by Stokely Carmichael's statement that "the so-called state of Israel was set up by white people who took it from the Arabs."[58] This placement of Israel as "part of the white world" was further summarized by two images that accompany the piece: the first of Palestinians massacred in Gaza in 1956, and the second of Gamal Abdel Nasser and Muhammad Ali with nooses around their necks, each noose held by a hand with a Star of David on it. As Fischbach notes, the images were even more controversial than the text, especially as they seemed to suggest that there was a global Jewish conspiracy to target African Americans and Arab heads of state. While Carmichael did express regret at the way some Jewish comrades might feel the attack was expressed as "personal," it is also possible to read the image of the noose as a fundamental statement of solidarity between African American and Arab victims of white supremacy and colonialism.[59] Indeed, the caption under the first photograph of victims in Gaza expresses a far more ambivalent relationship to Jews and antisemitism, one that suggests structural rather than cultural forces: "This is Gaza Strip, Palestine, not Dachau Germany." While it might seem provocative so soon after the Holocaust to equate Jews to Nazis, the statement seems more about an analysis of white supremacy. As Carmichael said, "The persecution of the Jews came from the white man. There is no need for the Jews to turn around . . . and persecute the Africans and especially the Arabs," suggesting that whiteness is a relationship to power and colonial violence, not something intrinsically deployed by Jews.[60]

Amid "the Jewish backlash against SNCC," as Fischbach titles his chapter, it would probably have been more appropriate to say to Jewish liberal, or institutional, backlash against SNCC. While there was swift condemnation from Jewish financial backers of SNCC, the Jewish left, including the SWP and SDS, responded with offers of support. As Gilbert writes,

> SNCC, the most militant of the civil rights organizations, and some other Black organizations came out, quite justly, in opposition to Israel's war of conquest at that time. So did SDS, the radical student group based mostly in the North. SDS activists understood their tole not only as advancing an anti-racist politics, but understood their relative privilege to be a means to protect SNCC from "the furor and backlash [that] was overwhelmingly against the Black movement.[61]

For Eanet-Klonsky, who authored the articles in support of the forces of Palestinian liberation, that SNCC took a position on Zionism encouraged her rather than discouraged her. SDS saw itself as the "northern arm of SNCC" and fundamentally allied with the organization both in its anti-racist work in the US and its later turn toward anti-imperialism. Once SNCC came out, Eanet-Klonsky remembered, "we had to say something."[62] The SWP, which had long been critical of Israel, was one of the few international socialist organizations to vocally oppose the Soviet Union's support for Partition in late 1947, so its support of Palestinian liberation was in line with already-developed policy positions. Anti-Zionism in the SWP, particularly Jewish anti-Zionism, went back to its founding. Trotsky had long been critical of Jewish nationalism and saw Zionists as reactionaries aligned with forces on the far right. Hal Draper was another Jewish SWP member who was critical Zionism and felt that the Soviet support for Partition was yet another attempt of Stalin to not only deny Jews a rightful place in the Soviet Union but use them as pawns in the Soviet geopolitical game. And above all, like most who were critical of the Zionist project, the SWP was acutely aware of Israel's reliance on and service of imperialist interests in the West. Furthermore, the SWP was an early supporter of Black Power on the left, backing Malcolm X when he was still in the Nation of Islam. As Suzanne Weiss recalls in her memoir, the SWP office would often play recordings of Malcolm X speeches from their office on loudspeakers, much to the wonderment and occasional outrage of passersby.[63] Supporting SNCC also came as second nature to Jews in the SWP.

Peter Buch was the author of most of the SWP's long-form material on Palestine in the 1960s. Raised as a labor Zionist in Hashomer Hatzair, Buch not only broke with Zionism, but devoted much of his life to debunking the socialist claims Israel made about itself. In his best-known 1967 pamphlet, *Zionism and the Arab Revolution*, offered in the context of the 1967 war, Buch dissects the claim that Israel is a progressive, even socialist, project and should be supported for that reason by the global left. Opening with Robert Kennedy's remarks that Israel is an "outpost of democracy and civilization," Buch punctures the widespread myth of Israeli democracy and socialism by noting how all such nominally leftist projects are subordinate not only to rigors of conquest but to Israel's fragile position as a client to Western states. Taking on first the seeming paradox of a country with a democratic socialist government supporting the US invasion of Vietnam, Buch notes that these policies "flow from the character of Israel as a capitalist and colonizing society."[64] The image of Israel as a socialist country hinges on the social democratic nature of its ruling party at the time, the MAPAI, but also its founding institutions, the national labor union, Histadrut, and the collective farms, the kibbutz. Noting that both the Histadrut and the kibbutz made the decision to exclude Arab workers from their ranks, and were always subordinate to the goal of state creation, the primary division in Israeli politics for Buch was not between the left and right, but "between the Zionists and anti-Zionists."[65] This claim of Buch's was addressed to the liberal press, which loved to hail Israel as the "only democracy in the Middle East," and to Jewish leftists in particular who were inclined to view Israel as a progressive project, in line with the long history of European Jewish socialism.

For Buch, the need for state creation subordinated all the elements of a progressive society to military expenditure, the creation of a homogenous national culture, and the colonial racism undergirding such exclusions, meaning that even originally Communist-aligned Zionist organizations such as Hashomer Hatzair, in the last instance, supported the ethnic cleansing of Palestinians and legalized discrimination against the Arab citizens of Israel. "The history of the kibbutz (indeed the entire history of the Zionist left)," writes Buch, "is the history of a Social Democracy corrupted by capitalism and the harsh economic realities of a capitalist economy."[66] While the SWP was alone among all anti-Zionist organizations on the left in that it supported left-wing organizations such as Matzpen that could be a nucleus for the "de-Zionization" of Israel, Buch acknowledged, "At present this organization has little influence on Israeli politics (though its very existence is a pressure on the CP and non-Zionist nationalists)."[67] The opening image of the pamphlet, in some ways, is the closing image: "the conquering armies of Israel" on the Suez Canal and the Jordan River, after their successful "blitzkrieg attack" on neighboring Arab countries, are greeted with "rejoicing" from the "palaces of General Ky" to the "Pentagon."[68] The image of militarism and even an echo of the invading armies of the Third Reich are not hard to miss, especially as the victory of Israel over Egypt, Jordan, and Syria unites the US empire under a single banner.

In 1971, the SWP issued a series of resolutions that clarified the organizational position toward the PLO and the ongoing existence of an Israeli state. The adopted resolutions and supporting materials, later published as a small book of around eighty pages, was chiefly authored by Gus Horowitz, one of the few Jews in the SWP who had grown up in an orthodox, Zionist household. While Horowitz had made up his mind about Zionism after the 1967 war, he described the experience as "wrenching," especially as he had always seen Jews historically as having a "feeling for the underdog . . . for the equal treatment of peoples," and it was clear to him that Israel was on the wrong side of history. Like many in the New Left, Horowitz described his "north star" as the Black liberation movement, first with the civil rights movement, and later with a full embrace of the Black Power movement. Horowitz said that he saw Israel through the lens of Black Power—that is, as a European colonizer violently dispossessing a colonized people. Horowitz makes the analogy clear when arguing against some SWP members who felt that Israeli Jews, while wrong to have invaded Egypt, Syria, and Jordan and to deny rights to Palestinians under occupation, still had the right to a nation-state, just like the Palestinians. Horowitz offered the analogy to white leftist support for Black autonomy, suggesting that even if leftists support Black self-determination "the whites will not have the right to decide the state relations *vis-à-vis* the Black nationality . . . to do so would contradict self-determination for Black people."[69] In this sense, like SDS organizers, Horowitz felt that his relationship to Palestine would be analogous to his relationship to African Americans in the US. Not only was the Black struggle seen as having its own autonomy, it was seen as a vanguard movement, the course of which white revolutions should follow and support.

In this sense the SWP was generally aligned with SDS and with Black Power positions on Israel-Palestine. And like in SDS it was largely the Jewish members who argued and debated the policy on Palestine, at least in print—Peter Buch, Pete Seidman, Gus Horowitz, and Jon Rothschild. In part this was explained by the need to defend the organizations against claims of antisemitism. But it also seemed to come from a sincere desire by the Jewish members to not only shield the organization, but also address the ways in which the SWP's position is derived from a long, proud history of American Trotskyists taking a principled stand against antisemitism and against fascism, even when other Marxists were quiet. Horowitz's pamphlet offered two major lines of argument—the first, that the Palestinian movement for self-determination was, unlike Nasserism and Ba'athism, a democratic people's movement of the broader Middle East, and as such, an "advance" over the anti-colonial bourgeois nationalism that had come before in the region. And because the movement was democratic in nature, Horowitz argued, it had a real chance to "appeal to the Jewish masses" and win them "away from Zionism." While SDS approached Israelis through the lens of "white skin privilege," Horowitz tended to view the Israelis as being exploited by nationalism at the same time as they formed an "oppressor nationality" in relationship to Palestinians. Arguing that the SWP is not only the strongest voice "against Zionism" on the left, but also the "strongest opponent of anti-Semitism," Horowitz observes that Zionism "does not advance the interests of the Jewish people—in Israel or anywhere else in the world." While Horowitz grants that Zionists have constructed their own "Hebrew nationality" that is distinct from diasporic Jewish identity, a Jewish-only state aligns Jews with "imperialism" and with their own bourgeoisie.[70] It is for this reason that Jews in Israel do not have an independent working-class movement, fear invasion from the Arab world, and fear their growing pariah status globally—Israelis have sacrificed the possibility for peaceful cohabitation with their neighbors for a violent bourgeois nationalism. Yet unlike the Arab national governments that are not serious about Palestinian liberation and will deploy antisemitic rhetoric, Horowitz argues, the democratic nature of the Palestinian liberation struggle offers a place for Jews within it, if they are willing to give up on an ethnic state. The fear that Palestinians will drive Jews into the sea is not the fear of antisemitism, but fear of revolution: "to consider that the Arab revolution will necessarily threaten the national oppression of the Israeli Jews is an unfounded *fear of the revolution itself*, a fear which is incited for counterrevolutionary reasons by the imperialists and Zionists."[71] The situation for Jews in Israel, Horowitz concludes, is not that of a religious or ethnic minority as it is in other countries, but that of an oppressor—and the liberation of Palestinians will be their own liberation.

While neither Eanet-Klonsky nor Horowitz identify themselves as Jewish in their articles, nor do their articles claim a particular Jewish subjectivity, they, as well as the other two dozen or so New Left revolutionaries I interviewed, understood their socialist anti-imperialism, including their anti-Zionism, as a continuation of, rather than a rupture with, their Jewish sense of self. Some such as Horowitz, Saks, and SDS activist Steve Goldman identified primarily as Marxists and anti-imperialists yet, toward the end of the interview, echoed similar sentiments, that the "Jewish tradition" is to "side with the underdog" and "the oppressed," and because of this, most Jews are "less inclined to anti-communism," and probably "more likely to sympathize with people of color."[72] This position—that they were inside a tradition they could define yet also not defined by the tradition—was a common, perhaps the most common, sentiment among the activists—so much so I might almost call it a kind of Jewish subjectivity itself. Linda Loew, who like Saks came from a red diaper background, summed it up simply by saying that she liked being part of a multiethnic movement in which she could organize with farmworkers, students, and civil rights activists, while not feeling that she was burdened by a sense of identity—which she thought of as her father's intense sensitivity around perceived and real antisemitism.[73] Yet she also prided herself on being the kind of Jew who opposed Zionism, and felt very much that she was carrying on the legacy of her parents. "I didn't feel there was a break," she said, between her life in the New Left and her parents' life, either in the kind of revolutionary work she was committed to in the SWP, or with her sense of what it meant to be Jewish. Saks remembers inviting his friends to talk politics with his father, who had been in the Communist Party, and Loew describes her uncle as a particular mentor of hers. Like Rudd's narrative—in which he "calls home" at the moment of a revolutionary act—the generational narrative of the 1960s rupture did not hold true for many if not most of these activists.

For many I interviewed or whose memoirs I read, their revolutionary politics and their Jewish sense of identity in the world did form both ideological and affective unities. Such unities were not usually expressed in programmatic statements about Jews; more often, their expression of Jewish identity was revealed in their visceral response to Israel and to Zionism. Dick Bernstein, one of the early members of SDS, expressed with a kind of sardonic playfulness that "Israel didn't seem kosher to me." He continued with a remembrance of the first Israelis he met:

> I didn't like [them]. They seemed like arrogant pricks. I met this guy who said he had shrapnel still in his neck from a battle. And instead

of being agonized over the violence of war, he was proud of it. Made him feel manly. He liked being tough. And I thought I wanted nothing to do with that, if that was what it meant to be Jewish now.[74]

Embedded in this brief portrait of an Israeli citizen is a long line of diasporic thinking about the role of militarism and masculinity. As Jonathan and Daniel Boyarin write in their seminal essays on diasporic thinking, the diaspora itself is conceived as a non-binary modality of existence, opposed both to phallic masculinity and the nation-state that requires such forms of masculinity to exist.[75] Being an "arrogant prick" and enjoying battle are both, to Bernstein's mind, products of nationalist thinking—and opposed to his sense of what being Jewish means in the world. Unlike Zionists who took Jewish pride in Israel's swift victories, Bernstein recognizes the price of such a nation-state is the Jewishness it claims to represent.

While Bernstein later elaborated on what a non-Zionist Jewish identity meant for him, his visceral disgust, Jewish diasporic disgust I might add, was shared by other former SDS and SWP members I interviewed. As SDS and later Revolutionary Union member Joel Beinin articulated, his experience on a Hashomer Hatzair kibbutz was deeply alienating. Not only did he hear racist language against Palestinians on a regular basis, his entire sensibility as a member of the Jewish left was foreign to his fellow kibbutzim in ways that were both comic and profound. Telling the story of watching *Hair* dubbed in Hebrew, he remembers he and the other Americans clapped during the burning of an American flag—while the kibbutzim sat stone-faced and disapproving. Beinin was confused: Weren't Hashomer Hatzair Communists? Weren't they against the war in the Vietnam? And it occurred to him then that his Israeli counterparts on the collective farm were nationalists—not Jewish socialists as he understood the term. For them, he said, nationalism meant respecting flags, and respecting the military. "However critical they might be of Israel, the occupation . . . whatever they might say in the end, it's kind of meaningless because they went to the army, they do their reserve duty every year. They do it willingly and with pleasure."[76] When Beinin heard Palestinians being referred to with a racist slur he finally left the kibbutz, but this anecdote stuck out to him as evidence of the vast divide between diasporic radical Jewish culture and Jewish nationalism. And he wanted nothing to do with Jewish nationalism.

As SDS member and child of Communist Party members Dick Flacks joked, "You can't get a good bagel in Israel."[77] Underneath the joke about the foreignness of Israeli culture was a far more serious and chilling experience. Dick Flacks and his wife, Mickey Flacks, both traveled to Israel in the mid-1970s, in part to see one of the few museums of Jewish partisan culture in the world. In some ways, Dick expressed a sense of homecoming, as they felt "the Jewish underground partisan resistance during the war had been greatly neglected and obscured ... but here was this place that really was, you know, restoring memory of that." To add to the sense of communality, the curator of the museum even offered to give the Flacks a late tour of the collection in exchange for a ride back to Tel Aviv. On the way back, Mickey and the curator began speaking in Yiddish about the political situation in Israel. "And pretty soon," Dick related, "he's talking about, Oh, you people are the lefties and you don't understand that we have to ... and he literally said, clean out the Arabs. And Mickey pointed this out, what he had said, you know? And he was not really apologetic ... So I would say ten times a day, we had these contradictory experiences ... Yes. I can understand why people feel being at home. And at the same time feeling quite alienated, like Israel is not a good place for the Jews." Dick further elaborated on the irony that at a museum for partisan resistance the curator used language that one would hear deployed against Jews in the Holocaust. Like Beinin and Bernstein, the limits of Flacks's nationalism were felt viscerally, personally, and on the level of acute and profound disgust. "Not good for the Jews," in a country founded on the idea of "what is good for the Jews" is perhaps the coldest indictment, but also a statement that for Flacks, Beinin, Eanet-Klonsky, and others, "Jewishness" was located in international solidarity, not ethno-nationalism.

Interestingly enough, the Yippies featured even more prominently in the minds of the Jewish liberals and the Jewish right than SDS, especially among the dignitaries at the Arden House conference. The Yippies' outrageous politics, as well as their obvious Jewishness, were on clear display for Glazer, Howe, and others who opined at the 1970 gathering. They heaped the most unaffected scorn upon Abbie Hoffman, "the accredited clown of the movement" who chanted "praise to the bombs" of the Weathermen and the PLO, in the words of Howe.[78] What is often unspoken however, and what may lie behind such scorn, was the fact that Hoffman and Jerry Rubin were committed anti-Zionists, with Rubin writing in 1971, "if Moses were alive today, he'd be an Arab guerrilla."[79] Fischbach also notes how Rubin's wife and cofounder of the Yippies, Nancy Kurshan, remembered years later, "Jerry was definitely supportive of the Palestinian struggle as was I . . . We viewed it as a struggle similar to the Vietnamese or perhaps the American Indian Movement in the country." Other Yippies agreed: "Our pro-Palestinian sentiments came from the fact that the Yippie core were all pretty much rebellious Jews," recalled Judy Gumbo Albert. "We identified with all the liberation movements of the day of which the Palestinians were one." Hoffman was similarly sharply critical of Israel. "I hate Israel and want to see the Palestinians triumph," he once wrote his wife, Anita. Attending protests at the Democratic Party's 1972 national convention in Miami, Hoffman later opined, "I am very pro-Jewish, but anti-Zionism." His post-Yippie letters to his wife in the early and mid-1970s revealed a visceral anger at Israel. In December 1974 he wrote, "I am violently anti-Israel and no longer believe they have a right to exist. During the past ten years they have forfeited any right they might have 'earned.'"[80] While not always spoken so forcefully, "pro-Jewish" and "violently anti-Israel" was the predominant mood on the radical Jewish left.

I Saw Myself among the Dead: From Holocaust to Days of Rage

> Mr. [Abbie] Hoffman: Your idea of justice is the only obscenity in the room. You schtunk. *Schande vor de goyim*, huh?
> The Court: Mr. Marshal, will you ask the defendant Hoffman to—
> Mr. Hoffman: This ain't the Standard Club.
> The marshal: Mr. Hoffman—
> Mr. Hoffman: Oh, tell him to stick it up his bowling ball. How is your war stock doing, Julie? You don't have any power. They didn't have any power in the Third Reich, either.
> The Court: Will you ask him to sit down, Mr. Marshal?
> The marshal: Mr. Hoffman, I am asking you to shut up.
> Mr. Rubin: Gestapo.
> Mr. Hoffman: Show him your .45. He ain't never seen a gun.
> The Court: Bring in the jury, Mr. Marshal.

> Mr. Rubin: You are the laughingstock of the world, Julius Hoffman; the laughing stock of the world. Every kid in the world hates you, knows what you represent.
> Marshal Dobkowski: Be quiet, Mr. Rubin.
> Mr. Rubin: You are synonymous with the name Adolf Hitler. Julius Hoffman equals Adolf Hitler today.
>
> — Abbie Hoffman et al.,
> "At the Chicago Conspiracy Trial"[81]

Early in the research for this project, I interviewed a longtime comrade in Chicago, Joel Finkel, whom I knew as a socialist, Fourth Internationalist, and active anti-Zionist with Jewish Voice for Peace (JVP). Eager to learn how his socialism, anti-Zionism, and Jewish identity intersected, I sat him down for a nearly three-hour-long conversation at the famous Jewish deli in the strip mall zone west of the Loop, the last fragment of what used to be a thriving Jewish neighborhood before urban renewal and the expanding University of Illinois obliterated it—a reminder that the suburbanization of Jews was done as much by bulldozer as it was funded by racially restricted FHA housing loans. Like a number of other Jewish activists of his generation I have known through the years, Joel downplayed how much his Jewishness was central to his becoming a revolutionary: he wasn't religious, his parents were progressives but not in the Jewish left, and he underscored that the primary movers of his political life were objective and historical events such as the war in Vietnam and the civil rights movement. He had a clear analysis of the contradictions of capitalism, the historical conjuncture of the 1960s, and the role of Zionism in global imperialism, and thought of questions of personal identity as slightly foreign to his ears, as if I had asked him about his moon sign. And then, perhaps two hours into the conversation about how he got involved in the movement and developed his political outlook, he choked up, flushed, and almost sobbed, "We couldn't let it happen to anyone else." "It?" I asked. "The Holocaust. It couldn't happen again."[82]

Finkel's formation is one I encountered often while reading memoirs and interviewing Jewish activists who were part of the New Left of the 1960s and early 1970s. In another interview, Eanet-Klonsky explained her own dedication to Palestinian liberation through Holocaust memory. After talking for several hours in her northwest Chicago home about her Jewish upbringing, about her father who was a founder of a liberal temple in Washington, DC, and about how that related to her anti-Zionist writings for the SDS newspaper *New Left Notes*, she finally explained: "We couldn't be good Germans."[83] Jews, she said, more than anyone, should know the price of the world's silence as a genocide is taking place. Tellingly, Mark Rudd also framed his resistance to the Vietnam War in the same way in his memoir of SDS, saying he couldn't "be a good German"—"In my home, as in millions of Jewish homes, 'Hitler' was the name for Absolute Evil," Rudd went further to say, "only this time, it was us, the Americans."[84] Like Eanet-Klonsky, Rudd evoked the Holocaust not to suggest that Jews are special victims of a unique tragedy or to justify or rationalize their behavior, but to explain why they felt a personal responsibility to oppose fascism and colonialism done in their name, either as Jews and/or Americans. Shortly after her release from prison, Weather Underground member Kathy Boudin recollected that her decision to support the Black Liberation Army's campaign of bank robberies and jailbreaks rested on her analysis that America was in the process of committing multiple genocides, and that she, like Rudd and Eanet-Klonsky, thought "a lot about Germany" during the Holocaust: "How do you live a life when your government is doing what it's doing?"[85] In other words, she too could not be a "good German."

The idea that there is a particular Jewish responsibility to oppose fascism and the genocidal race theory behind it was expressed clearly by another member of SDS and early friend of Rudd, David Gilbert. "For myself and many other Jews in the movement," Gilbert writes in his memoir, "the bedrock lesson from the Holocaust was to passionately oppose all forms of racism," explaining also that because of the Holocaust, he could "never join the oppression of other people." And even though Gilbert describes his parents as apolitical, he asserts "they taught me racism was wrong" a conclusion drawn from witnessing the violence of antisemitism.[86] Rudd also locates the meaning of the Holocaust not only with the destruction of European Jewry, but specifically with "racism; that's what anti-Semitism was."[87] "Racism" as an explanation of antisemitism does not locate antisemitism as something unique to Jews, but as part of a larger structure of white supremacy, insofar as it connects the persecution of Jews to the oppression of people of color. In this way Rudd connects his support for SNCC not only with a political project, but with his own personal story. "With the solipsism of a child," he writes of reading Anne Frank's diary and looking at the death camp tattoos of his relatives, he saw himself "among the dead."[88] For Rudd and for many Jews in the movement, their attachment to fighting racism was a way of articulating their own feelings about being Jewish. Historian Arlene Stein suggests that she "developed an intense, vicarious identification with the struggles of African Americans" as a means to better understand "the collective experience of trauma" after the Holocaust.[89] While Stein articulates this as a form of displacement, for Rudd and others it was a way to passionately connect with and honor their Jewish heritage.

In this sense, the deployment of the Holocaust by Rudd, Eanet-Klonsky, Gilbert, Hoffman, and Finkel speaks to ongoing and present debates about its meaning and relevance in the politics of Jewish memory and identity. There is a growing consensus that supposed silence among American Jews around the Holocaust was at best partial. Scholar Hasia Diner counters the narrative that the Holocaust was "unspeakable" until the late 1960s and that Jews refused to remember or honor the dead out of fear of antisemitism, or shame of victimhood.[90] Diner documents how memorials, religious ritual, journal articles, and art were created and disseminated by Jewish organizations and synagogues, and in private homes and community events. Far from distant from the minds of Jewish Americans, the Holocaust reconstructed Jewish American life in personal and public ways. Indeed, the Holocaust was a common enough reference point in Jewish life that Philip Roth's first published story in the late 1950s not only evokes the genocide but also uses it as the punch line of an ironic joke. Grossbart, the Jewish private who wants to avoid combat in the Pacific and leave base for *treyf* egg rolls on Passover, manipulates the scrupulous Sergeant Marx by suggesting Jews "let themselves get pushed around" in Germany and needed to "stick together."[91] Indeed, one can read the entire collection of stories in *Goodbye, Columbus* as a kind of meditation on the Holocaust, from "The Conversion of the Jews" to "Eli, the Fanatic." The Jewish community in "Eli" is so desperate not to attract antisemitism they wish to ban a yeshiva, but also so concerned about Jewish cultural continuance after the Holocaust that they do whatever their children ask of them, even convert to Christianity. In evoking the Holocaust with irony and complexity, Roth signals less a silence on the topic and more an intimate knowledge of it and of the many ways it complicated and animated Jewish American life—a near decade before the 1967 war.

Even scholars like Diner acknowledge the "myth of silence" is a construction, however there is an assumption that the Holocaust made the Jewish community fundamentally conservative and assimilationist. As Norman Finkelstein documents, the 1967 Arab-Israeli War sparked a wave of support for the victorious Israeli armies, and government officials from the State Department to the Pentagon began to understand how Israel could be a strategic ally. "The Holocaust proved to be the best defensive weapon deflecting criticism of Israel," Finkelstein writes.[92] In service of Israeli nationalism, the Holocaust, he argued, was transformed from a fascist genocide that was part of a larger far-right racial project to something very particular and "unique" that happened only to Jews.[93] European historian Enzo Traverso takes this analysis a step further to suggest "the Shoah closed a cycle of European intellectual history, in which Jews had been a central part," transforming Jews from a "pariah" class to an integrated part of Western culture. It is Henry Kissinger, for Traverso, not Trotsky, who inherits the meaning of the Holocaust in global politics.[94] Citing the ways the Nuremberg Trials and American triumphalism celebrated the inclusion of Jews into the fabric of mainstream American life and Israel into the sphere of the capitalist West, "the Jew" for Traverso had gone from being counter-modality to European modernity to its most ideal subject. Citing both Israel and human rights law, Traverso argues that the "former trouble makers and disrupters of order had become its pillars.[95] Historian of antisemitism Paul Hanebrink frames it another way: as the victory over Nazi Germany became absorbed into the narrative of global American power, so did the Jews go from being a "Judeo-Bolshevik menace" to part of the "Judeo-Christian West."[96]

In an essay in *Protocols*, Mark Tseng-Putterman argues that the mobilization of the Holocaust not only justifies the state of Israel for a Zionist Jewish establishment, its very memory actually makes Jews less likely to see Israeli "culpability in the so-called conflict."[97] For Tseng-Putterman, Holocaust narratives create a kind of "Jewish-exceptionalism" that serves as the ideological infrastructure for Zionism and, more broadly, blinds white Jews to ways in which they mobilize their own whiteness. "Far from progressive," Tseng-Putterman continues, "the absolution of Jewish participation in white supremacy" that develops when the Holocaust is centered as the singular event defining antisemitism "halts opportunities to challenge Jewish complicity." Indeed, the essay argues it is precisely through the American narrative of the Holocaust that Jews have been conscripted into the institutional relations of American liberalism and American empire. That the US can place itself as the protector of the Jews reinforces and can be understood to be the modality through which a liberal white supremacist state maintains is legitimacy. Not only are the Nuremberg Trials part of the legal superstructure of the global American empire, the incorporation of a certain kind of Jewish suffering is the way the state disavows its own history with eugenics and genocide. There is "an order" to state violence, the author declares, and by centering the Holocaust as a primary part of that order, Jews literally whitewash their own complicity with whiteness and empire as well as allow the state to benefit from Jewish investments in a normative history of antisemitism. In the order of state violence, the Holocaust is low on the hierarchy, and more silence, rather than less, is necessary. The article suggests that Holocaust narratives cannot be mobilized outside of a context of whiteness and cannot but help, in such a context, redeploy it.

"Just as organized Jewry remembered The Holocaust when Israeli power peaked, so it remembered The Holocaust when American Jewish power peaked," Finkelstein argues, suggesting that the Holocaust not only deflected criticism of Israel, but also deflected white Jews from criticism of their whiteness.[98] As Jewish studies scholar Ben Ratskoff wrote in *Jewish Currents*, Jewish analogies to the Holocaust are the "narcissistic" means by which Jews "disavow" concern for their complicity in white racism and the normative violence of liberalism. Tseng-Putterman writes that "2017 may have offered a strange solace," and poses that antisemitism actually reassures Jews of their safety in the world rather than threatens it, as it mobilizes the state in their defense. Jewish memory of antisemitism exaggerates the threat of antisemitism, and antisemitism is the very means by which Jews align their interests with the state—antisemitism is a form of state power. Antisemitism, in this formation, makes white Jews whiter; it solidifies their relationship to narratives and institutions of American power. One may look no further than attacks against Jeremy Corbyn and progressive American socialists to see the ways in which a discourse of antisemitism protects the powerful and is deployed as a weapon against democracy.

Rudd, Eanet-Klonsky, Gilbert, and other New Left radicals articulate, however, a challenge both to the mainstream Jewish establishment's Zionist conscription of the Holocaust, and Traverso's and Tseng-

Putterman's narratives about post-Holocaust memory and Jewish identity. While Traverso, Finkelstein, and Tseng-Putterman are certainly accurate to point fingers at an increasingly reactionary Jewish establishment, and I suspect their analysis is largely directed toward larger Jewish foundations, their narratives tend to evacuate other possibilities for progressive Jewish life outside of or even oppositional to such institutions, with a logic, history, and subjectivity of its own. Such discourse tends to flatten Jewish experience into an expression only of large—if quite powerful—Jewish institutions. As Michael Rothberg documents, Holocaust memory is "multidirectional," and emerged in the context of anti-fascism and de-colonial discourse in the 1940s and 1950s long before it emerged as a pillar for a muscular Israeli and/or US nationalism.[99] While widely divergent in their political commitments and perspectives, both Hannah Arendt's *Origins of Totalitarianism* and Aimé Césaire's *Discourse on Colonialism*, published in the early 1950s, locate the origins of fascism and the roots of the Holocaust in European imperialism, in transnational or perhaps supra-national projects of economic expansion and political repression. Indeed, as Norm Fruchter wrote for the summer 1965 edition of *Studies on the Left*, the wide-ranging anger at Hannah Arendt for her condemnation of both Jewish nationalists and Jewish leadership during and after the Holocaust was a marked *departure* for an American Jewish community that substituted the "secular values . . . of social justice, use of intellect, the pursuit of knowledge" for Zionism and its "myth of the victim which Jews tend to substitute for their history."[100] Thus for Rudd and Eanet-Klonsky, who do not wish to be "good Germans," the violence of fascism is not something that happens only to Jews, or can be accounted solely through Jewish history or Jewish victimization. The violence of fascism is a structural part of imperialism, whether the genocidal levels of violence deployed against the Vietnamese during the US invasion, or the ethnic cleansing and militarism of the Israeli state. The question for Jews is not how to memorialize the Holocaust as a uniquely Jewish tragedy, but rather what ethico-political stance the Holocaust requires of a Jew.

As Gilbert makes plain, Jewish survival is not the primary lesson the Holocaust imparts. While it is clear that Gilbert, Eanet-Klonsky, Rudd, Deutscher, and others understood Jews to be targets of fascist violence, they also understood that social solidarity, not Jewish particularism or nationalism, was what Holocaust memory should mean. As Deutscher writes, "I am a Jew by force of my unconditional solidarity with the persecuted and exterminated."[101] Note the construction—it is not solidarity with other Jews that makes Deutscher Jewish, it is the particular "force" that marks his passion and his solidarity. It is the depth of commitment against persecution and extermination that makes the Jew. While Gilbert does not explicitly say this, one could possibly derive that the lengths he was willing to go to, eventually to a life sentence in prison, mark the "force" of his solidarity, and hence his Jewishness. Yet Gilbert is also clear to normalize such feeling. His parents, whom he describes as apolitical—his father an Eisenhower Republican, his mother a relatively liberal but not zealous Democrat—explicitly articulated that the lesson of the Holocaust was to stand against racism. That this was the opinion of Jews who were otherwise politically unremarkable suggests less their idiosyncrasy than their shared set of convictions by the articulation of an anti-racist Jewish common sense in the decades immediately following the Shoah. When Rudd writes, "I saw myself among the dead" when he imagined the Holocaust as a child, it did not lead him to think Jews were exceptional—rather it led him into the struggle to oppose genocide and imperialism wherever he encountered it.

A number of small Jewish socialist collectives sprouted in the chaos left by the splintering of SDS from 1968 to 1970. While I will discuss them in greater detail in chapter 4, it is important to note that the former SDS members' explicit turn toward Jewish identity in the wake of the New Left's upheaval deepened rather than diminished an internationalist interpretation of Holocaust memory. Jewish Radical Community (JRC), an organization founded by self-described Jewish revolutionaries in 1968, handed out a Passover flier on the UCLA campus explicitly comparing the My Lai massacre to the Holocaust. The pamphlet opens, "Genocide has no concern for numbers. Had Nazism killed 'only' three million Jews, would it have been less of a crime? Auschwitz: 1943 My Lai: 1968."[102] Not only does the pamphlet explicitly place the Holocaust in line with a far-broader scope of colonial mass murder, it calls into question the very premise that "genocide" can only refer to crimes against humanity that occur on the industrial scale of Auschwitz. In addition to undermining Holocaust exceptionalism, the flier further attacks American exceptionalism, noting that Roosevelt expressed "apathy" and thus "moral responsibility" for the murder of 6 million Jews. In this framing, the United States is neither the savior of Jews nor the enemy of fascism, but rather its facilitator, and now its inheritor. Brooklyn Bridge Collective, founded in 1971, also by Jewish veterans of the New Left, proposed an identical framing on the front cover of their third magazine issue. "Genocide Then/Genocide Now" reads the title, under which are images of the dead from Nazi death camps and dead Vietnamese people, killed by US bombs.[103] The bottom of the cover reads "Resistance Then/Resistance Now," above which are images of Apache guerrilla fighters and members of the Vietnamese NLF. Again, the function of this cover is to mark the Holocaust in an archipelago of modern genocides, as an expression of the racial logic of capitalism and racial colonialism. The US is not merely adjacent to this history, but rather at the very center of it. This rewrites the Holocaust from the paradigmatic genocide to rather its exception, occurring at the heart of Europe rather than in its colonial or settler peripheries. The Chutzpah Collective takes this a step further to suggest that, within Israel, Holocaust memory still plays a subversive role, even as it's deployed by the state to legitimize its dispossession of the Palestinians. In a story about *New Outlook*, the "doves" in Israel— the New Left "peace camp"—Chutzpah notes that war resisters are often depicted through antisemitic stereotypes denoting the "effeminate" nature and "weak knees" of the peacenik, associating such "trembling" with "the galut," the prewar diaspora.[104] The implication, of course, is that the Holocaust was not an act committed by a racial state but rather emanated from the weakness of Jews, who lacked the martial vigor of a nation. Slyly or perhaps not, the *Chutzpah* editors paired this article with an article on the facing page about growing Holocaust denialism.[105]

Perhaps the most sustained engagement with the radical usable past of the Holocaust is Suzanne Weiss's memoir, *Holocaust to Resistance, My Journey*. Weiss, a Polish survivor who spent the last years of the war in hiding and then in a Jewish orphanage in France, emigrated to the United States when two Jewish members of the Communist Party in New York adopted her in 1950. The first time Weiss articulated herself as a Holocaust survivor in public, however, was many years later, during an official state visit by Ariel Sharon to Toronto in 2003. Framing her own experience as both unique yet at the same time part of larger structures of racialized state violence, she spoke the following at a rally outside of Sharon's hotel:

Hitler's Holocaust is unique in history; nothing is "similar" to it. Still, many Israeli techniques—the expulsions, the ghettoization, the pervasive checkpoints—have a disquieting resemblance to Nazi methods. To oppose Sharon is *not* anti-Jewish . . . a united resistance can, like the anti-Nazi Resistance of my childhood, win out against the aggressors.[110]

Figure 2.1. *Brooklyn Bridge* 1, no. 3 (May 1971), cover.

That Weiss commits the Holocaust to public memory only as Sharon embarks on a state visit to Toronto turns much of the Holocaust narrative, left and right, on its head. It is not the Holocaust that justifies the state of Israel, it is rather Israel's crimes that require us to remember the meaning of fascism. It is Sharon that forces Weiss to remember the Holocaust, because it is Sharon, and all he represents, that threatens to erase it.

Before Sharon's visit, of course, Weiss was no stranger to politics: she had been a member of the SWP since her teenage years, and had organized anti-war demonstrations, visited Cuba on an official delegation, and worked in heavy industry trying to form unions among other workers. Yet it wasn't until she undertook a personal journey first to Poland, then as a social worker among Holocaust survivors, that she articulated the meaning of her experience: "I wondered whether Holocaust survivors differed from survivors of other traumas, tragedies, or genocides, such as Palestinian families subjected to daily terror, the destruction of their families, and the loss of their homes, possessions, and homeland," she writes. "Holocaust survivors, I concluded, must be addressed not through comparison with other historic disasters . . . Yet working with Holocaust survivors sharpened my awareness of the suffering of all peoples emerging from genocide and societal traumas."[111] In this double turn, Weiss recognizes that the specificity of Jewish trauma does not make it perfectly analogous to other forms of oppression, yet her increasing awareness—unlike Traverso's and Tseng-Putterman's claims—increases her feelings of solidarity with other oppressed people, especially with Palestinians.

It's also clear in Weiss's narrative that her conclusions regarding the Holocaust are not a rupture with her family's past or her experience, but rather, as she articulates it, a final culmination. Throughout her text she sprinkles comments from her mother, such as "Jewish people have a natural affinity to Negroes seeking human dignity," on walking past a lunch-counter protest, or "The Ku Klux Klan hated Jews just as much as they hated Blacks," noting a synagogue was dynamited the same week as a Black church.[112] During the Suez crisis in 1956, Weiss's father confirmed his continued critique of Zionism by noting "Israel is on the wrong side again," aligned with imperial West.[113] Weiss's most succinct articulation of a Jewish anti-Zionist subjectivity was in high school. Troubled one day when a Jewish friend ask if she was a Zionist, she replied "No, I'm Jewish." For Weiss, her Jewish identity preceded the question of Zionism and also excluded it. When she asked her red-diaper-baby boyfriend about the incident, he explained that a "Zionist is anyone, Jewish or not, who defends the settlement of Israel as the Jewish homeland."[114]

With the neat separation of Zionist politics from Jewish identity, Weiss's sense of Jewish identity was reaffirmed, reflecting that Jews will experience antisemitism wherever they go, no matter the location or country; she couldn't see how a nation-state would solve such a question. She asks rhetorically, "Wouldn't it be a convenient place to get rid of us all at once?" In this way Weiss articulates an anti-Zionist common sense, in which Zionism is something alien from her point of view, but also troubling: she didn't understand why it seemed important to her friend when it was something that seemed so far away, so removed. And her response, though equally laconic, was common diasporic reason—antisemitism is global; it makes sense then to be a global and dispersed people, on the move. More than anything else, it is the brevity of the passage that is remarkable—in less than a page in a 300-page memoir, the question of Zionism was settled in her mind. *Are you a Zionist? No, I'm Jewish*, seems paradoxical, yet it is a governing logic of the 1960s Jewish New Left.

While the central political "journey" in *My Journey* is from Holocaust survivor to revolutionary, the physical journey Weiss undertakes is from Poland to France, the United States, and then finally, in the 1980s, back to Poland. While one cannot call it a kind of reverse aliyah back to Europe, it is clear that Weiss finds a sense of emotional and historical closure by visiting the towns in which her family once lived. For Weiss the return back to Poland is filled both with melancholy and optimism. She travels to the Jewish cemetery in Piotrkow, where her mother and grandmother ran a bakery. Finding the cemetery "overgrown with weeds" and the townspeople unconcerned with its upkeep, Weiss writes, before returning to Warsaw, "Alone, I listened to the melancholic murmur of the breeze swaying leaves."[115] Yet while in Warsaw she is heartened to learn that the Solidarnosc movement, which the SWP supported, printed "anti-racist leaflets and posters . . . as proof that the union stood firm against xenophobic sentiment."[116] Weiss's twin feelings about the murder of her family and their erasure from Poland, and the "Polish Spring" of the Solidarity movement, suggest that whatever her fight around Jewish identity and the Holocaust may be, there are European problems to be resolved in Europe. The entire journey of the text, from survival to finally awakening to the political implications of the Holocaust, live within a political cycle around questions of capitalism, fascism, human rights, the state, and Jewish memory. Israel's only presence in the text is as an interloper, literally—as Ariel Sharon visits Toronto, much to the dismay of Weiss and her comrades.

New Left Anti-fascism and (Jewish) Red Scare Memory

One reason for a Jewish left to oppose Zionism during the 1960s while also affirming a Jewish subjectivity may have been the way progressives tended to see postwar prosperity in terms very different than those of large mainstream Jewish institutions such as AJC and ACJ and their adherents. As Marc Dollinger writes, "American Jews celebrated the postwar consensus," enjoying their "integrating into the suburbs" and finding "common ties" with their new, often white, Christian neighbors.[117] Along with this new consensus, of course, there was also a rapid rise in class ascension, fueled by the GI Bill, university entrance in greater numbers, and the beginning of the end of restrictive covenants backed by FHA loans—all things, it should be noted, denied to most African Americans during the same period. Yet while large numbers of Jews ascended into the middle class, for the many hundreds of thousands of Jews on the Communist and socialist left of the 1940s and 1950s, the era, of course, looked quite different. For Jews on the left, whether in the Communist Party, as members of Communist-affiliated unions and organizations, or simply people with strong left sympathies, the era appeared less as the birth of a new postwar consensus and more like the emergence of a postwar fascism.

Several years before Philip Roth ironized Jewish assimilation in *Goodbye, Columbus,* Jewish Communist writer Howard Fast published a different tale about Cold War Jewish life in the United States: *Peekskill USA*. The short book is a first-person narrative of Fast's role in the infamous Peekskill riots of 1949, in which gangs of right-wing vigilantes twice attacked the concertgoers and supporters of Paul Robeson. Fast was part of the initial concert-organizing committee, using his name and reputation to help publicize the event, and on the first night he was also one of the concert attendees who organized resistance to the mobs. He and two dozen other men fought off the fascist attackers, protecting the concert space while others fled to safety. Fast's analysis, supported by the Civil Rights Congress that urged him to write it, was that this event was the opening salvo of a new form of fascism that was emergent in American life. Fast writes, "The *Peekskill* affair was an important step in the preparation for the fascization of America and for the creation of receptive soil for the promulgation of World War III." It was a way, he concluded, to both prepare the US for necessary "violence" to put down the left, and also begin preparations for new military conflict. It was one of the many instances of "force and violence against the *left*." Fast saw the coming Cold War, what Dollinger refers to as "consensus," less as a coming sign of integration and liberal democracy and more as a right-wing purge of the left, and the intensification of a militarized state.[118]

The racial and political coordinates of the vigilante violence were quite stark to Fast. The crowd that assaulted the concertgoers shouted racist and antisemitic slurs, "screaming ... in a full frenzy ... full of the taste of death," promising "Every n- bastard dies here tonight! Every Jew bastard dies here tonight." Fast cites both the ACLU and the Civil Rights Congress documentation of how both riots were premeditated and took place in full view of local and state police. Fast not only witnessed police intermingling with the vigilantes, he watched as a cop "beat the windshield of [a] car in with his club while he drew his revolver with another hand," while "another policeman" was "smashing in the windshield of a car that asked for directions." The racist and antisemitic rhetoric Fast also documents as systemic and premeditated. Stickers were printed and plastered all over town reading "COMMUNISM IS TREASON. BEHIND COMMUNISM THE JEW," and a statement from one of the groups organizing the riot read, "You Jews, and we mean you Communist Jews, have made yourself obnoxious and offensive to the American people, and you are only using the American Negro as a 'Front' in your criminal un-American activities."[119]

Fast additionally documented an attempt to assassinate Robeson, with a sniper's nest discovered in the trees behind the stage, and even before the full assault on the concertgoers, Black people were dragged out of cars in town and beaten in broad daylight. Fast described the mob not as "lumpen" but as "prosperous-appearing men, well set up, well dressed, real estate men, grocery clerks, lunch counter attendants," not a rabble but "decent citizens" and civic leaders.[120] It was an organized assault, from the top down.

Fast later said he wrote the book to wake Americans up, for he felt Americans have an "amazing resistance . . . toward" the "acceptance" of an "unmistakable phenomenon—the cultivation and growth of American fascism. We simply do not believe it." As if to prove his own point, Fast himself documents multiple moments in the text when he either refuses to recognize what he is seeing, or refuses to listen to advice from people who had a better understanding of what transpired that week. Frequently "Mrs. M.," his children's nurse and a Black woman, admonishes Fast for not understanding how "white folks behave" and left town before the second concert.[121] Likewise, the night of the second concert, Fast frequently documents how he fails to comprehend what he sees:

> Then suddenly we had to slow down. The car ahead of us had fared worse than we; every window was smashed, even the rear window. I remember saying to R—
> "The road is wet. They must have gotten the gas tank or the radiator."
> There was a dark wetness that flowed out of the car ahead of us; and then we realized that it was blood, but an enormous flow of blood that ran from the car that way and into the road.[122]

Even at the level of Fast's sentence, the "but" creates an opposition between what he sees and the enormity of it, revealing his own sense of unreality as he faces yet again another barrage of violence on the way out of the concert grounds. Through his Black nurse and his own feelings of unreality, Fast quietly documents not only the slowness of his own perceptual response, but the much longer lineages of fascism his nurse seems far more aware of: "how white folks behave."

Indeed one of the stranger ellipses in the literature on Jewish racialization is the absence of any mention of the antisemitism of either the Red Scare or postwar immigration restrictions. While the literature on

Jewish whiteness generally states that the elimination of legal restrictions to buy property in the suburbs and to enter elite universities facilitated Jewish upward class and social mobility, 1945 is often treated as the terminus of state oppression against Jews. As Amy Kaplan documents, Congress and the State Department actively limited the number of Holocaust survivors who could immigrate to the United States on the grounds that they could not assimilate and would likely be Communist sympathizers, often forcing them to emigrate to Palestine whether they wanted to or not.[123] British foreign secretary Ernest Bevin noted with some acerbic wit that the hundreds of thousands of surviving Jews displaced after the Holocaust were only shipped to Palestine because the West didn't want them: "Regarding the agitation . . . for 100,000 to be put in Palestine, I hope it will not be misunderstood in America . . . that that was because they do not want too many of them in New York."[124] In addition to antisemitic immigration restrictions, the Red Scare, which started in earnest in 1947, mobilized antisemitic tropes and actions, from dog-whistle global conspiracies to actual accusations against Jews. From the late 1940s to the mid-1950s, over half of Americans associated Jews with Communist espionage. In 1952, two-thirds of people questioned in the McCarthy hearings were Jewish, despite Jews being under 2 percent of the American population. Six members of the Hollywood Ten were Jewish, and Congressman John Rankin delighted in "unmasking" the Jewish names of Hollywood actors and directors under HUAC investigation. And of course, the only two people ever executed on federal espionage charges, the Rosenbergs, were Jewish.

That the Red Scare didn't substantively end until the HUAC showdown on the University of California's Berkeley campus in 1960 suggests that its impact on the Jewish New Left has perhaps been understated, not only in terms of the Jewish New Left's relationship to official institutions, but also to their own Jewish subjectivity. Many of the people who came of age in the 1960s whom I interviewed had lives deeply touched by the Red Scare, and their perspective on the function of the state and the Jews' place within it cannot help but have been touched. Many, including Dick and Mickey Flacks, Dick Bernstein, Joel Beinin, and Pete Seidman remember the vigilante threats against Communist-affiliated Camp Wo-Chi-Ca, and either attended or knew people who attended the infamous vigilante assault on the Peekskill concert.[125] Seidman recalls a window smashed in with a brick at the concert as one of his first childhood memories; he also talked about the "great fear" that lined his mother's face as the HUAC hearings intensified. Naomi Allen, who was an SWP activist and is now a member of Jewish Voice for Peace, described how her father had a heart attack when he was called before HUAC, and that nonetheless, he lost his job and was blacklisted from finding another.[126] Seidman, an SWP member who wrote the organization's pamphlets on antisemitism in the early 1970s, witnessed his father lose his job and start work for the New York City mob. Dick and Mickey Flacks mention in their autobiography how important it was that SDS refused to couch its revolutionary vision in anti-Communism, allowing Dick and other Jewish red diaper babies to participate: Dick said he could breathe freely for the first time as a leftist in his memory.

For many members of SDS who were not red diaper babies, the story of the Red Scare was also a family and neighborhood story: "Remember Benny Schmirnik," Rudd's father said of a friend who was blacklisted, a story Rudd "had heard often in [his] childhood."[127] For many Jews, the lesson of the Rosenberg trial was as much about anti-Communism as it was about antisemitism, or perhaps the conflation of the two. "Anti-communism and the Rosenberg execution warned Jews not to step out of line," April Rosenblum writes.[128] And as Cheryl Greenberg notes, liberal Jewish organizations such as the AJC and ADL were all too happy to reinforce such a message by distancing themselves from the Rosenbergs. There was a sense among the mainstream Jewish press that the Rosenbergs' sentence was extreme precisely because the judge and defendants were Jewish: Judge Irving Kaufman had to prove Jews were not Communists, precisely by being hard on Jewish Communists.[129] Yet Greenberg also quotes from the *Daily Forward* that "Jews and African Americans" were most numerous at organizing meetings for the Rosenbergs' defense, and that rabbis and Jewish congregations were chief among those protesting their execution—clearly there was a great distance between Jewish institutional life and the grassroots.[130] The message, as former Communist Sid Resnick said to me in an interview, was that if you were Jewish and a Communist, you could be killed by the state, and the Jewish establishment wouldn't "give a damn."[131]

There is also something unnervingly familiar in Dick Flacks's description of his parents' attitude after they were both fired from the New York City school system during the anti-Communist purge. Recounting the sudden removal of all visible left-wing material from the home, including books, magazines, pamphlets, and posters, Flacks describes the bearing of his parents about their Communism as rather similar to the way many Jews describe their observance: "Be proud of the rightness of our faith, but be very careful how much of it you reveal to others."[132] Flacks's description of Communism as a "secret faith" is a formulation that tracks closely to the way Jewish poet Yehudah Gordon summarized the Haskalah in his famous phrase: "Be a man in the streets and a Jew at home." This is not to say that Flacks embraced the universalist ideals of the Jewish Enlightenment, so much as to say the formulation, that one in public is unmarked yet in private engages in subversive acts, would be familiar to a historic Jewish sensibility. Indeed, in the Flacks's account of the Red Scare in New York City, there was a great deal of ambiguity as to whether the wholesale purge of the Jewish and Communist Teachers' Union was done primarily by Catholic administration as a result of their antisemitism, or their anti-Communism, or the conflation of the two.

The sense of the personally fungible nature of Jewish and Communist identity was highlighted a poem by Jewish Communist author Mike Hecht, published in the January 1947 edition of *Jewish Life*, documenting a man who was tortured to death by the Nazis. Was he a "Jew or a Communist," Hecht poses as a question, "I forget which . . . it don't matter nohow."[133] There is a sense in the poem that the dead man's public identity as a Jew or Communist is of no distinguishable difference, indeed they may even be the same thing. Obviously, in a Jewish magazine, the difference is one to ironize as much as to claim. But that the poem also slips into slang when it feigns or confesses that the speaker cannot remember the dead man's identity suggests the extent to which the equivalence is common sense, and perhaps is of no real importance to either the man or the author. Jews and Communists, the speaker seems to say, have a shared sensibility, a shared fate, and often quite literally share the same political and cultural outlook. In the end of the poem, it is not revealed if the man is a Jew or a Communist, other than that he is nonetheless dead. This poem serves as an unspoken political unconscious for Jews assimilating in the 1950s, that these identities were seen as interchangeable, at least for readers of *Jewish Life*.

In a memoir by Marianne Ware, she remembers the tension in her household as the Red Scare began winding up. For the narrator and the narrator's father, Communism and assimilation into a Christian whiteness were understood to be the same. While the story opens in a cramped apartment in which everyone has to awaken early for work after sleeping poorly due to crowding, the only objection the narrator offers is that she must take pumpernickel as opposed to the "white bread" her classmates eat.[134] The tension about her poverty and her parents' Jewish Communism is intensified as her father refuses to acknowledge her desire to celebrate Christmas and also her desire to give charity to a homeless man in the cold. Her father's Communism, represented by an unyielding ideology (and subscription to the *Daily Worker*) that cannot bend to give alms or partake in celebrations around them, is also coded as urban and Jewish: pumpernickel inspires the same loathing and shame as her father's difficult public performances of his ideology. While, as Dollinger suggests, many Jews "celebrated" the new consensus and the new prosperity, for Jews on the left, assimilation was as Rosenblum framed it, "an offer they could not refuse" or that perhaps seemed tied to both the pleasures and pressures of being forced to eat white bread, celebrate Christmas, and stop reading the *Daily Worker*.

In this sense, both Jewish and Black radical interest in anti-fascism in the late 1960s had not only a clear logic to it, but a very recent precedent in Communist and Marxist analysis of the American Red Scare. As Chris Vials notes in his postwar history of anti-fascism, the 1960s and early 1970s witnessed a resurgence of anti-fascist rhetoric and organizing. The Black Panther Party (BPP), with which the majority faction of SDS was allied, published a broadside in the SDS paper *The Old Mole* in 1969, calling for a "United Front against Fascism" conference in East Oakland.[135] As a follow-up, *The Old Mole* documents that the conference was called in response to the violent white backlash against the left, the assassination of Martin Luther King Jr., and especially the repression of the Panthers themselves. "Wherever they have organized," the report begins, "the Panthers have been hit hard by the Man: beaten, framed, jailed, held under huge ransoms, murdered."[136] The Panthers theorized that this backlash was the precursor to a fully fascist state, the beginnings of which they were already starting to experience. Like David Gilbert's analysis of fascism, theirs did not specifically target one racial group in particular, but rather found that it was a structure of state violence, rooted in the power of concentrated capital and its need for an ongoing war machine. The Panthers' analysis of the state led them to open their conference with a speech by Penny Nakatsu, a Japanese American woman born in an internment camp or, as Nakatsu insists, a concentration camp.[137] "The lesson I hope we can learn from 1942," Nakatsu warned the conference, "is not to wait until we have positive, irrevocable proof of . . . the all-encompassing determination of our monopolistic capitalist system to suppress all movements."

Gilbert in his autobiography came to a similar analysis: as the loss in Vietnam began to unravel the US economy, he predicted that "reactionary forces would do their best to mobilize masses of white people on a . . . racist basis to reconquer 'our' wealth and resources."[138] Calling the mass mobilization to "regain empire" the "heart of fascism," Gilbert justified not only a focus on anti-imperialism as the means to undermine American capitalism, but his own submersion into the Weather Underground Organization (WUO) and its symbolically violent and destructive acts. As Alberto Toscano has argued, many on the left in the 1970s shared the analysis that the defeat in Vietnam would trigger a society-wide backlash that would imprison or suppress a wide swath of social movements.[139] According to imprisoned Black Panther George Jackson, fascism was a kind of "delayed counter-revolution" evident in the already-present manifestations of prisons, surveillance technology, and the widespread use of police—one that would soon intensify as the revolutionary organizations gained more ground. Herbert Marcuse, the German Jewish refugee from Nazi Germany and member of the Frankfurt School made a similar argument when he suggested the New Left experienced a "preventative counterrevolution" that was part of the totalized system of control in an advanced capitalist society.[140] In some ways, fascism tout court was no longer necessary, since the "frightening reservoir of violence in everyday life" that organized monopoly capitalism was content to target people on the margins, "black and brown people, hippies, radical intellectuals," only.[141] This "proto-fascism" was a structural feature of late capitalism that could promote liberal freedom, prosperity, and authoritarian control simultaneously: one could be both a Jewish radical victim and a beneficiary of the postwar order at the same time.

Rudd, who did not want to be on the side of the "good Germans" also said by 1969, only a year after joining the Columbia strike, "We had determined that there were no innocent Americans, at least no white ones. They—we—all played some part in the atrocity of Vietnam, if only the passive roles of ignorance, acquiescence, and acceptance of privilege."[142] Rudd arrived at similar political conclusions, writing that witnessing the mass atrocities in Vietnam and the assassination of Black Panther Party members including George Jackson and Fred Hampton led him to conclude he had the moral responsibility of one living in a fascist state. And given the level of FBI, CIA, and National Security Agency coordination to undermine, disrupt, arrest, and murder members of the left through J. Edgar Hoover's COINTELPRO program, one might forgive the young Rudd for thinking that such desperate measures were necessary. He writes, "Literally hundreds of individuals and groups whom FBI director J. Edgar Hoover deemed subversive were destroyed, jailed, or otherwise neutralized by completely illegal clandestine COINTELPRO activities." To him this justified not only revolutionary acts but the underground nature of the WUO. Many Panthers agreed with the analogy. As Gilbert reported,

> Panthers were fascinated by the Holocaust and often asked the Jewish members of our group why there hadn't been more widespread resistance. They understood the U.S. treatment of Black People as genocide and were determined, even at the cost of their own lives if necessary, to stop it.[143]

While the WUO's decision to dissolve SDS and go underground is often regarded as reckless, it should be remembered that only a decade and a half before, the Communist Party, faced with similar repression at the hands of the Cold War Red Scare, decided as well to take a large segment of their leadership underground when it believed the United States was about to turn fascist. In that sense, the BPP invitation of Jewish Communist scholar Herbert Aptheker to give a keynote address suggests the Panthers were aware of a longer Jewish and Communist analysis of fascism that emerged in the 1930s and 1940s. It was common in the 1930s and '40s for left-wing Jewish writers such as Mike Gold to refer to the Klan as fascists and suggest anti-labor vigilantes wanted a "Nazi Germany" east of Los Angeles.[144] Communist-sponsored Jewish publishing houses such as Yidburo and Morgen Freiheit routinely published pamphlets that connected "Jewish survival" both before and after the Holocaust to defeating fascism in the US and abroad. In a pamphlet published in 1945 in response to the Holocaust, Jewish Communist writer Alexander Bittelman wrote that for the "uprooting of fascism" one must "resist all reactionary and fascist theories and ideologies of 'race superiority,' 'white supremacy,' the superiority of 'western civilization,' and 'Anglo-Saxon' domination of the life of the American people."[145] In particular Bittelman focused, much like the BPP, on how the "national aspirations of the Negro people" are connected to the struggle against imperialism and Zionism, the abolition of both necessary for the full flourishing of the Jewish people around the globe. As the Jewish Communist magazine *Jewish Life* observed in November of 1946, the Ku Klux Klan are the "American SS" and "the fate of the Jew is tied to the fate of the Negro, the trade unions, and the general fight for democracy."[146]

Perhaps the most important Communist organization to make the connection between the US and homegrown fascism was the Civil Rights Congress (CRC). Founded in 1946 to replace the International Labor Defense, it took an explicitly anti-fascist approach to organizing against racism and anti-union suppression. Placing the Holocaust at the center of its analysis of capitalism, William Patterson, its director, compared the fate of African Americans in the United States to Jews under the Holocaust. Furthering the analysis of Negritude theorist Aimé Césaire, Patterson held that the origins of fascism lay in colonialism and slavery, systems that in an era of crisis returned back to Europe to form fascism. Following this logic, perhaps the CRC's most famous and controversial act was the We Charge Genocide petition delivered to the United Nations in 1951, claiming that under the UN charter, the United States was committing genocide against African Americans, and UN intervention against lynching and Jim Crow was necessary. What was remarkable about the CRC was that it was one of the few organizations with a sizeable grassroots Jewish and African American membership and leadership to denounce the Rosenberg trial as a site of fascist violence. One might even say that because of its Jewish and African American members and leadership, it was uniquely suited to make such comparisons. Unlike the American Jewish Committee (AJC) and the NAACP, which both denounced the Rosenbergs, the CRC connected the execution of the Rosenbergs to lynchings of African Americans in the deep South and Nazi genocide in Europe.[147] The CRC, like the

Communist Party and later the BPP, saw the violent backlash against Communism, including the execution of the Rosenbergs, the bloody riot at Peekskill against Paul Robeson, and the jailing of Communists under the Smith Act as signs of incipient fascism. Had the CRC not been banned in 1956 as a "subversive organization" under the same act, it is very possible that it would have been among the groups sponsoring the BPP's United against Fascism conference.

Stanley Aronowitz's 1960s pamphlet on the specificity of American fascism likewise connects the Holocaust to the "systematic and conscious genocide against generations of blacks, both North and South," linking the Nazi mass murder to "lynchings" and the "brutality" with which "American Indians" were treated by an "advanced industrial country."[148] Aronowitz, who came out of the left-labor tradition and was not allied with SDS, nonetheless saw in the Panthers' description of the United States as fascist something that aligned with a longer left tradition in the United States. Fascism for Aronowitz is not merely a kind of lower-middle-class populism, but a modality of rule that arises when the traditional modes of parliamentary hegemony are no longer sufficient to resolve contradictions or quell rebellion. But rather than a departure from normative modes of rule, fascism exists within and is an expression of US liberal institutions, founded as they were on forms of capitalist violence. Thus Aronowitz concludes, much like the CRC, the "anticommunist purges" of the late 1940s and 1950s constituted a "prefascist stage" of American capitalism, which culminated in the "public trials of countless communists . . . the murder of the Rosenbergs . . . witchhunts against trade unions . . . and the McCarren Act," which banned any organization affiliated with the Communist Party.[149] Unlike the Zionists who might refer to the Holocaust as a form of Jewish exceptionalism, or radicals such as Tseng-Putterman who would order the Holocaust on a hierarchy, the CRC, Aronowitz, the CP, and others think of racial genocide and fascism in its many intersecting forms as a totality of capitalist rule.

In this context, it makes sense that the most serious left-wing pamphlets and articles on antisemitism in the 1960s would be produced by Marxist organizations. While most New Left organizations had significant Jewish presence, their considerations centered on defending groups like SNCC and the BPP against charges of antisemitism for their calls against Zionism. In part because there is a lengthy Marxist literature on antisemitism, and in part because of their own analysis of the role antisemitism plays in the construction of fascism, both the CPUSA and SWP devoted extensive resources to discussing the present role of antisemitism in America and its relationship to Zionism and the right. CP and SWP publications do not single out antisemitism as a transcendent evil, or mark the Holocaust as a singular event in human history. Like Marcuse and the BPP, they locate the Holocaust within the larger structures of capitalism and imperialism and see antisemitism as a structural and reoccurring feature of capitalist life. In a collection of essays in the late 1970s on antisemitism and Zionism from *Jewish Affairs*, Communist author Hyman Lumer documents the still-active presence of antisemitism in American life. Quoting from a University of California study, Lumer writes that two-thirds of Americans are antisemitic: one-third hold such views "private," one-third are "outspoken antisemites," and, of these, a tenth "advocate doing something to take 'power' from the Jews."[150] Lumer roots antisemitism in capitalism and imperialism, and in doing, places the "Nazi Holocaust" alongside the "millions of Africans" who "suffered death at the hands of slave traders" and the "genocidal extermination of the Indian people in the Western hemisphere."[151] Like Hannah Arendt, Lumer locates antisemitism in the economy insofar as he documents Jews' exclusion from "top executive and administrative positions" in banks, corporations, and elite universities, but he primarily aligns antisemitism as part of a political formation, the far right.[152] "With a sharp swing toward reaction on the part of the Nixon administration . . . fascist elements . . . rise in an open, virulent expression of antisemitism," Lumer argues, further documenting the "desecration of synagogues" in recent months.[153] Lumer, who was one of the members of the Communist leadership who went underground in the 1950s and was later arrested and jailed for a year under the Taft-Hartley Act for "conspiring to lie about membership in [the] Communist Party" as an organizer in a labor union, was very familiar with both the fascist and antisemitic nature of the American state. Like generations of Marxist critics before him, Lumer locates the rise of antisemitism as a means to deflect attention from the power of global capitalism and shield the ruling classes from scrutiny.

The specificity of antisemitism, for the left, was not then simply an afterthought but rather a necessary articulation that linked their anti-facist politics with their anti-imperialism. Pete Seidman, a red diaper baby whose father lost his job during the Red Scare, wrote the position paper for the SWP on antisemitism. While Seidman had been personally aware of antisemitism from a young age, as he was bullied at school and his father was a blacklisted former Communist, it was the experience of being attacked by the ADL for the SWP's support for Palestinians that goaded him into serious study on the question. What is perhaps most remarkable about Seidman's study is the emphasis it places on the failures of liberal democracy to protect Jews from structural antisemitism both before and after World War II. Antisemitism, for Seidman, is less a means for market liberalism to disavow the racial modalities of capital accumulation, as Tseng-Putterman and Ratskoff suggest, than a structural part of the liberal state itself. Focusing on the Roosevelt administration, Seidman shows how even while Roosevelt made token gestures toward Jewish inclusion and courted Jewish leaders of well-heeled organizations, on its most fateful policy decision, whether to allow Jewish refugees from Europe fleeing fascism, Roosevelt collaborated with assimilationist Jewish organizations to keep Jewish refugees out. Not only did the Roosevelt administration not raise quotas, it intervened to ensure that even existing quotas were not filled, even after Kristallnacht made the Nazis' plans quite clear. This did not change even after the full scope of the Holocaust was widely known: Roosevelt and later Truman's policy of keeping Jewish refugees out of the United States remained because they feared that Jews, as the Nazis felt, would bring with them Communism and other "unassimilable" ideas. For Seidman, the Roosevelt administration's refusal to allow Jewish refugees was entirely in line with the antisemitic culture of assimilation enthusiastically embraced by many Jewish organizations including B'nai B'rith and the AJC, which felt that becoming "good Americans" was more important than rescuing Jews from the Holocaust. Seidman goes so far as to accuse the Roosevelt administration of conscious antisemitism, noting that despite his "carefully cultivated reputation as a friend and benefactor of the Jews," Roosevelt placed a known antisemite and fascist sympathizer, Breckinridge Long, in charge of the administration's Jewish refugee policy.[154]

For Seidman, the US's increasingly vocal support for the state of Israel after the 1967 Arab-Israeli War was not a sign of Jewish inclusion, but rather a new form of state antisemitism. Far from making Jews safe, Seidman argued, much as Arendt did two decades earlier, Israel created a "haven" only by "militarily conquering" a "nation of two and a half million people" and conducting an "endless war with the refugees it created."[155] Further, Israel depends "for its survival" on "aid from U.S. imperialism," allying "the Jewish people" with an empire that the "oppressed peoples around the world" regarded as an "enemy." To secure this allegiance and to ensure that Jewish refugees arrived in Israel and not the United States, from the 1930s through the Holocaust, Zionists agreed "any struggle against ... immigration policies might interfere with Zionist attempts to woo U.S. support for their plans."[156] Further, Seidman documented, Zionists allied with the right wing of the Jewish establishment who, for their own reasons, "believed any influx of Jewish refugees from Europe would undermine their assimilation into U.S. society."[157] Embittering the Palestinians and allying with both reactionaries and the US empire, the state of Israel, Seidman felt, was objectively antisemitic both in its foundation and in its practice. This proposition that Zionism feeds the very antisemitism it says it exists to defend against was apparent from the very inception of the state. Turning the metaphor and history of the Holocaust on its head, Seidman wrote that it is precisely because the Zionist state existed that the people of Israel would "face Munich-like dangers or worse."[158] For Seidman it was the cruelest of ironies that the SWP was labeled as antisemitic by the ADL as, he argued, it was Trotskyists and other radicals who opposed fascism in the US and in Europe, while it was the Jewish establishment and Zionists who tacitly or even explicitly allied with fascists on the condition they supported a Jewish state in Palestine.

As the SWP Marxist intellectual George Novack wrote in 1968 upon reviewing the posthumous publication of Deutscher's *Non-Jewish Jew*, worries about antisemitism might seem "unduly alarmist to those privileged and short-sighted Anglo-American Jews" who had been "sunning in the prolonged prosperity and social stability of the post war decades."[159] Novack is acknowledging here that for most white American Jews, the terror of Nazism and even Peekskill seemed but a distant, far-removed echo. Like "proto-fascism" in Marcuse's analysis, repression does not have to be total to be racialized and reactionary: that some Jews experienced antisemitic state violence at the height of the Cold War while others experienced prosperity is not so much a contradiction of late capitalism but a condition of its function.[160] Yet there is always a danger that at some moment, the counterrevolution against fascism may not be deemed to be sufficient, and, echoing Fast's experiences in Peekskill, Novack quotes Deutscher:

> Let this society suffer any severe shock, such as it is bound to suffer; let there be again millions of unemployed, and we will see the same lower-middle-class alliance with the Lumpenproletariat, from whom Hitler recruited his following, running amok with anti-Semitism. As long as the nation-state imposes its supremacy and as long as we have not an international society in existence, as long as the wealth of every nation is in the hands of one national capitalist oligarchy, we shall have chauvinism, racialism, and, as its culmination, anti-Semitism.[161]

For many of the New Left activists with whom I spoke, there was a particular urgency to their antiracist work that was not solely explicable by political calculus or benevolence alone. For many of the two dozen or so interviewees, there was a special importance, only a decade and a half after the Holocaust, less than a decade from the Red Scare, to work in the civil rights movement. David Gilbert remembers his youthful attraction, still an adolescent, to hearing MLK speak; Linda Loew remembers it was the power of Malcolm X's autobiography that brought her into contact with the anti-racism of the SWP; Phil Passen relates how joining the Freedom Rides dedicated him to a life of struggle. Many, like Geoff Mirelowitz, remember their parents taking them to their first protest (in Mirelowitz's case, a picket in Chicago for the desegregation of the schools).[162] That these activists would connect the Holocaust to anti-racism and anti-fascism and then also to anti-Zionism did not strike them as wholesale inventions of the present—they were, for the most part, intuitive connections. They were part of the Jewish world in which they were raised. That they seem strange, or forced, or even nostalgic today suggests how much Zionist propaganda and historical amnesia has clouded Jewish memory, specifically, memory of the left. As Mirelowitz himself said, such ideas did not need to be spoken to him aloud to be absorbed—they were simply in the air, in the Yiddish jokes, in the aura that was around him growing up. Rudd's story thus remains exemplary in a sense: that he might "see himself among the dead" of the Holocaust, and then throw himself headlong into the struggle against racism and imperialism. The Holocaust, in this frame, does not provide one safety and security via a new relationship to the state, as sought after by the ADL and later Zionist organizations. Holocaust memory, rather, serves as a means by which other forms of racism and state power can be understood and opposed.

3

Exceptional Whites, Bad Jews: Class, Whiteness, and the Racial Politics of the Anti-Zionist Jewish New Left

Racial Reassignment; Racial Conscription

No story about the radical 1960s can be told without considering the ways Jewish revolutionaries were formed by and reacted to changing Ashkenazi Jewish racial dynamics in the postwar era. There is something of a cottage industry dedicated to figuratively or perhaps literally fleshing out the contours of these new social relationships: How did Jews experience, as Grace Paley put it, their rise like a "surface-to-air missile" into a white (ethnic) middle class?[1] The metaphor is a telling one, as it links the expanding postwar racialized middle class to the Keynesian warfare-welfare state, with its suburbs, urban renewal, compulsory anti-Communism, and conservative unionization tied to military production and the maintenance of a dollarized global empire.[2] It is also an image that is deeply uncertain: on the one hand it connotes a kind of phallic power and determination; it also connotes a kind of dizzying speed, a rush into a vast and heretofore-unknown space. The uncertainty of the metaphor expresses much of the ambivalence Jews felt about their sudden acceptance into the widening sphere of middle-class probity. Hardly passive, Jews moved en masse into newly developing suburbs of New Jersey, northern Chicago, and West and North LA, much as they eagerly sought out work in the expanding cultural middle class of universities, think tanks, newspapers and other media, social work, and civil service, all arenas in which Jews remain overrepresented. Yet the loss of cultural ties and urban communities and the broad effect of the Red Scare meant that this newly achieved whiteness was as much sought-after as it was compulsory, an ambivalence expressed in films and books, from the Coen brothers' *A Serious Man* to Philip Roth's *American Pastoral* and Chana Bloch's *The Past Keeps Changing*.

While few progressive scholars doubt the general contours of Karen Brodkin's argument that European-descended Jews experienced a "racial reassignment" as they ascended from low-paying industrial jobs in factories, slaughterhouses, and the garment industry to jobs requiring increasing levels of education, there is an ongoing discussion about how Jews may have experienced these changes and how, politically, they responded. As Brodkin notes, the story of race is the story of class, at least insofar as Jews appear to be an exemplary case: classified as "Hebrew" and barred from entry to the US by racialized immigration quotas, Jews from the late nineteenth to the mid-twentieth century were not by and large seen as fully "white," and this is apparent not only in their assignment within layers of the working class, but in restrictive real estate covenants, limits to their numbers at prestigious universities, immigration restrictions, and antisemitic norms in civic and commercial culture.[3] Changing racial attitudes that began in the Depression-era labor movement emerged in non-discrimination clauses of the New Deal, and finally exploded into popular culture when the anti-Nazi rhetoric of World War II created enough of a consensus that most official forms of explicit legal and cultural discrimination against Jews began to fade. With entrance into suburbs and top universities, Jews rapidly began to see their class—and their racial assignment—change. Jews were now included in the expanded circle of "white people." Or as Frank Sinatra sang in the 1945 propaganda film, Jews were now in the house I lived in quite literally, as zip code and racial identity, if not objective correlatives, at least bear very strong correspondence.

How even this transformation was, how much of it was by threat and how much by choice, and how stable Jews' racial reassignments were are up for debate, but a consensus exists among scholars that by the 1950s, American Jews enjoyed "the privileges of inclusion," as Marc Dollinger articulates, at least in terms of economic success and political representation.[4] Yet this new inclusion in the middle classes was greeted by its beneficiaries with more than a bit of ambivalence. As Brodkin writes, some Jews worried that their assimilation into a hegemonic "white" form of Jewishness might betray a personal or collective sense of ethos, or perhaps ethnos; others worried that the US's sudden embrace of the Jews would be short-lived, insincere. For Dollinger and Goldstein, this ambivalence was expressed in a kind of normative racial liberalism, in which Jews could express their distinctive ethno-religious heritage through a belief in American inclusion, tolerance, and multi-racial belonging.[5] Anti-racism became a kind of postwar Americanism that Jewish Americans could embrace as both a positive marker of their newfound belonging and a self-interested political struggle to ensure a kind of progressive liberalism remained hegemonic.[6] Or as David Verbeeten frames it, when Jews assimilated into the mainstream of American life, they did so Jewishly.[7] Not only in the limited sense that Jews often moved into Jewish suburbs and entered professional fields in which there was already a Jewish presence, but also in that they hoped to remake American liberalism in their image: secular, inclusive, anti-racist, multicultural, meritocratic. Jewish voting patterns and political sensibilities seemed to bear this out: Jews were far more likely to support liberal Democrats and also support civil rights measures than non-Jewish white Americans and, even by the mid-1960s, were alone among white respondents to be evenly divided in saying civil rights progress was moving "too slow."[8] If Jews were going to assimilate, it seemed, into the house Sinatra lived in, the hope was that it was not burning down too fast.

Much of this ambivalent relationship to whiteness has been mediated through both the historiography as well as the metaphor of "Black-Jewish relations." As Cheryl Greenberg writes, "No other racial/ethnic group formed as long term collaboration as Blacks and Jews."[9] Pointing to the Jewish involvement with the foundation of the NAACP, the high rates of membership of both African Americans and American Jews in the Communist Party, as well as the AJC's collaborations with the NAACP in the civil rights movement, Greenberg traces the material and institutional means by which Blacks and Jews not only formed an alliance but helped construct a liberal consensus on multi-racial democracy. This alliance is often memorialized by Jewish liberals in relation to the murders of Schwerner and Goodman, Rabbi Heschel's march with Martin Luther King Jr., and, for the more radical, the defense of the "Scottsboro Boys" headed by a Jewish lawyer. What is compelling about Greenberg's analysis is precisely that it was not discursive: the Black–Jewish alliance she describes was founded on deep institutional collaborations, and coalitions founded in prominent organizations and political parties. While she could have gone further to point out how radical organizations such as Civil Rights Congress and large left-wing labor unions such as the United Electrical Workers and the National Association of Substitute Letter Carriers made these alliances not only through dominant organizations, but through radical social movements, such movements reflected less a break than a continuum with Jewish racial liberalism. While it might seem shocking now, polling data recorded a higher Jewish support for civil rights than for Zionism in the late 1950s—liberal anti-racism was, for Jews at least, postwar Americanism.[10]

As important as this mid-twentieth century Jewish–African American alliance may have been in shaping Jewish and African American culture as well as American politics, another stream of historiography examines the ways in which Jews ascended, or perhaps descended, into whiteness at the literal and discursive expense of African Americans. Michael Rogin's *Black Face, White Noise* tracks Jewish use of blackface minstrelsy in Broadway and film, noting how Jews were accepted as white to the extent they could participate—and did participate—in the dominant racist culture of the day.[11] They could be white by proving in essence that they were not Black or, perhaps, anti-Black. This view that Jews succeed to the extent they refuse blackness, as Brodkin discusses, was concretized by liberals turned neocons such as Nathan Glazer and Norm Podhoretz who deployed myths of Jewish work ethic and moral probity to explain why Jews succeeded in the US and African Americans did not. In Glazer's *Beyond the Melting Pot*, he embraces Jewish "model minority" status to show how strong family ties, hard work, and communal cohesiveness were the vehicles of Jewish success, while African Americans' failure was their own fault for not inculcating these values.[12] Beryl Satter's *Family Properties* articulates the material foundation for Jewish whiteness, as she explores how, even for progressive Jewish Chicagoans, white flight had an economic imperative that was difficult to resist, as urban disinvestment often meant that remaining in increasingly African American neighborhoods entailed losing the value of their homes.[13] While one could say that Jewish homeowners and small landlords were caught in the middle of a racist system, willing or unwilling, Jews could leave for racially exclusive suburbs to protect property values, and African Americans could not.

As Feldman, Dollinger, and Goldstein and others narrate, these contradictions came to a head in the late 1960s as the rise of Black Power and group-based identity politics "seemed to evidence a fundamental break-down in a once-historic interracial alliance."[14] Often narrated as a larger breakdown of consensus around Cold War liberalism, Black Power not only rejected integration as an aim of a Black freedom struggle; given the prevalence of Jews in the civil rights movement among white people, it was felt with great anxiety in liberal and sometimes even left-wing Jewish communities. Whether SNCC letting its white, mostly Jewish staff members go, or a rhetorical embrace of armed resistance, as Seth Forman articulates, Black Power was "perhaps the most unsettling development for American Jews," as it revealed Jewish liberalism and African American political and cultural movements were moving at "cross purposes."[15] Even Abbie Hoffman, a key activist in SNCC in the mid-1960s, published an attack on Black Power during SNCC's "purge" of white activists, only to be gently corrected by comrades, including Julius Lester and Stokely Carmichael, who talked him out of his position.[16] According to Feldman, Jewish conservatives and liberals shared "deep anxieties" about Black Power critiques of Jewish liberalism that went far beyond just the civil rights movement and to the entire project of Jewish nationalism.[17] Many Jewish progressives felt a deep betrayal by both SNCC and the BPP when both articulated a critique of Zionism as a form of white supremacy. And if anything, such historical retrospectives downplay the anger and even disgust of many Jewish liberals at the BPP and other Black Power organizations, who all but accused left-wing Jews who supported BPP of being race traitors and "sycophants to the Blacks" for not breaking with such organizations.

In a sly rejoinder to scholars who accuse Black Power of fostering the end of the golden age of Jewish civil rights activism and those who conversely blame Jewish racism for its demise, both Dollinger and Goldstein offer a perhaps more original synthesis of two ideas. Even while "Jewish leaders sounded the alarm over the rise of Black militancy," Jews found inspiration in Black Power to rearticulate Jewish politics on similar ontological grounds.[18] Jewish activists, Dollinger writes, were "inspired by the unapologetic approach of Black Power," and were "modeling tactics employed" by movements that were widening the "limits of acceptable group expression" in the 1960s and early 1970s.[19] In what was sometimes referred to as the Jewish Renewal Movement, Jews,

Dollinger argues, "turned inward" to rearticulate a more expressive, more expansive view of identitarian politics. Whether that meant demanding Jewish communal day schools, a democratization of religious culture, or a celebration of Jewish culture or Jewish looks, Jews eschewed the liberal universalism of an earlier generation to promote a kind of "Jewish pride movement." As Goldstein articulates, Jews ceased looking to "racial liberalism as a surrogate for ethnic distinctiveness" and focused rather on a "group-centered political agenda."[20] On the left this might look like organizations such as the Chutzpah Collective and Brooklyn Bridge Collective that embraced both left-wing politics and positive Jewish identity, while also rejecting the firm anti-Zionism of SDS and the SWP. On the right, this looked more like JDL, which explicitly modeled itself on the Black Panthers and Black Liberation Army. "[If Black nationalists] can walk around saying black problems come first for blacks—beautiful! Right on!" claimed Kahane. "Then Jewish problems come first for Jews," including, and perhaps most saliently, Zionism.[21] As Dollinger framed it, Black Power allowed Jews to become more Zionist, rather than less.[22] Not only did it provoke a right-wing backlash against left internationalism, it allowed Jews to feel more comfortable with their own nationalism, and their own sense of group identity. While Dollinger does not quite come out and say it, he seems to imply that the "Black-Jewish alliance" may have dissolved materially, but it has been reborn at the level of discourse, and perhaps in an ontological age this will provide a new basis for solidarity.

While the narratives of Dollinger, Goldstein, and others describe a wide swath of American Jewish life, as they themselves articulate, they leave out the story of the Jewish New Left—organizations such as SDS, the Yippies, and SWP that were not self-consciously Jewish yet had sizeable, even outsized, Jewish membership. For SDS and other organizations of the New Left, Black Power was not seen as threatening, but rather a welcome advance over what before had been understood as partial and far-too-slow progress on civil rights. Rather than harmful to the New Left, Black Power organizations such as the BPP were seen as advancing the racial and political analysis in the movement, embracing Third World revolutionary politics over the civil rights frame of the nation-state. African Americans in the movement understood themselves, much like SDS saw the world, less as minorities in a multiethnic nation than as colonized peoples in a worldwide struggle against

American imperialism. As Rudd states in his memoir, "We saw the black-power movement, led by the Panthers, already fighting a revolutionary war from within the United States."[23] The BPP were living corollaries to the anti-colonial NLF and *focos* of the Cuban revolution. As Gilbert—one of the architects of SDS's theory of imperialism—articulates in his memoir, "The 'Black Power' slogan also became a fountainhead for the development of a revolutionary tendency within the white student movement," galvanizing the student left to go beyond anti-war demands to a larger framework of anti-imperialist struggle.[24] While both Rudd and Gilbert and others in SDS and later Weather Underground would come to modulate their theories as events on the ground shifted, such analysis came out of their lived experience. It was their concrete experience with the Columbia strike—the unity among Black students, Black community members, and the anti-war student left—that encouraged their understanding of the potent relationship Black militancy could have with what they referred to at the time as the "white left." Rather than see white organizations developing their own separate, even separatist agendas, the largely Jewish leadership of SDS saw organizations such as the BPP and the newly emergent Black student unions as setting the political agenda for white (and very often Jewish) student organizations to follow. While these Jewish students agreed with the Jewish Renewal Movement insofar as the hegemonic liberalism of the 1950s no longer expressed their subjectivity, it was not Jewish separatism that inspired them, but Third World and Black revolution.

Following from a global analysis of the historical moment, SDS embarked on a serious internal and external debate about race and whiteness, and indeed, much of "whiteness studies" as we know it today emerges from this debate within SDS. As SDS activist and writer turned historian Noel Ignatiev (writing as Noel Ignatin) articulates in a widely shared open letter to SDS members, it was not enough simply to be anti-racist if one was a member of a revolutionary white-led organization. Writing an open letter to the Progressive Labor Party, which promoted a "class first" analysis of the struggle against capitalism, Ignatiev offers that the PL not only misunderstands racism, but misunderstands the role of "the Negro workers" in the struggle for the "future of the American working class."[25] Ignatiev argues, "The U.S. ruling class has made a deal with the misleaders of American labor, and through them the masses of white workers.[26] This "sweetheart deal" has origins not only in the New Deal and the compromise reached with labor unions in the 1930s and 1940s, but in the "special privileges befitting . . . white skin," including property in white neighborhoods, white schools, and access to higher-paid jobs.[27] These privileges not only bind white workers to the political and economic system through wages and secure jobs, they also blind them to their real interests in overthrowing the system. Describing "white skin privilege" as both "material" and "spiritual," Ignatiev suggests that white workers have more to lose than their chains.

Not only does Ignatiev challenge the PL's central argument that working-class demands would benefit Black workers—as a greater share of Black people are working class—he suggests universal demands are racist, as they would keep Black workers in their place. More importantly for his argument however, Ignatiev challenges the *role* Black workers play in the struggle. The PL, Ignatiev accuses, places Black workers in a "limbo," as accessories or "allies" in the primary working-class struggle waged by white workers, rather than as the most dynamic and revolutionary element of the entire working class. It is up to white workers not to lead the struggle but rather to follow militant Black organizing that understands racial capital for what it will and won't offer Black labor—the "sweetheart deal" open to white workers. Ignatiev closes on an image of John Brown as a "careful student of American social reality," someone who saw "white supremacy" as the central challenge for his time. That John Brown dedicated his life to the violent overthrow of white supremacy was not lost on SDS. As a domestic corollary to their analysis of global capitalism, SDS posited Black workers and anti-colonial guerrillas as poised to lead the struggle not only subjectively but also materially against the "neocapitalism" of the postwar age. It was the role of SDS to support them.

Psychologically and physically, as Gilbert expresses in his memoir, the task of a white revolutionary was not only to support Black revolutionary struggle, but also to throw off the shackles of whiteness in their person: from a respect for authority to what George Lipsitz would later refer to as a "possessive investment" in the property that undergirds the white middle class. As Gilbert writes, "We enthusiastically borrowed Panther rhetoric . . . A prime example, quickly adopted by white street kids, was to rename the police 'the pigs' . . . This term played a provocative role in breaking the mental shackles of the day."[28] This also included confrontations with police and a willingness to engage at least symbolically in acts of violence. While Marshall Berman has derided such politics as a "romance of marginality," for SDS members such tactics were not merely personal displays of bravery; they carried with them a logic about race, class and revolution. As SDS activists described it, it was their role to "share the costs" of the struggle against racism and imperialism: "Since Black revolutionaries are already engaged in armed struggle, it was the role of whites to support them"—especially given the relative protection white skin and middle-class status might provide.[29] Such an approach not only mobilized what Ignatiev would later call "white skin privilege," it also would set an example for the white working class, who many in SDS felt were bought off and acted only with their short-term interests in mind. While most in SDS did not abandon a critique of wage labor and exploitation as fundamental to capitalism, they did feel whiteness allowed white workers to imagine—even if they were incorrect in the long run—that they had more to lose than their chains should the revolution succeed. As the inverse perhaps of the accusation that Jews in SDS had assimilated, Gilbert wryly formulated later, "We had seen ourselves as 'exceptional whites'—the rare handful of white people who were sincerely anti-racist."[30] It was the role of such "exceptional whites" to protect Black revolutionaries who were being murdered by police in ever-greater numbers, and also to commit "propaganda by the deed" behind enemy lines—that is, use their whiteness to infiltrate and disrupt the system from within.

Exceptional Whites, Bad Jews

One could ask if there was anything particularly *Jewish* about SDS's theorizations of race apart from the ethno-cultural heritage of many of the authors and actors. As Dollinger and Goldstein point out, this "racial reassignment" from liminally white to white was disorienting for many on the left, and the embrace of Jewish ethnic identity politics could be seen as one response to it. The Jewish Renewal Movement could be seen as a disavowal of whiteness while at the same time an anxiety that expressed itself in appreciation for simultaneous political rejection of Black nationalism. To recast one's ethnicity as "Jewish" rather than "white" was to retreat from positions held by the Panthers while also embracing a logic of racial-identity formation. As Gilbert says, there was something equally solipsistic about SDS members' understanding of their whiteness—that while it aided them politically in forming alliances with Black radicals, it also included naïve assumptions and romantic ideas about race. Concerning the feeling of many SDSers that they were "exceptional" in their understanding of whiteness and ability to transcend it, Gilbert writes,

> There was a double error embedded in the "exceptional whites" perspective: First, it led us to abdicate our responsibility to organize other white people in an anti-racist way; and secondly, it expressed the conceit that we were now magically free of racism. So the "exceptional white" vanity ... was more about promoting ourselves than about building the strongest possible solidarity with people of color.[31]

While Gilbert may be accurate when he discusses the political limitations of his approach to race, it seems equally possible that, for Gilbert and others, "whiteness" was felt with a certain kind of ambiguity. While I do not want to collapse or equate the rejection of the Panthers or an embrace of Zionism with SDS or even the Weather Underground, there is for both a sense that these Jewish activists were not quite like other white people. For Gilbert that was a call to solidarity; for many in the Jewish Revival Movement who embraced Zionism it was, as Dollinger refers to it, a turn inward.[32] Either way, whiteness—as a felt material transformation in the generational lives of these Jewish activists—was the source of a constant political and personal struggle. Nearly all of the SDS and SWP memoirs—as well as personal interviews I have conducted—expressed a disquiet between normative Jewish liberalism and recent memories of the Holocaust, the Red Scare, and the state-sanctioned antisemitism of US anti-immigration policy. Yet it was also this critique of whiteness that allowed activists in SDS to understand that whatever misgivings they might have, solidarity with SNCC and the Panthers over questions of Israel was unwavering and foundational.

One can hear a kind of dialectical echo, a unity of opposites, in Gilbert's framing of SDS Jews as "exceptional whites" and Glazer's formation that Jews are prefiguratively white. As Brodkin suggests, Glazer openly adopted anti-Black racism to highlight Jewish postwar assimilation, suggesting that it was Jewish cultures of hard work, educational attainment, and in-group solidarity that enabled Jews to thrive in the years following World War II, unlike African Americans who were mired in what Daniel Patrick Moynihan referred to as "cultures of poverty."[33] As Brodkin frames it, Jews for Glazer were "pre-figuratively white" insofar as their cultural values allowed them to excel and perhaps even exceed their Protestant betters, who honored Protestant values only in the breach. In some ways, Glazer offered a racialized version of Slezkine's thesis that, as Marx wryly suggests in "On the Jewish Question," Jewish emphasis on diaspora, mobility, fungibility, assimilation, and secularity make them suited for modernity, or perhaps, has made modernity Jewish in their own image. While Slezkine's and Marx's theses are, to put it generously, grand and sweeping, Glazer's comparison between African American and Jewish children's value of education and capability for abstract and impersonal thought locate Jewish modernity within a postwar ethnic framework for success.[34] Gilbert's insight that the largely Jewish SDS and later Weather Underground were "exceptional whites" echoes Glazer's ethnic framework in an inverted mirror. While Gilbert would never explain either Jewish presence in SDS or their critical distance from whiteness in ethnic terms, one could see both Glazer and Gilbert circling around the radical upheavals of race and ethnicity the postwar era brought. How does one explain the rapid and epochal shifts of Jewish racial identities, while at the same time explaining how so many young white people wanted to reject this order?

Not all engagements with changing Jewish identity during the New Left era framed class solely through the modality of race, as Stuart Hall famously phrased it. In Shaul Magid's critical and theoretical biography of the far-right ultra-Zionist leader and Jewish Defense League founder Meir Kahane, he notes how Kahane spoke to "lower middle class Jews" in New York City's outer boroughs who did not attend well-heeled colleges such as Columbia or the University of Chicago.[35] In Magid's telling, these "lower middle class Jews" who "suffered from latent and overt antisemitism" in "racially mixed neighborhoods" were left behind by the New Left both materially and discursively. As the New Left prioritized anti-imperialism and called out working- and middle-class Jews for their whiteness and racism, particularly during the Ocean Hill–Brownsville teacher's strike, so the narrative goes, working-class Jews often felt their own needs were unmet and that they were abandoned by their well-heeled Jewish betters. Magid goes so far as to call Kahane's approach to class "Marxist" insofar as he particularly called forth Jews who were politically disenfranchised and underrepresented by both liberal and radical left-wing politics.[36] While calling Kahane's approach to class Marxist is, to say the least, rather unorthodox (Kahane was not anti-capitalist and indeed did not see laboring for capitalists as a form of exploitation), it is nonetheless true that not all Ashkenazi Jews were lifted gently from their marginal and working-class status by the great transformations of the post–New Deal era.

As I discuss in the next chapter, with the rise of Jewish socialist collectives after the collapse of SDS, members of the Brooklyn Bridge Collective and Chutzpah foregrounded their working-class roots. Myron Perlman, former member of SDS and one of the founders of the socialist Chutzpah Collective, writes that it was the "myth" of Jewish middle-to-upper-class status in the 1960s that led him to work summers and be exploited by Jewish bosses, as he assumed—as a Jew—class exploitation was someone else's problem.[37] Jewish religious and communal life, as he experienced it as a child in his Chicago neighborhood of West Rogers Park, both celebrated wealthy donors to his shul and gave special recognition to the children of well-to-do Jews. Yet, Perlman recounted, the discursive framework of Jewish unity and emergent Jewish nationalism there and elsewhere not only elevated wealthy Jews who could donate money and make gifts to a narrow range of Jewish causes, it also tended to blind the Jewish community as it blinded Perlman to his own working-class background and the class backgrounds of his Torah school classmates. Perlman observed, "My father wore a white collar to work every day." He believed that his button-down shirt worn as a "salesman in a small men's clothing store" in the Chicago Loop made him middle-class, even when the Perlman family could not afford to send Myron to summer camp or a prestigious university, or even take vacations.[38] For Perlman, this disjunction between his own class background and the class background of the Rogers Park Jewish community fostered his interest in working-class history and organizations, leading him not only to explore the role of unions in Jewish life but also to write numerous articles about the Jewish Workers' Bund of Eastern Europe.

The Brooklyn Bridge Collective highlighted the continuity of working-class Jewish life by profiling the Jewish Student Union (JSU) at the Community College of Philadelphia (CCP). Observing that the CCP's JSU was the "strongest and most dynamic" in the region, the Brooklyn

Bridge Collective argued that was because of and not despite the class roots and parochial neighborhood life of its Jewish members.[39] Jewish students at CCP were from "lower income families," and not insulated from the "physical abuse, slander and anti-semitic hieroglyphics" that might have been more muted at wealthier institutions. Yet for Brooklyn Bridge, this exposure to antisemitism propelled them to make alliances with other ethnic and religious student organizations on campus. Rejecting the Zionism and right-wing populism of Kahane's Jewish Defense League as "full of shit," the CCP JSU hosted speakers from the radical Puerto Rican Young Lords, the Black Student Union, and Black Muslims. By the end of the year, they boasted having 1,300 members, some of whom were not even Jewish—attracted to the JSU's progressive politics, diverse alliances, mutual aid work, and militant anti-racist tone. Not only did JSU organizing get the "anti-semitic graffiti in the bathrooms to come down," it also provided a space for working-class Jews to express their class identities as part and parcel of their Jewish identities.

Working-class Jews become, in this framework, a kind of vanguard for a new Jewish left for these socialist collectives. Too class-focused to be Jewish nationalists yet not privileged enough to avoid overt antisemitism, these Jewish socialists enjoyed their own place of "exceptionality," from which to see through and also organize outside of the white middle-class American center. In a way, class for Chutzpah and the Brooklyn Bridge Collective becomes much like race for the Weather Underground: a standpoint, as Hungarian Marxist Georg Lukács argued, at which one can see oneself doubly, as conscripted to participate in forms of dominant power but also outside of them.[40] Perlman argues that Jews occupy "middle" positions on the social ladder that are high enough to be visible—professors, social workers, teachers, doctors—but in Marxist terms these neither control the means of production nor determine the conditions of labor for themselves or others. He notes that there are still few Jews in the commanding heights of key industries, but that CEOs of boards may have actual power yet remain very much hidden in the background.[41] Thus middle-class Jews—while facing antisemitism as professionalized workers—also have too much invested, literally and figuratively, in their newfound class status to fully reject the white middle-class ascension into which they have been half invited, half pushed.

While New Left Jewish organizations that formed in the early 1970s after the collapse of SDS framed a recovery of Jewish working-class politics in the name of Jewish working-class history—from the International Ladies' Garment Workers' Union to the Workers' Bund of Eastern Europe—a faction within SDS led by Jewish members including Gilbert, Robert Gottlieb, and Gerry Tenney formulated class struggle in a quite different way. The Port Authority Statement, framed as a Marxist answer to the famous inaugural 1962 Port Huron Statement, was an attempt to move past intra-left polemics between social democrats and sectarian groups on the left by offering a new vision of the material, class-based resistance of students and white-collar workers against the postwar "affluent society" and its expanding imperial-military state. Beginning with a broad description of US transnational corporations—as large as city-states in many cases—the Port Authority Statement methodically documents the ways in which the new college-educated technical and cultural workforce, at universities and mass cultural industries, is dominated by capital and alienated from their labor and connection to others. "Massification," quoting the French New Left writer André Gorz, does not necessarily exploit and dominate through privatization, as nineteenth-century socialists argued, but rather through the routinization of mental labor, commercialization of desire, commodification of nature, and militarization of technology, so that within the expanding state and corporate apparatuses of Western capitalism, even the college-educated middle class lacks freedom and self-direction. In one sense, the Port Authority Statement is a distillation of postwar Marxism, fusing Marcuse's *One-Dimensional Man*, André Gorz's Gramscian analyses of the incorporation of labor into ruling social democratic coalitions, and newly released works by Marx, including the 1844 manuscripts' penetrating analysis of labor alienation under capitalism. It replaces the Port Huron Statement by locating the anti-war movement, the civil rights struggle, and the rise of a student left in a context in which the conditions of economic prosperity are widely achieved for many yet come at a price: a permanently subordinate underclass, imperial wars, and alienation for all but the ruling elite.

It should also be noted the title of the document—the Port Authority Statement—is a discursive return from the Midwest of Port Huron, the fabled America that SDS founders such as Dick Flacks and Mark Rudd felt they had discovered by embracing Tom Hayden as their spokesperson or, in Flacks's case, moving from the Lower East Side to Michigan. Not only does the text return to (Jewish) New York, it locates their struggle in the urban materiality of a famously dirty bus terminal rather than the United Auto Workers' lakeside conference center and resort, long a symbol of the UAW's move into the comforts of the middle class. Yet this New York articulation of class is far removed from either the Progressive Labor Party's embrace of industry or the Brooklyn Bridge Collective's evocation of the Jewish Workers' Bund of Eastern Europe. Rather Gilbert, Gottlieb, and Tenney argue that it is precisely the college-educated workers in culture and technological industries that are the new advance guard of the proletariat. It is not that college-educated workers and students are the most exploited, the statement argues, rather that, precisely because "they are being prepared to comprehend the productive process," students can "best perceive the over-all contradictions" of a system engineered to stop "control over the processes of shaping one's life."[42] Much like Georg Lukács's argument in *History and Class Consciousness*, the document states that the worker in advanced industry of the late nineteenth and early twentieth century is not the most destitute within capitalism, yet because of their position, at the center of industry yet objectified by it, they can see both the immensity of production and their exploitation simultaneously. "This new group," the statement continues, may "enjoy greater benefits" while they still "remain in a position of class exploitation (non-control over production and the quality of their lives)."[43] This disjunction or contradiction between the student or college-educated worker's benefits and their lack of freedom is, for Gilbert, Gottlieb, and Tenney, precisely the contradiction the new student movements—the New Left—emerge out of. That the New Left, in their estimation, demands greater freedom of expression, less violence, a say over state and colonial policy, and an end to racism is not a sign of their lack of class consciousness, but rather a sign of the class consciousness of their particular formation.

While only the title and the identity of the authors may suggest a Jewish unconscious to the Port Authority Statement, it is nonetheless an implicit rebuttal to the argument that postwar American Jews either nostalgized an earlier state of working-class Jewish poverty, or were middle-class rebels against affluence and authenticity.[44] Rather, the authors argued that the many first-generation Jewish Americans who attended prestigious colleges in significant numbers for the first time were responding to the new material conditions of their existence, perhaps in greater numbers only because of their relative latecomer status to such mass-cultural institutions as research universities, think tanks, corporate labs, publishing houses, television, film, and radio. Yet there is a reformulation, even so, of particular notes of American Jewish history. Citing the 1954 Communist Control Act by Anglo liberal senators Humphrey and Morse, the Port Authority Statement gives wide treatment to the effects of anti-Communism on American historical memory and foreign policy, an anti-Communism that affected the lives of many of the Jewish New Left activists in greater proportion than other members of the movement. And in the final pages of the statement, a new alliance between a Black "underclass" and a disempowered student left is imagined, refashioning the famed (and often defamed) Jewish-Black alliance here as one between outsiders who demand the necessities of life and insiders who are at the levers of the new machines. The Port Authority Statement thus grants to the new Jewish middle class not a politics of guilt or nostalgia, but rather a subjective agency all of its own, a new intermediary status on class terms, if not necessarily on racial terms.

One of the longest extended meditations on this question of Jewishness, anti-Zionism, class, and whiteness for the New Left is Abbie Hoffman's autobiography, written while he was still on the run from what he claimed (with good reason) were trumped-up drug charges several years earlier. While my take on Hoffman's presence on the New Left may be subjective, I would argue that Hoffman, perhaps more than any other single figure, represented metonymically the image and perhaps trajectory of the Ashkenazi Jewish radical of the 1960s and early 1970s. While his hair, nose, and accent were promoted by Hoffman himself as markers of Jewishness, it is also his move from civil rights and antiracist organizing to the New Left student and anti-war movement that tracks the trajectory of many of these activists. Starting as a dedicated organizer with SNCC, Hoffman deliberately used the organizing skills of the civil rights movement to politicize the counterculture. As he framed it, "Yippies were the new Wobblies of the cultural apparatus," suggesting that the IWW's direct action to stop work at the site of production was analogous to the Yippies' attempts to seize the media and turn it toward their own ends.[45] If it was "flower power," as Hoffman later said, it was a flower "held in a clenched fist."[46] Hoffman took the New Left analysis that cultural workers are the new working class to its logical conclusion: that outrageous forms of culture could themselves be a form a resistance, from committing to radical standup comedy, to "levitating the Pentagon," to burning money on the stock exchange, these were not just antics for Hoffman, but an attempt to use television and film for radical purposes. In E. L. Doctorow's fictionalized representation of Hoffman in *The Book of Daniel*, Hoffman tells the son of the (even more fictionalized) Rosenbergs that in the same way Castro made a revolution by toppling a corrupt gangster with no legitimacy, so the Yippies would make a revolution against the forms of sophisticated ideological control embodied in the cultural apparatus of modern America.[47] I say this not as a defense of the Yippies but rather to point out that Hoffman—despite or rather because of his reputation among Jewish liberals such as Howe and Glazer—was quite deliberate about his politics, and thought through questions of activism and identity with the comedy of someone who takes life deadly seriously.

"I came into the world," Hoffman writes in his autobiography, "acutely aware of being Jewish and I'm sure I'll go out that way."[48] Hoffman articulates his understanding of left politics through two distinct Jewish traditions, the traditions of "going for the money" or "going for broke."[49] "Going for the money" is something he acknowledges his own family embraced, the "social melting pot" of New England "gelt and assimilation." "Going for the money," he argues, is a long Jewish tradition of assimilation, fitting in, and embracing worldliness, yet in an American context this amounted to an embrace of whiteness and middle-class racism. Hoffman also suggests that Jews have other cultural resources. Five thousand years of living with "someone trying to break our backs" produces a countertradition of rebels, "wiseguys who go around saying things like 'Workers of the world unite' or 'Every guy wants to screw his mother.'" Hoffman's autobiography is, among other things, an ongoing dialogue between these two traditions of Jewish subjectivity: between whiteness and assimilation, and radicalism and rebellion. For Hoffman, who grew up lower-middle-class in Central Massachusetts and was a first-generation college student, such paths were open to him and represented not only personal existential decisions but metaphors for the American Jewish experience, caught liminally between whiteness and blackness, socialism and success, for much of the twentieth century.

As Hoffman decided to "go for broke," that is, become a rebel, many of Hoffman's antagonists were Jews who decided to go for "gelt and assimilation," or money and whiteness. Hoffman's most famous Jewish antagonist is Judge Julius Hoffman from the Chicago Seven trial, a "German Jew who had risen to acceptance by the gentile community of Chicago's Gold Coast."[50] As the "tale of two Hoffmans," it was for Abbie a tale of two Jews: calling Judge Hoffman a "token Jew," Abbie noted how Judge Hoffman made a point to mispronounce their Jewish lawyer's name, noting that it was "as if the judge were unconsciously dredging up all the Jewish nose-pickers holding back the Tribe's assimilation and laying them on poor Lenny."[51] Famously calling Judge Hoffman a "*schtunk*" and a "*shanda fur da goyim*," it is clear that Hoffman wanted to publicly make a display of his own Jewish identity as well as the judge's, playing out these two traditions for an international audience—and hoping to defeat Judge Hoffman's decisively. Perhaps Hoffman's most tinged barb against Hoffman was to invoke the name of the Rosenbergs when pleading the Fifth, reminding Judge Hoffman that it was another Jewish judge, and prosecuting attorney, who condemned the most famous Jewish Communists to death a decade earlier. It seemed that Hoffman humiliated his judge and namesake not just to make a political point and radicalize the trial's viewers, but to begin an argument with America's Ashkenazi Jews, as if to say, "This is what one participates in when one takes the side of whiteness and power." One becomes executioner of the poor and marginal, but also participates in a trial that was clearly antisemitic, if only slightly less than it was aggressively racist, given the large number of Jews on trial. Hoffman even made up baseball-style programs and called it the "official pogrom."[52]

For all of the ways activist Hoffman antagonizes Judge Hoffman, he also expresses a certain amount of structural sympathy, perhaps even pity, for the judge's position. "You don't have any power," Hoffman tells the judge. "They didn't have any power in the Third Reich, either."[53] This comment is telling, uttered only twenty years after the Holocaust. Hoffman is deploying the metaphor of the *kapo*, the Jew who escorted other Jews to the gas chambers and was often gassed in the end themselves. But given there is no Holocaust in America, at least of Jews, one has to ask what this is a metaphor precisely for. On the one hand, many on the New Left saw the US state as proto-fascist; they understood the war in Vietnam as a genocide, and further understood the oppression of

African Americans to be like the oppression of Jews under Nazi Germany—in this sense, much like the famous photo of Hoffman under a portrait of LBJ in a Nazi uniform, Hoffman understands Judge Hoffman to be on the side of fascists. Yet there is another thread here in which Hoffman understands, even sympathizes with, Judge Hoffman, as representing a uniquely Jewish dilemma. Not for nothing did Hoffman say he ran his court like his grandfather ran his candy store: "If you came in the door you were there to buy."[54] In some ways Judge Hoffman represents the dilemma of success: like a petit bourgeois store owner, his own harshness and grab-instinct comes from his precarity, his relative newness to his class and to the country. Hoffman opposed his judge and namesake, but also seemed to offer that, in the long run, trying to succeed as a Jew in the United States was like trying to succeed in Hitler's Germany: you didn't have any power there either. Hoffman said he viewed the trial as a theatrical experience—it was for the New Left, but it seems there was also a message about the Jewish relationship to whiteness.

Abbie Hoffman's condemnations against "gelt and assimilation" Jews didn't begin and end with Judge Hoffman. Hoffman describes his role, while a student at Brandeis, in the Committee to Abolish Football negotiating with Benny Friedman, Brandeis's famed football coach. Portraying Friedman as the epitome of "gold and whiteness," Hoffman describes him as a "bronzed and dapper senior-citizen ad for White Horse Scotch" in contrast to Hoffman's own look as an "unshaven bo with a green book bag."[55] The political implications of this contrast Hoffman makes clear when he quotes Friedman's defense of football thus: "Sonny, you know the two greatest things that ever happened in the history of the Jewish people? . . . The first was when the Jews got up an army and walloped the living shit out of the British, and the second was when I made All-American twice at Michigan State."[56] At this equation of athletic success with Zionist military prowess, the young Hoffman "quietly tiptoed out of the room." Hoffman continues such analysis in a mock letter apologizing for his "crimes," where he lists a number of right-wing and often non-Jewish cultural and political positions, including "Jesus died for us all, even the Jews," "Pat and Debby Boone introduced me to Jesus in their swimming pool," "Communism is evil . . . you can see it in Karl Marx's beady eyes, long nose, and sneering smile," before adding, "I love Israel as the protector of Western civilization."[57]

Israel for Hoffman is not only equated to crimes against humanity or the abrogation of Palestinian rights, but is clearly associated—like Benny Friedman and Julius Hoffman—with whiteness, money, antisemitism, and Christianity.

It's important to also note that Hoffman didn't understand himself to be a Jewish iconoclast, nor did he understand all Jewish history as binary. "The drive for money is obstructed by the ethical ambiguities of Jewish teachings," Hoffman argues, suggesting for most Jews the binary "going for money" or "going for broke" is not absolute: "it's this and it's that" and "neither here nor there." And while "destined to end in unhappiness," this liminality and ambiguity, this dialectical pull between rebellion and assimilation, is the source of Jewish "curiosity and humor."[58] In this sense, Hoffman never fully rejects the Jewish community or his parents, nor does he even see himself as outside of Jewish tradition or Jewish norms. Hoffman's grandmother, in a gesture of understanding after Hoffman went underground to evade arrest, said on her deathbed that her own brother was "a leader of the Bolshevik Revolution" and "dismissed all [Hoffman's] mishigas with a scowl and a wave of the arm." He took her gesture as a Yiddishkeit "great compliment" and a sign of her sympathy.[59] Hoffman further acknowledged the wider, unmarked, and normative Jewish presence in the New Left by noting casually that Mark Rudd had an assimilated "stage name" like his (Hoffman's original family name is "Shaposhnikoff," like Rudd's "Rudnitsky"), and that "Columbia's new rock and roll singer" was a "member in good standing of the 'International Jewish Conspiracy.'"[60] Rudd, for his part in his own memoir, recalled Hoffman fondly from a night they spent in jail together, remembering his "Jewish nose and wild curly hair," his "humor and spirit": "He probably didn't remember me from that encounter, but I sure remembered him."[61]

In this sense, we can see Hoffman quietly recovering a very different kind of Jewishness *and* whiteness than Dollinger or Gilbert articulate: Hoffman neither sees himself as exceptional nor understands Jewish assimilation, or the rejection of assimilation, as particularly new; rather they are currents within a longer history he mobilizes to give himself a sense of purpose, direction, and place in the world. In many ways we can read through Hoffman's text a kind of theory of solidarity and a theory of change. "History, stubbornly refusing to repeat itself in the exactly same way," Hoffman concludes of the '60s, "doesn't offer a precise prescription of social change. Mostly it's a catch-as-catch-can affair, and the activists who can best judge the mood of the times will always be the most effective."[62] One can also read this as a theory of identity: what Jewishness, whiteness, or power may mean is conjunctural, subject to change or to break apart in strange ways at a given moment. Hoffman did not, at least in his telling, become a Yippie because he discovered LSD; he became a Yippie because he saw an opening to reach disaffected (mostly) white people and channel them to a political project. But Hoffman's reading of Jewish whiteness is also contingent. As I mentioned above, Hoffman was initially outraged at SNCC's purging of white activists, until he noticed "praise coming from quarters I mistrusted."[63] Engaging with his comrades, including Julius Lester and Stokely Carmichael, Hoffman quickly changed his mind and also turned over keys to the Liberty House to Black organizers: not a statement of Hoffman's exceptional whiteness or his exceptional Jewishness, but rather an acknowledgment that history moves through us, and as activists, as subjects of history, we need to change. Hoffman's political understanding of Israel, however, never wavered.

Non-Jewish Jews: Jewish Marxism and a Particularist Universalism

The one text most frequently cited by Jewish radicals I interviewed, when I asked them to describe themselves as Jews, was Isaac Deutscher's "The Non-Jewish Jew." Indeed, it was cited enough to be derided by Arnold Forster and Benjamin Epstein in their classic of reactionary thought, *The New Anti-Semitism*.[64] Originally a speech delivered in 1958, the essay appeared shortly after Deutscher's death in a 1967 collection of essays by the same title. It might seem a strange essay to be on the lips of New Left radicals, as Deutscher was from a previous generation, but a number of people cited it as being a personal description of their own Jewish subjectivity. Joel Beinin, who was a member of SDS and later, in the 1970s, joined the Revolutionary Union (RU) after he broke with Hashomer Hatzair as a young man, found the essay so resonant with his experiences that he read it aloud at his wedding.[65] Pete Seidman, who authored the SWP's major pamphlet on antisemitism, recalls seeing Deutscher speak at the teach-in at Berkeley against the Vietnam War.

"That's me," Seidman said to himself after reading Deutscher's essay. Referring to his role in the SWP, Seidman felt that Deutscher named for him the tradition, "part of the revolutionary international rootless intellectual world." He added: "[The essay] was part of the formation for us."[66] Another SWP member, Linda Loew, herself the daughter of Jewish Communists, devoted an entire second interview with me to the essay, as she also expressed how Deutscher's work made her understand how her own internationalism engaged with her strong sense of Jewish identity.[67] Geoff Mirelowitz expressed that Deutscher's essay, and Deutscher's relationship with major Jewish Trotskyist intellectuals in SWP such as George Novack, helped him to break with Zionism and understand that was the right political stance, and also conformed to his own sense of being Jewish in the world. Beyond the 1960s left, the essay continues to have an afterlife: Adam Shatz cites it in the introduction to his anthology of anti-Zionist writing, and opens the book with Deutscher's essay; Christopher Hitchens called himself a non-Jewish Jew when openly opposing Zionism.[68] Most revealing of all perhaps, in a recent book-length defense of liberal Zionism, Susie Linfield targets the essay for special fury, suggesting that Deutscher's formulation would make him an "Uncle Tom" for any other ethnic group.[69]

The very personal responses to Deutscher suggested something I suspected but hadn't quite put into words. While Deutscher of course creates and then places himself in a kind of secular Jewish prophetic tradition, it seems clear to me that he is also telling a generational story. It does not reflect, as Linfield describes, the desire to hold on to a "prewar outlook" out of nostalgia, but is rather an accurate description of the world where left-wing Jews of the 1960s lived. Like Deutscher himself, thousands, tens of thousands, of young Jewish Americans experienced their parents walking away from their older Jewish communities and into the formerly off-limits wider world as the first generation to go to college, especially elite colleges, in large numbers. Rudd expresses, "We were peasant children right out of the shtetls of New Jersey and Queens screaming, 'You want to know the truth about Columbia University, they're a bunch of liberal imperialists!'"[70] In other words, the story that Deutscher narrates is not so much a transcendent story of Jewish radicalism as the story of a particular Jewish American generation that moved from fairly homogenous Jewish communities and onto the global stage of the New Left and the elite campus—only to respond with revulsion, outrage, and anger at the hypocrisy and perhaps their own sense of displacement. They experienced themselves as both Jewish and not Jewish, white and other, inside and outside of the world they lived in. If, as Staub suggests, "the 1960s were Jewish" insofar as revolutionary Jews were rejecting the "goyish" world of the suburbs, for many Jews on the left, the discovery of their Jewishness was through revolutionary activism in a wider leftist project, not despite it. What looked like assimilation and self-hatred to Nathan Glazer, and is merely unintelligible as Jewishness to historians of Jewish New Left history, was actually a historically and culturally coherent form of Jewish radical practice. In that sense Rudd and others were more like than unlike their parents and grandparents. As revolutionary queer anti-war activist Emily L. Quint Freeman articulates in her own memoir of the New Left, joining the anti-war movement as a revolutionary may have been a rejection of her middle-class parents and their dreams of material acquisition, but in doing so she invokes her grandfather Joseph, a peddler who escaped conscription in the tsarist army and traveled halfway around the world, always in motion.[71] As with the generation of Jewish Communists during the Great Depression, being a socialist first is a way back to, and not away from, a certain modality of Jewish experience.

The power of Deutscher's essay is not that he declares a historical lineage of Jewish radicalism, but that the very title is a kind of riddle: as I asked in chapter 2, is Deutscher talking about *non*-Jewish Jews? Non-*Jewish* Jews? Or non-Jewish *Jews*? The power in some way is that for Deutscher, and many of the Jews of the New Left, it is all three in a tense alternating dialectic. Deutscher's experience of leaving the closed, scholastic, and insular Jewish community yet retaining a Jewish subjectivity, a certain universality, is one particular to him, but spoke to a generation for whom their Jewishness was both essential and contingent, both felt and invisible, yet informed so much of their perspective on the left. "Their manner of thinking is dialectical, because living on the borderlines of nations and religions, they see society in a state of flux," Deutscher writes of Jewish radicals from Spinoza to Marx to Luxemburg.[72] This was also a position that he himself embodied: Deutscher was a Polish émigré who was first an exile from his orthodox Jewish community for becoming a Communist, and then an exile from the Communist Party, which expelled him in 1932 for trying to prematurely alert the party to dangers of fascism. As an exile from the

Holocaust—his entire family was murdered—Deutscher had no home to return to. Yet even in England, as someone who made both a public and popular reputation for himself as a writer and scholar, he could not find an academic appointment, perhaps because of, rather than despite, his refusal to take sides during the Cold War. And one suspects perhaps that George Orwell's naming of names to the British MI6 had a touch of English antisemitism, as if Emmanuel Goldstein for a moment to Orwell were real: there was real suspicion that Deutscher's former membership in the Communist Party, and his identity as a Jew, followed him even in the English left. Speaking multiple languages and living in multiple countries, Deutscher was an image of the diasporic "comrade Shylock," as historian Enzo Traverso once described Trotsky.[73]

Historian Viren Murthy compares Deutscher to another Jewish Marxist a generation younger than him, Moishe Postone, to ask if Deutscher and Postone could posit what one could call a "Jewish Marxism."[74] On some level one could suggest the term would be a scandal to Deutscher, not only because it recalls the fascist "Judeo-Bolshevik," but also because it suggests a Marxism rooted in a kind of ethnos, the capitalist logic of the nation-state. But for Postone and Murthy, it is precisely the Jewish transcendence of the nation-state that makes their subjectivity particularly suited to a Marxist project. For Deutscher, the creation of a Jewish nation-state was not only a humanitarian crime against displaced Palestinians but an ironic tragedy, as the nation had become an anachronism at the very moment Jews hinged their hopes upon it. The nation offers inclusion, but only on the terms offered by European antisemites to begin with, as if the "bourgeois Christian . . . took a fresh look at Shylock and hailed him as a brother."[75] The non-Jewish Jew is precisely the kind of dialectical, anti-teleological form of identity out of which a new socialist humanity could form, beyond the garrison of borders, both from somewhere but with no fixed end-point of destination. Comparing a "Jewish Marxism" to a "Christian Marxism," Murthy offers that it is the non-totalization of the non-Jewish Jew that points to a strand within Jewish tradition as well as a particular Jewish contribution to an open-ended, non-deterministic Western Marxism.[76]

His open-endedness, internationalism, and hostility to phallocentric national projects also put Deutscher in line with many of the cultural and political turns of the New Left. Deutscher influenced the British

New Left, especially as a prolific contributor to the *New Left Review*, and it has been said that he translated "classical Marxism" to a postwar audience, free from its allegiances to Stalin and the foreign policy of the Soviet Union. And while it is true that the 1960s was the heyday of the SWP and organized Trotskyism, especially in the US, to call Deutscher a "classical Marxist" is to miss Deutscher's novel reading of the contradictions of the Bolshevik Revolution. For Deutscher it was neither a counterrevolution nor an inherent flaw in the Bolshevik Party that generated the rise of Stalin. Rather, for Deutscher, the failure of the revolution to sweep Europe after World War I sentenced Russia and its former colonies to a perpetual isolation, in which its status as both culturally overdeveloped and industrially and economically underdeveloped was the fundamental contradiction that led to the rise of an autocratic state. As Trotsky himself understood, it was only military force that won the civil war in Russia, and only military force could achieve the "primitive socialist accumulation" that led Russia out of its backwardness—yet such requisite violence doomed the project to an anti-democratic, authoritarian future. In some ways, Deutscher's reading of the Soviet Union was not unlike the situation of the Jew: both inside and outside the West, both behind and ahead of the society that rejects it, both prostrate and vulnerable, feared yet loathed, a symptom but not quite yet a cure. In this sense, the dialectical style and way of seeing Deutscher offered went far beyond simply his stance on Stalin or his novel expression of Jewish identity: one gets the sense that Deutscher saw the Soviet Union as a little Jewish, yet also saw the world revolution through Jewish eyes.

In this sense one can conceive of Frankfurt School philosopher Theodor Adorno's comment on the "non-identity" of dialectic thinking as more than just a comment on epistemology.[77] As Adorno spells out in the final chapter of *Negative Dialectics*, his magnum opus on dialectics, history, and Western philosophy in light of the Holocaust, it is precisely the shadow of the Shoah that leads Adorno not toward an affirmative Jewish national identity, but rather to theorize that "pure identity" is a "philosopheme of death"; that to fix on identity is to demonstrate a politics of destruction. This non-identity, for Adorno, is a perspective at remove, not "bourgeoisie objectivity" but the only perspective possible when one has realized their own death as the apotheosis of Western Civilization.[78] This "spectator" and "specter" of life is precisely the non-space of resistance, as it refuses to be what would be seized by the barbed wire yet also refuses to look away and refrain from impassive judgement. Written directly after World War II, Adorno and Max Horkheimer's *Dialectic of Enlightenment* poses the same question from the point of view of Western intellectual and economic history: the Enlightenment, even in its own self-conception, is a project of mastery by instrumentalism and objectification. The "incommensurable," in such a formula, "must be exterminated." Jews in such a schema, precisely because they were perceived as incapable of assimilation into rationalizable things, in the greatest epic of irrationality, were targeted for elimination.[79] Their perspective as European Jews, as modernity's victims and, in the US, modernity's defenders through the process of assimilation, leads one only and again to an in-between non-space of critical inquiry.

As critic Santiago Slabodsky suggests in his exegesis of anti-colonial thought in and through a nineteenth- and twentieth-century secular Jewish tradition, there exists a long history of seeing the process of modernity not as the immanent unfurling of progress, but rather as the concretization and intensification of dehumanization and violence. Of course, such a tradition is inescapable, from the concretization of antisemitism in the nineteenth century via religious persecution, to a theory of Jewish racial otherness, a transformation that coincided with the secularization of European states. Yet as Marx points out in "On the Jewish Question," the secularization of European states implies not the liberation of religious and ethnic minorities within their borders, but rather their conscription into normative and now supposedly universal ideas of citizenship, which also just happen to force Jews into a path of assimilation. That Marx felt the abolition of all religion—and the capitalist state—would end the entire question of assimilation simply meant that he still believed in the progress of revolution, if not the progress of the modernizing European state. For Slabodsky, Walter Benjamin takes Marx's fundamental insight a step further to completely subvert the terms that "On the Jewish Question" wrestled with: there can be no assimilation into European civilization, as European civilization and its ideals of progress are fundamentally a form of "barbarism."[80] Turning the savage/civilized binary on its head, Benjamin suggests it is not Jews who must assimilate into Europe—or even into a bold European revolutionary future. Rather, the task of the Jewish historian is to read "against the grain" in order to find the means to fight against the "homogeneity" of progress. As Slabodsky notes, when Benjamin writes history from the point of view of Europe's victims and not its victors, he is "thereby discovering the forgotten sources of the vanquished that are not understood as documents [and finding] . . . a place for Judaism."[81] For Benjamin, like Deutscher, Jewishness is less an identity than a modality of reading against the racial history of European and American progress: a non-space, much like Adorno's, of critique.

Daniel Bensaïd tackles this dialectical Jewish perspective through the metaphor and metonym—and also lived history—of the Marrano, the Jews forced to convert to Christianity after the Spanish conquest of Al-Andalus in the late fifteenth century. Bensaïd, one of the foremost Trotskyist theorists to emerge out of the Parisian student left of the late 1960s, was the son of a working-class Algerian Jewish father and a Franco-Catholic mother who "discovered (or invented) a distant Jewish ancestor."[82] As leader of the student left and the global Fourth International movement, Bensaïd was also an important figure for the Marxist student left in the US, someone who fused a sharp Marxist theorization of politics and economics while retaining a critique of both the Soviet Union and the "hasty" urgency of the New Left. By Bensaïd's own accounting in his memoir, *An Impatient Life*, his own Jewish ancestry was a "ghostly haunting" of the Holocaust; many of his cousins were deported to Nazi death camps and did not return; his adolescent sister was sexually molested by the Gestapo.[83] Yet Bensaïd recalled that his father was in no way religiously or culturally Jewish, at least insofar as he refused Kaddish to be said at his funeral, and Bensaïd remembers no celebrations of the High Holy Days, Passover, Hanukkah, or any other Jewish holiday or observance. "I was bound to inherent a lack of belonging" he wrote of his Jewish heritage.[84] For Bensaïd, the sole positive legacy of his heritage—up until the formal end of the New Left in the 1990s—was merely, if also defiantly, the recognition that the Holocaust imparted "an intransigence" against any expression of racism or xenophobia, especially against any expression of antisemitism: a lesson imparted fiercely by his parents, regardless, they let him firmly know, of the consequences.

As much as Bensaïd's own history would seem to point to a waning meaning of Jewishness in the postwar context, if not via assimilation into French Republican *laïcité*, then into universal revolutionary egalitarianism, Bensaïd's writings on Jewishness are singular insofar as they acknowledge the appeal of such teleology yet also underscore that such expectations of order should be suspect. Bensaïd's memoir, *An Impatient Life*, is among other things a meditation on the non-linear antinomies of history, appearing at once to have resolved the Jewish question through the long unfolding of the French Revolution's formal equality, and thus launching, as so many socialists believed, the revolution's second act through the abolition of wage labor and the end of colonialism. At the same time, however, Bensaïd bears witness to not only the Holocaust, but the end of the New Left and its promise to finish what the Russian Revolution started, and also, convergently, the emergence of a settler-colonial Jewish state. As Bensaïd writes at the beginning of his memoir, "We belonged to a landscape threatened with disappearance ... We had all grown up on the historical sequence opened by the Great War and the Russian Revolution ... Can the light from extinct stars still travel on?"[85] Titling the opening chapter "Fourth Person Singular," he begins by questioning the perspective he uses to tell his life story: is it self-construction, eyewitness, the subject of history, history itself? This question posed itself with all of its furious ontological uncertainty first when Bensaïd attended a series of protests organized by left-wing Jews against the Israeli invasion of Lebanon, and later in 2000, when he signed a letter authored by dozens of prominent Jewish intellectuals in protest of Israel's sabotage of the Oslo process by their expansion of West Bank settlements. "A few years ago," he writes, "I could not have imagined one day being associated with an initiative of this kind, claiming the legitimacy of a particular origin to justify a political position."[86] Yet rather than simply claim political expediency, Bensaïd offered an interpretation of the non-religious, non-communitarian yet publicly identified Jew both within a tradition of the Marrano and also as a condition of history: that history did not solve the "Jewish question" as it had once promised.

"Is it possible to define a 'Jewish identity'?" Bensaïd asks after signing a letter critical of Israel with a number of other French Jewish intellectuals.[87] In a 1980 essay, "The Jewish Question Today," Bensaïd grapples with one side of this question, the historical. Picking up where the Trotskyist intellectual Abram Leon left off, Bensaïd clearly notes that one epoch of European American Jewish life is over. Leon, who defined Ashkenazi Jews as a "people-class" insofar as their economic and social function formed a cultural unity across the diaspora, predicted, even as the Holocaust was to begin in earnest, that Jews would find new avenues for emancipation with the twentieth-century proletarian revolutions. Yet clearly, observes Bensaïd, the Jewish question was neither liquidated in the camps, nor did it evaporate in the clean air of the American suburb. "Does the Jewish question die out with the breakup of this people-class, torn between proletarianization and the rise of big capital?" Bensaïd asks. "Once the social vector of the people-class is dynamited by capitalist accumulation . . . would the Jew, as such, survive as a ghost, or as a pure product of Zionist manipulation?" In other words, if one takes "identity" as such as produced only through material classes, then by all rights, the diasporic "Jew"—aside from its figural specter on the far right or in the fidelity demanded by the state of Israel—should not on some level exist, or at least exist as a subject separable from others in a meaningful way.

The essay ends as much with a question as it does an answer. On the one hand, Bensaïd acknowledges the historical rupture of the Holocaust, a rupture that, however, did not end the Jewish subject but rather gave "the Jewish question" a "new lease on life." The "phoenix" of Jewish nationalism arose from the ashes of Auschwitz: "The genocide, Stalinist anti-Semitism, the founding of the State of Israel: these are the three reasons which are making the Jewish question resurface, contrary to historical predictions at the beginning of the century," Bensaïd writes. If one considers all the potential solutions to "the Jewish question" at the turn of the nineteenth century—assimilation, socialism, and Zionism— it would seem each of them carries with them irony, upset, and contradiction. The history Trotsky envisioned in his famous 1905 argument with the Bund did not come to pass: years later, Trotsky admitted that "the course of history had reversed, contrary to all expectations, the prospect of a rapid withering away of the Jewish national question." Yet to suggest that Zionism is an untroubled answer to the "Jewish question" would ignore that the new "Hebrew nationality in Palestine" is "today an oppressive nation" at the "expense of the Palestinians." By the same token, the understandable "objectives of the Palestinians who want precisely the abolition of this entity with a mono-ethnic and colonial base established on their territory" deny both the material and cultural reality of the "new Hebrew nation" that has formed since 1948, a "cohesion of indigenous Jewish populations to the Middle East and European settlers" that may not be legitimate or even legally on the land, but nonetheless exists. "The alternative to Zionism will only be effective if it is posed simultaneously by Jews within Jewish communities," Bensaïd concludes, thus circling back to the very act of identity production he was so reticent to make in the beginning.

While the paradoxes of history may have guided Bensaïd's hand to sign "En tant que juifs" despite himself, Bensaïd offered instead a kind of hybrid ontology—or perhaps hauntology—of Jewishness that takes as its starting point the double negations of the Holocaust and Zionism. Bensaïd finds this "paradoxical identity" in the "emblematic figure of the Marrano, a Catholic without faith, Jewish by choice but without knowledge."[88] This non-Jewish non-Jew is not a stable figure, s/he is "a rent and divided being, attached to perpetuating a Judaism adulterated by the obsession of secrecy and torn by repressed doubts," who "belonged without belonging, and painfully lived this unbelonged belonging, this training in modern liberty." It is a condition that is described on the one hand as a "lack of faith in Christianity" while on the other, both a "defective knowledge of Judaism" and a lack of adherence to "Jewish communitarianism."[89] While the "lack of faith" in Christianity is hardly particular to half-assimilated Jews, for Bensaïd in addition to literal atheism it might also refer to a certain skepticism regarding liberal Christian ideals of progress: both the Holocaust and Zionism are enough to suggest that history neither moves in a straight line nor includes salvation, but that its own projected solutions re-create the cul-de-sac from which one escaped: Israel is again, as Hannah Arendt described, the "new pariah state."[90] While one might say Bensaïd merely documents the forms of exile that Edward Said describes as the "condition of modernity," there is a special attention to the assemblage of memory for these Jewish exiles from both Christendom and Judaism. Calling it a "faith of memory," scholar Josep Maria Antentas locates the specificity of "Marranism" in Walter Benjamin's countercurrent of memory, cutting "against the grain" of the orderly establishment of states, populations, and rational ideals of progress, whether this means the citation of the Holocaust to the West and its own self-conceptions, or to Israel and its oppression of Palestine.

In this sense, Marranism for Bensaïd is not the same as nationalism or assimilation (that is, fascism or formal equality in the West), the twin and binary oppositions secular Jews are often offered in response to both the Holocaust and the Haskalah. The Marrano is a "hauntology" to use Derrida's phrase, or a "spectre" to quote Bensaïd, neither in one world nor the other, located in both the past and the future. As a memory project, Marranism is "refractory to roots and rootings," as Bensaïd calls such an identity formation, an "intimate wound," one that recalls the history of Jewish suffering and resistance in "transition and passage" without having to "return to an identity" or "rally to the cause of the victors."[91] This "third option" for Bensaïd is a welcome "inheritance," not as "a good, a wealth that is received and banked" but rather as a memory of Jewish history that speaks to the "active, selective affirmation that can sometimes be reanimated and reaffirmed more by illegitimate heirs than by legitimate heirs": a kind of fidelity to a tradition that is also apart from it.[92] In one sense the Marrano is simply a "Communist"—a laying claim to rebels in history, such as Marx and Spinoza; but to say Marranism is just Communism is too simple. It is an arriving at Communism through the negation of pure identity and cosmopolitanism simultaneously. While in one sense one could say Marranism is Adorno's "non-identity," it is rather a dialectic between two poles that is neither. "One does not go towards the universal," writes Bensaïd, "one does not universalize, without going through particularities and singularities." Perhaps one could say Marranism is just another method of articulating a politics of diasporism, but in a way that would be too easy. For Bensaïd, his Marrano politics are a recognition that history did not solve "the Jewish question" but rather laid it at the feet of survivors—as Bensaïd's family was—who are placed outside of both resolution or community. Marranism is the recognition of failures: the failure of both assimilation and nationalism to resolve the crises for which Jews have been a vector, but also a refusal to accept that such in-between place is a permanent landing.

If there is such a thing as a "Jewish 1960s," surely these Marxists—Deutscher, Bensaïd, Postone—articulate a subjectivity of Jewish radicalism that goes beyond abstract solidarity. The meeting between the universal and the particular, as Bensaïd puts it, is true for all internationalists, and yet for these Jewish leftists, this meeting is not merely an intersection but a place of its own. Not a nation but perhaps a pathway; not roots but routes, as Paul Gilroy famously phrased it. It is perhaps what Myron Perlman, the former SDS member who went on to found the Chutzpah Collective in the 1970s (and whom I will discuss in the next chapter), meant when he said Jews have "a kesher with the left," a bond, that goes beyond mere transactional politics or cycles: the left itself is a Jewish modality of articulating a point and politics between identity and solidarity. For other Jews in this chapter—Gilbert, Rudd, Eanet-Klonsky, Hoffman—solidarity, dedication, worldliness, and internationalism were the words they lived by, yet it is clear they also held on to some part of their Jewish heritage that was present and necessary, as Deutscher put it. One could say they are non-Jewish Jews, or Marranos, or specters, but like a Marrano or a specter, their ghostly presence can neither be removed nor substituted for something else. While it is tempting to offer that this particular perspective has been eclipsed by identity politics or assimilation, I would suggest, rather, that it has been reformulated by new forms of diasporic politics for left-wing Jews, whether Judith Butler's "ethics of the Other" or Daniel Boyarin's "diasporic nation of memory." While these point in similar directions, one also has to ask if rooting one's politics of solidarity in an ontology of being—diasporic belonging to another, or a collective of shared ritual and narrative—causes anything to be lost or gained. Surely Deutscher and Bensaïd benefit from a clear understanding of the dialectic, a process without a center or teleology, that may take the form of a diaspora but cannot be located in any one particular thing or be said to be nothing. Whether the specters outlast their hosts remains to be seen.

4
A Kesher with the Left: Jewish Identity Politics and the Remaking of a Diasporic Left, 1970–1980

> Diaspora is not equivalent to pluralism or internationalism. It is egocentric.
> —Daniel Boyarin, *Powers of Diaspora*

The Identitarian Turn

At a Students for Democratic Society (SDS) reunion in 1977, Dick Flacks—one of the o]riginal attendees at the inaugural Port Huron meeting in 1962—noticed something about the ten remaining members sitting with one another on the grass: they were all Jewish. Most of the ten were red diaper babies, children whose parents were members of the Communist Party or other organizations in and around the 1930s and 1940s left.[1]

In an odd way, this meeting of Jewish revenants on a grassy lawn in California was the exact opposite of the original Port Huron gathering, in which Flacks and another Jewish attendee from NYC, Steve Max, commented to each other how gentile the meeting at the UAW conference center was. While the number of Jewish attendees at Port Huron would seem high by any other standard, from their perspective, that over half of the attendees hailed from places outside NYC seemed a promising sign. "We had broken out of the ghetto," Dick suggested in an interview, delighting that, for once, there were so *few* Jews at a socialist conference.[2] "We had made it into America," he later reflected. Flacks and Max were of course correct about the potentialities of SDS's explosion outside of the Red Scare confines of (Jewish) Manhattan, yet what to make of the SDS loyalists on the grass some eight years after SDS's implosion in 1969? When I asked Flacks this question, he expanded by saying the same question had animated their own discussion, especially as some of these ex-SDSers were beginning to find their way to Jewish community in the waning of the 1970s. "What do we do in the long haul?" Flacks posed. "What are things we can commit ourselves to . . . to get rooted, build a life around?" Flacks seemed to be posing a question that many Jewish veterans of the New Left themselves asked: After the end of the SDS and the fragmenting of the New Left, where do we go? And is there a particularly Jewish answer to this question?

As Michael Hardt and Tariq Ali have both observed in their own ways, 1970 marked the end of an era. To paraphrase Ali, 1968 was the last cresting shock wave of the Bolshevik Revolution: not that Communism or Marxism have ceased to be relevant or ceased to have passionate and consequential adherents, but rather that the 1960s was the last generation for which the Bolshevik Revolution was still lived as a conscious reference point, the revolution something to be directly continued or reformed.[3] Janus-faced, Hardt expresses this conjuncture looking to the future, arguing that the 1970s marked not only the formal end of the Bolshevik era, but "the beginning of our time." "Our time" includes the "great tectonic shifts" of post-Fordism, neoliberalism, identity politics, and what Hardt refers to as the "end of mediation," the hard turn away from the Keynesian compromises of the postwar social democratic order.[4] Hardt is correct to point out that revolutionary movements did not cease in the 1970s; in many ways they grew more militant. The Weather Underground, the Black Liberation Army, and the American Indian Movement in the US took up the question of armed struggle, while one of the largest wildcat strike waves swept the US in the early 1970s. Yet even Hardt—who champions the "subversive '70s"—acknowledges that the left faced state suppression and reactionary backlash, an ending. The end of SDS and the violent suppression of the Black Panther Party did mark the closing of one chapter of the US left even as, he argues, it may have opened another.

For the Jewish left, the contradictions were even more dramatic and sweeping. The rise of Zionism in the wake of the crack-up of SDS inaugurated powerful and inexorable cleavages between the new left—which held anti-imperialism at the center of its ideology—and wide swaths of Jewish liberals and progressives in the US. In 1974, Arnold Forster and Benjamin Epstein of the ADL would issue the opening salvo in what would become a decades-long attempt by the Jewish establishment to equate anti-Zionism with antisemitism and, as importantly, to locate the "new" antisemites not with the Christian church or far right, but rather with Black Power movements and the left. Following the 1970 conference at the Arden House in which many members of the liberal Jewish literary establishment, including Irving Howe, Leonard Fein, Seymour Lipset and Nathan Glazer, bemoaned the turn of Jewish youth to the seductions of the New Left and Black Panther Party and away from American liberalism and Zionism, the ADL concretized this anxiety into a formal theory.[5]

Forster and Epstein's *The New Antisemitism* begins by announcing an epochal shift in the history of Jewish life in the West: Christian antisemitism had given way in the US to "genuine ecumenicism" after the Holocaust, as the Vatican had renounced their previous stance on "Jewish deicide" and mainline Protestant churches in the US accepted Jews as part of the "Judeo-Christian West."[6] In addition, the "social acceptance" Jews experienced in their economic mobility meant a broad respect across the political spectrum and among other religious traditions. To the ADL, the postwar order was one that American Jews could thrive in; its normative model of liberalism gave rise to a common sense of "orderly social progress" and the "decent treatment of all citizens."[7] Further, Israel's place among Western nations meant that Jews no longer experienced life as marginal outsiders in their nations, but as people with a Western, US-allied country of their own. In the orderly march of capitalist liberalism, Forster and Epstein observe, only a radical or a racist could find fault with Jewish institutions or the Israeli state; in such a world, only paranoid leftists or Islamofascists could find flaw with American democracy. Understanding Jewish institutions at home as the "liberal" enemy and Zionism abroad as the "colonial" enemy, the left, they argue, has replaced the right as the primary threat against democratic "Jewish interests" around the globe. The New Left and radical Black Power organizations are thus transformed from erstwhile defenders of the Jewish people to their primary enemy.

As Stuart Hall notes in his lecture "Old and New Identities," "class" as the "main locator of social position" gave way to a freer and more discursive play of differences during this period.[8] This new construction of identities would have major impacts on both US politics and Jewish life. As Matthew Frye Jacobson writes in his history of white ethnic revivalism in the 1970s, the "white backlash" in the 1970s spoke an increasingly ethnic language. No longer was "whiteness" simply expressed as anti-blackness, it was also articulated in forms of white ethnic pride: Italian American, Irish American, and, as the ADL posed, Jewish American forms as well.[9] White America's complex cultural absorption of Black nationalist texts such as Stokely Carmichael's 1967 *Black Power* and mid-1970s television sensations such as *Roots*, based on Alex Haley's text, led many white people to dive into their own their identities, rather than and often to the exclusion of exploring new avenues for solidarity with African Americans. From Rocky Balboa to the Irish American busing riots, the expression of white ethnic pride often seemed tinged if not laden with explicit racism. As critics such as Shaul Magid, Marc Dollinger, and Eric Goldstein suggest, liberal American Jewish response to the rise of Black Power tracks many of the same trends: at once a libidinal and political reaction against Black demands for autonomy and reparations, as well as a kind of emulation and adoption of many of its slogans, if not its revolutionary politics.[10] Perhaps most famously, right-wing rabbi turned militant Zionist Meir Kahane's Jewish Defense League (JDL) articulated a "resonance with Black Nationalism" insofar as the JDL claimed a militant style, Jewish autonomy, a criticism of assimilation, and an embrace of ethnic nationalism.[11]

The ADL's turn from targeting Nazis to targeting the anti-Zionist left suggests the wider Jewish institutional world in the US was fast adopting not only a Zionist framework, but a particularly virulent form of Zionism seen only a few short years before as beyond the pale (pun perhaps intended). As Shaul Magid articulates in his critical biography of Meir Kahane, Kahane's radical identitarian Zionism has been adopted and "embraced by present day American Jewry," at least at the institutional level.[12] Kahane's obsessions, a muscular Israeli nationalism that allowed for no criticism, ethno-nationalism and the narrowing of Jewish identity, and more than anything else, a claim that antisemitism on the left was "threatening Jewish survival" were once seen as fringe in the 1960s. By the end of the 1970s, according to Magid, these positions were adopted by major Jewish foundations and organizations. Kahane's rise was not in a vacuum, or solely to be found autochthonously in the Jewish community. Kahane's embrace of both Jewish identity and Zionism were part of a wider politics of white ethnic reaction, and Kahane's JDL—while styled after the Black Panther Party—had more in common with white nationalist militias that were rapidly on the rise in the 1970s. The New Antisemitism's origins were as much in Zionism as they were in a rising tide of right-wing reaction and racial revanchism.

It should be noted the JDL (despite rhetorical flourishes and berets) and Kahane were neither anti-capitalist nor saw themselves in solidarity with Third World anti-colonial movements. Indeed, one of the JDL's first public protests in 1969 was to prevent SNCC activist James Forman from speaking at a Brooklyn synagogue, at which he was to demand reparations from Jewish institutions for African Americans.[13] Kahane, as a true reactionary, felt liberalism itself, to say nothing of the radical left, was a threat to ethnic continuity and ethnic nationalism. "Marxist-Leninists are the deadly enemies of Jews and Judaism, seeking spiritual and national genocide," Kahane opined in the late 1960s. "Let us remember this the next time we feel constrained to protest United States defense of Vietnam and remember that, there but for the grace of God and the United States military, go we."[14] The JDL's antipathy to the left and to Third World nationalism went so far as to threaten both Jewish socialists and members of the Young Lords Party with violence if they showed up to a 1971 anti–Ku Klux Klan march in New Jersey.[15] The JDL often assaulted New Left Jewish organizers and broke up radical meetings, on the grounds that Jewish leftists were in league with Black Power movements that were a threat to Jews and to Israel.[16] Some organizations such as the Radical Zionist Alliance tried to square the circle by claiming that Zionism is a form of radical anti-colonial liberation, yet as many radical Zionists such as Kahane were all too aware, most anti-colonial movements, from the Black Panther Party to Cuban revolutionaries, were in solidarity with Palestinians and understood Zionism to be a form of settler-colonialism.[17] Even as Black Power and Third World solidarity movements offered what seemed like a portable repository of metaphors and iconography to Jewish nationalists, such Zionist groups either were forced to ignore

Black Power critiques of Zionism or, as with the JDL, find themselves locked in a militant opposition to them.

Such dramatic changes were also fracturing Jewish progressive movements. Joyce Antler notes that anti-Zionism split apart the women's movement, the leadership of which—like the New Left—was heavily Jewish. The 1975 World Conference on Women hosted by the UN in Mexico City became a major flashpoint among Jewish feminists and the anti-colonial left. Finding themselves alienated by two UN resolutions, one in 1973 and the other in 1975 that equated Zionism with both South African apartheid and racism, many Jewish feminists felt that "Jewish women who opposed anti-Zionist measures found themselves outsiders to the global women's movement."[18] While there were certainly many Jewish radicals who remained anti-Zionists throughout the 1970s, key Jewish figures in the feminist movement including Betty Friedan, Congresswoman Bella Abzug, Esther Broner, and Letty Pogrebin came to share the feeling that the New Antisemitism thesis was correct: the anti-colonial left was not only anti-Israel, but antisemitic. "To many Jewish women . . . the bitterly familiar 'Zionism-is-racism' plank" of the Mexico City conference, Antler summarized, "seemed 'another victory for anti-Semitism.'"[19] As feminist scholar Brooke Lober notes, "liberal Zionist feminism was instituted as the normative mode of US Jewish feminism."[20] The energy around forming a "Jewish feminism" led to the rise of Jewish feminist publications such as *Lilith*, which under the editorship of Susan Weidman Schneider promised a robust debate among Jewish feminists, only to devote the initial issue to Friedan's assessment that the anti-colonialism of the UN Conference on Women was indeed antisemitic. Having broken with SDS over New Left sexism, wide swaths of the Jewish feminist movement seemed to also be breaking up with the anti-imperialist left over its anti-Zionism. As Michael Fischbach suggests, there was a common perception on the left in the 1970s that one could either be a Jewish anti-imperialist or a Jewish identitarian—one could not be both.[21]

It would seem to many then, by the end of the 1960s, that any articulation of Jewish identity would need to come at the expense of solidarity with Third World liberation and ultimately the left. As Walter Laqueur posed it, "Jewish radicalism is a form of assimilation," insofar as Jewish radicals from SDS to the Communist Party privileged antiracist revolution over particularist Jewish cultural or political expression. "Good Jews" for Laqueur—that is, Jews acceptable to the Anglo Christian establishment and to Black Power activists alike—were Jews who forwent any claims to group needs and surrendered their identity to ideals of universal justice.[22] As Robert Alter argued, solidarity with Black Power required a "self-effacement before black militancy."[23] The Ocean Hill–Brownsville teachers' strike in 1968, which pitted a Jewish union president and many Jewish members against both Black nationalists and the New Left, seemed to bear this proposition out. To Laqueur as much as to Kahane, it was a zero-sum game: Black group rights would come at the expense of recently won Jewish class advancement; Black expressions of identity were a threat to Jewish expressions of identity. Perhaps the firmest blow against the concrete politics of Black-Jewish solidarity occurred in 1977, when three prominent and ostensibly liberal Jewish organizations, the Anti-Defamation League, the American Jewish Committee, and the American Jewish Congress all wrote a "friends of the court" brief against affirmative action in *Bakke v. Regents of the University of California*.[24] It would appear that expressions of Jewish group interest could only further Jews' implication and imbrication in a white power structure. It would seem that the Jewish ethnic revival—"Jewish Renewal"—like white ethnic revival in Jacobson's analysis, could only further solidify the already broken forms of alliance that once existed within the ranks of the Communist movement or on the streets of Selma. Zionism was now for these voices the essence of Jewish identity.

Yet other members of the New Left took the lessons of solidarity, identity, and the left quite differently. Stokely Carmichael's call for white people to "organize in their own communities" was taken seriously by many members of the New Left, and seen as an advance over earlier politics of liberal integrationist organizations. As historians James Tracy and Amy Sonnie document, the move from the "integrationist" politics of the early civil rights movement to Black Power was felt as an invitation by many white leftists to join in coalition with Black radicals, rather than as a rejection or a challenge. Drawing a line between the narrow "nationalism" of the Nation of Islam and the "internationalism" of Third World anti-colonial revolutionaries, groups such as the Panthers felt that racial autonomy was a means, rather than an impediment, to work in coalition with other organizations, from members of the student left to ethnically and racially defined organizations with equally revolutionary goals. In other words, the turn to identity among white people need not *necessarily* be reactionary, as the Rainbow Coalition dramatically demonstrated. In Hardt's reassessment of the "subversive" 1970s, radical movements did not so much diminish as take on questions of "autonomy," "multiplicity," and "democracy" as their organizing principles, favoring smaller, diverse coalitions over broad-based populist movements.[25]

The Rainbow Coalition, for its brief life, was perhaps the most successful expression of "revolutionary internationalism" organized within the US left, among the Black Panthers, Young Lords, and Young Patriots in Chicago. This coalition of Black radicals, Puerto Ricans, and working-class whites stood together to fight for issues they had in common—police brutality, affordable housing, the war in Vietnam—as well as to share resources for their own community service and radical educational programs.[26] Rather than feeling alarm at an all-white organization on the left, the Panthers and the Lords thought a group of young white working-class radicals on Chicago's North Side were valuable insofar as they might win over poor whites to the revolutionary cause. Black Power's call to "organize in one's own community" did not, of course, preclude solidarity and, for the Black Panther Party, was the basis of solidarity. The Young Patriots' newspaper, *The Patriot*, called on white people to "abandon racism, unite the vanguards of other oppressed communities, and fight the 'real enemy.'"[27] The fact that the city power structure and the FBI found this coalition a clear and present danger was all the more reason for many within the post-SDS New Left to feel they were headed in the right direction.

More recently, there has been renewed attention given to the Combahee River Collective's (CRC) theorization of solidarity and identity during the same era. A group of Boston-area radical Black feminists who are credited with coining the term "identity politics" in the mid-1970s, the CRC framed "identity politics" in ways to avoid "exclusionary" politics.[28] For the women of the CRC, like for the Panthers, group identification was a means toward solidarity, intended to strengthen the political commitments from other groups by asking them to reflect on how their own struggle is related to a common goal of ending capitalism. Defining themselves as socialists, they wrote in their manifesto:

We realize that the liberation of all oppressed peoples necessitates the destruction of the political-economic systems of capitalism and imperialism as well as patriarchy. We are socialists because we believe that work must be organized for the collective benefit of those who do the work and create the products, and not for the profit of the bosses ... We have arrived at the necessity for developing an understanding of class relationships that takes into account the specific class position of Black women who are generally marginal in the labor force, while at this particular time some of us are temporarily viewed as doubly desirable tokens at white-collar and professional levels.[29]

Thus their formulation that "if Black women were free, it would mean that everyone else would have to be free" does not imply that the liberation of Black women is at the expense of Black men, the working class, or other marginalized groups.[30] Rather, they stated, since Black women are "triple-oppressed" as women, African Americans, and workers, then by freeing working-class Black women one would by necessity have to end capitalism. Yet the CRC also understood that if they organized under the banner of other causes or groups, their own perspectives and needs would likely go unmet. Breaking with the National Black Feminist Organization for its inattention to both gender and class in its attack on white racism, the CRC understood their version of identity politics as a means to expand the analysis of capitalism, rather than to restrict it.

In the year after the dissolution of SDS, some Jewish veterans of the New Left—from SDS, the Venceremos Brigades, radical feminist collectives, and anti-war mobilization—formed socialist collectives as at least one way to form Jewish answers to questions and invitations raised by the Rainbow Coalition and CRC. The organizations formed spontaneously and seemingly independent of one another yet nonetheless articulated very similar core principles and beliefs about Jewish culture, its relationship to the left, and the need to organize within their own communities. Jewish Radical Community in Los Angeles, Chutzpah Collective in Chicago, and the New York City Brooklyn Bridge Collective are the three largest and most influential of the radical Jewish collectives formed between 1969 and 1971, and emerged as a means to keep New Left momentum growing after the collapse of SDS as well as to answer the challenge the Student Nonviolent Coordinating Committee had posed a year earlier: What would it mean for white people to organize in their own communities? The three organizations also formed out of a sense that the New Left—while central to their formation as activists—was not only fragmenting, but could not address the needs and challenges of its Jewish members, from the nature and structure of antisemitism, to communal belonging, a sense of continuity, and a nuanced anti-imperialist politics that could engage what seemed to them a then-promising Israeli New Left.

Such organizations are sometimes referred to as the left fringe of the Jewish Renewal Movement, an attempt by religious members of the Jewish community in the US to find a more spiritual, diverse, and relevant form of Jewish practice in light of postwar Jewish assimilation. While there are overlaps between these Jewish collectives and Jewish Renewal, Chutzpah founder Miriam Socoloff recalled, "We thought of ourselves as part of the New Left; I was not even aware of Jewish Renewal until much later."[31] Creating vibrant newspapers and pamphlets, organizing protests and trips to Israel and Palestine, educating community members about radical Jewish history, and exploring the radical content of Jewish ritual, these groups not only attempted to rebuild a new New Jewish Left, they also formed a bridge between SDS and later Jewish progressive organizations such as New Jewish Agenda in the 1980s and Jewish Voice for Peace in the 1990s. Indeed, if one had to conceive of a direct predecessor to Jewish Voice for Peace, it would be less SDS than the Chutzpah Collective and Brooklyn Bridge: organizations that, while on the left, led with a Jewish identity that fused Jewish religious and secular traditions.

It is clear to the members of the Chutzpah Collective, Brooklyn Bridge Collective (BBC), and other radical Jewish organizations that arose in the early '70s that they saw themselves as continuing, rather than breaking with, the left by embracing their Jewish identity. Members of Chutzpah and BBC did not see themselves as Magid phrased it, "Jews who had abandoned the New Left and became New Jews," but rather as Jews who articulated a Jewish subjectivity as a way to carry forward the next conjuncture of the left.[32] The forms of identity and solidarity expressed by the CRC and BPP were not only inspiration, they informed, as one member framed it, the "common sense" of the age.[33] As activist Sheryl Nestel remembers, as she walked across the UCLA campus there was something particularly compelling about the idea of a "Jewish Radical Community," the name of a new left-wing organization forming in Los Angeles handing out pamphlets at Royce Hall one spring day in 1968. As Nestel remembered, her attraction to the pamphlet and later the organization did not come out of a particular need to express herself as Jewish, but rather, an understanding that, for the radical left of the late 1960s, ethnic and racial identification were the primary entry points to revolutionary activity. "It was Black students, it was the Chicano students, it was the Asian students and it was the Jewish students," Nestel recounts of the coalition to save Angela Davis. "We were completely accepted, completely, you know, integrated into the coalition."[34] Rather than finding it an impediment to work with other revolutionary groups organized around racial identification, Nestel remembers thinking, "Everybody else had a place, here is my place." Contra the JDL and other right-wing Jewish nationalists, a focus on Jewish particularity was the means for Nestel and other young Jewish radicals to form coalitions not against, but rather with revolutionaries of color—even if those revolutionaries had anti-Zionist politics.

Myron Perlman, who at the time of founding the Chutzpah Collective with several other Jewish radicals had been active in the anti-war movement as a member of SDS in Chicago, expressed a desire to create a socialist commune in the city with other Jewish activists in the city.[35] Other initial members of what Robbie Skeist called a "Jewish Liberation Collective" found each other through their writings in small New Left publications—Skeist himself was recruited after he published a piece on meeting with Jewish Cubans while volunteering with the Venceremos Brigade, a New Left organization dedicated to supporting the Cuban Revolution. Indeed, it was Skeist's Passover celebration in Cuba as a supporter of the revolution that rekindled his desire to form Jewish community: not only did the Cuban government provide resources for the meal, the few remaining Jews in Havana expressed their support for revolutionary politics. It's important to underscore that, if in hindsight such groups as Chutzpah may seem to have been engaged with what we might call "identity politics" today, from their own vantage point, the members understood their forming of Jewish socialist collectives as moving the New Left forward, as a project of the left, aligned with other organizations also on the left.

In a 1971 editorial in *Brooklyn Bridge*, the BBC's magazine, member Lee Weiner frames the BBC less as a Jewish organization committed to radical politics than an organization whose Jewishness was a crucial part of the "revolutionary nationalism" of the era. Opening with a critique of American nationalism, he poses that Americans are nationalists whether we like it or not, cheering for "John Wayne and his 7th Cavalry" or participating in the Hollywood restoration of the Confederacy.[36] These forms of white American nationalism are foundational not only for American capitalism and militarism, but for forming a common political weal and even a sense of selfhood. Defining the imperial nation-state as a vehicle for capital unification and class suppression, Weiner outlines how important it has been for the labor movement, the Wobblies, and both socialist and Communist movements not only to reject "Americanism," but to reject Americanism for an alternative ethic of counter-hegemonic ethnic belonging. The Wobblies "printed their leaflets in 64 languages" he notes; the Communist Party had "ethnic sections" building on "their own people's shared sense of common heritage . . . teaching people about their common enemies." For Weiner, all new social movements against the US empire—and many in the US—speak the language of "revolutionary nationalism" whether they are aware of it or not. While Weiner cautions against the "chauvinist isolationism" of "cultural nationalism," which privileges narrow benefits for their own nationality against all others, he celebrates "radical" or "revolutionary nationalism" that unites separate ethnicities and peoples in a "common struggle against exploitative class relations and structures."[37]

Sounding a great deal like the CRC, Weiner writes, "Blacks, Women, Puerto Ricans, Jews, Gay, and young people are all now involved in asserting their rights . . . they must construct a viable politics . . . in which their individual national interests are secure while at the same time . . . waging a common struggle towards revolution."[38] To put a finer point on it, on the cover of the third issue of *Brooklyn Bridge*, they lined up on one side images of Jewish and Vietnamese dead under the banner "Genocide Then/Genocide Now," and below that, images of Apache warriors with images of Vietnamese guerrillas under the banner "Resistance Then/Resistance Now." The issue included stories of the Buchenwald death camp, gay liberation, and the UFW lettuce boycott, and a favorable story about the Israeli Black Panthers (IBPP). Firmly drawing a line between the two forms of nationalism Weiner discusses, the issue concluded with a conversation with a member of the JDL who would not march with the BBC against Klansmen if the BBC march included members of the Young Lords or the Panthers. For the BBC, like the Black Panthers, solidarity began with a rejection of whiteness and an embrace of one's cultural, political, and ethnic heritage in solidarity with all other non-white or white-rejecting communities.

Chutzpah's Myron Perlman further takes on Kahane and the JDL's form of "nationalism" in his essay "The Jewish Stake in Vietnam," provocatively titled after Kahane's book by the same name that appeared five years earlier. Kahane argued the "Jewish stake" in supporting the US war effort in Vietnam was both to prevent antisemitic accusations that Jews are anti-militarist, and to defeat forces around the globe that threatened Israel.[39] As he writes in *Never Again*, the defeat of the US in Vietnam, like Weimar Germany, will be blamed on disloyal Jews that "stabbed the nation in the back," and Jewish over-representation in the peace movement only invites such attack.[40] More importantly, Kahane argues, the same people who support "Victory for Hanoi" also support "Arabs and their war on Israel."[41] "The Left," Kahane warns, with its "Marxist-Leninist dedication to internationalism," is the "deadly enemy of the Jews" as such internationalists as Black Power in the US see Jews as forces of colonialism and whiteness. Perlman's reply to Kahane begins with no mention of Jews or Jewish interests—rather, Perlman offers a colonial history of the Vietnamese people attempting to liberate themselves from three successive empires, Japanese, French, and now the United States—and the US reply under Nixon, which was to intensify its terror campaign from air and sea.[42] "As Jews," Perlman concludes, "we can, and must relate to the genocidal acts of Nixon against the Vietnamese people . . . racism is the basis for what happened . . . to the 'kike' or the 'gook.'"[43] A pamphlet produced by JRC takes Perlman's argument a step further to argue that the massacres at My Lai and Auschwitz were both "genocides" and that both groups of victims must "resist oppression everywhere."[44] The expressions of "Jewish interest" or perhaps, one could say, "Jewish identity," between the JDL and these Jewish radicals are so radically different as to be incommensurate: Jews are a de-territorialized subject whose fate is bound up with the least powerful, or Jews are an exceptionalist people whose fate is threatened by any other claim to injury.

In other words, what Dollinger describes as the "turn inward" to identity tends to obscure how, for Jewish socialist collectives such as BBC and Chutzpah, "the left" itself was understood as a modality of Jewish experience. That is, it may be better to see Chutzpah and BBC not as Jews who broke with the left in order to lead more "authentic Jewish lives," but rather as Jews on the left who wanted to see a renewal of *a Jewish left*. As Myron Perlman put it, even in an interview in which he is critical of what he sees as the left's blindness to Jewish concerns, "we have a kesher with the left, a connection to the left, even an anti-semitic left."[45] There is a sense that "the left" is a kind of homeland itself, an identity formation that goes beyond political positions to be an ontology of Jewish belonging. "We were leftists," Socoloff stressed to me on this point, "we were not part of other Jewish revival groups. Our home was the left."[46] As a counterpoint to Zionists who understood Israel to be "home"—or even US liberals for which the United States was a "homeland"—Chutzpah and the BCC articulated the left itself, cosmopolitan, transnational, locational, as their site of belonging.

In practical terms, it meant that *Chutzpah* articulated a different politics of Jewish interests than Kahane. In a *Chutzpah* article criticizing the 1977 anti–affirmative action lawsuit of Allan Bakke against the University of California, author Arden Handler's title, "Tsuris of a Jewish Leftist," signals the ways in which, to be a Jewish leftist, one must also at times take positions against the short-term interests of other Jews. Framing Jews as "caught in the middle" between a WASP elite and proletariat of color, Handler acknowledges Jewish establishment support for Bakke, presumably because "quotas" may take opportunities from Jews who, unlike wealthier applicants, have fewer alternatives.[47] Yet Handler frames taking a "leftist" position on the Bakke decision as inseparable from Jewish "self-interest," as he sees "attempts to eliminate affirmative action as part of the overall ... right-wing backlash ... extremely menacing to the Jewish people." In other words, Jewish identification with the left—and with people of color—is of greater self-interest to Jews than what, in the short term, might materially benefit Jewish people. If this is an "identity politics," it is one that is dialectical, in conversation, in which relational politics are as important, if not more important, than politics of immediate self-interest.

One way Perlman and other Chutzpah members defined their commitments to the left was using what they referred to as the "Moishe-to-Mao continuum": on any issue, they often debated between the most narrow Jewish nationalism, "Moishe," and the member(s) with the most expansive vision of left internationalism, "Mao." Yet the continuum also implies a necessary connection, that "Moishe" and "Mao" are part of the same discursive and material world. Thus it is not despite the fact but rather because Chutzpah and BBC saw themselves as primarily on the left, that many articles in their magazines begin with a critique of the "antisemitism on the left," and end with a sense of their necessary connection to the left. For Chutzpah and BBC, left antisemitism is less based on classical tropes of Jewish power or Jewish money than as the refusal to grant Jews their own "self-determination," which might be better described as "autonomy"—that is, to allow Jews within left coalitions to have their own position on Zionism, fascism, and antisemitism that would be aligned with the left but not necessarily always in agreement.

Chutzpah often expressed the Moishe-Mao continuum as a set of contradictions, claiming, for example, that it was necessary for the left to recognize the right of a "Jewish state" yet supporting anti-Zionist organizations such as the Black Panther Party and Young Lords, or declaring support for the Israeli left with left-Zionist groups such as Gush Shalom and New Outlook, while also supporting the anti-Zionist Israeli Black Panthers and the mostly Palestinian Israeli Communist Party and meeting with members of the PLO. Many have described Chutzpah and BBC as non-Zionist (a point I will discuss further), which is true after a fashion, but it would be more accurate to say that both were militant particularists and supporters of a Jewish left, in ways that often appeared in dialectic contradiction. As Chutzpah member Maralee Gordon framed it, "It made sense for the Black Panther Party to support Palestine in the same way it made sense for the Chutzpah to support the Israeli left. And because we live in the US, it also made sense for Chutzpah to support the Panthers."[48] If Chutzpah and BBC were Jewish identitarians, they were identitarians in ways that often saw Jewish interest as inseparable from the interests of a broad left, one that often regarded Jewish claims for self-determination as a form of racism.

Chutzpah's and BBC's seemingly contradictory positions,

universalist and particular, Zionist and anti-Zionist, internationalist and local, Jewish but not exclusionary, might seem like a historical curiosity—an attempt to square, perhaps impossibly, the new American Jewish investment in Zionism after 1967 with a historical commitment to the Jewish left. On the one hand, Chutzpah's position in favor of negotiations with the PLO, a two-state solution, and the right of return for Palestinians marked them on the left edge of what was sayable within the Jewish community and, more often than not, beyond it— and for Chutzpah, that was the point: moving the Jewish community from within seemed far more valuable than joining a far left, which at that time was quite marginal. For Perlman, a political project that united the PLO, the Israeli Communist Party, the Israeli New Left, and the US Jewish left was far more winnable than a maximalist position. However compromised that may appear, however, in hindsight one can draw a straight line—both ideologically as well as through the roles of particular influential individuals—between Chutzpah, BBC, and later developments on the non-Zionist and eventually anti-Zionist Jewish left. From New Jewish Agenda (NJA), which included many members of BBC and Chutzpah, to Jewish Voice for Peace and IfNotNow, all owe their ontology if not their continuity as much to organizations such as Chutzpah as to SDS, which sought to develop a human rights position on Zionism and Israel from within the Jewish community.

In constructing revolutionary and explicitly Jewish organizations, one could say Chutzpah and others engaged in a left-wing version of Jewish adaptation that Lila Corwin Berman describes as "revising the terms of Jewishness" to meet changing political, demographic, or cultural shifts in the US.[49] While Berman charts the ways rabbis and professional Jewish intellectuals attempted in various moments of US history to redefine religion and Jewish community to appear acceptable to changing ideals of Americanism, so too one could say that Chutzpah and BBC adapted their Jewishness, and their revolutionary commitments, to be legible to other revolutionary organizations such as the Panthers, CRC, and Young Lords. Yet it is important to note that groups such as Chutzpah did more than merely adapt strategically to emergent paradigms. They also developed a flexible, relational form of political commitment that fell under the cultural framework of diasporism, the historical Jewish modality of belonging in societies in which Jews are religious and ethnic minorities. Yet diasporism also accounts for ways in which Jewish minoritarian status is complex and contradictory. Jewish whiteness, while incomplete and sometimes contingent, meant that at times groups such as Chutzpah could insist on a particular Jewish subjectivity, as when engaged in cultural expression or when confronting antisemitism, yet in other moments subsume "Jewish self-interest" when it was necessary to address other forms of inequality, such as anti-Black racism or US imperialism.

Diasporism, further, is a complex formation. While liberal Jewish writers such as Philip Roth articulated a Jewish diasporic sensibility critical of Zionism and Jewish nationalism, Roth's diasporism was rooted foundationally in the freedom of a middle-class white male individual subject. Within groups such as Chutzpah and BBC, a diasporic sensibility emerged at the precise moment that Jewishness was being conscripted by both nationalism and right-wing political backlash. In other words, one could see Chutzpah and BBC as either running with the tide of the Jewish turn to identity or perhaps struggling against it, holding on to a different conception of being Jewish in the world as the Jewish world was rapidly changing. Even if one could say Chutzpah was too late, in another way one could say that history has finally caught up to them. Their form of Jewish diasporic thinking is echoed by Judith Butler's 2012 articulation of a Jewish group identity conceived in "relationship to the other," and Daniel Boyarin's theorization of a "non sovereign" form of nationalism articulated "in solidarity" with oppressed people.[50] On the one hand, their embrace of the Jewish diaspora was framed as a rejection of what they perceived to be two forms of reactionary Jewish identity, both assimilation and whiteness, as well as reactionary forms of Jewish identity they saw in both the JDL and Zionism. On the other hand, their diasporism was also a particularly Jewish modality of left-wing expression, both as outsiders to US mainstream life with a particular history of exclusion and discrimination, and as white people who in recent decades had experienced rapid class advancement. This doubleness, duality at the heart of Jewish identity, was Chutzpah and BBC's own contribution to both the left and the idea of identity politics in the 1970s.[51]

It may seem strange to devote an entire chapter to three Jewish socialist organizations in the 1970s that remained small and, one could argue, relatively marginal throughout their decade or so of existence, at least in the shadowed Götterdämmerung of mass organizations such as SDS and the Communist Party. Yet I would argue that the small size of Chutzpah and BBC belied their influence. Not only did their newspapers print stories, histories of the Jewish left, analyses of global revolutionary politics, and information about the Israeli New Left and PLO, their readerships reached far beyond the size of the organizations. Perhaps more importantly, many of the members of Chutzpah and BBC became founding members of New Jewish Agenda and had lasting influence on founders of Jews for Racial and Economic Justice, Jews against the Occupation, and Jewish Voice for Peace. In that sense one can think of Chutzpah and BBC as organizations that filled an interregnum between the New Left and later social movements of the 1980s and 1990s, as well as articulated—theoretically and practically—the ideological terrain of a post-1960s left, perhaps a post-Communist left as well. Groups such as Chutzpah were amalgamations—one part a continuation of the New Left, another part looking forward to identity formations such as New Jewish Agenda and Jewish Voice for Peace that would organize not in the name of a class or global political horizon, but rather in the name of a particularly Jewish subjectivity. Yet because Chutzpah and BBC were new, the questions they posed were, if not unheard of, novel queries that would direct Jewish organizing and Jewish left community for the coming conjuncture: What does it mean to organize as Jews? What would it mean to break down the secular/religious divide in Jewish left organizing? Is there a Jewish perspective on the left? Is the left itself a Jewish perspective? What is a Jewish identitarian perspective on Israel? Antisemitism? Solidarity? And so on. What is refreshing and perhaps invigorating about such groups is not only the urgency and openness with which they explored such questions, but their perspectives, not as professional intellectuals but as activists attempting to work out such perspectives in real time. Chutzpah, BBC, and JRC no longer exist—but I would argue that the Jewish left is now as much, if not more, their world than SDS's or the SWP's.

Neo-Bundism: Historical Memory and the Remaking of Diasporic Jewish Working-Class Politics

On the front cover of the 1971 inaugural issue of *Brooklyn Bridge*, there is a collage of four images. In the foreground and center is a bank with marble columns and dollar signs on its Roman-style façade, topped by Egyptian-style runic figures in togas carrying skulls. Inside the bank is an ominous black sun. Surrounding the bank, its black sun, and its army of Egyptians are fragments of Hebrew script, bordered by an NYC subway map. Under this complex image, in which US financial capitalism is the new "pharaoh" at the center of a marginal Jewish world of text and urban transit, is the caption "We Are Coming Home."[55] The caption is the first line of the Brooklyn Bridge Collective's manifesto, in which they clarify that they are "coming home" to Brooklyn. The notion of "home" doubly, perhaps triply, signifies in this manifesto and the image: on the one hand, "coming home" is not emigrating to Israel, it is not a return to Europe, North Africa, or the Middle East, nor is it a return to one of the Jewish suburbs surrounding New York City that became popular in the era of "white flight" a generation earlier. The notion of "home" offered by the manifesto is thus ambiguous. On the one hand, it promises a return to a radical, unalienated form of Jewish life and to a revolutionary, anti-capitalist political project; on the other, its "home" is presented as a form of exile, in pharaoh's Egypt of US capitalism, in a country in which, they pose, Jews are a small minority. It is one image of a reconstituted diasporic politics.

Like many of the "nationalist" or "identitarian" New Left organizations to come out of the 1960s and early 1970s, BBC's project was to define a cultural "nation" as well as to "return" to or perhaps reinvent a past. In much the same way Walter Benjamin articulates that revolutions are historians of a kind, seizing the past "singled out in a moment of danger," Chutzpah and BBC set out to define a usable past for Jewish revolutionaries in the US.[52] In Benjamin's formulation, history is not "how it was," but rather the memory of past class struggles held by the oppressed as they emerge in particular conjunctures to "fan the flames of hope" in moments of crisis. In the way the Bolsheviks called upon the memory of the Jacobins, or the Movement for Black Lives "remembers" the Black Panther Party, so Chutzpah and BBC turned to the memory of

Figure 4.1. *Brooklyn Bridge* 1 (February 1971), cover.

Jewish radicalism in what they perceived as a moment of crisis and radical struggle. Unlike such white-ethnic revival texts as Marin Scorsese's documentary *Italianamerica* (1974), Elia Kazan's *America America* (1963), or Irving Howe's *World of Our Fathers* (1976), Chutzpah and BBC rejected the narrative of immigrant success as well as the implied racism that opposed solidarity with Black Power, urban uprisings, and affirmative action. Rather, they posed, it is Jewish success that turns American Jews into a "buffer zone" between the ruling class and working class of color. Rather than side with a "Jewish establishment," Jewish nationalism in Israel, "assimilation," or the gentile elite, Chutzpah and BBC reached back into a global Jewish radical past to find other models for Jewish organization and Jewish life that were anti-capitalist and still articulated a Jewish particularity, political and cultural distinctiveness.

In this way, the many articles in *Chutzpah* and *Brooklyn Bridge* devoted to memorializing histories of the Jewish left, in particular anti-fascist resistance to Nazis during World War II, the US labor movement, and histories of the Jewish Workers' Bund, were not just histories but interventions into a dialogue about what it meant to be a Jewish socialist in a moment of crisis and reorganization. While these histories may be commonplace now, it is important to remember that in the late 1960s and early 1970s, much of this history was suppressed by the decades-long Red Scare, class ascension, and cultural assimilation, particularly the erasure of Yiddish as a working-class vernacular. Indeed, it is probably fair to say that Chutzpah and BBC were the first radical non-academic groups in the 1970s to attempt to offer historical memory about the Bund and diasporic Jewish socialism to a wider English-speaking Jewish audience than the few remaining secular Yiddishe shules run by the Workman's Circle.

Beginning two long articles about the Jewish Workers' Bund in early editions of their magazines, both *Chutzpah* and *Brooklyn Bridge* narrate their return to Bund politics in almost identical ways, through the logic of cultural forgetting. "Most Jews," *Chutzpah*'s Perlman writes, "know something of their biblical past, and a little about Zionism and the state of Israel. Unfortunately, few know anything about the Jewish labor movement, or groups like . . . the Bund as it came to be known."[53] "It is not very surprising that most people, even most Jewish people, know nothing about the Bund," the *Brooklyn Bridge* article begins, before concluding more vehemently that it is "rather disgusting . . . American radicals, *especially Jewish American radicals* know nothing about this party."[54]

For BBC and Chutzpah, the danger of assimilation is not just cultural uniformity but the loss of rich sources of radical belonging and practice.

In particular, these groups lamented that Jews exchanged for whiteness not only a sense of collective belonging, but a radical cultural heritage that could promise an alternative to racism and class ascension. As Chutzpahnik Jeffrey Mallow describes in "Growing up Yiddish," "America made one demand on its immigrants: an acceptance of the myth of the melting pot."[55] In a *Brooklyn Bridge* article, "Giving Up Assimilationist Privilege," the unnamed writers lament that Jews "have been sold on the Amerikan dream . . . of the great Amerikan melting pot."[56] "All a white person had to do was change his name, get rid of his accent, and the streets were paved with gold," the authors pose, suggesting that the trade-off for "gold" was "shame" over ethnic features and ethnic accents, and a silence over "anti-Semitic remarks." While Chutzpah and the BBC could be likened in many ways to what Jacobson refers to as the "white ethnic revival," what makes this form of cultural revivalism different from the JDL or the Italian American Civil Rights League is that Chutzpah and BBC are nostalgic not for the days before civil rights legislation, but rather for the multiethnic left; they want to call back to the days of working-class Jewish revolution.

That is, the Bund was not memorialized as simply a pre-assimilation Jewish organization; it was articulated as a precise intervention into the historical conjuncture. It was Chutzpah and BBC's attempt to construct a working-class, non-Zionist identity politics that could challenge what they felt to be the erasure of Jewish concerns from SDS, and also the ultra-Zionism of Jewish liberals and the right.

The Bund, one could say, was revolutionary identity politics before identity politics. While the General Jewish Workers' Union of Russia and Poland was at its height, it was the largest revolutionary organization in eastern Europe, organizing general strikes and "battle squads" to fight against pogroms, and playing a major role in the 1905 Revolution, though its cultural role for the 1970s Jewish left may have been even more important. As Perlman articulates in *Chutzpah*, "The Bund was a new kind of organization . . . based on national feelings and class oppression rather than religion. It was the first modern Jewish political party."[57] Constructing an analogy with the gender and cultural politics of the feminist movement, "Bundists developed a revolutionary lifestyle," as Perlman phrased it, that included the equality and inclusion of women in the social, political, and educational life of the party—as well as a radical democracy that eschewed other Russian revolutionary organizations' cult of personality. One could say the Bund created the first global radical Jewish subculture.

The Bund served thus as a "usable past" as well as a historical model of organization for Chutzpah and BBC, as they sought to practice a kind of diasporic nationalism that constructed Jewish identity and community in ways inimical to the majority of their co-Marxist left as well as to Zionists. As Ruth Balser posed in an early edition of *Chutzpah*, "Why form a separate Jewish movement when there is already a Movement in this country fighting against everyone's oppression?"[58] Stating that "as a woman" she saw firsthand that "there would still be sexism after the Revolution (witness Cuba)," Balser analogized that African Americans realized "an integrated movement would remain racist," and "Jews must fight for Jews." Yet unlike Zionist nationalists, the Bund was a group of "Marxist internationalists," to quote Perlman, who wished to organize in solidarity with other workers where they lived. Indeed, when the Russian Civil War began in earnest after the October Revolution, many Bundists happily joined the Red Army in support of the revolution.

It should be noted that while Chutzpah and BBC did promote Yiddish and Yiddishkeit (as well as on occasion Ladino), the "Bund revivalism" was primarily political: What in a Jewish past can serve as a model for the present? In this sense we can think of the words of perhaps the most provocative section of *Brooklyn Bridge*'s introduction to Bundism—an interview with Emanuel Scherer, executive board member of the Bund, and the Bund's representative from Poland during World War II. In some ways Scherer's inclusion is as much a commentary as what he says, suggesting that the Bund, and its absence in American Jewish life, is far more a present concern than one might imagine: there are living Bundists still among us. Scherer's argument about the Bund is that they were not idealists; they were "adapted to the condition of life" around them, "the first Jewish mass organization that said, Jews are a nation or a nationality without a state of their own and apart from religion."[59] In other words, the Bund's radicalism is its radical presentness, its *doikayt* in Yiddish: that political movements are made from the grounds on which people live, not utopian and far-off places. That Chutzpah and BBC are making a Jewish nationalist politics in the United States is not utopian, they would argue, but rather the Jewish adaptation to the radical cultural nationalism of the 1970s.

Nowhere did "neo-Bundism" manifest more dramatically and

materially than in Chutzpah's fight against Chicago Nazis. The Warsaw Ghetto Uprising Coalition (WGUC), a group pulled together by Chutzpah in 1978 to oppose Nazi organizing in the suburbs of Chicago, is most famously recalled as the group that confronted a Nazi march in Chicago in 1978. The confrontation is memorialized in popular culture by both the ACLU's courageous (or ignominious) defense of Nazis' free speech rights and the equally bizarre 1980 *Blues Brothers* scene of the black-jacketed pair running "Illinois Nazis" off of a bridge in their iconic 1974 Dodge Monaco. The truth is far more quotidian and perhaps disturbing: the Nazi Party—and far-right racists—had been active in Chicago's working-class South Side and Southwest Side neighborhood for quite some time, and were part of Chicago's political fabric.[60] Most famously recalled by the incident where a brick hit Martin Luther King Jr. in the head during his 1966 Fair Housing March in Cicero, white racist mobs were so vicious King reportedly said that he had never seen "mobs as hostile and as hate-filled as I've seen in Chicago."[61] Much of the violent activity both during and after King's visit focused on keeping Black Chicagoans from the white conservative communities that they were slowly buying homes in, and escalated to arson and the murder of a Black Chicago motorist who was dragged from his car and stabbed repeatedly by a group of white men to keep the communities segregated.

Frank Collins's Nazi Party of America was assumed to be behind many of these arson attacks on the Black community of Marquette Park, just east of Cicero, and his party frequently held public demonstrations in Marquette Park's green space, openly terrorizing local residents. When the city struck back by charging Collins for "insurance," Collins announced his plans to move his march to the Jewish postwar suburb of Skokie, a neighborhood produced through the paradoxical confluence of white flight, destruction of Jewish neighborhoods, antisemitic covenants restricting Jewish mobility in Chicago, and Jewish refugees of the Holocaust. When it seemed like Collins would eventually be permitted to march, Skokie's city council, in league with the Jewish Federation of Metropolitan Chicago and the ADL, were far more concerned that Collins and his small group of several dozen Nazis might be torn limb from limb by a crowd that was expected to be in the thousands, than with the real terror and dismay felt by Jewish residents over the Nazis' plan to march through their town.

CHUTZPAH

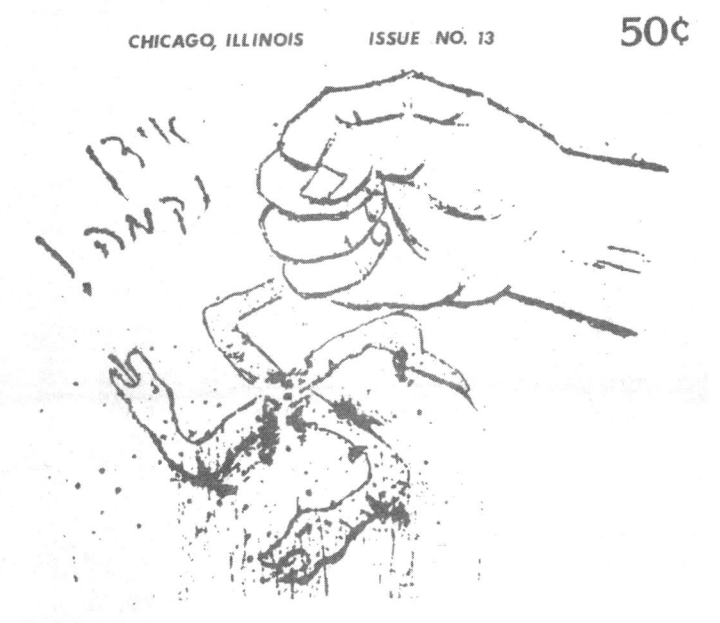

CHICAGO, ILLINOIS   ISSUE NO. 13   50¢

Smash Nazism, Fight Anti-Semitism

"JEWS REVENGE!" FROM "YUGNT BUND ZUKUNFT", A NEWSPAPER OF THE
JEWISH RESISTANCE TO THE NAZIS IN WARSAW, POLAND.   **THE FIGHT CONTINUES.**
SEE PAGE 5

Figure 4.2. *Chutzpah* 13, cover, with image taken from a Bund flier.

The Warsaw Ghetto Uprising Coalition organized in this cauldron, holding their first of several demonstrations in Skokie when it seemed the Nazis might march a day earlier than they had announced. Ultimately Collins and his American Nazis cancelled, yet the WGUC described a militant gathering nonetheless. *Chutzpah* reported the presence of "Holocaust survivors" with "iron pipes under their sweaters" as well as Jewish and non-Jewish anti-fascist groups carrying "canes" and "baseball bats"—while "most of the mainstream Jewish groups stayed away." The WGUC led some "spirited chants" threatening the Nazis, and led the crowd in "a Yiddish resistance song from the Vilna uprising."[62] Highlighting the distance between the "Jewish establishment" and the anti-fascist demonstrations, *Chutzpah* noted with disgust that the ADL not only lied to the Jewish community about the number of Nazis in the Chicago region, but told Jewish protesters to stay home. The Skokie city council and Jewish Federation equally seemed more concerned with Jewish quiescence than opposing the far right, and "worked together with the police to make sure the crowd stayed orderly," trying to move the crowd from shouting "anti-Nazi slogans" to "singing pastoral Israeli songs."

Indeed, prior to the march, it was the experience of trying to organize with official Jewish leadership, who seemed more interested in keeping everyone calm than Jewish safety or solidarity with African Americans, that led Chutzpah to formalize the Warsaw Ghetto Uprising Coalition to begin with. As the magazine reports, "(WGUC) was called together by Chutzpah to confront the Nazis" as a "coalition of progressive and socialist groups" founded on three points of opposition: "(1) anti-Semitism as exemplified by the threatened Nazi march into Skokie; (2) frequent Nazi attacks on Black people in Marquette Park and the Englewood area, and (3) the Nazi ideology which threatens other ethnic minorities, women, gays, workers, and all supporters of human rights."[63] Yet it was not only the Jewish institutional right that Chutzpah contended with when forming the coalition, it was also groups on the left. The most salient was the New World Resource Center, which opposed the coalition's focus on antisemitism and centering of Jews. The resource center argued that Jews were not the only target of Nazis, and that "calling attention to anti-Semitism and choosing a Jewish name for the coalition" would ironically "isolate the Jews," even as it strove to center them. "Identify instead," Chutzpah was told, "with the struggles in South Africa and elsewhere."

Chutzpah balanced the tension between a Jewish-centered politics and the politics of solidarity in two ways. In an editorial after the march, WGUC member Les Friedman articulates an "identitarian" critique of subsuming Jewish concerns with calls for international solidarity. Borrowing the feminist phrase "the personal is political" to describe Jewish relationship to the Nazi threat in the editorial's title, Friedman writes, "The only true allies anyone has in life or death matters, let alone Jews, are other people facing the same fate and consequences for their acts . . . In the face of any possibility of Nazi resurgence, the non-Jewish components of the left (the best allies we have aside from ourselves) simply do not face the degree of hatred [or] the same fate for their actions as do Jews."[64] While Friedman is clear that "fascism" is not "imminent for America," he does articulate that for Jewish people, their "personal" stake in opposing Nazism is greater than for white leftists, perhaps even as great as for African Americans (though he hedges a great deal at this comparison). Thus for Chutzpah, it made sense for Jews to lead the coalition against a Nazi threat in Chicago, even if there was an explicit acknowledgement that for other issues, Jews should not necessarily take center stage. Even so, the coalition that did agree to organize under a Jewish name and with Jewish leadership included groups such as the socialist New American Movement, Substitutes United for Better Schools, News and Letters Committees, and International Socialists, as well as other groups that signed on but were less heavily involved, including Chicago Gay Socialists, Americans for a Progressive Israel, Minyan Sheni, Tim Berry Irish Republican Clubs, Mobilization for Survival, Gray Panthers, Oak Park War Resisters League, and Gentiles Against Anti-Semitism.[65]

Yet while the WGUC centered Jewish politics, their largest and perhaps most important march confronting the far right was not led by Chutzpah, but in coalition with residents of Marquette Park. At a meeting in a church in Englewood—the Black neighborhood adjacent to the eastern European white neighborhood of Marquette Park—the groups included the PUSH Coalition, the Urban League, many members of the community, and the state senator Harold Washington, soon to be Chicago's first African American mayor. As one anonymous *Chutzpah* writer expressed in the pages of the magazine after the meeting, in the church "with its windows broken out by fascists" he felt he was witnessing the "Black-Jewish working class communist united front" he had always dreamed of. The next day, he adds, he "was privileged to experience the first taste of a fighting unity" among "thousands of Jews, Blacks and leftists . . . ready to brave . . . flying bricks and bottles in common physical defense."[66] And while the march in Skokie received much more media coverage and has been memorialized by the Illinois Holocaust Museum, the march among this diverse coalition was far more violent, far larger, and included the arrest of several Chutzpah members and a South Side Chicago minyan as they tried to push past the police and confront the gathered white racists.

In the words of Chutzpah member Jerry Herst, it was a "heterogeneous" march with college students, older members from the Gray Panthers and Emma Lazarus Clubs, members of socialist and Communist organizations, and African Americans with signs against racism and fascism. Herst, who had arrived late, found the march disorienting at first, meeting "a Holocaust survivor who was really shaken by the hatred and sick familiarity of the day's events."[67] Watching the crowds of "white power T-shirters standing outside bars," he (metonymically perhaps) kept his "nose clean" and "tried not to look too obviously Jewish." Yet as Herst walked back from the park and past the "Nazi storefront" and "dozens of police" on Western Avenue, he "finally felt safe again, back in the Black ghetto": "That feeling of safety there is one I hope not ever to forget." This final note seems an important place to pause, as it highlights both the dialectical contradictions as well as the promise of Chutzpah's "neo-Bundism." Chutzpah organized in language of their own self-interest and Jewish autonomy, but used their communal organization to build one of the largest marches against fascism in Chicago history in a primarily Black South Side neighborhood.

This diasporism, as Daniel Boyarin articulates it, is "partaking always of the local, but by definition never confined to it . . . a place where that interaction can be grasped."[68] For Chutzpah and BBC members, the "adaption to the condition of life" is the American contradiction that they felt: they wanted a particularly Jewish organization, but also one that was on the left without having to sacrifice its Jewishness. Against the Jewish right, the Bund expressed a desire to organize within a Jewish community without having to accept Zionism. Opposing the "Zionist and Orthodox movements," such movements "contradicted the basic premises on which the Bund was founded . . . independent, anticapitalist political action by working people and international solidarity."[69] And in an American context, the Bund allowed Jews to reject both assimilation into whiteness and the dissolution of Jewish particularity in the name of other struggles. To organize as Jews in Skokie as one small member of a larger coalition in Marquette Park was practical common sense, and displayed a relational and diasporic sense of identity. "Coming home" to Brooklyn was in some ways coming "home" politically to Bundism—neither exile nor the belonging of assimilation.

One could suggest that "diasporism" of this kind was Chutzpah's own theoretical contribution to the question of identity. Much like the CRC, for whom solidarity is premised on organizing separately as Black women, Chutzpah's neo-Bundism stressed that Jewish organizational autonomy was the means by which members could join larger communities of struggle. Yet it should be noted that Chutzpah's identity formation was not fixed, nor was it essentialist. In certain contexts, Chutzpah placed Jewish concerns first; in others, Jewish concerns would be subsumed within a broader movement for justice. This notion of "identity" is relational, dialectic, and based on contingent relationships with both the left and other marginalized groups. The diaspora, then, for Chutzpah and BBC, is a place between and among all these contradictions, neither resolving them nor allowing them to overwhelm the particularity of either group. Diasporism is neither exclusively identitarian nor a flattened, universal subject; it is the nexus between their "kesher with the left" and their own search for Jewish community and Jewish interests.

New Antisemitism, or the Class Politics of a New Right?

The anti-fascist marches organized by the Warsaw Ghetto Uprising Coalition took place at a propitious moment, in which the definition of antisemitism was under rapid revision in the Jewish institutional world. In context of the "New Antisemitism" thesis, it is little surprise that the ADL and the Jewish Federation are among the villains of the "Nazi Skokie" march, not only for their institutional timidity, but more importantly, for what lay behind the ADL's message of caution: an analysis of the origins of antisemitism and its connection to the US right. Chutzpah's clear sense of urgency around the rising threat of an active Nazi party in Chicago, solidarity with African American activists, and insistence on singing Yiddish songs from the diaspora rather than Israeli songs, all mark a sharp rebuke to the "New Antisemitism" of the ADL and others. An essay that appeared in *Chutzpah* shortly after the series of anti-fascist marches in Chicago and its suburbs places the threat of antisemitism squarely on the "New Right." While Chutzpah confirms its earlier perspective that the appearance of Nazis in Chicago is "the most serious threat" to American "Jewish people since World War II," they come to the conclusion through their "struggles and confrontations" that the dangers faced in the present moment are "past the actual Nazi Party" and are part of a "rising New Right" that includes but extends far beyond Nazism.[70]

Offering an economic analysis of the late 1970s conjuncture, *Chutzpah* gives a concise analysis of what the economist Robert Brenner refers to as the "profit squeeze" or "overcapacity" thesis, in which Western economies, now facing competition from a rebuilt Western Europe as well as colonial economies that have "de-linked" from the capitalist market, confront spiraling inflation, oversupply of commodities, and labor unrest that can no longer be assuaged through endless expansion.[71] "Particularly crucial in the rise of the Right in this country is the breakdown of the American dream," Chutzpah writes. "Job security is at a low and . . . many persons in the middle class are facing downward mobility."[72] Noting how in Europe "the decline of Western capitalism is reflected" in "a world-wide revival of fascist movements—against 'coloured' immigrant workers in Britain and against Algerian workers in France," Chutzpah concludes that the same economic pressures are at play in the United States and are felt widely across the "forces of liberation" in the United States: attacks on feminists, gay rights activists, affirmative action, and labor rights. In a moment of crisis, such groups—who represent the disempowered—become easy targets and explanations for the sense of social disarray and calamity, whether it be experienced as economic struggle within the nuclear family, or white workers' inability to sustain their previously high standard of living.

As noted earlier, Chutzpah argues that Jews occupy "middle" positions on the social ladder, high enough to be visible—as doctors, lawyers, school teachers and social workers—but that they hold very little actual economic power. Owing to the US role supporting Israel against other Arab-majority states in the Middle East, Americans may further think that "Jewish interests" play an outsized role in determining the economy and US imperial policy. Yet even while the Chutzpah Collective hears echoes of the "world political situation in the 1930s," they conclude with a far different message than the ADL. While the "capitalist system pits man against woman, black against white, Jew against non-Jew," Chutzpah says movingly and with great hope, "we are not alone in this struggle."[73]

All the "threatened groups" can "stand together," unite to "meet the threat" of a rising right, and realize they share a common oppression they can address collectively.

Unlike Zionist feminists and the ADL, for whom adherence to the state of Israel formed the basis of "Jewish identity" in the words of Pogrebin, Chutzpah and BBC attempted to articulate a different ontological ground for Jewish identity practice. Jewish identity for Chutzpah and other like-minded groups was theorized through a diasporic subjectivity that included elements of cultural nationalism while rejecting the need for a Jewish-only state. By defining themselves not only at odds with the Jewish right, but as the right's ontological enemy, Chutzpah, BBC, and other such organizations were able to articulate a different modality of Jewish identity in a moment of right-wing identity formation. And ultimately their definition suggests why certain contradictions that might frustrate or baffle some Jewish identitarians made perfect sense to Chutzpah and BBC: their Jewish identitarian politics are not immanent within Jewishness itself; they are relational, in dialogue, in alignment with other groups and organizations on the left. The power of Jewish diasporic thinking, Boyarin writes, "is to never fit into a dichotomy" of Jew and non-Jew, but rather to see the diaspora as the site in which "the interaction can be grasped."[74] Jewish socialism, for Chutzpah and BBC, is Jewish diasporic thinking, as it can never be viewed outside of its relationship to the other—especially those whose interests in justice can be understood to find alliance.

Indeed, perhaps the largest difference between Chutzpah, the BBC, and the ADL—and even Jewish studies historiography—is the way they understand not only the politics of the right, but also the politics of the Jewish right. Michael Staub's magisterial *Torn at the Roots*—the first monograph to mention, if briefly, organizations such as BBC—notes Meir Kahane and the JDL's animus toward the Black Panther Party and to Black Power more generally. Yet Staub frames Kahane as one wing of a generic "Jewish radicalism" that swept through the 1960s, linking him to the "anti-establishment" politics of the 1960s and early 1970s.[75] In Shaul Magid's equally crucial recent monograph on Kahane and the JDL, Magid makes an important note of how the Jewish establishment, including the ADL and the Jewish Federation, first opposed the JDL yet came to adopt much of Kahane's platform, centering defense of Israel and criticism of the far left in Jewish institutional politics. While

Chutzpah and BBC would clearly agree with much of this analysis, especially the extent to which the Jewish establishment embraced "Kahanism" even as they rejected the messenger, their own language regarding Kahane was far different.

Missing from Staub's and Magid's accounts is the extent to which the JDL—even Kahane himself—physically attacked radical organizations, specifically targeting not only Black Power and the left, but radical Jewish organizations. *Brooklyn Bridge* naturally published more on the JDL, given its origins in NYC, and initially many of the writers expressed curiosity about the militant style of the JDL and their willingness to physically attack Nazis. "Every Jew a .22 was a slogan I could really dig," one BBC member recounts, thinking of the ways their own organization stressed Jewish militancy and revolutionary autonomy, urging other Jewish radicals to "stand up and fight for yourselves."[76] Yet the BBC quickly soured on JDL, reporting how Kahane "literally led a charge into a group of Bundists . . . attempting to engage him in a dialogue" at a speech at City College. At Brooklyn College, the BBC reported the JDL "fomented a riot" when they attacked "a group of Black students" and "destroyed a potentially unified protest against Rockefeller's budget cuts." These same tactics played out at local NYC school board meetings: "JDL has been going to . . . open meetings and causing bedlam, making it impossible to get anything done." Chutzpah reported similar attacks against progressive Jewish organizations, such as the group of JDL activists who broke into a hall where the liberal Jewish peace organization, Breira, held their inaugural meetings, overturning chairs and tables.[77] Even after Breira's security ousted JDL activists, the JDL chanted "Death to Breira" and "Breira is PLO" outside of the meeting. Rather than frame the JDL as a "radical" organization, *Brooklyn Bridge* concluded that they were an "assimilationist" one, using "anti-communist propaganda" to "assimilate the Jew into traditional Amerikan racism." They are "anti-Black and racist," a *Chutzpah* contributor noted, and unwelcome at anti-fascist protests, as they broke up coalitions with African Americans and queer allies.[78] Ultimately, *Brooklyn Bridge* came to regard the JDL as "fascist," opening an article on the JDL with the question, "Does fascism begin where nationalism ends?"

In Chutzpah's analysis, the "passive revolution" moving the "WASP elite" toward the right requires the legitimacy of a populist force, from the Nazis to the JDL, to both disrupt working-class alliances as well as give the ruling class the semblance of democratic legitimacy.[79] Chutzpah and BBC make little distinction ultimately between the Jewish fascists and non-Jewish fascists, noting that both wish to usher in reactionary, racist, and antisemitic ruling-class domination. The literal street fighting between BBC members and the JDL merely underscores this point.

While regarding the JDL as either "fascist" or "radical" may seem like a rather subtle distinction, it nonetheless reveals both the lineages as well as the identifications of groups such as Chutzpah and BBC. Rather than seeing themselves as a Jewish organization rebelling solely against a complacent liberal establishment, as the JDL framed itself, Chutzpah members saw their Jewishness as an articulation of their socialist politics and their socialism as a particular form of Jewish belonging. Thus the JDL is not an analogy to Chutzpah, but entirely anathema to it—more of a danger to Jewish thriving than a force for its continuation. The JDL is not, like Chutzpah or BBC, another form of Jewish radicalism, but rather a radical form of Jewish alignment with the capitalist elite. "Jewishness" is not only an identitarian formation for Chutzpah, it is also an ensemble of relations including class, gender, political orientation, alliances, and relationships to other social blocs. In what Stuart Hall refers to as a "combination" within a "social formation," the meaning of Jewishness is not only defined by Jews, or Jewish organizations solely—it is also a set of relationships, a modality of being that is dependent on its self-awareness within hegemonic and resistant groups and organizations.[80] The contested form of Jewishness for Chutzpah and BBC is not only a question of separateness or assimilation, in which JDL and Chutzpah may vie for space, but also a question of political and social affinity: Jewish socialism is not just a different form of Jewish separateness but rather an entirely different form of understanding the meaning of the term "identity" and its relationship to Jewish people. The *identity* of Jews, for Chutzpah, is made *in their relationship to the oppressed*, not in competition with them. To say Kahane is a "fascist" is thus to put him outside any form of Jewish identity that Chutzpah would positively recognize. For Chutzpah, the JDL is not another form of identity politics but an obliterattion of the meaning of Jewishness altogether.

Bundism and the Politics of Class after the New Left

Entirely missing from discussions of Chutzpah and BBC, let alone the JDL, is the contradictory resurgence of class politics in the late 1960s and early 1970s. Ethnic studies scholars such as Matthew Frye Jacobson as well as New Left journalists and theorists such as Todd Gitlin and Noel Ignatiev tended to see the reemergence of class politics among white workers in the waning of the 1960s as reactionary. Familiar reference points in the white working-class backlash narrative include the infamous "hard hat riots" in 1970, the George Wallace campaign, and white working-class resentment against affirmative action. Yet the class politics of the era were far more complicated. As Jefferson Cowie charts in his magisterial work on labor and culture in the 1970s, the late 1960s and early to mid-1970s saw a wave of walkouts, wildcat strikes, and labor actions that broke through the so-called "labor peace" of the 1950s. In 1970 alone, 2.4 million workers went out on strike, and some work stoppages involved tens of thousands of workers.[81] While *Time* magazine and other outlets heralded the new "blue collar worker" and a return of Depression-era militancy, the 1960s labor revolt took many shapes and forms, some of them countercultural—as with the "hippie" strikes at GM's Lordstown plant, others tied to progressive reformers, such as Jock Yablonski's attempt to democratize United Mine Workers, which ended in his assassination. The 1960s and early 1970s also saw the formation of radical Black union caucuses in the United Auto Workers, the often multiracial coalitions that produced public-sector unions, and the rise of "pink-collar" unions led by working-class women in offices and hospitals. While some of this working-class discontent was siphoned off by Wallace and the Hell's Angels, it is fair to say that one of the least memorialized upsurges of the New Left happened at the office and on the shop floor.

The rise of "white ethnic" populism in a moment of working-class uprising should come as little surprise. As Michael Denning phrases it in his encyclopedic work on the 1930s left, *The Cultural Front*, "ethnicity and race had become the modality through which working-class peoples experienced their lives and mapped their communities" during the working-class upsurge a generation earlier.[82] In other words, the expression of class in the US is almost never an unmediated category: it is expressed as often through ethnic identification and race as it is in terms of labor alienation or workplace solidarity. Perhaps a better way to say this would be: workplace solidarity often moves through race and ethnicity as it expresses class outrage and class power. Thus one way to conceive of the fight between Meir Kahane's JDL, which organized working-class Jewish New Yorkers initially, and Chutzpah and BBC is to think of them as competing class-conscious expressions of Jewish life, or perhaps Jewish expressions of class. For Kahane, like George Wallace, expressing racial or ethnic identity became a means to articulate a working-class challenge to a newly diverse workplace and demands for racial justice; for Chutzpah, a Jewish expression of class was primarily a means to articulate solidarity with other racially and ethnically marked workers, and to offer a cultural history to Jews about a Jewish labor tradition as the modality of their solidaristic offering.

It's important to point out that unlike other key figures in the Jewish Renewal movement, even the JDL, the organizers of Chutzpah and Brooklyn Bridge were by and large not members of the professional classes, let alone Jewish professionals in the organized Jewish world: key figures such as Arthur Waskow on the left and Meir Kahane on the right were rabbis. Of the founders of Chutzpah, Myron Perlman was a cabdriver and later a union carpenter; Robbie Skeist worked as a nurse after being expelled from the University of Chicago for protesting; Miriam Socoloff was a teacher; Maralee Gordon taught nursery school and Hebrew; Adar was a speech therapist. Their sense that Jewish issues are also working-class issues, that Jewish left politics needs to be rooted in class critique of capitalism, was not a theoretical question. As Perlman articulated to me while offering a ride home from a protest in 2012, "People on the left, especially the Jewish left, are often surprised when I tell them I am a retired carpenter. That's just ideology."[83] Chutzpah members' attempt to construct a working-class consciousness among Jews was both an expression of their own personal politics and part of the ethnic undercurrent of the massive wave of organizing workers, especially working-class women in pink-collar jobs.

While Chutzpah published numerous articles and essays on the history of the Jewish labor and socialist movement both in the US and abroad, perhaps their greatest intervention was that they did not assume working-class issues or Jewish members of the working class were simply a matter of the past. In a long personal essay by Myron Perlman, he details how the myth that "all Jews are rich or at least middle-class" "trapped" him for many years as he internalized his own lack of relative success as something he needed to compensate for by "working harder."[84] Perlman narrates his humiliation working as a caddy for wealthy Jews in the Bryn Mawr Country Club, which required that he have the "back of a donkey" and that he "shuffle" like "a slave" before the patrons.

Part of the reason he was willing to accept the humiliation of his job, he recounts, is that he believed, as a Jew, that he was middle class, even when his father and mother both worked low-wage jobs for long hours. Thus, whatever humiliation he received at the hands of his economic betters was temporary, something personal he had to overcome. "Most of the Jews and non-Jews I hung around with in college were of the same class background . . . sons and daughters of park district workers, office workers, small shop owners, and union organizers." These, like Myron, had dreams of success brought about by hard work, even if they were slated to go to the local state college rather than "Knox, Michigan, Wisconsin, or Urbana." Yet it was his final pre-college job working for a moving company that specialized in wealthy homes that jolted him out of his middle-class daydreams: "I was part of the moving equipment to them . . . I decided to stop trying to catch up with the middle class and have some fun." He chucked both his job and a good part of his college savings on a spontaneous trip out east. He concludes by saying, "I'd rather work toward the day when no one will have to work as a pack animal, or shuffle with humility in the presence of their employer."

Marian Neudel, another member of the Chutzpah Collective, filled the back page of issue twelve with a long poem about gig working, in the 1970s still a new phenomenon. "Temporary" is not about Jewish middle-class anxiety, but rather the entrance of women into the office-wage economy as "a kind of secretary" and, she argues, a "scab," a replacement worker. Much like other analyses in *Chutzpah*, the framework offered by Neudel is not merely her own oppression as an underpaid, gendered temp—though that is clearly rendered in her description of the tedium and anxiety of a man "who hands me papers for the Xerox/and stands there watching," worried "his manhood would drop off" if he touched the "lowly . . . machine."[85] Yet the poem begins with her awareness that the "temporary" worker lacks agency—and thus becomes an agent of her own oppression—as a feminist, socialist pacifist who must type "gentleman," "help the Army," and "type praises of Free Enterprise." And further the temp is a replacement worker, a "scab," someone hired to remind other workers they can be replaced. While the poem ends on a note of personal despair, "Yes, a kind of woman/—Temporary/A kind of life," it is also fundamentally relational: the working-class (Jewish) woman is gendered by her boss, but also in competition with other workers. The poem's Jewishness is perhaps its contingent relationality.

The intervention groups such as Chutzpah wanted to make was not only to inflect a "Jewish" subjectivity on the left, but also to bring a working-class, socialist subjectivity to Jewish movement and community spaces. In a manifesto of sorts, Chutzpah laid out its vision of a better society in "The Joy of Socialism, the Heartbreak of Capitalism," in which the profit, or in Marxist terminology, "surplus value" extracted from workers, not only creates vast polarities of wealth, ecological devastation, manufactured needs and desires, automation, and mass unemployment, but also fosters and fuels racial and economic tensions as the social world is remade in the image of capital: competition for scarce resources. Reflecting the moment in which it was written, Chutzpah further distinguishes between various kinds of socialism— noting how all have their internal contradictions: the health and literacy improvements under the Soviet Union and Mao's China, even while they are not democracies; the failures of democratic socialism in Scandinavia to prevent capital flight and the underfunding of social services; and Allende's Chile, which was "not strong enough" to prevent an economic blockade from the US and ultimately a fascist coup.[86] The manifesto concludes that given both the current horizons for socialism and the increasing economic despair wrought by capitalism, the "persecution of Jews and other minorities" will increase; the task of Chutzpah is both to work within the Jewish community "for solutions to common problems" and to defend the right "of Jewish self-determination when working with other left groups." The final line comes from a Bundist slogan, "democracy without socialism is not democracy; socialism without democracy is not socialism," evoking both their commitment to socialism and the uniquely Jewish cultural resources Chutzpah encourages Jews and non-Jews on the left to embrace.

In practical terms, Chutzpah's and BBC's class politics often meant forming caucuses or tendencies within broader umbrella organizations. When Breira, a Jewish pro-peace organization affiliated with Israel's Gush Shalom, formed in the early 1970s, Chutzpah members led an effort to form a separate "socialist caucus," as they perceived the organization to be not only "liberal," but run by male, professional members of the Jewish world.[87] As Ezra Nepon notes, Breira struggled to find roots in the Jewish community not only because of its progressive stance on Israel and Palestine, but because "it never truly built a grassroots movement."[88] In Chutzpah's language, "the high volume of intellectual bullshit" at the first Breira meeting reflected its insulation as an organization from the Jewish left as well as Jewish women's groups and the Jewish working classes. Printing their statement next to reportage of Breira's first meeting, Chutzpah declared that Breira should ban the JDL from the organization, noting that the JDL attempted to disrupt the conference, and that the "racist and fascist" movement supported the "expulsion of all Arabs" from Israel and the suspension of all democracy. The further statement called for the inclusion of working-class Jews and working-class Jewish concerns, noting that it would be difficult to sustain a peace movement with mass support if the organization did not concern itself with the immediate needs of the wider community. Finally, Chutzpah called upon Breira to recognize the Palestine Liberation Organization as the "legitimate and recognized representative of the Palestinian people," suggesting that if Breira limited itself to discussions only with Israelis, it would reinforce the segregation of Israeli society.

The Brooklyn Bridge Collective took a slightly different approach to emphasize the importance of Jewish working-class politics. Reporting on the rise of the Jewish Student Union at the Community College of Philadelphia (CCP), the "strongest and most dynamic in Philadelphia," they argue that because CCP was "not largely cosmopolitan," as was Penn, nor was it "solidly middle class like Temple," it was very militant.[89] Jewish students at CCP were from "lower income families," and are not insulated from the "physical abuse, slander and anti-semitic hieroglyphics" that might be more muted at wealthier institutions. Describing the JDL and its approach to solving antisemitism as "full of shit," the JSU not only pushed back against the "violence" and "bullying" some of their members received, it hosted speakers from the Young Lords, the Black Student Union, and Black Muslims. By the end of the first year, nearly 50 of the 1,300 members were not Jewish, and "the anti-semitic graffiti in the bathrooms" had come down. For BBC, the strength of the JSU was precisely because of its class roots: not only were the members of the JSU "not comfortable" with or capable of renouncing "their Jewishness" as they were "reminded of it every day," their proximity to other working-class communities meant the JSU was capable of doing work that Jewish organizations at other more elite institutions could not.

Their emphasis on class nature pitted Chutzpah and BBC against bourgeois Jewish institutions such as the ADL and the Jewish Federation, and formed a basis of their critique of the New Left as well. As Myron Perlman articulated, "vanguard" groups such as the Weathermen were really "anti-white working class people," which meant that as the revolutionary "period started to wind down," disaffected white Jews might be drawn toward the JDL and other reactionary Zionist movements. And like other aspects of Chutzpah and BBC's critique of the New Left, their embrace of working-class politics—as part of a wider wave of working-class organizing—allowed them to continue to function within the left and the Jewish community at the same time. Robbie Skeist, another Chutzpah member radicalized by his trip to Cuba with the Venceremos Brigade, also remembered organizing at a community college in Chicago after his anti-Communist expulsion from University of Chicago, and found that among people "more likely to be drafted," organizing had a far more immediate quality to it. Thus Chutzpah and BBC's politics were much in their mind like the Bund: organize the community where it is, and build the movement from within it, even with all of its contradictions. The *hereness* of neo-Bundism also demanded that a Jewish organization not only take on issues of global significance such as the war in Vietnam or Zionism, but also organize among working-class Jews not represented by large Jewish institutions. That Chutzpah and BBC were instrumental in founding New Jewish Agenda—the largest multi-tendency left-wing Jewish organization to exist since the collapse of the Jewish People's Fraternal Order—suggested that their impulses would later come to bear fruit.

The Limits and Promise of Non-Zionist Diasporism: Chutzpah and Brooklyn Bridge Engage with Palestine

Chutzpah cofounder Myron Perlman recalled the first time as a teenager he was aware of meeting a Jewish Zionist. She was "very strange," he remembered. Israel was "foreign" to him since he was living in the West Rogers Park neighborhood of Chicago.[90] In a conversation I had with

Perlman around the same time as his interview with the American Jewish Peace Archive, he further elaborated that this young woman who wanted to make aliyah was how he came later to understand the Marxist theory of ideology: the replacement of something abstract for something concrete; the privileging of something far away over something close; the construction of self-as-object rather than subject. The Brooklyn Bridge Collective offered a similar construction of Zionism in their inaugural manifesto, in which they declare they are "coming home" to Brooklyn—and implicitly, not to Israel. They add:

> I am a Jew. I am not an American (though I am a "naturalized" American citizen), nor a German (country of my birth), nor a Pole (country of my parents' birth). I am not an internationalist although my people have been murdered in almost every country on the face of this earth. I am not a Zionist because I do not know what it means to be a Zionist except in Israel, which I am not. I am a Jew. I am tired of being ashamed . . . it is my source of strength and joy. And if anyone made a problem out of being Jewish it wasn't me or my people.[91]

Like in Myron's response to his high school classmate, Zionism is denaturalized in this construction as the logical or teleological end point of Jewish life. It is not the "negation of exile" but rather another place in which Jews must understand how to cohabitate with non-Jews. Zionism is something foreign that bears little relationship to Myron's life or the BBC collective's particularist "life here." Yet neither construct the United States as an alternate "homeland," let alone a site for belonging. The territorial boundaries of Jewish life are negated entirely—Israel is no more an "end to alienation that has lasted 1,000 years" than the US is; alienation or lack of fixity is the ontological condition of the term "Jew."[92] Such a statement also rejects an easy American pluralism; global life for Jews is a history of being temporary guests, in places where they have been murdered, rather than a search for permanent and rooted national polity. Israel may be a place where Jews live (and are murdered or commit murder), but it offers no telos of security or answer for global Jewish existence.

Chutzpah and BBC's diasporism did not, however, imply that they rejected a Jewish state. Indeed, these two tensions within BBC and especially Chutzpah—which was far more engaged with the politics of the Middle East than BBC or JRC—are often unresolved, even as the groups attempted to defend both Jewish and Palestinian rights for self-determination. Chutzpah was an early adopter of the "two-state solution," and attempted to square its support for Palestinian independence with what Keith Feldman and Steven Salaita have referred to as the "becoming-native" of settler colonialists, posing equal rights and equal claims to the land from both settlers and the indigenous inhabitants.[93] The "Jewish right for self-determination," as Chutzpah and BBC phrased it, was perhaps the most complicated and contradictory part of their "kesher with the left." As numerous editorials and essays in *Chutzpah* and *Brooklyn Bridge* stated, they viewed the left's hard anti-Zionism as an erasure of Jewish subjectivity and Jewish political life. Yet unlike many of the former leftists and liberals who turned against the left and Black Power in favor of Jewish nationalism, Chutzpah and BBC felt that their place was both on the left and in the Jewish world; straddling this line often meant skating both the edge of the left and the edge of the organized Jewish progressive community.

To put Chutzpah's call for "Jewish self-determination" in context, it should be remembered that their audience was not only the anti-Zionist left in SDS, the SWP, and the BPP, but Zionists on both the left and right. As organizations such as the previously non-Zionist American Committee on Judaism, American Jewish Committee, Jewish Federation, and ADL turned toward Israel in their fundraising and messaging after the 1967 Arab-Israeli War, Chutzpah and BBC were unsparing in their critique of these organizations, primarily for presuming Zionism and support of Israel should trump all other issues for diaspora Jews.[94] From lambasting the ADL for singing "Hatikvah" at an anti-Nazi march, to criticizing the Jewish Federation for honoring the pro-Israel weapons manufacturer Henry Crown, to their portrait of the institutional Jewish elite as blind, bourgeois nationalists, these Jewish socialists echoed the Bund's reservation about Zionism: that the Zionist state would be "just another class-ridden society in which Jewish workers would have to fight Jewish bosses."[95] As one *Chutzpah* editorial bluntly framed their feelings about "wealthy Jews" and Jewish institutions, "No one is rounding up Jews in America, and your behavior offends and scares me."[96] And while Chutzpah and BBC did not explicitly call out emergent left-wing Zionist groups such as the Radical Zionist Alliance (RZA), it is clear their views on Zionism, the Israeli state, and the diaspora were radically at odds. For the RZA, life in the US was "life in exile (galut)" and lived as a "perpetual contradiction"; for Chutzpah it was a site of vital cultural thriving and possibilities for engagement with progressive organizations. To the RZA, Jews who criticized Israel were "psychically disfigured" by the diasporic need to please non-Jews.[97] The slogan of the RZA, "Be a revolutionary in Zion and a Zionist in the revolution," not only implied a total rejection of the possibility of an affirmative political life in the United States, it also implied that only a singular revolution in the Middle East was possible. While critical of some anti-Zionist Palestinian groups and at least nominally supportive of a Jewish state, in both their politics of the diaspora and Zionism, Chutzpah and the BBC rejected Jewish isolationism and tended to see the Jewish community, and Jewish state, as deeply engaged with the world and dependent on their relationship to all marginalized communities.[98]

What makes Chutzpah's politics more complicated, dialectical, and in motion than a simple binary between Zionism and anti-Zionism was their willingness to engage with the Israeli left (including the anti-Zionist Israeli left), as well as to recognize the legitimacy of the Palestine Liberation Organization long before anyone in the liberal or even left Jewish community would see such engagement as anything short of treasonous. In addition, they were also quite open to an Israeli state taking many different forms, many of which would not, by the 1970s, still be considered Zionist. Neither Chutzpah nor BBC aligned themselves with the Israeli state or felt that Zionism, beyond declaring Jewish cultural and political rights, was bound to a particular form of existence. As one *Chutzpah* writer framed it, "self determination embodied in a state does not automatically imply support for the particular state of Israel."[99] And while such a position aligned itself broadly with the Israeli anti-war left, specifically Uri Avnery, and the New Left "New Outlook" movement—which argued for full rights for Palestinian citizens of Israel, de-militarization of Israel, and peace negotiations with the PLO and neighboring states—they also wrote about and made contact with far more radical organizations in Israel, most notably the Israeli Black Panther Party (IBPP).

Founded in 1971 by Jews of Arab and North African descent in the former Palestinian neighborhood of Musrara in Jerusalem, the IBPP protested against poor living conditions for Mizrahi and Sephardic Jews, racial discrimination, and lack of cultural and political representation.

They also saw their own struggle materially linked to the struggle for Palestinian self-determination, developing links to the PLO as early as 1972, arguing that the "needs of the Mizrahim and the Arabs are intertwined ... When we are fighting for Palestinian rights we're also fighting for our rights."[100] Chutzpah and BBC ran numerous articles about the IBPP, noting the exclusion of Mizrahi and Sephardic Jews from the mainstream of Israeli society, as well as embracing their entrance into the political sphere, observing, "Sephardim are ... conspicuously absent from the Israeli left and support tough stances against Arabs."[101] The emergence of a "Black Panthers national conference held last September in Beersheva," which declared "the key to peace is recognition that Israel and Palestine is the homeland of two peoples," was welcomed as a means to bring non-Ashkenazi Jews into the New Left. Further, the emergence of the Moked Party, led by a member of IBPP in coalition with Hadash, the mostly Palestinian-Israeli Communist Party, was heralded by Chutzpah as a sign of the possible emergence of a "new humanist society in which Israelis and Palestinians live with one another in peace and dignity."[102] Far from the ultra-nationalism of either ADL, JDL, or RZA, Chutzpah and BBC approached Zionism from the pragmatic perspective that if Israel is to exist, what would it look like, and who would have to be organized to transform it into a democratic and peaceful country?

"We were looking for anyone we could work with," Myron Perlman said of his trip with several other Chutzpah members to Israel and the West Bank. "Mostly this included members of New Outlook and Peace Now," Perlman said, but they also talked with Yasser Arafat's soon to be mother-in-law Raymonda Tawil, Communist Party mayors of West Bank towns, and other Palestinians who worked within the PLO orbit.[103] The widest divergence between the left diasporists and explicitly Zionist Jewish groups at the time was their treatment not only of the Israeli state, but also of Palestinian resistance to Israel. In defiance of Golda Meir's famous quote, "There is no Palestinian people," and the RZA's insistence that Zionists are the indigenous inhabitants of land west of the Jordan River, *Chutzpah* devoted significant pages to PLO leader Yasser Arafat's statements and the various positions of Palestine liberation groups. In a long 1978 article on Arafat, *Chutzpah* addressed the way the PLO's political positions, rhetoric, and organization transformed, suggesting that fixed and rigid insistence on one Zionist, or anti-Zionist, line would not be helpful. First noting that Arafat was open to a "peaceful solution to the conflict" through land transfers and negotiations, *Chutzpah* mocked Israelis who still thought it was the "Arab nations' goal to 'drive the Jews into the sea,'" adding that it was the Israelis and not the PLO who refused to negotiate.[104] In something of a rebuke to Zionists who imagined they were the victims of Palestinians, they quoted Arafat saying, "[Israel] scares all of its Arab neighbors with its armies and nuclear weapons... Taking into consideration the aggressiveness Israel has shown... it is us, the Palestinians, who need guarantees for peace." Arafat's final point is one that could have been made by Chutzpah, given their dialectical analysis of the *relational* meaning of social movements to one another, capital, and the state. "We are not a revolution," Arafat concluded. "Once we become a state we will be taking a different form." Much like Chutzpah's relational ethos, any given articulation of the principle is in dialogue, motion, and change, both within Jewish communities and among Palestinians.

In an earlier interview with both the PLO and Democratic Front for Palestine guerrillas, *Chutzpah* even expressed an openness to the armed fighters, though the interviewer says "[they] hate us." The interviewer, an Israeli New Left activist, acknowledged that the guerillas were not "madmen," even if devoted at that moment to armed revolution. The interview concludes with the guerrilla leader saying, "As much as we would like to go back to 1948, we really can't... 'here' includes three million Jews... We have to live with them and we want to live in a secular democratic state."[105] In some ways their position is not entirely removed from that of Chutzpah, which argued in their "Principles" that as "two-thirds of Israel's Jewish population [was] Mid-East born" or refugees from "oppressive conditions in Arab lands," the national character of Jews "must be defended," regardless of what state formation such defense might ultimately take.[106] It seems clear that Chutzpah wanted to conclude the interview on a positive note, suggesting both transformation and a utopian future in which one would find peace with the other.

Perhaps the clearest vision of this balance was offered on the cover of the "Israel and the Palestinians" issue, with four images: a smiling soldier, young kaffiyehed militants with rifles, an old man with a bandage on his head holding a small child drinking milk, and a smiling woman also holding a child. With the exception of the kaffiyeh-wearing guerrillas, it is impossible to know if anyone in the photo is Israeli or

Palestinian, and the binaries between soldier and militant, old man and young women, seem to occupy the framing more than nationality. The up-close portraits of faces, smiling or brooding, frame their complex inner reality and subjectivity. This final point marks a sharp departure even from the diasporism of progressive religious figures such as Arthur Waskow, whose critical engagement with the Zionist nation-state elides or dismisses Palestinian voices, faces, and political organizations. As ethnic studies scholar Keith Feldman writes, Waskow's criticism of Israel and nationhood still preserves intact the "absent-presence of Palestinian subjects endowed with a complex personhood."[107] "We tried to make no assumptions and keep an open mind," Perlman recounted. "Ultimately no matter how far apart a person was, they were going to be a neighbor to an Israeli or a Palestinian." It is this openness to the other that allowed Chutzpah to consider breaking with a Zionist state altogether, if conditions allowed for it: "Perhaps living in separate states for some time, a bi-national state would be desired by both groups," Perlman wrote in *Chutzpah*.[108] "Palestinians would need to recognize the peoplehood of the Jews," he concluded—yet not, importantly, their *nationhood*.

It's fair to say, however, that while Chutzpah moved along the "Moishe to Mao" continuum in its coverage of Israel and Palestine, its center of gravity or perhaps natural twin was the Israeli New Left, particularly among the early "refuseniks"—Israeli soldiers who refused to serve in the West Bank and Gaza—and the "New Outlook" movement and journal. In December 1976, Chutzpah and Am Chai, a *havurah* of progressive-minded Jews in Chicago, invited David Shacham, one of the editors of the Israeli journal *New Outlook*, after which the faction of the New Left movement was named. Many of the points in Shacham's speech were points that articulated Chutzpah's own position: a withdrawal from territory seized and occupied in the 1967 war, direct negotiations with the PLO, demilitarization of Israel, and the right of Israeli soldiers to refuse service in the occupied territories, among others.[109] It should be remembered that while the "two-state solution" was seen by factions of Palestinian guerrillas such as the PFLP and much of the US New Left as liberal, in the mid-'70s, within the Jewish community in the US and Israel, it was "la la land," as Chutzpah's Perlman put it. "It was completely outside of the realm of possibility," he added, especially as it would mean recognizing the PLO, still regarded as a terrorist organization by most Israelis and Jewish institutions in the US. Whether Chutzpah and New

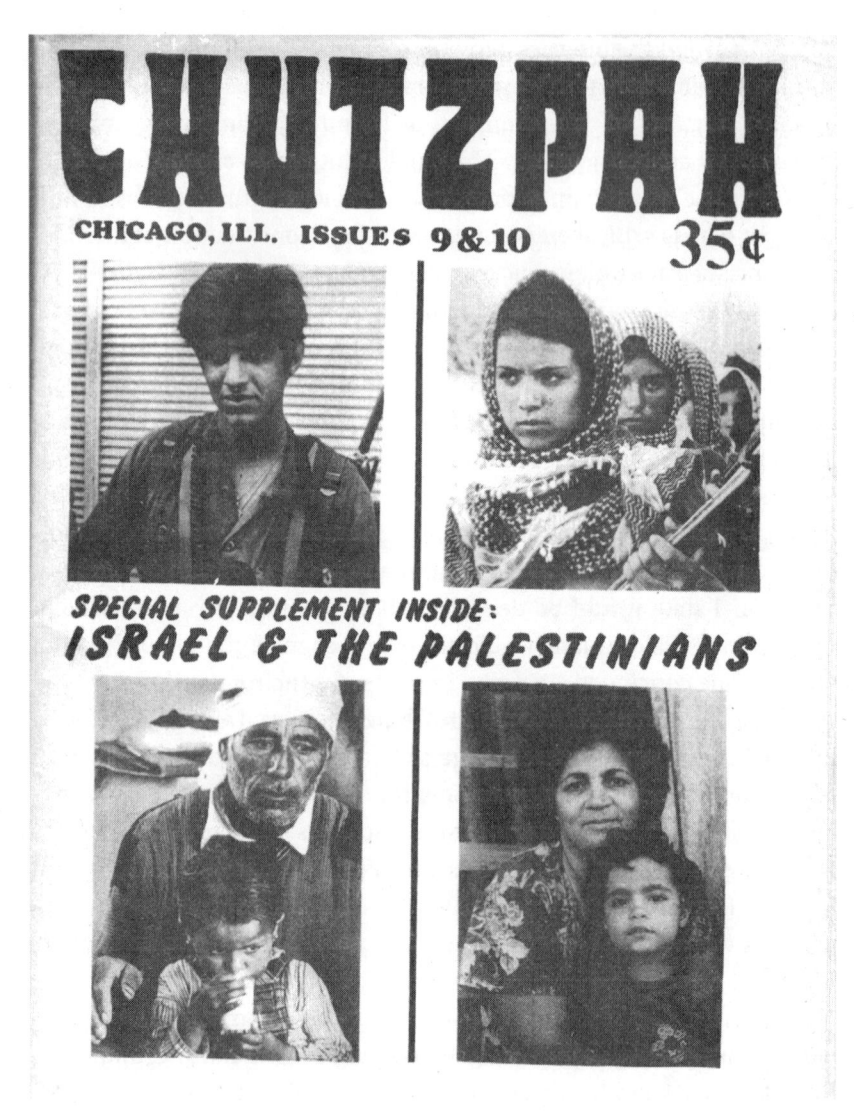

Figure 4.3. *Chutzpah* 9–10, cover.

Outlook regarded the two-state solution as optimal or simply the best that could be done given Israeli and Jewish American opinion depended on the member of the group with whom one spoke. From Chutzpah's point of view, these were not separable issues: as Shacham pointed out, since only a fifth of Israelis supported what was seen as the far-left "peace" position of total withdrawal from the West Bank, East Jerusalem, and Gaza, it would be politically impossible and utopian to push for more.

Yet what aligned Chutzpah with New Outlook beyond their shared positions was their analysis of Israeli society and its relationship to its own Jewishness. As Shacham points out, the Israeli right, the "hawks," described the Israeli Jewish left in openly antisemitic terms:

> The whole image of the dove became one of the intellectual with a bent, hunched back; someone from the Galut, somebody who doesn't believe in our mission, in our strength. The whole symbolism of the dove became anti-masculine. There is a joke about the national erection of the hawks. They were talking about standing firm, strong, and upright; while doves are those who are bent, with weak knees, and they tremble.[110]

The notion that the lack of a Jewish nation-state produced effeminate, over-intellectual men was a staple, of course, of antisemitic European discourse for centuries. The association of this supposed diasporic state with the left was an addition of the more recent European post-Dreyfus right, which suggested that Jewish effeminacy did not make Jews merely incapable of self-governance, but morally and politically dangerous to state interests as well. Thus the Israeli right not only saw progressive Jews as political opponents, they increasingly saw them in ways not unlike European reactionaries: as enemies of the state. Chutzpah's claim of the diaspora as a place to thrive not only articulated a non-Zionist positionality to the world, it also recognized a fundamental incompatibility between the increasingly rightward drift of Israeli nationhood and a progressive vision of world Jewry.

It makes sense then that former members of even the most Zionist of the left-wing Jewish socialist collectives, Jewish Radical Community (JRC), would shift positions as Israeli politics lurched from an implicitly expansionist labor-left to the eliminationist right. To quote Sheryl Nestel, a former member of JRC, she held a "two-state" Zionist position in the 1970s but moved to anti-Zionism some forty years later as it "seemed Israel's policies were untenable." Former Chutzpah member Miriam Socoloff said something similar: she realized Israel had made the two-state solution "impossible" through settlement expansion, and all that was left was "democracy" in a binational state.[111] In this way, one can see how Chutzpah and other diasporic Jewish socialist collectives of the 1970s— while to the "right" of the New Left on Zionism—nevertheless laid the groundwork for later Jewish organizations that would go on to finally break with Zionism totally. The 1980s progressive organization New Jewish Agenda, of which Chutzpah and BBC were founding members, led the first protests against the Israeli invasion of Lebanon, and hosted Israeli refuseniks through the 1980s. Jewish Voice for Peace (JVP)—the largest Jewish anti-Zionist organization—also grew out of the ferment left in NJA's wake when it was founded in the early 1990s. JVP also moved, like members of Chutzpah, from a "pro-peace" position to explicit anti-Zionism, in dialogue with social movements in the US and Middle East. While correlation is not causation, it is fair to say that the organized Jewish left, increasingly anti-Zionist, owes its origins as much to SDS as to the groundwork laid by Chutzpah, JRC, and BBC, which created Jewish groups funded and organized by Jewish leftists to work within the Jewish community, creating solidarity with Palestinian activists and civil society. It was a long game, perhaps, but one that may have more or less paid off. One can see Chutzpah as a kind of vanguard of the neo-diasporism of groups such as IfNotNow and Jewish Voice for Peace, less in their individual positions, but in their willingness to challenge the organized Jewish community while staking their place in it.

Philip Roth and Melanie Kaye/Kantrowitz : Two Visions of Post-1960s Diasporic Thought

> *I believe in the Diaspora, not only as a fact but a tenet. I'm against Israel on technical grounds. I'm very disappointed that they decided to become a nation in my lifetime. I believe in the Diaspora. After all, they are the chosen people. Don't laugh. They really are. But once they're huddled in one little corner of a desert, they're like anyone else: Frenchies, Italians, temporal nationalities. Jews have one hope only—to remain a remnant in the basement of world affairs—no I mean something else—a splinter in the toe of civilizations, a victim to aggravate the conscience.*
> —Grace Paley, "Two Sad Short Stories from a Long and Happy Life," *Collected Stories*[112]

As part of the cultural and political efflorescence of American Jewish life in the 1960s and 1970s, a discussion emerged on the meaning of Jewish diaspora: the idea that Jews constitute a historical and global people yet who share neither a contiguous nor stable territory. The debate between Jewish diasporism and nationalism was not new, and indeed, many cultural nationalists from Bernard Lazare to the Jewish Workers' Bund were also diasporists, and some, if not many, diasporists accepted at least in theory and to a lesser or greater degree Jewish national aspirations in Palestine and elsewhere. The emergence of the debate in the late 1960s over diasporism had little to do, then, with an immanent change in Jewish self-conception or threats to Jewish security in the United States; indeed, one could say Jews had never felt a sense of belonging in the US such as they did in the 1960s and 1970s and, it could be argued, may or may not feel such a sense of homecoming again. Rather, the emergence of diasporic thinking had everything to do with the institutional embrace of Zionism after the 1967 Israeli victory over the combined forces of neighboring Arab states. It could not be ignored any longer that Jews were not only a nation, but one acting with the aggressive force of the European nationalisms from which Jews earlier fled. Claiming Jewish diaspora functioned as both a critique and at times a disavowal of Israel's national stature, which seemed perhaps for the first time willing and able to eclipse American Jews' sense of their uniqueness. At the most fundamental level, the (re-)embrace of diasporic thinking in the late 1960s and 1970s was a denial that Israel was the "collective Jew among nations," as one scholar framed it, acting in the interests metonymically of Jews around the world.[113]

Yet there is also a sense for Jews in the 1960s that their ghettoization in the US was coming or had come to an end: there was little choice but to engage with the gentile other; indeed, there was also a fear that they were about to become them. The "breakthrough narrative" of the 1950s and early 1960s, as literary critic Benjamin Schreier frames it, with the emergence of iconic Ashkenazi Jewish writers such as Philip Roth, Bernard Malamud, and Saul Bellow, contains both versions of these narratives simultaneously. If the emergence of a Jewish literature into the American mainstream signals Jewish paradigmatic success *as Jews*, it at the same time ends Jews' distinctiveness as particular ethnic or cultural expression: the paradigmatic Jewish novel becomes the paradigmatic American novel, according to Schreier.[114] The scene in which SDS activist turned Weatherman Mark Rudd bursts into Columbia president Grayson Kirk's office with a dozen other activists, and is immediately stunned by the opulence and artifice he sees, recalls that he experienced the office occupation less as a revolutionary storming the halls of power than as a "Jewish kid from New Jersey" finally entering the inner sanctum of "the goyim."[115] Yet there is an ambivalence to this entrance, as Rudd must ask if he is occupying the halls of power, or preparing for them. For a young revolutionary, it marked an important psychological moment: no longer was the WASP elite an object of intimidation, or even desire: in their own chambers, they were just paper tigers. Rudd went on to call President Grayson "shithead" in public speeches, inscribing the WASP intellectual with an appropriate Freudian reversal.

In an analogous moment at the foundation of SDS at Port Huron, Michigan, in which—as I mention earlier in this chapter—several of the Jewish attendees felt like they had finally burst into the "real America," one can think, like the young Rudd at Columbia, they were bursting upon the scene: no longer in their East Coast left-wing Jewish ghetto of New York City or, in Rudd's case, Jewish suburb in New Jersey. While SDS is not merely a Jewish story, there is more than one Jewish activist—and more than one gentile observer—who suddenly noticed the large number of Jews very visibly in places they had not been seen before: in the South as Freedom Riders, in prestigious universities loudly protesting, and as the 1960s closed, on "most wanted" posters for political terrorism, as in the case of David Gilbert and Bernardine Dohrn. And perhaps most surprising to the Jewish establishment, Jews who were not bursting into the inner sanctum of their goyish university president were instead bursting into the Jewish Federation building in Washington, DC, demanding the federation actually represent working-class Jewish interests, especially for solidarity with African Americans and anti-war protesters.

Thus the question of diaspora emerged as both a reaction to nationalism and perhaps also a reaction to assimilation. In this context, it seems helpful to mention that positive and even normative descriptions of Jewish diasporism in the 1960s and 1970s were not limited to the left. Philip Roth, who never identified with the New Left (if also never disavowing it completely like Saul Bellow or Irving Howe), sketched both dimensions of the question or, perhaps, in a sense, that they are both the same question: Zionism is the other side of assimilation. Roth, who launched onto the scene with wry, ironic stories of Jews who assimilated, if all too well, was criticized by Jewish establishment figures for his representation of Jews who mock the Holocaust, for showing Jewish men having affairs, for exposing both the snobbery as well as the garish arrogance of class-ascending Jews toward their poorer and/or *frum* brethren. Roth, whose 1969 novel *Portnoy's Complaint* made him a household, or perhaps bathroom, name, went on to be condemned by the likes of Irving Howe for being antisemitic, as he offered the middle-class Jewish family as an object of ridicule and portrayed Jewish men as sexual deviants obsessed with having sex with Christian women. Whether these initial stories of Roth's should be read as Jewish provocation, satirical send-ups of Leon Uris or Henry James, autobiography, or autoeroticism is up for debate, but regardless, Roth seemed to intuitively grasp that the era of the other Roth (Henry) and ghetto pastorals was over: consider him Lenny Bruce for the University of Chicago set.

Of equal or perhaps even greater importance, Roth's diasporism and his gender politics fell far short of Chutzpah and BBC. Again, Roth was not a leftist; in many ways he does not belong in this book, unless only to suggest the meaning of margins by refracting back on the liberal Jewish middle. Roth was not of the left, yet he was made possible by it. Thus Roth's writing, if not exactly from the center, the cultural heights, seemed to understand that this Jewish explosion into America was also happening simultaneously from below on the left, and from above on the right, and they were at odds with each other if also dialectically linked. As young Jewish students were protesting the war in Vietnam and segregated lunch counters, the Jewish establishment began to vigorously embrace an expansionist form of Zionism and to declare war on its erstwhile allies and sources of moral strength: the African American liberation struggle and the radical left. While few of Roth's early novels delve into the explicit politics of the 1960s, except in passing, their portrayal of Jewish libidinal desire to "stick it up the backgrounds" of the WASP elite forms a kind of sexualized homology to what SDS did on the streets: expose, figuratively, that the emperor is wearing no clothes. Yet Roth, alone among Jewish authors in the 1960s, also ridiculed not just the goyim, but the sententious, even goyish desire to become a nation at the expense of both Jewish liberalism and the indigenous inhabitants of Palestine. Roth's novels offer the diaspora back to itself in their rejection of Jewish nationhood.

Whether he knew it or not, Roth captured this dialectical motion of Jewish experience. And perhaps more interestingly still, Roth's novels seemed to capture, if they did not perhaps understand, this radical Jewish energy much in the same way Chutzpah and BBC did: as embedded in both a very particular *Jewish* memory of the left and a diasporic sensibility that can only be expressed as a minority in relation to a Christian other. That Roth was *not* part of the New Left allows this expression to float through his novels as, at times, a disassociated metaphor, perhaps allowing for a greater expansiveness, if also denying his work an ultimate political meaning or a positive counter to Zionism. For Chutzpah and Jewish writers in the orbit of the 1970s Jewish socialist left such as Melanie Kaye/Kantrowitz, "diaspora" was not only opposed to an identification with a state, it was also a kind of political meeting place, a modality of encounter, and a relationship to otherness: a kind of left politics embedded in a Yiddishkeit minoritarian socialism from below. Unlike Roth, for Chutzpah and Kaye/Kantrowitz, diasporic thinking is not merely against a masculine state formation, but rather a way of theorizing solidarity and relational existence. Roth's diaspora is always one of comic subversion that is radical insofar as it undermines the premises of Jewish ethno-nationalism; yet beyond tweaking the nose of Menachem Begin it remains strictly libidinal, a source of creative passion, yet limited to the horizons of the liberal (male) individual subject and his private rebellion.

Toward the end of *Portnoy's Complaint*, the "breakthrough" novel about a "nice Jewish boy" who is on a quest to sleep with "shiksas," there is a telling metaphor. Comparing his mother to the mother of a thuggish, yet enviably aggressive, teenage neighbor, the young Alex comments, *"He has a mother who works.* Mine . . . patrols the six rooms of our apartment the way a guerilla army moves across its own countryside."[116] While it might seem that this is a metaphor about his masculine fears of his mother's feminine authority, there is an open question about how to read the affective register of this description. If Alex's mother is a guerrilla (and it should be noted, this is the one reference to the Vietnam War in the entire text), what is she a guerrilla *against*? On a similar note, we might ask by comparison what it is Alex is rebelling against. The "complaint" in *Portnoy's Complaint* should be read not as the title implies, a binary between a "nice Jewish boy" and a libidinal conqueror of women, but rather perhaps in league with his mother's own sense of Jewish gender subversion.

It should be remembered that Alex describes his own libidinal desires for "shiksas" in terms that evoke his mother's sense of insurgent domesticity: after his "daring" visit to the family of "Christian blondie" in

"Ioway" during Thanksgiving, Alex describes his journey to the faraway Midwest as a kind of reverse "manifest destiny." That the final WASPy "shiksa" Alex describes in detail he hails by the name of "The Pilgrim" further suggests that his libido, much like his mother's gender-blurred domesticity, is an act of insurrection. That he describes his first sexual encounter with The Pilgrim as a boxing match between his swarthy body of "undigested halvah" as opposed to the "fair fuzz" of "Republican refinement" suggests as much libidinal desire as it does racial conflict.[117] All this while Alex is working for the congressional committee that exposed Charles Van Doren the "ur-WASP" as a "fake" in much the same terms Rudd denounces President Grayson.

In this way, we might recover Alex's love for his mother—highly sexualized and pathologized by the narrator—by suggesting Alex carries out a particularly Jewish gender threat to the WASP social order. Both of Alex's parents violate the expectations assigned to "European gender norms," as Jewish studies scholar Daniel Boyarin frames Jewish masculinity and femininity, that prized both "effeminate and bookish men" as well as "aggressive and masculine women."[118] Unlike Alex's father who defers to Alex and allows him to verbally lash out, Alex's mother verbally dominates him, and exposes him to both her sensual body—her menstrual blood, her garters, her underwear hanging on the line—as well as her bodily desire for Alex as her child.[119] While nothing Alex's mother does approaches incest, her embodied frankness violates the European, Christian feminine ideal of a chaste, sexless mother figure separate from the sexualized, pagan, or de-Christianized temptress.

As a young Alex laments, the gender relations are reversed in the Portnoy household: "Christ . . . if my father had only been my mother! My mother my father! But what a mix-up of the sexes in my house!"[120] "Christ" in some ways is right. As Boyarin suggests, psychoanalysis along with Zionism were two means by which Jewish members of the intelligentsia sought to answer anxieties about Jewish masculinity in the early twentieth century.[121] Alex's confession to Dr. Spielvogel should not be read as a window into his subconscious and therefore more honest mind, but rather a performance in which Alex is attempting to order his libidinal desires into their proper gendered form. Alex's ostensible rejection of his mother and late embrace of his father's baseball playing not only elide the rebellion against WASP culture and an undoing of its gendered manifest destiny, but also bury the affinities between his mother's "guerilla" warfare against proper Christian motherhood and Alex's own rebellion against his proper masculine role.

Yet it seems, given Alex's quest and his identification with the rebellion of his mother, we are invited to read *Portnoy* against its gendered grain. In this way, we can also understand that Alex's crisis over his final "shiksa" lover, Mary Jane Reid, aka "the Monkey," is precisely because she is *not* a "shiksa" like the college-educated, professional-class "blondies" who attended Vassar and whom Alex has declared libidinal war upon as "the Schnoz." Not only is "the Monkey" from rural Appalachia and functionally illiterate, the very name Alex bestows upon her—due to her act of eating a banana that had been on the ground—suggests less a class difference between the two than a racialized one. Tellingly, while trying to "educate" Reid about the political implications of her own background, Alex offers her classic 1930s Popular Front literature by Communist and Marxist writers such as James Agee and Louis Adamic, and he recalls while with her his support for Henry Wallace, the Progressive Party candidate that was in many ways the last gasp of the socialist left before the Red Scare foreclosed such possibilities.

While one could interpret Alex's "gifts" to Reid as part of his arrogant, "virtuous" public face, they also suggest a pre–Cold War, pre-suburban Jewish experience, in which the class and racial solidarities of the Communist Party and affiliated organizations would have made a romance between Reid and Alex not only acceptable but perhaps even laudatory. It should be stressed that Reid is also the only girlfriend of Alex's that he actually has "feelings" for—unlike The Pilgrim, whose "frailties . . . accomplishments . . . family" provoke Alex's intolerance.[122] Rather than consider his mother's imagined admonitions, one can consider that it isn't difference Alex runs from, but actual sameness: "the Monkey" is in many ways an outsider in America just like he is. By racializing her, Alex underscores how limited his rebellion against WASP America really is, or perhaps simply redefines its meaning. Alex is not wrestling with being a "nice Jewish boy" or a Don Juan with a taste for blond women; Alex wrestles with whether or not he embraces being fully white. He can sexually rebel against the daughters of the WASP elite, but can he embrace in solidarity—and risk his own liminal whiteness—the daughter of unemployed mine workers?

We can consider *Portnoy* to be in many ways a rewriting of the other US-to-Israel Jewish bestseller in mid-century, Leon Uris's 1958 novel,

Exodus, the story of Jewish victims of pogroms and Nazi extermination rediscovering their masculinity and pride by engaging in frontier-style war against Palestinians and other Arabs. In this novel of the "New (militarized, masculine, sabra) Jew," the protagonist, Ari, sheds his shtetl and his Jewish effeminacy by waging war against the "Arab mobs" who, critic Amy Kaplan observes, are "Orientalized" in Uris's "racist" depiction.[123] As Kaplan points out, Ari lives out not only a Zionist narrative of Jewish "regeneration through violence," to borrow Richard Slotkin's memorable phrase, but also an *American* frontier narrative, in which a nation is constructed and reborn through continual confrontation against the savage other, who fights the frontier protagonist but also reconstructs him to shed his urban softness and equivocation.[124] Roth reportedly found Uris's novel and the depiction of the Jew as a "patriotic warrior" so absurd and offensive that it was "not worth disputing."[125] At least not via argumentative essay. For it is hard to read Alex's journey to Israel, otherwise gratuitous, as anything other than a pointed refutation of the masculine "New Jew" thesis in both racial and gendered terms. Alex's first observation in Israel is particularly loaded given the entire literal and figurative thrust of the novel: "here [in Israel], *we're* the WASPs!"[126] This association of Israel with *whiteness* rather than Jewish redemption or gendered regeneration runs through a chain of associations for the young Alex: the self-possessed and most importantly "humorless" kibbutznik Alex attempts and fails to seduce and her retort that he is a "schlemiel" and is attracted to "ghetto humor" when he makes a self-deprecating comment suggest that the "New Jew" is, in fact, against the very notion of Jewishness the novel sardonically embraces.[127] Alex's failed erection in Israel—"I just can't get it up in this country"— suggests that his sexual "guerrilla war" against the WASP elite—contra radical Zionists—can find no expression in Israel; indeed, it renders the entire war moot: that is, "we're the WASPs now."

For all the sexist futility and infantile nature of both Alex's sexual rebellion against WASP culture and his backhanded embrace of the diasporic schlemiel, it is important to note that the novel poses a kind of diasporic utopia in the lost or perhaps suspended and displaced middle-class New Jersey neighborhood of Newark. That this diasporic ideal, or perhaps idyll, is located in a place and time both delineates the meaning of diaspora for Roth's Alex, and freezes it in the past. Alex tells his unrealizable Israeli object of desire that his kibbutz is a "victory garden," placing the Jewish socialist collective both in the United States and, more importantly, in the Popular Front war against fascism that animated the American Jewish community, from leftists to liberals, from the 1930s to the Cold War. Alex's sentimental evocation of the adult male softball game ("I want to grow up to be one of these men!") is inextricable from his childhood memory of Henry Wallace, the last great hope of the (Jewish) anti-fascist alliance to emerge out of the Popular Front before the long night of the Red Scare.

Even so, it is hard to miss that the sentimental longing of Alex for his socialist collective of Newark is related to the failure to achieve proper European-American masculinity in Israel: it is not that the softball-playing men are rebels so much as their masculinity is presumably comfortably restrained and shaped by the "guerrilla army" of the Jewish domestic matriarchy. Softball is opposed to Galil rifles; sweating, grimy men playing a game rather than digging trenches; helping the "poor and oppressed" of Newark rather than fighting Palestinians or Egyptian soldiers.[128] If one thinks of *Portnoy's Complaint* as a gender satire of Zionism, then the diasporism of the text—much like the rendering of 1940s Newark—is not a joke, even if it is unclear how our hero, returning to the US, can manifest it.

As Nathan Zuckerman, Roth's occasional fictionalized avatar, writes to his brother who has moved to an Israeli settlement, his "landscape" wasn't "the Negev ... it was the industrial, immigrant America" of Newark. While this scene in *Counterlife* was published nearly two decades after *Portnoy*, it is in many ways a kind of explicit decoding, or perhaps working out, of the implicit politics embedded in Alex's much more prurient journey in the 1960s. While *Counterlife* poses three different plots in five chapters, three of the five chapters feature Nathan's brother Henry fleeing to a West Bank religious-Zionist settlement after a nervous breakdown—much like Alex's after a fashion—following a spell of impotency and a potentially life-threatening surgery to correct it. Much of the same analysis of Zionism that is offered in *Counterlife* appears in *Portnoy*: while Zionism proposes to solve the problems of diasporic life, Zukerman suggests that Zionism solves merely the problem of modernity, perhaps to limit its dizzying possibilities. Henry goes to Israel in order to escape from, in many ways, his own success: he has a lucrative profession, a devoted wife, a plentitude of women with whom he can have affairs. He goes to Israel to restore his self-ideal as a "model husband" or to retreat from the idea of a self entirely and become a "model boy" with the far-right Zionist Mordecai Lippman as a substitute father.[129] Henry's potency as a father or lover is replaced with an ostentatious pistol he now carries as he travels in the Occupied Territories of the West Bank. "I was totally obsessed by that gun," Zuckerman notes.[130] For Zuckerman, the gun represents both a totemistic phallus—the other side of Alex "not able to get it up" in Israel—and a kind of normative and violent WASPy masculinity. And for Zuckerman, the totem-phallus is the entire country: looking out over the desert, Zuckerman sees a single red light that looks like the "wrath of an Almighty God," yet a second later he understands it as an Israeli missile battery: it is malevolent, violent metal erections all the way down.

The gun also represents to Zuckerman the ideological hollowness of Zionism. As Zuckerman approaches Henry (now Hanoch) at his illegal West Bank settlement, he notices a young woman with a New York accent and when he asks if she is an American, she responds flatly, "I am a Jew." Similarly, this prompts Zuckerman to recount the limits of Henry/Hanoch's commitments to Jewish life as a young man, which he curtly summarizes as attending a Hillel event or two in college and playing basketball with a Jewish fraternity. As Henry/Hanoch's mentor regales the elder Zuckerman with the perils of Jewish life in the diaspora and its emptiness, Zuckerman turns to Henry/Hanoch and asks pointedly if "living under a volcano" is what his brother experienced as life in the United States, to which Henry/Hanoch can only reply "no."[131] The diaspora for Zuckerman is precisely this "no," that he could not "think of any historical society that had achieved the level of tolerance institutionalized in America," and that essentially, Jews had it pretty good in the US.[132] Zionism isn't just an erasure of the forms of creativity and libidinal rebellion that give Jewish (men at least) their metaphorical and perhaps literal hard-ons, it is an erasure of the material of Jewish success and *acceptance* in the United States. The "counterlife" is the myth that Henry/Hanoch, and perhaps all Zionists, could create as a "counter parable" of Jewish life, and "un-Jew" themselves to world applause; they would create a "fabulous utopia" with the "reality of a gun."[133] That Zuckerman's Israeli friend wryly comments that Israel is now "the homeland of Jewish abnormality" suggests how much the joke is on the teller in this case.[134]

The real Jews for Zuckerman are in one sense quite ordinary, "the kitchen table in Newark," but their practical desire to move to the United States to "save their skins" is their modest and very diasporic form of courage. In this sense it is hard to see if Zuckerman offers any meaning to his diasporic Jewish life beyond the internally self-referential "Diaspora Abbott and David Costello" relationship he has with his brother—Zuckerman's diasporism only existing in relationship to what it is *not*, Henry/Hanoch's religious nationalism. While Zuckerman "comes out" as a Jew in England in response to his wife's blue-blooded antisemitism, he cannot supply it with any meaning outside his own liberal individualism:

> I am not one of those Jews who wants to hook themselves up to the patriarchs or even to the modern state; the relationship of the Jewish "I" to their Jewish "we" is nothing like so direct and unstrained as Henry now wishes his to be . . . England's made a Jew of me in only eight weeks, which, on reflection, might be the least painful method. A Jew without Jews, without Judaism, without Zionism, without a temple or an army or even a pistol, a Jew clearly without a home, just the object itself, like a glass or apple.[135]

The homelessness that Zuckerman experiences is the homelessness of modernity, the condition of everyone in America wanting to be who they are not, "Chicanos who want to look like Texans . . . Middle Western Wasps who, believe it or not, want to talk and act like Jews."[136] There is no Jewish collectivity, only the endless expanse of American liberalism, in which identity is a lone monad and a person is just an object "like a glass or an apple." While Roth's invocation of diaspora is a welcome rejoinder against the ideological assumptions of Zionism, Roth's diaspora is like his nostalgia for Newark: something frozen in the past, but able to offer no generative meaning. His rebellions may be symbolic, but they remain at the level of the atomized individual. Unlike Chutzpah and Brooklyn Bridge, Roth's notion of *doikayt* is privatized in the personal mobility of a white, male subject: rather than a collective notion of struggle or a socialist desire to transform the "hereness" of Jews into a more just society, Roth's "doikayt" is rooted either in childhood nostalgia or liberal and masculine ideals of personal freedom.

The activist and author Melanie Kaye/Kantrowitz edited a volume of essays by radical Jewish women entitled *The Tribe of Dina*, which was published in the same year as *Counterlife* and posed many of the same questions Roth does against the concepts of diaspora and nationalism. Kaye/Kantrowitz, while not formally part of the Brooklyn Bridge Collective or other Jewish socialist projects of the 1970s (though years later helped found a kind of sister organization, Jews for Racial and Economic Justice), said of herself that she was "born" of those movements and came to both political and personal maturity through them.[137] In her essay "To Be a Radical Jew in the Late 20th Century," Kaye/Kantrowitz describes an upbringing not entirely different from the upbringing of many of Roth's male protagonists: in Jewish Brooklyn, not Newark; the child of left-wing activists, not left-liberals; conscious of being Jewish but not strictly observant. "Jewishness" was to her, like Alex and Nathan, simply part of the world she inhabited, the air she breathed, and also, she added, "took for granted."[138] When meeting other Jews in activist spaces in the city, she would relate to some, but others seemed indistinguishable from the "WASPs" she encountered; when hearing about a "Jewish caucus" at a feminist conference, she did not find herself curious: "I couldn't relate to it." Yet only upon arriving in rural Maine to find a swastika "smeared on her bedroom door in what looked like blood" and "swastikas and crosses spray painted on doors" did Kaye/Kantrowitz begin to question her earlier aloofness from Jewish community. Likening her resistance to seeking Jewish community to her "pre-feminist" resistance to seeking out the intentional community of women, she concluded "she needed Jews." Her encounter with antisemitism, unlike Roth's, did not leave her feeling even more isolated but rather in search of active community.

Beyond a vision of Jewish collectivity, Kaye/Kantrowitz also theorizes Jewish collective practice in its historical conjuncture. That is, the sight of swastikas on her house in rural Maine reminded her not only of her solitude away from Jewish community, but that the political conjuncture had radically shifted between the heyday of American liberalism in the 1960s and the rise of the New Right. "The liberalism I had for years seen as the real danger," she writes of her New Left activism, "was being superseded," and "the right was gaining power, with all of its Jew-hating, racist, sexist, homophobic capitalist thrust." That is, the rise of antisemitism in the 1980s is not something that happens to her particularly as a Jew—it is something that is part of a larger social formation that includes antisemitism—but she assumes solidarity to be the response to racism, rather than individual retreat. Indeed, Roth's embrace of Jewish diaspora is predicated on his embrace of the United States as a paragon of "tolerance" for Jews. While Roth's statement could certainly bear more scrutiny (did the Rosenbergs, for instance, find the US a beacon of tolerance?), it more importantly assumes that the measure of US "pluralism," as Roth phrased it, is its treatment or acceptance of Jews into normative whiteness. While Kaye/Kantrowitz does not deny ascription/conscription of Jews into social, economic, and political formations of whiteness, especially after World War II, her linkage of antisemitism to the rise of a New Right after the hegemony of fifty years of liberalism suggests a fundamental interconnection between antisemitism and other forms of politicized racism.

Thinking through her need for Jewish community not only as an individual subject, but as part of the historical time of politics, Kaye/Kantrowitz offers a political ontology radically different from Roth's. For Roth, Jewishness is something he simply experiences as an individual—and he often articulates his sense of Jewishness through the privatized memory of a family life in Newark that is also locked, lost to the past, with no translation or correlative for the present. Indeed, Roth's resentment against Israel is precisely that it does not allow for the liberal individualism Roth experiences as a successful writer in the United States: his "kitchen table" Jewishness is a family affair. For Kaye/Kantrowitz, Jewishness is relational, expressed only in community and in dialogue with both Jews and non-Jews. As Judith Butler summarizes in their reading of Emmanuel Levinas and Edward Said, at the heart of Jewish liberatory tradition, beginning with Moses, is both the relationship to the contingency of being Jewish (Moses becomes Jewish through his relationship to Jewish victimization) and more importantly, the relationship to an other, the "burden" of the "ethical relationship" in our "relationship with others."[139] As Kaye/Kantrowitz articulates, guilt and solitude are actually part of the dominant white Christian cultural formation against which her socialist politics militates:

> Let me say something which in this (christian) culture may come as a surprise: what is best in people is not self-abnegation. What is best in people is sturdy connection between respect for self and respect for the other: reaching in and out at the same time. If I am not for myself, who will be? If I am only for myself, what am I?"[140]

By closing her call for solidarity with Rabbi Hillel's famous injunction, Kaye/Kantrowitz conjoins Jewish collective practice with traditions of solidarity bound by Marxism, Black liberation, and labor traditions of activism in the US: not reducible to these traditions but also inextricable from them.

In Said's theorization of diaspora, he places a non-Jew and Egyptian who comes to lead the Jewish people from Egypt at the center of Jewish tradition and Jewish peoplehood. Moses's Jewishness is entirely relational: it emerges not out of introspection or genealogical data, but rather his choice to defend a Jewish man from a beating and his later adoption by Jews as their leader. Moses in turn comes to make Jews not only a fleeing mass, but a coherent people.[141] This dialectical formation, in which a non-Jew becomes Jewish through his decision to relate to the other, and in turn produces the very other he defends, is the creative site of diaspora that Kaye/Kantrowitz would bring into emergence: one that sees Jewish belonging as a relation to self and other, each of which brings the other into a fuller being. It is also the dialectical process of becoming, what Boyarin refers to as the site where "interaction can be grasped," a place of meeting and transformation, not fixity and stasis. Boyarin and Said's diaspora is radically ulterior to Roth's nation/individual binary in which the nation can only be opposed by retreating from its historical totality into a privatized self. And it is, of course, even more radically opposed to the Zionism that allows otherness only as an outside to be feared or dominated.

For Chutzpah and the Brooklyn Bridge Collective, Jewishness is equally defined by their relationship both to Jewish history and to non-Jews, to what Boyarin refers to as the site between genealogy and contingency. This double relation, between and among the powerful and powerless, is less the intermediary of the European Jewish ghetto than a site of gathering and dispersal, making and remaking. Chutzpah and BBC suggest, through their practices regarding political action in the US and their writings and advocacy in Israel and Palestine, that their politics and their concept of what Jewishness means are under constant revision and development as their engagement with Palestinians, African Americans, and other Jews—the historical conjuncture—opens and changes. While Chutzpah and BBC certainly articulated ideological coordinates—socialist, internationalist, antiracist, against antisemitism, for Jewish autonomy—the position they were required to take, politically and as Jews, transformed. As the leaders against the Nazis in Skokie or as one part of a coalition against Nazis in Marquette Park suggest, what is "Jewish politics" is relational and contingent, in dialogue with other communities, not something experienced in solitude. Likewise Chutzpah and BBC's politics changed in conversation with Palestinian resistance, and in response to the ideas of Israeli activists and the Israeli state. That many of the original Chutzpah Collective have abandoned the "two-state solution" for a post-Zionist "one state" is not for them ideological but rather a practical assessment of the changing relationship among all three: Jews, Israeli state, and Palestinians. Or if it is ideological, it is the ideology of socialist diasporism. Ironically, while the Jewish left such as it exists has come to absorb a position regarding Zionism closer to the New Left's than Chutzpah's original "two-stateism," it is the relational nature of Chutzpah and BBC, framed as part of Jewish identity, that is the true inheritance of these organizations. Jews have become anti-Zionists in organizations such as Jewish Voice for Peace or Jewish Solidarity Caucus *as Jews* first, in relationship with allies in the US and Palestine, rather than anti-Zionists who form such relationships later. For Roth, to be a citizen of the world is to leave one's collective Jewishness in a nostalgized Newark past or a perverse, reified Zionist future; for Chutzpah and Melanie Kaye/Kantrowitz, to be Jewish is to be a citizen of the world.

5

The Antinomies of Jewish Liberalism: Socialist Memory and the (Re) Emergence of Jewish Anti-Zionism

In the final moments of Tony Kushner's 1992 epic, *Angels in America*, Palestine makes a brief appearance. Louis Ironson, the play's queer Jewish voice for secular liberalism, pauses to assure his friends that his Hebrew prayer for healing will not have "Zionist implications."[1] Receiving a rare nod of approval from his critic on the left, Belize, Louis quickly changes course and adds, "We do recognize Israel's right to exist," before he and Belize digress from the blessing into an argument about the size and nature of a future Palestinian state. Belize, the voice for racial justice throughout the play, of course argues for a larger state and Louis a smaller one, before Belize undercuts Louis's hypocrisy in trying to have it both ways: denying "Zionist implications" while also forcing Belize to accept "Israel's right to exist." Louis says with no small amount of chutzpah that "no one cares more about Palestinian rights" than he does, and is met with Belize's comeback: Than the Palestinians? Louis, as both the voice of liberal orthodoxy and its supposed universalism, is caught here as he often is by Belize, confusing universal truths with his own (in this case Jewish) self-interest; that is, trying to have it two ways at once.

Prior, whose deteriorating condition from AIDS drives the narrative of the play, interrupts Louis and Belize to prophesize that they will survive. "We will be citizens." Abandoned by Louis when his HIV became symptomatic, Prior speaks, one could say, from the point of view of history's victims: someone who while not stateless is nonetheless the victim of a late twentieth-century holocaust. Louis's abandonment of Prior and his later attempt to return function very much as Louis's two conceptions of himself: at once someone who acts in the name of his own self-interest and privilege, and someone who lives in the memory of queer Jewish history and Jewish trauma. Louis, his Jewishness, and his queerness live on both sides of the liberal world, as its universal subject and its exception. While Prior's benediction refers to those infected with HIV, it is hard not to hear echoes of Louis and Belize's argument about Palestine, in which the majority of the population lack not only equal rights but any basic guarantee of citizenship status, and are subject to mass death. Louis, as a gay man, a white man, and a Jew, has more than one relationship to Prior's messianic message for the future, as he does with himself.

Perhaps, then, it makes perfect sense why Palestine and Zionism appear in Kushner's epic of the HIV/AIDs pandemic, that is, why, in perhaps the most famous work of Jewish literature in the last forty years, Palestine appears in the final moments. Of course, *Angels in America* is about far more than a pandemic: it poses the question of how to think about the end of history for people who lack basic rights, who live under the shadow of state-sponsored violence, whose humanity is under question. The play poses this question against the backdrop of world historical events—the imminent fall of the Soviet Union, the right-wing backlash of the Reagan era, the era of global warming—and in the particular context of American Jewish radical history. *Angels* is perhaps the only significant work of American Jewish literature to address both the Red Scare and the Communist Jewish Left as important sites of Jewish memory, and to connect them implicitly with contemporary crises, from the post–New Left backlash to the question of gay rights, and human rights more broadly. In other words, Kushner proposes it is precisely this memory of the Jewish left and the Red Scare that can provide one answer among many to both the AIDS pandemic and Palestine.

In many ways one could say Kushner's play summarizes a paradox: it is both the best of times and worst of times for the Jewish left. As historian Dov Waxman notes, the consensus over Israel that emerged after the 1967 Arab-Israeli War was short-lived. As of the Israeli assault on Gaza in 2014, nearly one-third of American Jews hold that Israel is an apartheid state, with one-quarter of American Jews accusing Israel of genocide against Palestinians; nine years later, in 2023, over one-third of American Jews considered Israel's assault on Gaza a "genocide," twice the number of other Americans.[2] According to Waxman, the so-called "golden age" of American Jewish identification with Israel ended with the Israeli invasion of Lebanon and several years later, the harsh crackdown on the First Intifada.[3] Some of the first widespread Jewish protests against Israel, organized by members of New Jewish Agenda (NJA), took place during Israel's invasion of Lebanon, marking the first time since the 1940s that open and widespread dissent by members of the liberal Jewish establishment—not just the left—was visible on the street and in the media.

Yet this newfound, or perhaps rediscovered, dissent over Israel happened in an otherwise odd conjuncture. While there has never *not* been an over-representation of American Jews on the US left, by the late 1980s the Jewish Marxist and socialist left was in a state of retreat. Daniel Bensaïd, writing in the 2000s, asks if the "historical sequence" that began with the "Great War and the Bolshevik Revolution" is now over, "if light from our extinct stars still travels on."[4] While SDS and the Chutzpah Collective would see themselves to some degree as breaks with the 1930s and 1940s Jewish Marxist left, there was perhaps far more continuity with the three generations of Jewish socialists than there was rupture. From Mike Gold to Bernardine Dohrn to David Gilbert to Myron Perlman, the idea of both a Jewish left and a socialist left, with revolutionary aims and agendas, shared a common vocabulary rooted in both anti-imperialism and Marxism. While this chapter will explore continuities from the socialist Jewish left to the many Jewish lefts of the present, it seems worthwhile to take some time to explore what appears to be a *liberal* rupture with Zionism, as ambivalent and incomplete as it may be.

As Waxman points out, Jewish support for Israel emerged at a time when Israel appeared not only to represent US imperial interests abroad, but to be molded on a liberal vision of American Jews themselves, at least if one did not look too closely. Ruled for decades by Labour governments, with a high rate of union density, gender equity, secularism, and freedom of expression, Israel appeared as if a borough of progressive NYC had been exported six thousand miles over the sea to the Mediterranean. While this vision had always been challenged by a multiethnic left, by the 1980s this veneer of liberalism had begun to wane considerably even for a Jewish liberal mainstream, not least because Israel was under far more scrutiny precisely because of the newfound primacy of American Jewish support. Not only did the 1982 invasion of Lebanon and harsh crackdown against the First Intifada shock American Jewish liberals, it prompted the first open, public street protests against Israeli policy, organized by a liberal Jewish organization. NJA, formed only a year earlier by an amalgamation of liberal Jewish professionals, intellectuals, rabbis, and post–New Left activists, organized a public letter printed in the *New York Times* and signed by forty rabbis. Nothing like it had been done before.

While it's become almost a cliché to note the normative liberalism of American Jewry, less has been said about the ways in which politics itself functions as a modality of ethnic and cultural belonging.[5] As sociologist Laurence Kotler-Berkowitz points out, "liberal politics" forms the "structural basis of cohesion for many Jews," particularly for Jews whose communal life is not oriented around daily religious observance.[6] In other words, liberal politics is not just something American Jews, especially "Reform and secular Jews," as Kotler-Berkowitz frames it, engage in to advance material interests, but an expression of Jewish communal life and belonging. Or, as one conservative writer dismissively put it, liberalism is the "civic religion" of American Jews.[7] Perhaps even more devastating than Israel's highly unpopular and controversial invasion of Lebanon, after which Israel could no longer even plausibly suggest it was the underdog acting in self-defense, was Israel's election of Menachem Begin's far-right Likud Party in 1977. The year that Waxman declares is the end of the formal Jewish American and Israeli alliance is simultaneously the year Israeli Jews elect a government that sounds more like Ronald Reagan than Bella Abzug. As much as any other single event, the election of a right-wing government to the Knesset forced a realization among American Jewish liberals that Israel was not a country "like us." The political landscape among American Jews and Israel "had completely changed."[8]

Yet as much as Waxman declares the honeymoon period between US Jewry and Israel over in terms of popular Jewish opinion, the institutional Jewish world experienced at the same time, perhaps in reaction, a hardening of Zionism consolidation. As scholar Shaul Magid writes in his biography of right-wing Zionist ultranationalist Meir Kahane, many positions that Kahane staked out on the extreme edge of Jewish nationalism in the 1960s, such as the annexation of the West Bank, the rise of an explicitly racist Jewish Supremacist movement in Israel, and most saliently in the context of US politics, the definition of antisemitism as primarily anti-Zionism, are now adopted as orthodoxy among mainstream, once-liberal Jewish institutions such as the Anti-Defamation League (ADL), Hillel, and the Jewish Federation, to say nothing of explicitly Zionist organizations such as America-Israel PAC and the Jewish United Fund.[9] Even as the consensus of support among US Jews for Israel can no longer be assumed, the institutional consensus among Jewish elite institutions has grown even more bounded and narrow. One visible sign of this rift has been the explicit attempt by Jewish Zionists to demonize Jews critical of Israel, from the Chicago Reform rabbi who declared anti-Zionist Jews "Jews in name only" and the "primary threat" to Israel, to the Zionist magazine *Tablet* that declared anti-Zionist Jews "un-Jews," to another op-ed in the same magazine that declared that Jewish liberalism is engaged in a "great replacement"—replacing Jews in the US with people of color, and Jews in Israel with Palestinians.[10] While these are extreme positions, they point to a growing anxiety among leading Jewish religious, cultural, and political institutions that the Jewish masses in the US are "detaching," in Antonio Gramsci's words, from the institutions that once guided them.[11] While one response might be to open the doors wider, the increasingly right-wing Jewish institutional world is slamming them shut.

In this sense, *Angels in America* captures the contradictions of this conjuncture, as it appears the American Jewish left is in retreat while the right is ascendant, at the very same time its decades-long critique of Israel is slowly moving, if not into the mainstream, at least into the language of American Jewish liberalism. In some ways, *Angels* appears as a kind of homage and farewell to the mid-century Jewish American left. Roy Cohn, its executioner, lies dying with AIDs, and Ethel Rosenberg is called from the grave to sing him, in his last moments, a Yiddish love song. While Ethel ostensibly emerges to gloat over Cohn's death, her final act makes it seem as if they share more of a world with one another—a kind of cultural secret—than Roy does with Louis or the presumed reader/viewer of the play. Cohn is more, however, than simply an unlucky villain. As critic Emily King suggests, we should read Kushner's Cohn as a kind of trickster figure, volatile, performative, aware of the ways in which identity can mobilized, and erased, to achieve power, whether he's cynically denying he is a "homosexual" (while admitting he sleeps with men) to preserve his place in a heteropatriarchal pecking order, or tricking, in his last minutes, the ghost of Ethel Rosenberg into singing him a Yiddish lullaby.[12] Aside from the elderly rabbi who eulogizes Louis Ironson's grandmother, Cohn is the only figure who speaks Yiddish, eats Jewish food, and articulates himself without qualm as a Jewish victim, under threat of disbarment by country-club lawyers who see him as a "filthy little Jewish troll."[13] While King sees Kushner's Cohn as a trickster, he is also cast as the play's Shylock (and tellingly, Al Pacino played both Kushner's Cohn and, a decade later, Shylock on film): not only the last closeted gay man who articulates clearly the politics of the closet, but the last Jew, who takes Ethel Rosenberg to the grave with him.

The invocation of Ethel Rosenberg's ghost is doubled not only by Cohn's long, kvetching goodbye, but by the solitary soliloquy of Aleksii Antedilluvianovich Prelapsarianov, "the World's Oldest Bolshevik." His name and patronymic, puns on the time before the fall, link him to the angels that visit Prior and beg him to join them in their attempt to stop the world and end the progress that has brought modernity but also a deadly disease. Now "old and totally blind," he poses the question, "Can we Change? In time? And we all desire that Change will come."[14] Demanding that change cannot come without a "beautiful theory," he poses that the neoliberal capitalism already on its way under Perestroika—"Market Incentives? American Cheeseburgers?"—is the only alternative to Soviet Communism. "If the snake sheds his skin before a new skin is ready, naked will he be in the world . . . WE MUST NOT move ahead!"[15] Representing the forces of Communism as old, blind, and wishing, like the embodied angels that visit Prior, for a return to a time before "the fall," the figure of Prelapsarianov, like the figures of Cohn and Ethel, suggests a ghost haunting the present, frightened of the world to come. If Belize's vision of heaven, in which "race, taste and history" are "overcome" in "gender confusion . . . racial impurity [and] voting booths," does not include Cohn, one wonders if it also includes old Bolsheviks, Yiddish-speaking Jews, and the memory of Ethel Rosenberg.[16]

While Belize and Louis are posed as opposites, Black/white, femme/cis, spiritual/secular, their visions of a utopian future are in some ways quite similar. Belize mocks Louis's vision of a liberal end of history in which America, with "no spiritual, no racial past," will be experienced as a pluralist democracy and ever-expanding horizon of democratic participation, the "shifting downwards and outwards of political power to the people."[17] Even as Belize mocks Louis's vision as both racist and blind, his own vision of a San Francisco in ruins, with "race, taste and history" finally overcome in a kaleidoscope of "racial impurity and gender confusion," offers Louis's universal democracy, only in feather boas and sequins.[18] While Belize's vision of "heaven" is expressed through the negation of Roy Cohn, implying a kind of conflict with both racial and political enemies, the overcoming of history through Cohn's death and the blind Prelapsarianov bemoaning the end of the Soviet Union imply a future in which a universal subject, with "history finally overcome," is a vision the two frenemies share. Their final bickering over the shape of a future Palestine exists at the level of details; as Louis narrates a hope for democracy spreading over the former Soviet Union, there is a sense that the last apartheid state, Israel, will also blossom into a democracy. Prior turns down the angel and the angel of history, suggesting that there will be neither a revolutionary final showdown, nor what Benjamin described as an "emergency brake" preventing a final calamity.

Yet for a play that seems to embrace a kind of liberal end of history, everyone included—even a Mormon mother—it cannot quite extricate itself from the very history its characters want to distance themselves from. While he is mocked by Belize for his ambivalent liberalism and castigated by his ailing ex-boyfriend, Prior, Louis redeems himself by rejecting his new right-wing and very goyish lover, Joe. Joe, who works as a chief clerk for a reactionary judge and is a protégé of Roy Cohn, seems to find no contradiction between the right-wing, even homophobic decisions he authors for his employer and the discovery of his own queer sexuality. When Louis confronts Joe after learning about Joe's relationship with Cohn, Louis uses a quote from the HUAC army hearings: "At long last, have you no decency?" When it is clear Joe does not know the quote, Louis castigates him for the reactionary decisions he authored, denying gay army veterans their benefits and narrowing the Clean Air and Water Acts. Further, when Belize asks Louis to recite Kaddish over Cohn's dead body, Louis's objection rests not only on his "secular upbringing" but his "New Deal Pinko Parents in Schenectady" for whom Cohn is the figurative if not literal embodiment of evil.[19] In other words, it is precisely Louis's memory of not only his left-wing parents, but the anti-Communism of the Red Scare, that allows him to break with Joe and return, at least in a gesture of friendship and camaraderie, to Prior. Indeed, though this is a play about the end of history and the "approaching millennium," it is haunted with ghosts. The play, like Bensaïd's Marrano, is as peopled with specters—of Jewish radicals, of Jewish persecutors, of history that literally stalks characters in their sleep, or their nightmares—as it is with real live people.

Louis among all characters seems to believe in American history as a straight line of progress, the "shifting downwards and outwards of political power to the people" yet is filled with continual ambivalence not only toward his boyfriend's illness, but to questions of human rights and Jewish assimilation: the figure of Louis is more a question mark about the end of history than an answer. The angels in America are also the angels of history—posing implicitly that after the left, what is left? Are we entering a movement of universal human rights, as Prior suggests, in which we are "all citizens" and Palestinians will be gradually enfolded into this universal embrace? In which, along with queer men with HIV, the assimilation of Jews, and the end of racism, we will all be one? Or is it a confusing empty space of history, a continual tide of wracked ambivalence and false starts, with the angel of history watching the wreckage pile up at her feet and flung into an uncertain future? To what extent does Zionism outlive history? Or is it perhaps the new axis or fault line over which global conflicts will articulate themselves?

Despite a consensus among Jewish studies scholars that the history of Jewish socialism and the Jewish left is but "nostalgia" and "long over," it seems it is precisely the memory of the left that saves Louis and, perhaps by extension, a kind of Jewish liberalism.[20] In one sense Louis is a classic Jewish liberal, both in his distance from his Yiddish-speaking past as well as his utopian ideas about the inexorable forward motion of history toward a more perfected democracy. Yet Louis's liberalism is haunted, one could say, with what Bensaïd and Jacques Derrida refer to as a "spectre" or "hauntology" of radical history.[21] It is not for nothing that Belize refers to him as a young Stalin, or that he mocks himself by noting that the "fucked up grandchildren" of his immigrant foreparents now live in the same neighborhood, downwardly mobile.[22] "This is progress?" he says in a fake Yiddish accent to Joe, both ironizing his own life and also bringing the upwardly mobile assimilation narrative into clear question.

Joe, unaware of any of his history, let alone its irony, only comments that Louis's apartment is "dirty." It is precisely this dirt, one could say, that Louis is stained by, that creates limits on his ability to join with a right-wing lover, or to abandon his sick ex-lover and his Black drag queen best friend. Louis has been dragged by history back into old solidarities. Louis is not a liberal, as Belize reminds him, he is "ambivalent": at once white, at once Jewish, at once queer, at once passing, at once conservative, at once radical. And what, Kushner seems to ask, could be more Jewish that that?

A New Jewish Diaspora, but Where?

One expression of this current conjuncture has been a revival of the idea of "diasporism" both as a term and an organizing concept. The expression of the diaspora as against a Jewish nation in mandate Palestine is not new; indeed, it has been central to Jewish anti-Zionism on the left since the early twentieth century. Yet the emergence of the term as *the* articulation of a new anti-Zionism is an expression of this left memory, and also has to be seen as a kind of rupture with it. That is, even while diasporism has been evoked by Jewish intellectuals from Mike Gold to Walter Benjamin to the Chutzpah Collective of the 1970s, it has seldom been the primary way Jewish leftists have identified their socialist or Marxist commitments. In 2018, a *Jewish Currents* editorial captured the recent wave of enthusiasm around the term, and articulated its uneven contemporary significations. The history of *Jewish Currents* itself is a kind of stand-in for the historical ambivalence around the Jewish left. Founded as *Jewish Life* at the height of American Jewish Marxism in late 1946 by the Communist-affiliated *Morgen Freiheit* association, the magazine broke not only with its anti-Zionist position in the late 1940s, but eventually with the Communist Party over the Soviet Union's increasingly critical stance toward Israel. Taking the name *Jewish Currents*, the magazine remained on the fringes of the Jewish left, representing a Marxist Zionism even as it was on the decline globally as well as in Israel. Relaunched in 2018 with a new editorial staff of Jewish millennials and a glossy cover, the rebooted *Currents* broke with both its earlier Marxism *and* its Zionism. Replacing both with the concept of "diasporism," a 2018 editorial penned by publisher Jacob Plitman announced the arrival of the new *Currents* and itself became a marker for a new articulation of Jewish social movements in the Trump era.

Plitman notes the small explosion of new Jewish organizing and cultural expression as both Trump and the Israeli right put antisemitism and Zionism under an equal if dialectically entwined spotlight.[23] The editorial lists protests against Trump's Muslim ban spearheaded by longstanding Jewish progressive organizations such as Jews for Racial and Economic Justice (JFREJ) and Bend the Arc (BtA), the Jewish presence in the then rapidly growing Democratic Socialists of America, newly organized Sephardi/Mizrahi and Jews of color caucuses, and other newly launched progressive Jewish publications such as *Protocols*. Not mentioned by Plitman, but certainly evoked, were other cultural productions signifying on the term "diaspora," including Judith Butler's groundbreaking 2012 intellectual history of Jewish diasporist thought from Walter Benjamin, Hannah Arendt, and Emmanuel Levinas to the popularity of anti- and non-Zionist Yiddishkeit musicians such as the *Klezmatics* and Daniel Kahn, who himself wrote an important piece of diasporic theorizing, "Yiddish Song Smuggling."[24] Rising non-Zionist Jewish youth movements from IfNotNow to NeverAgainAction aimed to take Jewish activism from an inwardly focused nationalism to a broad politics of solidarity: their signification on key touchstones of modern Jewish history, from the Holocaust to Rabbi Hillel's famous ethical maxim, are contestations with nationalists who would use their legacies to defend Zionism.

Yet it is interesting to note that Plitman articulates diasporism as a *break* with a Jewish past, as much as it is continuity. Telling his own story as a collective narrative for Jewish millennials, Plitman begins the call for a new "diasporism" with a story many observant Jews might find familiar: he attended Jewish summer camps, put money in a tzedakah box for Israel, attended a Zionist synagogue, and lived entirely inside a Jewish world both insulated from the left and from any criticism of Israel. What awakens Plitman to the harms and hazards of Zionism has little to do with his own contact with US social movements or a memory of the Jewish left, however. Rather, Plitman experiences its limits as immanent within Zionism itself: "What the symbols and experiences of Jewish nationalism meant and still mean to millions of Palestinians living under occupation."

While the editorial evokes earlier 1960s Zionist skeptics such as Leonard Cohen, it isn't until the end that Plitman draws on a sense of

Jewish radical history. The single left-wing Jewish activist Plitman cites as a precursor to the present moment is JFREJ's Melanie Kaye/Kantrowitz, whom he credits with the coining of "diasporism." While, as a veteran of the Jewish New Left, Kaye/Kantrowitz did much in the 1980s and 1990s to re-theorize diasporism, the term did not of course begin with her, even as she was very much formed by and helped to form the bridge between the 1960s New Left and progressive Jewish activism today. One gets a sense that for Plitman the diaspora is a space of unlearning two nationalisms, American and Israeli, as much as it is reemerging in an unbroken continuity of a Jewish left that stretches back at least 150 years.

Of course, one can (and, I would argue, should) draw a line of continuity between "the emerging diasporism" and earlier Jewish left(s). While Plitman does evoke Kaye/Kantrowitz, her own development arose in the ferment of the New Left and Jewish socialist activism of the late 1960s and 1970s, such as I mention in previous chapters: Jewish socialist collectives Chutzpah and Brooklyn Bridge, both with widely distributed magazines by the same name, often promoted diasporic radical thinking, often opposed to the centrality of Zionism in Jewish life both at the time and as a connection to earlier global socialist politics. Kaye/Kantrowitz's own essay, in which she elaborates on a de-territorialized, non-nationalist yet Jewish-identified politics of solidarity, appears in a post–New Left Jewish feminist anthology, *The Tribe of Dina*, edited by Kaye/Kantrowitz and the poet and Yiddish translator Irena Klepfisz. And of course, if one delves into the early postwar archive of the magazine for which Plitman was publisher, *Jewish Life*, "diaspora" was evoked not only against Zionism but against other forms of right-wing nationalism, toward an internationalist working-class radicalism.

This is not to suggest Plitman's editorial wasn't itself an important document in a growing movement away from Zionism among Jewish progressives: indeed, it put a name on a diffuse yet vital structure of feeling among American Jewish progressives. But it is nonetheless necessary to mention that "diasporism" points both literally and figuratively to a space in between the Jewish left of the past twentieth century that called for a "diasporic Jewish socialism," and the diaspora evoked by Zionists, a place of golus or exile, a future by which, as through a time machine, one arrives in a Jewish past. Plitman's construction of two diasporas, the first a "diasporism marked by wandering: a permanent wrestling with uncertainty and anger" and the other a faint echo of a Jewish radical past that must be sought in books (as he suggests he encountered Kaye/Kantrowitz's use of the term), indicates much like Kushner's *Angels* a Jewish progressivism that is at once at the liberal end of history and at the Jewish radical end of liberalism: it is made both of memory and forgetting. This diasporism, as it is articulated here, like Kushner's Louis, exists between increasing anti- and non-Zionism among American secular Jews and the rise of a Zionist right, between the divorce from Jewish nationalism and a simultaneous divorce from a formal Jewish left, between the non-space of the historical present and a politics of radical memory: it is both and neither.

That *Jewish Currents* would, a mere three years later, castigate many of the same organizations including JFREJ and BtA for the "solipsism" of focusing too much on antisemitism suggests how ambivalent and divisive the term "diasporism" can be, even among anti-Zionist Jews. Taking aim at a coalition of Jewish organizations including Jews Against White Nationalism (JAWN), which included both JFREJ and BtA, the *Currents* editorial board charged that this kind of focus on far-right antisemitism was "navel gazing" and closes down real possibilities for solidarity, especially with communities facing racial and national oppression.[25] That *Currents* could celebrate Jewish-centric left-wing organizing in solidarity with other organizations on the left, and condemn it only a few years later, poses a large question regarding what we mean by a "diasporic" politics of "hereness" or *doikayt*. Is targeting the rise of antisemitism, even if in the name of defending Black politicians such as Raphael Warnock or Ilhan Omar, an act of solidarity, or is it the narcissistic self-regard of a community that insists on making its own issues central? Is white nationalism even primarily about antisemitism, or is such a focus merely centered due to the class and/or racial privilege of white Jews? Should the old/new diasporic politics be a politics of solidarity *only*? That is, should Ashkenazi Jews with their relative privilege deploy their Jewishness only as other white people, against racism? To what extent can Jewish issues, Jewish perspectives, and Jewish history exist at the forefront? How much should *doikayt* focus on Palestine solidarity, even if, by definition, Palestine is not "here" but "there," and the fiction of Zion's *hereness* is one of the terrible conceits of Israeli nationalism? And what does it mean, after all, to be rooted "here" when here, the United States, is itself a settler-colonial enterprise in which the vast majority of

American Jews are, belatedly perhaps, still beneficiaries to the general slaughter?

I bring these questions up not to abandon the term, but to tease out the many trajectories of Jewish anti-Zionism in the current moment, all trading in one way or another in the idea of an "emergent diasporism." Much like the tension a generation earlier between the cosmopolitanism of Philip Roth and the diasporic solidarity and collectivity of Melanie Kaye/Kantrowitz, so too this generation implicitly or explicitly wrestles with the term. One way to think of contemporary embraces of a diasporic anti- (or at least non-) Zionism would be to pose them as either a break with the past, or a continuity with it. Both frames have their antinomies: whereas one might see a continuity with generations of Jewish socialism, the 2021 *Currents* "Responsa" sees that continuity as one of Jewish inwardness and insularity. Where one might see a break with Zionism into something new, of course, one has to ask what it means to jettison, or not be aware of, how Jews have wrestled with these questions for over a century, if not far longer. Further questions emerge as well, such as the role of class and race both within Jewish communities and the larger social context in which Jews organize and exist, and to what extent anti-Zionist politics take leadership from Palestinian communities in the Levant, or how much anti-Zionism is primarily a relationship among Jews and other marginalized communities in the US and the left, or among Jews themselves?

As Daniel Boyarin notes in his 2023 manifesto, *The No-State Solution*, current Jewish diasporas no longer share common vernacular languages to create global if overlapping communities, as the number of Yiddish, Ladino, and Judeo-Arabic speakers has declined in years due to the Holocaust, the Hebrew-language Israeli state, and Jewish assimilation in the Americas, Europe, and the former Soviet Union.[26] This has led anti-Zionists such as Shlomo Sand to argue that outside of the insular ultra-Orthodox and those sharing an Israeli national culture, secular Jewish "peoplehood" is less a lived reality than a political construct designed to bind assimilated Jewish communities to Israel, and little more. While Boyarin is equally skeptical of "peoplehood" for both its natal imaginary as well as its inability to be clearly defined, he argues nonetheless that shared Jewish "narrative" or memory binds Jews of many races and cultures into a single if discontinuous, de-territorialized, and polyglot "diasporic nation."[27] Contra Sand, nations are not "empirical" facts that can be counted in numbers of synagogue attendees or Yiddish speakers; they are what Benedict Anderson refers to as "imagined communities" located in texts, stories, and shared frameworks of understanding.

That is, if nationhood is not defined by blood and soil, but rather a shared sense of narrative time, then diasporic Jews share common textual narratives such as Exodus and Maccabees, as well as overlapping if not identical experiences: antisemitism, the Holocaust, immigration, exile, and the simple fact of living as a religious if not cultural or ethnic minority. While Boyarin does not discount religious ritual as a binding framework for all Jews, he notes that most Jews, especially in Russia, Europe, and the Americas, are quite secular. Memory, as a kind of practice, is elevated to what Michael Löwy refers to as an "elective affinity" that unites Jews as a common if dispersed nation, a "mutual articulation" between narrative and the collectives it forms.[28] Boyarin's privileging of narrative over language or ritual then poses, of course, the necessary follow-up questions: Which narratives, and what readers/tellers of these narratives? Kushner's *Angels in America*, with its fragmented narrative frameworks and memories, from the "old" Jewish left, the Bolshevik Revolution, Jewish liberalism, Yiddishkeit, and immigration, is the structural homology for Louis's own fragmented and contradictory sense of himself: his "liberalism" is precisely the space in between competing narratives.

One has to ask, is "diasporic Jewishness" just a nicer way of saying "anti-Zionism"? And if it is, then why bother demarcating its *Jewishness* per se? Or perhaps "diasporism" is merely a way of announcing one's *Americanness*, that is, the extent to which the US—at least New York and Los Angeles—has become perhaps an alternative Zionism, a liberal cosmopolitanism? If so, then how is it really a diaspora at all, except in the way that all Americans, save the indigenous, are living out diasporic lives? Surely one wouldn't say we are in diaspora from Israel, for to say that would be to posit Israel as "home"; and one could not with any real conviction say that we are still "in diaspora" from the ancient Judean kingdoms destroyed by the Romans. Perhaps one way diasporism could mean something would be to say Jews have no home—not even the United States—in the sense that internationalists believe workers have no country, and also, insofar as Jews see themselves as Jewish first, not belonging to a state, even or especially a Jewish colonial state. But this would require a renewed commitment to Marxist internationalism and/

or a recommitment to a diasporic nationalism such as Boyarin outlines, a diaspora of *memory*.

Cul-de-sacs of History: The Empty Diasporas of the American Jewish Anti-Zionist Novel

If we take Jewish storytelling seriously, then one of the more notable developments, culturally and politically, has been the vast number of contemporary Jewish American novels critical of Zionism. Not since the 1930s could one find a broad Jewish literature as skeptical of settlement in mandate Palestine or of Zionism, or find so few novelists or comedians supportive of the project. Indeed as one Israeli critic put it, there is a "preoccupation of twenty-first-century Jewish American novelists with Israel and its destruction."[29] The critic continues that the "destruction is not . . . unfortunate" but rather "has given writers an opportunity to rethink their sense of self as Jewish individuals . . . over the ruins."[30] Unlike Mike Gold's 1930 *Jews without Money*, or even Kushner's *Angels in America*, however, the ideological commitments of these novels, including Jonathan Safran Foer's *Here I Am*, Nicole Krauss's *Great House* and *Forest Dark*, Joshua Cohen's *The Netanyahus* and *The Moving Kings*, Nathan Englander's *Dinner at the Center of the Earth*, Tova Reich's *The Jewish War*, Adam Mansbach's *The Golem of Brooklyn*, Michael Chabon's *Yiddish Policemen's Union*, and Jess Row's *The New Earth* remain less than clear. While none celebrate Israel and many seem to even desire its destruction, the diaspora is not framed as a vital space of radical continuity or solidarity, Indeed, many of these texts focus on metaphors of divorce, family separation and breakdown, personal loss and conflict, and the empty space between two nationalisms that resolves in a kind of private redemption or, more likely, private dissolution. While political labels conceal as much as they reveal, these novels perform a kind desertion of the private liberal subject from both the grand sweep of history that Zionism performed a reactionary side of, and—like Philip Roth—the saving grace of intellectual cosmopolitanism. Like Kushner's Louis, these novels contain radical ambivalence, a crisis or antinomy of liberalism; but unlike Louis's crack-up these cannot be resolved by their own generic means.

The last American Jewish novel to win the Pulitzer Prize, Joshua

Cohen's 2021 *The Netanyahus*—one of only thirteen other Jewish novels in a hundred years to win such a distinction—pits the Jewish diaspora against Zionism as an irreparable antagonism. It is perhaps as surprising a development historically as the unspoken premise of the text: one so elemental that it almost eludes saying, that Zionism is not greeted, at least by the American Jewish narrator, as a messianic savior let alone a solution to any of his problems. Rather, Zionism—in the fictionalized figure of Benzion Netanyahu, Prime Minister Benjamin Netanyahu's father—literally comes as an unwelcome guest to the very assimilated life and home of a Jewish historian at an elite, WASPy private college in upstate New York. Narrating Zionism as something foreign, in an era still in the blond embrace of Leon Uris and Paul Newman's *Exodus*, would be shocking enough, but to suggest Zionism is something only slightly short of a home invasion orchestrated by one's WASPy employer is yet another level of antagonism. While it is clear that we are not to take the American narrator as entirely reliable, let alone likeable, Zionism's *otherness*, its extradiegetic noise, its complete alienness to the material life and realities of American Jews, is a premise as counterintuitive as it is exceptionally provocative.

Narrated from the perspective of an upwardly mobile son of immigrant Bronx Jews who makes it all the way, in the 1940s, to the leafy and rustic enclaves of the elite private college, the novel casts Reuben Blum as a parody of assimilation. He begins his narration by informing the reader he is *an* historian, not *a* historian, and the rest of his painfully performative tale constructs such distinctions as a means to announce he has arrived to the Ivy Leagues from insular, provincial working-class Yiddishkeit beginnings. Not only is Blum the only Jewish faculty member, from his telling, he and his family are the only Jewish people in the small upstate college town. Yet Blum sees himself, and perhaps all of Jewish America, as beneficiary of not only American upward mobility but all of American history. American history "brightened with Enlightenment and steadily improved" until the past was "merely a process by which the present was attained," a "democracy" that "could only grow."[31] Jewish history, as he received it in his cheder, was "closed," lost in "mitzrayim," exiled in a dangerous and unchanging diaspora. Even Blum's body, as he compares it to his father's, was "taller ... wider" from the "benefit of American abundance."[32] Growing with America, America had "grown [his] bones": an observation Blum makes while defending his daughter's right to nose job. America can make noses disappear and the sons of Bronx grocers grow tall and strong. While Blum studies history, his own Jewish past is "useless." In America "interstates get paved, urinals are desegregated," Jews can grow hale and tall.[33]

Blum does not argue antisemitism no longer exists in his American utopia of progress. Indeed, the novel, set in rural upstate New York, is rife with both micro- and macro-aggressions, from Blum's car mechanic checking his head for horns, to his department chair cracking circumcision jokes in his office, to the country club "losing" his application, to strangers muttering ethnic slurs under their breath in his presence. The novel's narrative arc is set in motion by perhaps the most typical microaggression that still occurs, usually among faculty of color, at colleges and in boardrooms: the faculty ask Blum to sit on the hiring committee for an Israeli academic applying for a position—to ensure, as he is told by his chair, that Benzion would "fit in."[34]

While one could read the antisemitism Blum faces with narrative irony, Blum is not naive. Blum's proposition about America is far simpler and far more complex than liberal assumptions of progress would make it out to be. In perhaps the most grotesque of the humiliations Blum faces at the hands of his department, he is asked to dress as Santa at the annual Christmas party, with the utilitarian explanation that "it'll free up the people who actually celebrate the holiday to enjoy themselves." Upon this humiliation, Blum reflects:

> Mrs. Morse turned and showed me a sweetness that would've hidden me from the Klan, that would've hidden my whole family and never turned us over, on the condition that I annually donned the costume and slide down her chimney bearing gifts.[35]

Unlike his rabbis for whom history does not change, and unlike Netanyahu who argues antisemitism is eternal and unchanging, Blum hedges toward a proposition: "They will not murder me in this country" if, of course, he wears a Santa suit every year and pretends to enjoy it. For Blum this is not despair, but rather a social contract: fit in and, unlike Germany, America will really protect you, precisely because it is wedded to an Enlightenment future, and not the past of blood and soil. Unlike the students of color at his liberal arts college who Blum believes are too focused on "grievance," he reflects that to "assimilate and not differentiate" is a "reliable protection." Progress in the US was real.

For Benzion Netanyahu, there is no such progress, even so circumscribed. History, like Blum's cheder, is circular, yet the circularity of Jewish history points not to eternal exile but rather to a singular teleological trajectory. Reading Netanyahu's work "like a convert forcibly returned to the faith [he'd] left," Blum reflects on the "dogma" and "mysticism" of Netanyahu's history of European antisemitism:

> There comes a point in nearly every text he produces where it emerges that the true phenomenon under discussion is not anti-Semitism in Early Medieval Lorraine ... but rather anti-Semitism in ... Nazi Germany; and suddenly a description of how a specific tragedy affected a specific diaspora becomes a diatribe about the general tragedy of the Jewish Diaspora, and how that Diaspora must end—as if history should not describe, but prescribe—in the founding of the state of Israel.[36]

Needless to say, Netanyahu has little but contempt for the assimilated and successful Blum, who has his own theory of the diaspora and his place in it. "The history department must decide upon a Jew and so enlists another Jew to help," Netanyahu lectures Blum. "Their own Jew ... a court Jew." Netanyahu goes even further to suggest that while he would "die for Blum" in a war, it is the Blums of the world who "decide which one thousand" must go to the gas chambers, "the Elder of the Judenrat."[37] Netanyahu elaborates, adding that his differences with Blum are not personal, but extend to the entire Jewish diaspora, "your democracy, your inclusivity, your chances for survival, none at all." For Netanyahu, it is Zionism or cultural, spiritual if not literal death.[38]

Despite the fact that (or perhaps because) Benzion Netanyahu is not hired by Corbin, the novel ends with a distinct sense that he has won the argument, not through logic but by the brute force of his own victimization. When the Netanyahus through mishap, antisemitism, their own rudeness, or some combination of all three find themselves without a hotel room, they move into Blum's house without asking. Tzila Netanyahu, wife of Benzion, helps herself to Edith Blum's clothes and earrings. Most memorably of all, and most commented upon, the Netanyahus' "eldest boy," Jonathan, is caught in flagrante delicto with Blum's daughter Judy, "his headstrong rigid penis toggling with his stride ... pointing rudely out to spear" Blum. That the Netanyahus take over Blum's house and manage to seduce Blum's daughter suggests, if not a direct likeness to Zionism, at least an analogy, Jonathan's penis-as-weapon only underscoring such point. While Blum at one point compares entering the job-interview process to being a "lone gunslinger" of the Old West fighting off "desperadoes," it is clear that Netanyahu—happy to claim the imperial mantle of Zionism—sees Blum as one of the unfortunate casualties of conquest, perhaps even its target.[39] That he is nearly impaled on the young Zionist's hard-on seems, from the point of view of Zionism, a fitting and humiliating fate for a hen-pecked, apologizing, diasporic Jew.

Blum's response, much like his response to his department chair, is passive. He does not deny that he is a "court Jew," yet responds that his lack of personal agency is the experience of being a "father in a family of women," suggesting that it is the family structure of the diaspora Jew, not the larger social world, that is the source of his passivity. And while, as Daniel Boyarin has pointed out, there is a long history of diaspora Jews celebrating both passivity and feminization as positive markers of sexual desirability and scholarly insight, it is clear that Reuben's wife, Edith, finds him neither desirable nor insightful.[40] After he dresses up as Santa she refuses to sleep with him, and spends much of the novel angrily drinking martinis and rejecting Blum's advances and pleas for affection. As Blum himself describes, he cannot "make a fire" on cold winter nights, and if the metaphor were not clear, the "fire had the same problem as the family: a lack of oxygen."[41] Benzion, on the other hand, is so overheated he repeatedly turns down offers of galoshes and raincoats in the wet snow of upstate New York's winter.

As *Jewish Currents* editorialized on *The Netanyahus'* receipt of the Pulitzer Prize, the novel was far too "beholden to fixed archetypes" of the submissive diaspora Jewish man and aggressive Israeli to "respond to contemporary Jewish life."[42] Nathan Goldman argues that such tropes are "exhausted" and attempts at mocking the phallic antics of the Netanyahus—Jonathan's spear-like penis—ironically mark them as merely the sex-obsessed diaspora Jews of Roth's fiction: the circle comes to rest. While Goldman is clearly correct that the novel evokes the Rothian tropes of neurotic diaspora Jew and virile Israeli, one gets the sense that Goldman doth protest too much: How can we separate Cohen's evocation of the diaspora from *Jewish Currents*'? I would suggest that for Cohen, the deadness of the diaspora as narrated by Blum is the point: it is precisely his desire to assimilate and succeed at all costs, the novel suggests, that grants the Netanyahus and by extension Zionism its phallic power over American Jewish life. Unlike Roth, with his nostalgic evocation of Weequahic in the 1940s or his cocky self-possession in *The Counterlife*, Blum sees the diaspora as devoid of life and memory: his reactionary politics are seen as alternatively pathetic and anachronistic, yet nothing has come into their place. Cohen is done with Israel, it would seem: as he explains in the afterword, Revisionist Zionism of the kind Benzion preached, with its "walls . . . settlements . . . normalization of occupation and state violence," has triumphed, as carried out by Benzion's son, Bibi.[43] But he is also done with Jewish America. By the end of the novel, nose jobs—and Israel—have won.[44]

Cohen is far from the only American Jewish writer to announce the spiritual and cultural death of world Jewry at the hands of both New York City and Jerusalem. Jess Row's 2023 novel, *The New Earth*, moves Cohen's afterword in *Netanyahus* to the opening epigraph, explicitly dedicating the book to a "just, free and peaceful future for Palestine and Israel."[45] Following the benediction with quotes from Palestinian poet Mahmoud Darwish and Subcomandante Marcos, Row draws links between the Palestinian struggle for freedom and the indigenous struggle for land, much as Cohen does between eviction in New York and the demolition of homes in Palestine. From this opening, it should be of little surprise that *New Earth*, perhaps alone among American Jewish fiction, centers on an American Jewish peace activist who travels to the West Bank in an act of solidarity. If the novel were just the story of Bering Wilcox, a twentysomething American Jew from an upper-middle-class background, and the Israeli IDF sniper who kills her, it might be a more radical reversal of Cohen's *Netanyahus*, pairing an idealistic young American Jew with a cynical, unworldly, and cold-blooded Israeli killer.

In a heteroglossic narrative, in which each character in an ensemble of nearly a dozen speaks through their own voice, we hear Bering as a headstrong young radical, ruthlessly (if painstakingly) examining her whiteness, exploring her sexuality, trying to understand how the Jewish world, let alone the rest of the world, could allow such an atrocity as the ethnic cleansing and occupation of Palestine to continue. The Israeli, Yoav, is by contrast so matter-of-fact as to be almost robotic—it was a war, "[Bering] was not the first person I have killed"—and demands that no one tell him "it's more complicated."[46] He is a father by the time of the novel (set some years after the events), runs a car-rental agency in Ashkelon, and opines that he is "no longer involved." The story of her murder, to Yoav, is no more complicated than another day on the battlefield: in gastronomic distress from the terrible food on base, he sees what he thinks, and what his commander thinks, are two Palestinian snipers waiting to drop on the IDF, mistaking Bering and her host Heba's run to the bushes to urinate for a sneak attack. In perhaps the only Jewish joke in a novel devoid of humor, Bering and Yoav are united in only one thing: trying not to soil their pants on that given day.

Yet Bering barely appears in the text: her presence is narrated only through a few emailed letters to her family. Indeed, the novel centers not on Bering's trip to the West Bank, but the way her murder refracts and shatters her family. As Winter, the oldest, puts it: "This family has never had a coherent story to tell itself."[47] The family, "lox-and-herring-and-Sunday-Times" Jews with expensive educations and elaborate careers, first disintegrates when Sandy and Naomi, Bering's parents, separate; the younger children are revealed as committing self-inflicted wounds (including incest with one another), and both end up literally maimed as a result of their attempts to flee to the farthest colonial margins, Tibet and Palestine respectively. Winter is thrown in prison, albeit briefly, for trying to defend her undocumented partner, Zeno. While these are all rendered as personal events, one gets the sense that it is American Jewish history that "never had a coherent story to tell about itself," and the many crises are metonymic for a larger crisis in American Jewry, of which Israel is at the symbolic center.

Midway through the novel, Naomi reveals what could only be described as a kind of social secret, a metaphor for all the other forms of secretive violence the family both runs to and flees: Naomi's father is a Black man, and she is the product of a brief assignation in a Catskill summer camp between her mother and a Black musician. Naomi and thus her children's "hidden" blackness is a metaphor for both Jewish assimilation and Jewish otherness: one gets the sense that both Naomi and Bering are wrong when the former denies she is Black and the latter insists on it. All that is left of both Jewishness and otherness is the inert weight of an ultimately rather meaningless biology. Naomi and Bering argue about whether or not this makes either of them Black—Naomi, ever the scientist, says no, as they have not lived lives of Black people; Bering says yes, as she wants desperately to escape her own Upper West Side family narrative. Left unexplored is perhaps the most interesting side plot of the novel, a brief boundary crossing between Naomi's mother and her lover who, in one of the few references to the Old Left, are brought together at least in part by a mutual passion for Paul Robeson and the Jewish camp's relatively progressive racial policies for the time. Like everything in the novel, what might be interesting explorations of Jewish racial liminality or perhaps Jewish boundary crossing in American left-wing history are left as a kind of curious absence, refracted through the private neuroses of each character.

As Naomi says ironically and more than a bit caustically, "My children . . . are drawn to camps. The places on the far edge of the world where the dispossessed are just holding on. The Tibetans, the Palestinians, and the immigration offices." For that reason, they are drawn away from any sense that their own lives could be self-generative.[48] While the novel is unsparing in its look at the violence of the Israeli occupation of the West Bank, one gets the sense that Palestine is a symbol of the illness of American Jewry, what Bering refers to as the "willingly naive and obtuse" myths of "American Jews."[49] While Winter does marry Zeno, in perhaps the one optimistic story of the text, her marriage threatens to move her permanently to Mexico and away from her family, as Zeno is under constant threat of deportation. While Naomi's semi-Jewish wedding after her weekend in jail suggests perhaps one route to an ethical Jewishness, the extremity of her move and her exile from any sense of Jewish community make it one that would be difficult to replicate at scale. One is left at the end of the novel with a sense of emptiness, as if the last moment of Jewish meaning happened sometime in mid-twentieth century and is redeemable only in death or exile.

In Nicole Krauss's *Great House*, this loss of meaning is represented by a giant "foreboding" desk of enormous weight with a seemingly endless number of drawers, some locked (metaphorically), others wide open (equally metaphorically).[50] We learn throughout the course of the novel that the desk has made its way from the office of a dead Jewish Viennese Holocaust victim, to the possession of a radical Jewish Chilean poet who himself is murdered by Pinochet's regime, to the apartment of a lonely, self-involved Jewish writer in New York City who has a brief liaison with the Jewish poet, and finally to the son of the original owner, who is obsessed with re-creating an exact replica of his father's office the day before he was sent to a death camp. As a metaphor, the desk does its work: it is sought after by both Nadia, the writer, and the Holocaust victim's son, as the object that will either restore their vitality or, in the son's case, complete their sense of loss. Nadia engages in yet another doomed affair while in Israel, and her story ends ambiguously with a terrible car crash before she has recovered the desk, or her sense of self. The Holocaust victim's son does track the desk down in a New York warehouse and decides at the end it will bring him no solace. The novel's title, *Great House*, refers to the first temple, burned to the ground. One gets the sense that all the Great Houses, temples of Judaism, whether constructed on memory or a new Zionist state, will end but in loss, and that memory is irretrievable. Like in Row's novel or the novels of Cohen, there is a marked frankness about the un-redemptive project of Israel: Israel is a place marred by death and violence, Jewish, Palestinian, or both. The diaspora is, however, no point of redemption. In Cohen's 2017 novel *The Moving Kings*, David King—King David, as perhaps a metaphor so literal as to escape explanation—is unable to recite Kaddish for his dead Israeli employee while at a resort in Mexico. That our modern King David, as rough, violent, loutish, and chauvinistic as the original, is also lost and without cultural resources in mourning seems perhaps the best image to capture this generation of American Jewish novelists and their sense of the lack of vitality of American Jewish life, even as they reject the colonial violence of Israel.

Perhaps the most creative and generous engagement with this cul-de-sac of Jewish history is Adam Mansbach's *The Golem of Brooklyn*, which, as the title implies, imagines a Jewish luftmenschen, a pot-smoking, semi-employed art teacher in Brooklyn who fashions himself a golem.[51] The book is at once a retelling of the Golem of Prague, a legendary folkloric tale about Rabbi Bezalel, who, as the story goes, created a golem to defend the Jewish ghetto from antisemitic attacks, and a historic inquiry into our connection with a European Yiddishkeit past. The premise of Mansbach's novel is both playful and serious or perhaps, in the interstices between the two, asks what conjuncture of history Jews currently live in: Is the reemergence of a golem funny or serious? Is the golem a practical joke evoked by a Jewish hipster in Brooklyn much in the way cool Jews sew Yiddish partisan phrases into their jackets or tattoo them onto their forearms? Or are we in a serious moment of danger with the rise of the far right and the death spiral of Israel into genocide? The book stages this question as a dialogue between the golem's creator, Len, and his Yiddish translator, Miri, an off-the-*derech* queer ex-Chasid who, like Len, both belongs and does not belong to Jewish culture and community. Miri believes the golem should be used to kill white nationalists increasingly on the march since Charlottesville. Len believes the golem needs to be prevented from killing antisemites yet, curiously, does not destroy the golem immediately when it's clear what his purpose is. One gets a sense that for Len, the golem is his connection to Judaism, even if he and the golem seem to barely be able to tolerate one another. This ambiguity is never resolved, nor is it ever decided whether the golem was correctly or incorrectly summoned, whether the era in which the golem was constructed is now over. As compelling as the sense of historical antinomy is, one gets the impression that for Mansbach the golem is a kind of Jewish id, frozen—like the golem itself—in a ditch of Babi Yar, unable to wake up to current realities or face them in a complex, nuanced way.

One way to read novels by Cohen, Row, Krauss, and others is to conceive of them as negotiations with the newfound, disorienting role of Jews who want to stand in solidarity with victims of Jewish power in Palestine and as white people who inhabit the European side of the axial line between white and Black in the US. Row's Bering, who discovers the hidden Black person in her own family tree and throws herself headlong into the sights of an IDF rifle, is in some ways no more or less absurd than her mother, who goes on as if nothing has changed: both responses seem to suggest *Jewishness* can no longer express a sense of alterity on its own terms that includes boundary crossings, if not longer liaisons with Blackness, as part of, if not its constitutive nature, at least its historical experience in the US. They are novels of emptiness, one could say, and exhaustion: the long Jewish story of radical and even prophetic promise seems to have come undone in the policed suburbs of Highland Park that, in their way, can be seen as prefigurations of the militarized settlements in the West Bank. In this light, one can understand a novel like Tova Reich's *My Holocaust*, in which Auschwitz, its memory and representation, has been so thoroughly integrated into global capitalism and imperialism that Jews and non-Jews alike are fighting for the economic and cultural power of being associated with mass Jewish death. After all, look at the power it seems both Israel and Jewish whiteness derive from the invocation of their perpetual innocence. As one rabbi once sardonically said to me, "Jews get to have it both ways, white people and perfect victims"—a sweet spot that registers, like these novels, an ironic emptiness.

To the Cultural Barricades, All of Them, or None

In 2017 at the Unite the Right Rally in Charlottesville, torch-bearing white nationalists marched in the thousands chanting "Jews will not replace us" before one of them plowed their car into a crowd and murdered an anti-fascist activist. The same year, a sleepy socialist organization with only a few thousand members suddenly surged in membership and onto the national scene, electing open socialists to local and national office, joining in pickets and rallies, organizing tenants' unions and, the same year, voting to endorse a BDS resolution at its national convention with near unanimity of its 800-plus delegates. While liberal Zionists such as Deborah Lipstadt saw both of these events as part of the rise of global antisemitism—neo-Nazis and socialists embracing a boycott of Israel—for many thousands of young Jews, the rise of socialism, rejection of Israel, and call to anti-fascist militancy were all of a piece. The sight of Jewish socialists, some wearing kippot, standing and waving red placards to cheer the boycotting of the Jewish state, felt not only like a major milestone, but a shot fired across the bow of American (Jewish) political culture. The Democratic Socialists of America (DSA), while largely known on the left as being willing to work within the Democratic Party, was also known as the lone socialist organization in the US that was open to having liberal Zionists prominently in its leadership. That DSA should, unanimously, democratically, and almost without objection vote to endorse a boycott of Israel with open Jewish support seemed to be a break with the past in more ways than one: it seemed an entire political and discursive framework had been blown right open.

The Jewish Solidarity Caucus (JSC) organized in 2017 shortly after the election of Trump and the surge in DSA membership. It was an organization born out of what seemed like an entirely new conjuncture: not only were fascists openly marching in the street, so too were socialists meeting in the thousands, the tens of thousands. As one of the JSC's founders, Lane Silberstein, wrote for the *Jewish Currents* blog, he realized the need for a left-wing Jewish organization when he saw "far-right populism" on the march from Greece to Germany, the United States to Israel.[52] The latter two countries seemed perhaps the most important: neither Jewish assimilation in the US nor Zionist nationalism provided any answers. The meeting of these two antinomies in the body politic, the emergence of a new left and a fascist-adjacent reactionary taking the White House, called forth a new form of Jewish memory: a search for a usable cultural and political past that could orient and root young Jewish progressives as they felt encouraged to vocally reject Israel yet also confronted the realities of a new antisemitic right. For the first time in their lives, American Jews, far too young to remember the Red Scare, witnessed both the reemergence of fascism as a *national* phenomenon and the powerful, or at least wealthy, Jewish institutions' complacency in the face of it. As in the work of the liberal Jewish novelists, all the stories that American Jews had been told of their American Zion and the liberalism of the American state appeared to be falling apart at the seams. Like the hit show based on the Roth novel, *Plot against America*, it suddenly seemed "it could happen here." Yet unlike the characters in the works of the liberal novelists discussed previously, young Jews' experience of Kushner's "new millennium" created in them both anxiety and a kind of invigoration, producing a moment to challenge a moribund Jewish establishment over Zionism and to also challenge themselves to build new organizations and cultural resources.

In some ways it might seem almost prophetic that the JSC was first thrust into the national left spotlight when a group of new DSA members brought a BDS resolution to the 2017 convention floor in Chicago. Several of the members of the BDS drafting committee were current or soon to be members of the JSC, but more importantly, the JSC had published its manifesto on Medium days before the convention, stating clearly that "nationalism" and "Zionism" were "barriers" to creating "strong" and "autonomous" Jewish communities in the diaspora.[53] The resolution, which declared itself "in solidarity with Palestinian civil society's nonviolent struggle against apartheid, colonialism, military occupation and for equality, human rights, and self-determination" in full support of "Palestinian civil society's call" to "boycott, divest and sanction" Israeli business and the state, was passed nearly unanimously with a floor vote among delegates, facing almost no vocal opposition.

While Michael Fischbach concludes his history of debate on the New Left over Palestine with a statement by a Jewish member of DSA who resigned after the vote, such a statement seems, if not empirically inaccurate, not representative.[54] There were few Jewish resignations from DSA after the BDS vote. Indeed, members of the JSC were elated by the vote, and felt that it represented the kind of socialist organization they wanted to belong to. As two JSC members later related to me, the vote and JSC members' vocal support for it were among their reasons for wanting to join the organization.

While the BDS vote may not have been controversial among young Jewish activists in DSA, it is important to note how much of a break it was with DSA's foundation. DSA was created when the Communist-leaning New America Movement (NAM) and the Democratic Socialist Organizing Committee (DSOC) merged in 1982. The primarily anti-Zionist NAM and liberal-Zionist DSOC agreed to a detente over the issue of Palestine solidarity in their merger, and largely avoided it in statements and in their activism. The mostly electoral group worked within the progressive wing of the Democratic Party, and Palestine solidarity rarely emerged as an issue within the progressive bloc of Democratic officials, so the silence—and the detente—remained largely unchallenged through the '80s and early '90s. Yet it should also be noted, as longtime DSA activist David Duhalde recalled, that up to half of DSA's members were Jewish—and indeed, two of its most prominent members who represented either side of the split on Palestine, Dorothy Healey and Irving Howe, were also prominent members of the Jewish left. "The organization was so Jewish," Duhalde remembered, that in the '90s Jewish holidays were often observed, and Duhalde cracked jokes in Yiddish at conventions. Yet as Duhalde articulated, even by the late 1990s the consensus on Palestine had begun to shift.[55] As a Jewish member of the Young DSA, DSA's youth caucus, Duhalde recalled, a resolution in which young DSA members criticized the expansion of Jewish settlements met little opposition from the leadership of the organization—a resolution that would have been deemed controversial in years past for mentioning Palestine at all. While the surge of new members meant the membership was far less Jewish in total, Duhalde's sense is that DSA had finally caught up with the rest of the organized socialist left, and the generation for whom Palestine was the third rail of politics had mostly either retired or passed away. DSA's other resolutions at the convention—to create an Afro-Socialist Caucus, to end realignment of the Democratic Party as its electoral goal, and to formally separate from the moribund Second Socialist International—were all of a piece: to declare DSA had broken not from its socialist past, but from the most conservative wing of it that had muzzled the organization from the beginning.

Like with the vote at the 2017 DSA convention for BDS, the mostly millennial-aged Jews who joined the JSC viewed their politics on Zionism—or rather against Zionism—as part of a wider politics encompassing both the left and the Jewish community. Unlike recent accounts by some scholars and reporters on the rise of Jewish anti-Zionism, the process of "unlearning" Zionism was far more overdetermined than a simple conversion narrative might imply.[56] For many Jews who joined DSA and the JSC, their articulation of an anti-Zionist politics was not so much a rupture with either their sense of Jewishness or their political commitments as an aligning with them. As one JSC member, Benjamin S., said in an interview, he was "always suspicious of nationalism" as a political ideology, yet "never had a break moment" with Israel.[57] "It was more a steady evolution. If I've come to the conclusion that American patriotism is bad, then, you know, there is something wrong with quote, unquote, Jewish nationalism." For Benjamin, reading Noam Chomsky, organizing against the Iraq War, and rethinking his relationship to Zionism were not only all of a piece, they were natural steps in the direction he already felt he was heading. His break with Zionism came after he broke with American nationalism; his support for the boycott of Israel was an extension of how he already understood his relationship to the world. Sharona Gordon, who was an early member of the JSC and also a founder of the Jewish anarchist group Outlive Them, described attending synagogue as a child and being troubled by the presence of both Israeli and US flags on the bima, even as she felt moved by the singing and prayers.[58] Having grown up in New York City in a left-wing family that was itself ambivalent about Zionism, she nonetheless related seeing CUNY Hillel recruiting for birthright trips to Israel and instinctively feeling an affinity not for the blue-and-white flags but for the Palestinian students and their allies tabling near them, "with beautiful art, literature about political prisoners, and information about cultural resistance." One of the founders of the JSC, Lane Silberstein, said simply, "My Jewish politics are based in anti-authoritarianism" and so "naturally lend themselves to the left" and against both the United States and Israel. Or as Zac Goldstein, a JSC member who joined later, framed it, "I knew I was a left-wing Jew, and misled by Zionists to think Judaism was conservative." In other words, for many of the Jews in the JSC, their anti-Zionism was an expression of their socialist politics and their sense of Jewish identity, not a rupture with it. As Silberstein recounted, "When an attendee at our first meeting suggested we call ourselves 'the Anti-Zionist Caucus' my first thought was, you think just like a Zionist: that Israel is all there is."[59]

For members of the JSC, embracing a socialist Jewish identity was not an obstacle to their anti-Zionism, but a precondition for it. Zionism, as Silberstein explains in a pair of articles for *Jewish Currents* and *Cosmonaut* in 2018, functions as a kind of prosthetic identity for US Jews, offering a form of assimilation into the "liberal, civic nationalist status quo" of Americanism.[60] While Zionism proclaims that life in the diaspora is impossible, for American Jews it is exactly the opposite. It is through Zionism that many American Jews can express their identity without challenging the dictates of capital or the nation: a narrow elite in the Democratic Party, in the nonprofit industrial complex, and in think tanks and lobby organizations such as AIPAC and the Democratic Majority for Israel materially shape their status in the halls of power as brokers between the Jewish state and the Jewish community in the US. Yet, as Silberstein argues, the twin rise of an antisemitic fascism in the United States and the rightward turn of the Israeli government have meant that increasingly such forms of assimilation, linked to right-wing nationalism and whiteness, are no longer protections for Jews, but "companions to the rise of fascism." For Silberstein, the reclamation of socialist anti-Zionist Jewish community is the only way to fight fascism and lift "the barriers to truly being Jewish" that capitalism erects. When the Center for Jewish History, Silberstein argues (let alone Zionist nonprofits such as the Jewish Federation), can cancel a speaker for their Zionism or seriously question whether "Jews should fear socialism," then an important legacy of Jewish history been lost, along with Jewish resources to oppose fascism and antisemitism. When Chelsea Clinton can praise labor leader Clara Lemlich "without noting she was an ardent communist," then Jews are in effect stripped of a crucial cultural resource in the struggle for continuity. Putting this question in Gramscian terms, Silberstein frames elements of Jewish socialist culture—from American

Communism, to the Yiddish language, to memory of the Eastern European Labor Bund, to Mizrahi and Sephardic radicals from Iraq and North Africa—as "cultural barricades" against the political right and the Zionist capture of Jewish identity.

While the JSC are anti-Zionists, the JSC's manifesto does not claim that all is well in the diaspora. Indeed, this is perhaps one of the questions that undergirds many of the quiet rifts over the term "diaspora," or "diasporism." The JSC manifesto's claim that "under capitalism Jews cannot enjoy cultural autonomy" may seem at a glance to ignore both the unprecedented freedom American Jews have and the powerful, well-funded, and thriving cultural and religious communities Jews have formed in the US. Obviously a great deal rests on what the JSC means by "cultural autonomy"—clearly if one wants to create a *havurah* or lead a radical Jewish reading group, one can. And it is also clear that Jewish institutions function out in the open, are well funded, and have Jewish leadership. Yet it is also a standard claim of Marxism, to say nothing of Jewish Marxism, that the dominant cultural institutions under capitalism will be *capitalist* cultural institutions. For Jewish culture, this is evident in quantitative ways—from high synagogue dues, to expensive summer camps, to the cost of a Jewish education, to Jewish nonprofits that cater to large donors—and also qualitative ways, from institutional support for Zionism, to erasure of Jewish radicalism in novels, Jewish studies programs, and Jewish day schools. Ironically, or perhaps appropriately, the first text in which the question of civil society, religion, and state emerge in Marxism is the (in)famous "On the Jewish Question," in which Marx poses a similar formula to the JSC: under capitalism, secular civil society "presupposes" not only Christianity in the West but more importantly that all the cultural forms of capitalism including private property, the wage relation, and the distinction between public and private, constitute the basis of civil society as such. While Marx argues that only under socialism will we be free from cultural particularism, the JSC turns it around: only under socialism will cultural particularism be truly free.

For many members of the JSC, the failure of Jewish institutions was most evident in the election of Trump and the rise of the far right. Not only was such a moment a new conjunctural event in American politics, it constituted a new moment in American Jewish history: one that Jewish institutions from the ADL to the Jewish Federation seemed incapable of meeting with the urgency or force required. As Sharona Gordon expressed after the election, "I felt this spark reignite in me": "I have to find my people." She was feeling "politically lonely" and saw the JSC Twitter account and people "posting on ascendent fascism, nationalism, white nationalism" and "using Yiddish terms" and "shouting out Jewish radical history." She "didn't see anyone [her] age doing that." Another JSC member, Javier Miranda, described the moment in this way: "Bernie's running, Trump's running. I'm getting into Marxism for the first time . . . I wanted some, you know, broad thing to anchor myself in something larger than myself."[61] Zac Goldstein describes coming across the JSC platform at a similar time, during which he was wrestling with both his attachment to Jewish identity and his increasing interest in radical politics. "The JSC platform was the first for a Jewish group that combined both," including "anti-Zionism" as part of a wider reconception of Jewish life left vacant by Zionism and assimilation.[62] In this sense, the JSC brought forth Jews who already for the most part understood themselves as leftists or progressives and wanted a uniquely Jewish way to articulate their politics. The JSC manifesto is written very much in the spirit of that moment: an analysis of the rise of fascism and the role American Jewish progressives and leftists can play. "As Jews," the manifesto states, "[we continue] to play a key role in white ideologies of antisemitism." Also, "As Jews, we are uniquely positioned to challenge the nationalism that appears in our community as Zionism." Further, "as socialists" the JSC can mobilize the cultural resources of left-wing Jewish history to oppose "our community's role in a capitalist, white supremacist society."

As Lane Silberstein joked, the JSC saw itself as a "Jewish socialist Chabad" bringing in Jews who had strayed from the *derech*, or path. They had three main activities, he said: "reading groups," mostly on Jewish radical history and anti-Zionism; "street protest," including organizing Jewish radicals to attend the counterprotests at the Unite the Right Rally in Charlottesville; and cultural events, such as Shabbos dinners and a "Yom Kippur ball" modeled after the late nineteenth- and early twentieth-century Jewish socialist practice of celebrating instead of praying at the end of the Yamim Noraim. As Gordon describes, her first action with the JSC was to hold a Shabbos service at an ICE detention facility protest in New York City, drawing both Jewish and non-Jewish observers into the ritual. JSC members in New York also joined with members of the Muslim-Jewish Antifascist Front at the site of a homophobic attack to hold a memorial; in San Francisco, JSC members held a "Jewish resistance" banner as part of another anti-ICE detention protest; JSC members helped organize and spoke at an anti-Nazi protest in Bowling Green, Kentucky; and at a punk show in St. Louis, JSC members lectured about fascism and antisemitism. JSC members also joined protests against Israeli evictions of Palestinians from East Jerusalem and against the moving of the US embassy from Tel Aviv to Jerusalem. Perhaps most effective, or at least most widely circulated, were JSC defenses of Julia Salazar and Ilhan Omar against charges they were antisemites. The JSC most passionately defended Salazar, not only for her politics but because part of the smear campaign against her was that she was not really Jewish—a charge many in the JSC saw as an attempt to push left-wing Jews out of the Jewish community. "Nationalism" of the Jewish establishment by necessity implies "anti-socialism," and "ethnic nationalism" implies "imperialism," the JSC stated in its manifesto.

The florescence of the JSC also coincided with and was part of a flowering of radical Jewish culture. This small cultural explosion was often heavily inflected with the history of Yiddish language radicalism though also regaled in the histories of Iraqi Jewish Communism, subversive Sephardic philosophers, and critics from Baruch Spinoza to Albert Memmi. Perhaps the best known of this new cultural wave is the Yiddish-language musician Daniel Kahn, whose songs range from anti-Zionist Bundist rhymes from the 1930s and Soviet anti-fascist songs in Yiddish, to Yiddish translations of Leonard Cohen and Woody Guthrie, to his own revolutionary music that blends punk rock, folk, klezmer, Dadaism, and blues. His concerts also tend to be events for the radical anti-Zionist Jewish left, and his work is shared widely among left-wing Jewish social media accounts such as Jewish Voice for Labour, Cool Jews, and Sounds Like Hasbara but OK, and played at anti-Zionist meetings and among Jewish activists. One song that has become a kind of anthem for the era is part of a longer musical, *The Last Universal Diasporic Testament of Adam Spielman*, and often referred to just by its refrain, "The Jew in You."[63] The song is an elaboration of an essay Kahn authored in *Smithsonian Folkways* in part to answer the question of why he writes and sings in Yiddish, especially given that it is a language he did not grow up speaking as an assimilated Jew from the Detroit suburbs.

In some ways the question posed to Kahn is inseparable from the question that the JSC poses: Why celebrate or even attempt to revive radical Jewish traditions? The answer Kahn supplies is both metaphoric and conjunctural: while the language of transnational exile represented by the stateless Yiddish language refers to Jews, "there is much value in seeing it as a universally human condition" as "more people than ever before find themselves—as the writer Michael Wex puts it—'Shlepping the exile.'"[64] "The Jew in You" invites the listener to take a radical Yiddishkeit subjectivity, to "take the rootless cosmopolitan point of view," and "bring out the Jew" in everyone. In this sense the song invites the listener to think of Jewishness less as "blood and land" or even identity, and more as a radical perspective, as migration, displacement, destruction, and precarity are inherent features of global capitalism. Indeed, Jews may not even be "Jews" anymore. "We turned our backs on everything that brought our people through"; did it "really work to try to make a new Hebrew?" Yet the song also points to actual lived Jewish experience and Jewish cultural memory of displacement as radical resources not only for Jews, but the entire left, even the entire world. As the song predicts the end of "Zion" and the universalization of the destruction of Detroit, it concludes, "So learn to take it with you, learn to be a Jew"—a statement of cultural openness as well as a productive specificity of Jewishness.

Often performing in worker's overalls and singing radical songs, it's clear that Kahn is both remembering a radical tradition and reinventing it for a contemporary and contradictory moment. Sometimes he even plays two opposing versions of the same song together ("Israel is nothing/Israel is everything") or changes the lyrics of Bund anthems to indict the state of Israel or remind listeners that the remnants of the Bund perished in the Holocaust.[65] This play with signifiers of nation and diaspora signals that Jewish identity is caught in such a contradiction, having a rich and radical history to draw from, yet stuck in a present in which that history spoke to a far different material context. Eli Valley is another artist who revives diasporic traditions in a radical if ironic context, crafting sharp criticisms of Zionists, fascists, and members of the Jewish bourgeoisie in a style that evokes both Nazi tropes of Jewish physical deformity and the exaggerations of Yiddish theater.

It was clear that, among this bloom of radical Jewish culture, the JSC wanted to be more than just a hub for political activism. Its notes contain a list of recipes for "hamsick challah, zucchini-apple-sage latkes, Jess's cholent, Simcha's seitan, Talia's beef brisket" and also a far longer list of future projects including a "socialist shul," a "publication," a "MENA Communist Jewish History" seminar, a "map of donors to Jewish institutions," and "buying property/land." The JSC had ambitions to revive a radical Jewish culture and build Jewish cultural institutions, in addition to just turning people out into the street.[66]

It is impossible to talk about the revival of an anti-Zionist, radical Jewish culture without of course talking about the giant in the room, Jewish Voice for Peace (JVP). Founded in 1996 by three Jewish American college students at UC Berkeley in response to Israel's construction of the West Bank barrier, it has grown into a nationwide organization with over 10,000 members and a staff of over two dozen. Beginning as a group that organized rallies and educational events against the Israeli invasion of the Jenin refugee camp in 2002, the continuing expansion of Jewish settlements, the Nakba, and other crimes of Israeli apartheid, JVP went on in 2005 to become an early backer of the BDS movement. JVP's first nationally successful divestment campaign against Caterpillar and Veolia helped pressure the retirement fund TIAA-CREF to drop both from its social justice fund in 2011. JVP also worked with the Presbyterian Church to help pass its BDS resolution in 2014, and the Durham, NC, JVP chapter helped lead, in coalition with racial justice and peace organizations, a successful effort to have the city divest from G4S, a security firm with ties to the Israeli state. JVP also helps facilitate trips to Palestine to protect olive harvests from Israeli settlers, lobbies Congress and statehouses, and is present at nearly every campus BDS vote or church resolution on Palestine. It is fair to say, even though JVP often hesitates to say it for reasons that are both ideological as well as practical, that it has grown into the single most successful Palestine solidarity organization in the US (and perhaps in the Western world) over the last several years. Rather than moderate its stance, its success has challenged JVP to clarify and sharpen its position on Zionism. In 2019, JVP embraced anti-Zionism as its official position, declaring that Zionism, though it had many cultural strands historically, was in practice a "settler colonial" and "apartheid state" inseparable from either its genocidal violence or its white supremacy. In particular, JVP also pays attention to the ways in which the Israeli state discriminates against dark-skinned Jews, with African and Middle-Eastern Jews often facing poverty and social exclusion.[67] While JVP's formal embrace of anti-Zionism caught the attention of pro-Israel outlets and organizations such as *Tablet* and ADL, it is important to note that JVP saw little change in its membership nor much of an outcry: it was, as one member expressed at a meeting, simply an explicit acknowledgement of what they were doing already.

As scholar Atalia Omer writes in her monograph *Days of Awe*, JVP is at the center of a Jewish solidarity movement with Palestine that is itself constructing crucial "reimagination of Jewishness" and a new "narration of Jewish identity."[68] And indeed, JVP's right-wing critics tend to agree with its centrality and its importance in creating a new Jewish culture. A *Tablet* editorial by Natan Sharansky and Gil Troy shortly after JVP's vote accused Jewish anti-Zionist activists of being "un-Jews" who have "wormed their way into the tradition" to undo "American Jewry's Zionism-accented, peoplehood-centered constructions of Jewish identity." While Sharansky and Troy are incorrect about JVP members' commitment to Jewishness or their "worming" into Jewish tradition, they are correct insofar as they recognize that JVP's project is larger than simply a just resolution to the occupation of and apartheid system within Palestinian land. JVP, which now has nearly three dozen chapters in nearly every state where there is a sizable Jewish presence, and can list alignment with over a dozen synagogues, a rabbinical council, and an academic advisory board, is itself one of the more culturally and politically significant Jewish organizations in the United States. As Omer states, "Jewish Palestine solidarity activists and other critics of the occupation and Zionism constitute a social movement operating to transform the meanings of Jewishness."[69] Many JVP activists reject what Omer frames through Jewish rabbinical scholar Marc Ellis as "Constantine Judaism," Judaism that, like Christianity under empire, adopted Roman state policies and politics, replacing the "Roman empire" of Zionism with a Judaism of antimilitarism, universalism, and anti-nationalism.[70]

As one JVP activist and now member of its rabbinical council noted, for many in JVP, the group replaces the Zionist religious community in which they were previously members. As former JVP board president Jethro Eisenstein evocatively framed it, JVP is his "shul," especially as he left his temple over its Zionist politics. Indeed a great deal of JVP's cultural energy is devoted to remaking Jewish liturgy, observance, and ritual so that it provides spiritual affirmation for Jewish diasporic politics and also wrestles the tradition from within regarding Jewish nationalism and Jewish supremacy as it is exercised in Israel. Perhaps most central to both Jewish culture and the founding of a Jewish nation is the story of exodus. It is no accident that Leon Uris's *Exodus*, perhaps the single most influential Zionist text in US history, appropriates the epic biblical tale and the observance of Passover itself, to prophesy and offer legitimation for Jewish settlement in the Levant. In JVP Rabbinical Council members Ariana Katz and Miriam Grossman's "Maggid," the story of the Jewish flight from Egypt, they begin with the question of memory and power: Pharoah holds on to power only insofar as he can erase the Jewish people's memory of themselves.[71] And in that sense, the Israeli erasure of Palestine, the Nakba, means that the story of Passover has been inverted: it is the Hebrews who are the new Pharaohs and the Palestinians who are the new subjects of displacement and violence. Yet even so, the JVP "Maggid" addresses Jews in the United States who face antisemitism and other forms of racial, class, gender, or structural violence: the story does not belong in that sense to one people, but is rather one of resisting oppression. Similarly, in JVP's Tashlich guide by Dori Midnight and Joanna Kent Katz, personal sins on which one might reflect during the Days of Awe are not eclipsed so much as included along with promises to repair the particularly social crimes committed by Jews as a collectivity, or at least in Jewish names. "We commit," the guide reads, "to repairing the damages of colonization in the ways we are able ... through relationship-building and direct political engagement in solidarity."[72]

Omer describes such practices as "rescripting religiocultural meanings" in the name of a broad "multivocal" solidarity.[73] Such rescription has long precedent in Jewish liturgy and Jewish radical politics with, for example, the inclusion of Paul Robeson songs in Communist Passover seders, and NeverAgain action that deploys the metaphor of the closed borders during the Holocaust to combat US immigration restriction. Yet the singularity of JVP and its success—as the largest anti-Zionist Jewish organization in the United States—are owed to what Dov Waxman calls the "paradox of American involvement in Israel": the more US institutions identify with Israel, Jewish or not, the more Israel will come under scrutiny and appear as a symbol for issues here at home.[74] That is, part of the success of JVP's strategy is the increasing commensurability of Zionism with the politics of the United States. Laclau and Mouffe argued that metaphor has generous movement-building capacities; indeed, the language of apartheid, borders, and settler colonialism is often transposed onto US domestic border politics, legacies of Jim Crow, and ongoing struggles for indigenous land and sovereignty.[75] In Katz and Grossman's "Maggid," the displacement of Palestinian land is mapped paratactically alongside the #noDAPL water protectors, and the burning cities in Brant Rosen's Tisha B'Av lament are replaced with the racial and classed fault lines of deindustrial America and climate change.[76] Of course, there is a materiality to the metaphor that goes beyond just signifier and signified—the United States is not only a major funder and supporter of Zionism, both the US and Israel see in each other mirrors of a Western settler-colonial project. The refraction of the politics of Israel and Palestine, some argue, meet limits when one considers the incommensurability of both slavery and Jim Crow to Israeli ethnic cleansing, as well as the dissimilarity of Jewish immigration to the United States and to mandate Palestine and then the state of Israel.

Yet the political analogy of Israeli settler-colonialism and Jim Crow in the United States has a long and unbroken history, going all the way back to Jewish and African American Communists in the 1930s, and to SDS and SWP support for SNCC in the 1960s. JVP has made it a central part of its message and its identity formation to analogize the Israeli state with both the Black freedom struggle in the US and a critique of Jewish whiteness. "What we are seeing is nothing new," said Black Lives Matter organizer Zellie Thomas, explaining his support for Palestine to NPR.[77] Thomas cites a tradition of African American support for Palestine, including Angela Davis and the Black Panther Party. In 2016, a coalition of African American organizations including the Movement for Black Lives, Dream Defenders, and Black Youth Project 100 issued a statement declaring support for BDS and solidarity with Palestine. Like SNCC's statement in 1967 and the Communist Party's solidarity with anti-colonial revolution in the 1930s, JVP's analysis and activism centers forging coalitions among African American activists in the United States. This sense of urgency was heightened by the ADL's formal condemnation of the Movement for Black Lives' support for BDS. Launching the "Deadly Exchange" campaign, JVP highlighted the ADL's support of Israeli-sponsored police training trips. While it is questionable the extent to which Israeli support for American police has a measurable effect on police brutality and mass incarceration, the campaign was effective to the extent it highlighted Jewish institutional support for white supremacy. As one longtime JVP Chicago member, Lesley Williams, wrote for the JVP blog, "Many White American Jews are fond of reminiscing . . . about the old '60s alliance between Blacks and Jews, extolling the hallowed moment when Abraham Heschel locked arms with Martin Luther King, and when Schwerner and Goodman died alongside Chaney in Mississippi. These were indeed inspiring moments of solidarity—but they are in the past."[78]

It is important perhaps to note that Williams is one of a growing number of Black, Mizrahi, Asian, and other non-white Jews who comprise the activist base of JVP and are part of their Black, Indigenous, Jews of Color, Sephardi, and Mizrahi caucus (BIJOCSM). Much like the proposition to change the tradition from within through rescription, so too the BIJOCSM seeks to make Jewish organized life different from within Jewish organizations. While SDS, the Yippies, and the SWP may have been more diverse than is often thought in hindsight, remember, their strategy in general was simply to acknowledge they were the "white (Jewish)" left and to work in coalition with organizations such as the Black Panther Party and Black Student Unions from that standpoint. While JVP sees itself as in coalition with Palestinians as well as Black and Muslim organizations, its project is also, as scholar Santiago Slabodsky phrases it, to "decolonize Judaism," both in the language around its ritual practice as well as who is imagined as a Jew. "Showing up as Jews," which is one of JVP's catchphrases (a long-available T-shirt read, "Another Jew Supporting Divestment)," means also showing up in the complex ways Jews are both visible and invisible within the ocular schema of racial hierarchy in the US. Melanie Kaye/Kantrowitz's influential *The Colors of Jews* begins with the question: Are Jews white?[79] While Kaye/Kantrowitz equivocates (by asking this, she suggests, we are understanding the ways in which Jews reveal the unmarked nature of whiteness), nonetheless, the question itself suggests that along with Zionism, the racial identity of Jews is neither a given nor a non-political question: indeed one could say that racial solidarity and thus racial remaking is one of JVP's primary political projects. To remake Jews as a diasporic people, one also has to undo the material foundations on which Jewish whiteness stands.

Perhaps one way to think about the politics of JVP versus the JSC is to think of them as parts of two overlapping but distinct strains of US progressive Jewish culture. Another way to frame it might be as two overlapping but distinct traditions and conceptions of anti-Zionist diasporism. While JVP originated in the Bay Area in the 1990s (JVP's longest-serving director, Rebecca Vilkomerson, got her start as a housing organizer in San Francisco during the eviction crisis), JVP's focus on religious rescription, Jewish-inflected organizing, and the crisis in Palestine hearkens back as much to Arthur Waskow's 1969 Freedom Seder and Jews for Urban Justice as it does the Bund. As Waskow himself wrote, he moved from being a "Jewish radical" to a "radical Jew," finding within the Jewish religious observance a new form of radical, anti-capitalist culture.[80] As he writes in *The Bush Is Burning!*, Judaism is a "rich cultural heritage that has been forfeited to the American melting pot, to be replaced by an uneasy . . . quasi loyalty to a foreign state."[81] Dismissing secular Jews in the New Left as "marginal" and the Bund as "statist," Waskow looks to the Talmud for his "radical" message.[82] At the 1969 seder, set in a Black church in Washington, DC, on the one-year anniversary of the assassination of Martin Luther King Jr., Waskow rescripted traditional questions about freedom, slavery, and liberation to ask the Jewish community of DC about its commitment to racial justice and to place the Black freedom struggle at the center of his radical Jewish vision.[83] While the Haggadah included Jewish martyrs of the Warsaw Ghetto Uprising, the point of the seder was not to focus on "liberation of Jewish people" but to place Jewish narratives "alongside" Black narratives, as a means to "legitimate" Black revolutionary leaders such as Nat Turner and Eldridge Cleaver.[84] While Jews for Urban Justice, the DC-based Jewish organization that helped organize the seder, was not long-lived, it set in some ways the template for a "radical affirmation of faith" that was seen as impossible in "organized Judaism."[85] Like JVP, Jewish tradition was rewritten from the inside out to de-center the very subject of its origin: like the radical "Maggid" of JVP, the stories of Jewish liberation are deployed as metaphors to undo *Jewish* power in Israel, and white power in the United States, rather than focus on crimes done to Jews by antisemites.

While they are clearly in alignment on many issues and approaches (many members of the JSC are JVP members and many JVP members are DSA members or other stripes of socialist), I think it's important to point out JSC and JVP's different points of entry to Jewish identity and culture. In defining its first opposition to *capitalism* and not *Zionism*, the members of JSC posit themselves not only as Jews in solidarity with non-Jews, but also as workers who have their own class subjectivity within capitalism. While the JSC has a class critique of major Jewish institutions, which includes their commitment Zionism, questions of *Jewish power* are not posed as something shared by all Jews, articulated by singular Jewish community, but rather as class antagonism both inside and outside of the signs of Jew and gentile. As JSC member Javier Miranda put it, "Jewish power? Sure, man, how about some working-class Jewish power?" Miranda, who works construction in the renewable energy industry, talked vividly about his Jewish coworker and their experience as working-class Jews who live in a primarily non-Jewish world at their work but who must also negotiate the world of gentile and Jewish relationships with more vocal give and take: if people have thoughts about Jews they are simply said out loud. The primary claim made by the JSC manifesto ties Zionism to working-class exclusion through the single framework of capitalism: ordinary Jews are no more represented by the Israeli state than they are by the Jewish Federation. In this sense, Zionists are not only racists, but also bourgeois nationalists who wish to align ordinary Jews with the interests of the Jewish bourgeoisie. This is why fighting antisemitism frames the JSC statement: it's not that antisemitism is the deepest crisis facing Jews at the moment, but that the Jewish bourgeoisie as represented by the ADL, the Jewish Federation, Jewish studies programs, and so on, understands that opposing the right would jeopardize right-wing support for Israel and funding of their institutions. And it is not as though street-brawling Nazis are coming after *them*.

One metaphor that may bring this distinction to light is the difference between *memory* and *rescription*, between *class conflict* and *coming out*. The JSC is primarily a memory project, dedicated to restoring and reviving the memory of the Jewish left in a new context. As Marita Sturken points out, memory and history are different: memory is not a replica but a narrative of the present, posed in a dialectic against forgetting.[86] Paraphrasing Benjamin's famous treatise on memory, the JSC poses that memory is not universal, but reveals a class antagonism, as memory of the marginalized is by definition the memory of past struggles and defeats. Working-class socialist Jewish history is then a *counter-memory* that exposes the antagonisms within the Jewish community, not allowing it to speak in one voice or abstracting Zionism into the politics of identity. JSC activities including Marxist reading groups, a Yom Kippur ball, and even the quoting of Clara Lemlich and Walter Benjamin (rather than Abraham Heschel and Judith Butler) mark the project as one that steps out of the past and into the present in a very different way. One could say that fighting fascism and Zionism is in a sense a replay of the past: one could read 1930s headlines in the left-wing press about both "Zionist fascists" and "Nazis," and not have to struggle a great deal to make them applicable to the present. For the JSC, the revived language of class speaks urgently to a new moment not so much in Jewish working-class history, but more in the way that dominant Jewish institutions are integrated within the American bourgeoisie, from Zionism to Jewish studies programs.

In a 2009 zine, *Out*, the creators—in their own words, two queer Ashkenazi human rights activists in Palestine—conflate "coming out" sexually with ending the occupation of the West Bank and Jewish supremacy more broadly.[87] "Out" figures doubly, even triply, as a reference to queer sexuality, a politics of anti-colonialism, and "coming out" against Zionism. The process of "unlearning" Zionism is thus compared to the process of unlearning the binary between man and woman, or the politics of hetero-patriarchy. As many commentators have noted, there is more than a casual overlap between the anti-Zionist politics of JVP and the gender/sexual identity of many of its core activists. While Rabbi David Basior articulates this in sociological terms—that many queer activists are refugees of Jewish orthodoxy, Omer puts it in epistemic terms—queer subjects by a refusal of binaries and questioning of the violently gendered apparatuses of state power are by definition more likely to be critical of nation-building projects. Either way, Ilana and Aviva, the zine's authors, describe themselves as emerging from within the institutional Jewish world of "day schools and Zionist summer camps" and hailing from "upper middle class families." The "coming out" narrative thus relies on a certain beginning reference point from within a discourse: "out" implies, of course, an "in."

An interesting element of JSC members' stories is that their encounter with radical politics often preceded their anti-Zionism and even their formal engagement with Jewish organizing. For many in the JSC, it is not about the centrality of Israel, but rather its peripheral and marginal status in their lives as labor activists or anti-fascists. While they are anti-Zionists, they regard Zionism as something that emerged from the class nature of Jewish institutional life; thus, opposing Zionism outside of a larger politics of anticapitalism makes little sense. This is not to say that JSC were somehow less queer than JVP activists, but rather that their Jewish activism and anti-Zionism begins from a different epistemic entry point. As Benjamin S., one former JSC member, framed it, "there is nothing inherently left-wing about anti-Zionism. It is left-wing because of the outsized attention the issue receives from the right." While JVP is often characterized as left-wing and would, I believe, adopt that characterization itself, such a perspective suggests the diasporic politics of *hereness* is not a response to nationalism, rather that it is nationalism's oversized presence that forces a diaspora to politicize its ontological existence. This is perhaps the largest and most often unasked question on the Jewish left: Does Zionism require Jewish leftists to find a patronym before the foundation of Israel, or does Zionism require we reject a Jewish radicalism that has failed within the Zionist present to force a change? Is it anti- or ante-Zionism, memory or coming out that will point the way?

As Israel intensified its genocidal war on Palestine after October 7 with no end in sight—displacing nearly the entire population of Gaza, destroying homes, hospitals, and infrastructure, and killing tens of thousands—there was a convergence of the Jewish left calling for an immediate ceasefire, an end to US material and diplomatic support for Israel, and an end to Israeli apartheid. And while the convergence was born out of terrible necessity—to prevent not only a genocide of Palestinians but a further slide of American institutions into an undemocratic abyss—it seems important to also note that both JVP and DSA lay their claim to justice not only on universal principles, but different if overlapping articulations of Jewish memory. Leaders within both DSA and the JVP have issued statements or articles since the Israeli onslaught, broadly aligned in their criticism of Israel, Zionism, and the increasingly right-wing nature of Jewish institutions—yet have also called for these demands in different languages of Jewish left-wing history. A statement entitled "Not in Our Name! Jewish Socialists Say No to Apartheid and Genocide" signed onto by hundreds of Jewish socialists—most of whom are members of DSA—calls on the long history of Jewish resistance to antisemitism.[88] "As Jews," the statement reads, "we live with the memory of the Holocaust, along with centuries of pogroms, displacements, and inquisition," including "a rise in antisemitic right-wing parties and groups" that have used Israel's violence to lay blame on the Jewish diaspora for the "brutal class inequalities and endemic crises and insecurity" of "capitalism." The statement calls upon American Jews as "socialists and working people" to oppose Zionism not only out of solidarity with Palestinians, but also out of a Jewish and working-class self-interest in safety.

Rebecca Vilkomerson, former executive director of JVP, and Dania Rajendra, who is on the board of JFREJ, articulate many of the same criticisms of Israel and right-wing Jewish institutions that the DSA letter does in an op-ed published in *In These Times*: Israel is committing a genocide, and it is the right-wing Jewish institutions that are helping to facilitate it.[89] Yet the piece diverges in its casting of both antisemitism and Jewish tradition. Accurately noting that mainstream Jewish institutions manipulate fears of antisemitism into a "panic" to spread anxiety about Palestine solidarity protests, the op-ed references Jewish traditions of healing and world-repair in its calls for solidarity. Rather than calling upon Jewish memories of anti-fascist resistance or appealing to Jews as workers, the authors ask Jewish progressives to unite in solidarity with a multiethnic left, including unions, civil rights organizations, and anti-war groups, to end Israeli violence and democratize both the US and Jewish institutional life. While not explicit, the op-ed appeals less to Jewish self-interest among ethno-religious minorities or workers, and more to a turn toward Jewish practice and authenticity—describing Jewish practices of shiva and Shabbos as forms of religious devotion to a more just and caring world, and a way to join "a multi-ethnic working class majority." The op-ed reflects in some ways Atalia Omer's insistence that "for a Jewish reaction to be restorative and reparative, it also must decenter Jewishness," noting that Jews, while benefiting from a rich social justice tradition, are not the population currently facing state-sponsored discrimination and genocide.[90] While pointing to divergences between the two statements may seem a narcissism of small differences, these divergences do gesture to real and continuing points of emphasis in Jewish left and Jewish socialist politics: Do we remember our histories as minorities and our material conditions as part of the 99 percent, or do we emphasize Jewish values and relative safety as a site within which to call for solidarity and democracy? Do we center and build Jewish communities in the fight against Zionism and imperialism, or do we work in solidarity only, as allies? These differences are, of course, reflections of the kinds of organizations DSA and JVP are—socialists emphasize the self-activity of the working class, while JVP frames much of its work as a form of allyship that articulates progressive Jewish values. These are not, of course, necessarily incompatible frameworks for justice: they are overlapping and, at times, contingent positions. However, they do raise very real questions as Jews "detach," in Gramsci's phrase, from their increasingly right-wing institutions and spill out into the street: Which Jewish history, and which version of Jewish life, shall we call upon to move us into a more just and egalitarian world?

Jewish Politics or Politically Jewish: A Tale of Two Diasporas, Jewish and Puerto Rican

When I think of the absent-presence of Jewish working-class politics in left-wing Jewish culture, it is doubled in an uncanny way by the absent-presence in Jewish life of perhaps the most important left-wing working-class Jewish poet writing today, Martín Espada. While Espada has been widely anthologized as one of the preeminent Latinx poets writing in the US and has won awards including the National Book Award and the prestigious Lilly Prize, he is to my knowledge never included in anthologies of Jewish writing and seldom discussed—let alone widely known—as a Jewish poet.

While this alone might be worthy of remark, it is even stranger that Espada's poems are often used in left-wing Jewish ritual and protest. "Imagine the Angels of Bread" has been included so many times in Rosh Hashanah services and Haggadot—including Jewish Voice for Peace's—that congregants at the anti-Zionist Tzedek-Chicago have written multiple versions of their own, as a kind of Jewish midrash upon the original.[91] A friend and board member of Jewish Voice for Peace brings Espada's poems to daven; several rabbis have related to me how they routinely sermonize with Espada's poems from the bima. Espada related in fact that the first seder he attended—Robbie and Michael Meeropol's—he attended in part because they asked him to read one of his poems, which they had included in their Haggadah.[92]

Considering Espada as a Jewish poet from a working-class background with both anti-colonial (including anti-Zionist) Marxist politics and poetics, Espada's ubiquity amid cultural production of Jewish progressive life—as well as the absence of reflection on Espada's presence—suggests a kind of riddle to Jewish progressive culture. In a sense, there is a clear recognition that many Jewish activists immediately share with Espada's work. His poetry, at once prophetic and quotidian—about busboys, famous revolutionaries, pumping gas in rural New England, and doomed general strikes—speaks to longer traditions of the messianic and material on the Jewish left, including Anna Margolin and one of Espada's heroes and literary influences, Edwin Rolfe. His poem "Imagine the Angels of Bread" situates itself within the seder and the Jewish New Year seamlessly for its visionary call for justice as well as its evocation of the material injustices of life under capitalism, from roach-infested apartments to murdered union organizers.

Yet the presence of Espada's poetry in Jewish ritual speaks to the complicated way memory is constituted in popular Jewish texts. The presence of Jewish left memory can be substantive—as with the work of Kushner or Espada himself, yet more often than not it is citational, simply present as part of the texture of text yet without context or history. The most visible instance of this is in the Coen brothers' films, in which there are references to Schachtmanites (an obscure Trotskyite sect), the Port Huron Statement, and Marxist Group Theater of the 1930s. The Coen brothers are hardly alone among liberal Jewish filmmakers and writers in the twentieth and twenty-first centuries. One can also find the presence of Communists and Trotskyists in *Seinfeld*, Neil Simon's *Brighton Beach Memoirs* (1982) and Gene Saks's film adaptation (1986), Philip Roth's *I Married a Communist* (1998) and *Portnoy's Complaint* (1969), and Woody Allen's references to *Dissent* magazine. What is striking is less their presence than their absolute ordinariness; they are there in the way mail carriers and baseball fans are there, a recognizable if unremarkable part of their fictional world.

While it's clear Roth grants far more reverence to his communists than Woody Allen or Larry David may, these writers nonetheless share what I call the *citational presence* of the left in mainstream American Jewish literature. Whether the references come from liberals such as Roth or Simon or from leftists such as Jewish Voice for Peace's Haggadot, such citational presence, sometimes conscious and sometimes not, speaks to a familiarity with the left, if not always an active and conscious historical memory. This refracted memory is both an embrace and a disavowal. My sense is that for writers such as Simon and David, this refracted memory is as much a product of their upbringing as it is the precise nature and lineage of Jewish liberalism. Jewish liberalism, unlike perhaps its WASPish counterpart, emerges alongside and in active dialogue with an American Jewish left, at times competing, at times hostile, and at other times inseparable from one another. The porous boundaries between Jewish liberalism and the left are evoked in such texts while they are also obscured. Like Louis Ironson in *Angels in America*, they remember without remembering, discovering the importance of the Red Scare and Roy Cohn only yet crucially in a moment of crisis.

Perhaps in a sense we can think of Walter Benjamin's theory of history-as-memory as instructive. In the "empty, homogenous time" of the present, such citations serve as temporal placeholders, in which the past is evoked but does not threaten to reemerge.[93] The citation, as Benjamin reminds us, is not mimesis, it does not strive to awaken with an uncanny representation of the present. Yet the citation also retains, in a time of crisis, the possibility, golem-like, of reemergence into a new form of memory, a new way of reading the past into the present. It is the debt liberalism owes to the left, but often does not acknowledge. Such citational refracted memory is present in the move many liberal Jews have made in recent years toward a rethinking of Zionism and Jewishness: a move that recalls and is recalled by this assemblage of memory.

In terms of Jewish memory, Espada is something of a classic Marrano in Daniel Bensaïd's definition of the term: while born of a Jewish mother (if not father), Espada did not grow up with a traditional Jewish education, yet relates that he feels "at home" in the tradition of the Jewish left. This "home" is not one that Espada experienced as a direct inheritance from his parents, rather as a found trajectory of Espada's own political career. "I define myself as 'politically Jewish,'" Espada explained to me in an interview, "the tradition of Jewish radicalism in the twentieth century and writing about it. How better to learn about the Spanish Civil War, the Rosenberg case and the anti-war movement in the Vietnam era than from those who were there, who would bear witness, fight back, or heal the world?"[94] As Bensaïd wrote, the Marrano engages in a poetics of memory, a pastiche of tradition, not part of a formal Jewish community, but re-creating a vital Jewish lineage that defines itself through a rejection of dominant Western culture and history.[95] Espada clarified, "Embracing Jewish radical tradition was much more viable than embracing the Jewish religious tradition, since I'm an atheist with an aversion to ceremony." As importantly, his mother "obliterated that tradition" through her disavowal of it.[96]

It is important to note, it wasn't just Espada's own personal imagination that drew him to the Jewish left. In what Michael Löwy refers to as an "elective affinity," Espada both sought and found himself amid members of the Old and New Jewish Left as a young man in New York City and in the educational and political milieus of socialists. Espada relates how his father, Frank Espada—a known New York activist turned photographer—was personal friends with Shelly Zinn, the famous historian's brother. Espada's later mentors and friends would include the children of the Rosenbergs, Herbert Hill, the Zinns, the Abraham Lincoln Brigade veteran Abe Osheroff, and Espada's colleague Jules Chametzky, all of whom, Espada recounts, taught him left history and offered both mentorship and comradeship. For Löwy, elective affinities are not chosen traditions or voluntary families, but rather solidarities that cross over linguistic or cultural lines because of a structural or political moment of mutual recognition. For Espada, as an intellectual, writer, and young activist in the 1970s, the literary and political tradition of the Jewish left formed a complimentary half to the way he counts himself also as a "political Puerto Rican," the metaphorical son of Roberto Clemente and the Rosenbergs simultaneously, anti-imperialist and anti-Zionist. "I am," Espada is fond of saying, "the only poet who has written both of the Rosenberg case and Puerto Rican colonialism."[97]

Espada's poems about working-class left-wing Jewish life are nearly all biographies of people he knew personally, either as a writer and activist, or as a young man growing up in the Brooklyn projects. The biographical aspect of the poems seems crucial to the intervention into Jewish history he is making. For Espada, his Jewishness and his appreciation for radical working-class left-wing Jewish traditions is not primarily textual or religious: it is about lived and relational practices of solidarity and resistance. That is not to say that Jewish texts are unimportant for Espada—proletarian poet Edwin Rolfe (Solomon Fishman) is one of Espada's more oft-cited poetic forebears—but rather that Espada's representation of Jewish history is relational, material, intersubjective, and deeply historical. Of course, the subjects of Espada's histories, whether they are farmworkers, Patterson silk strikers, or Jewish revolutionaries, are often people who, while personally perhaps highly literate, are written out of or simply never included in published histories of Jewish life, which privilege established Jewish institutions such as the AJC and ACJ and authors who themselves produced or wrote within established traditions of Jewish letters.

Espada's poem "How to Read Ezra Pound" serves this double function. Relating an interaction between the Spanish Civil War veteran of the Abraham Lincoln Brigade, Abe Osheroff, and a panel of poets on Ezra Pound, Espada narrates how Abe "raised his hand" to say, "If I knew / that a fascist / was a great poet / I'd shoot him / anyway."[98] The poem exposes the gap between Osheroff's lived experience, as both a Jew and a veteran of the fight against fascism in Spain, and the professional discussion of literature. In doing so, the poem further suggests that literature, especially canonical literature, has no place for a figure such as Osheroff, and that his experience is worth less than the poetry of a writer who literally endorsed the Holocaust. Such a statement also suggests that Osheroff has some experience with shooting fascists, which of course he did, an experience not only beyond the imagination of academic panels on poetry, but also representative of the rupture of orderly historical narratives in which lives such as Osheroff's are rendered marginal. Osheroff's very presence is a challenge to literature, history, and the academic production of both. The image of Osheroff politely raising his hand at a panel to offer his death verdict also implies that he, like Espada, gestures to a world outside of literature but is also very much capable of entering the room and disrupting the party from inside.

Espada wrote two other poems about Osheroff, both longer biographical pieces. Written as an elegy to Osheroff and printed alongside "How to Read Ezra Pound" in Espada's 2011 collection *The Trouble Ball*, "Like a Word That Somersaults through the Air" opens with Osheroff's first political awakening: an eviction, 1930s, Brooklyn.[99] Describing one of the many anti-eviction protests of the 1930s, the poem shows neighborhood children carrying a sofa "in a procession" to "evict the eviction" and make the "landlord a lord no more." In an escalating series of inversions, the poem states that Abe's "life begins" when he "snatches" the gun from a "cop waving a revolver" to stop the anti-eviction party and faces death, "squinting into his first arrest." "Like a word that somersaults through the air and cannot be unsaid" in one sense refers to Abe's act of disarming the police officer and then facing arrest, which cannot be undone; it is also a meditation on the act of writing itself and its relationship to social action. For Osheroff, words are not merely words; words, if they are to mean anything, are also a form of action. Much as Espada is fond of saying himself, the political poem is one that enacts the world one is trying to change it into being: it is part of a prophetic tradition of writing. "Words that cannot be unsaid" are holy utterances, speech acts, and spells: Abe's act, which prompted the poem, in its quiet but determined way is a symbolic gesture like that of speech—undoing evil, unseating a lord, and preventing a murder, while going quietly, without resisting, to prison.

Many of Espada's poems about Jewish life conclude with Espada as an imperfect but necessary recorder of both Jewish working-class and revolutionary history. In Espada's earliest poem about Osheroff, he describes in dread detail the torpedoing of Osheroff's passenger liner to Spain, the *Ciudad de Barcelona*, on his way to fight in the Abraham Lincoln Brigade.[100] Titled "The Carpenter Swam to Spain," the poem is a litany of wartime horror: the captain of the Brooklyn College swim team trapped below deck and drowning; the boat "punctured like a rib"; the seven-minute collapse of the vessel so close to shore that took the air from so many antifascist fighters: "at every porthole a face trapped." Yet the poem is also a testimony to the forceful and practical heroics of Osheroff, swimming the last two miles to shore, aided by the local fishers offering "blankets and rum" for the survivors. It is also a celebration not only of the fighters' heroism, but their radical politics, singing union songs and raising clenched fists for the camera. The poem, however, does not end with final comments on Osheroff's fortunes during the war; rather it concludes with a line about the poet himself, "like a telegraph operator / with news of survivors." At once the final lines of the poem are about the role of the poet-historian, disrupting the homogenous time of the capitalist present: there are survivors, still, of the socialist fight against fascism, and the poem insists on their still-living presence.

In two other poems that chronicle working-class Jewish life in New

York City, Espada also positions himself as a kind of translator of experience. In "The Task of the Translator," Walter Benjamin describes a translator's role as producing a second life, an after-life, of the original work.[101] Espada seems to be both, expressing the world of these Jewish working-class figures while at the same time bringing them into a secondary medium as a way to offer their histories another and perhaps even more disruptive life as a poem. In "Bastard Son of King Levinsky," Espada—who calls himself "something of an expert on Jewish boxers"—offers a portrait of a now-forgotten Yiddishkeit heavyweight boxer who fought—and lost to—Joe Louis before going on to sell ties on the streets of Chicago.[102] Espada's portrait of Levinsky, however, is merely the opening for his memory of another even less well-known and less fortunate Jewish boxer: Herbie Wilens, "the Hebrew Hitter." Espada describes their brief friendship over beer in the stockroom, where Herbie would smash boxes with his fist on which the narrator would write his poems. Wilens was found dead in his midfifties, and Espada memorializes his unlucky comrade, "the bastard son of King Levinsky . . . middle weight champion of the stockroom," whose career lasted a single fight in Jersey City. Espada's memorializing of working-class Jewish life is expressed in another poem about the death and life of his friend, the critic Jules Chametzky, the son of a kosher butcher, someone he remembers through words, like his own working-class father's, that burn and vanish "like fireflies." Both poems, like the poem about Osheroff, offer poetry itself as a mode of radical memory, a stand-in for the fists of the "Hebrew Hitter" or the guns of the Abraham Lincoln Brigade members who did not arrive at shore.

Critics Bill Mullen and Janet Zandy locate Espada's work within the longer tradition of proletarian literature in the US, tracing this lineage from slave narratives to the flowering of working-class writing during the "red decade" of the 1930s.[103] Espada himself recognizes his work as carrying on this tradition, from both the Latin American poetry of Pablo Neruda and Roque Dalton to the US tradition stemming from the poetry of Edwin Rolfe, Tillie Olsen, and Muriel Rukeyser. It is a project that is as much a question of style—a prophetic realism—as it is ontological. As Zandy states, one of the primary subjective moves of proletarian literature is expansion from "I" to "we," the construction of a collective imaginary—both as speaker and object of the poem. Espada's poetry is in close familial relation to Mike Gold's 1921 essay "Toward a

Proletarian Art," in which Gold states that he is a conduit for working-class experience: "The tenement speaks through me," he says, making his own body a kind of medium for working-class experiences others cannot or have not expressed. It's fair to say, then, that Espada's poems create a collective imaginary of a Jewish radical subject, but also, if one reads Espada's entire corpus, a multiethnic polity, a Whitmanic America of which the Jewish radical is a part. In "All the People Who Are Now Red Trees," this collective radical subject is imagined as a forest, consisting of figures ranging from veterans of the Spanish Civil War, like Osheroff, to Sacco and Vanzetti, to Puerto Rican independence activists, all described as different variations of "red leaves," "red wreaths in the treetops," raising "branches / like broken rifles."[104]

In Espada's poem to the Rosenbergs, he imagines a dream sequence in which the narrator—a tenant lawyer—cannot, as the judge demands, offer an eleventh reason for the Rosenbergs to be spared, after he has offered ten. In one of the pieces of "evidence" the narrator offers, "We will glimpse the electric chair on television / and shriek Jew, Jew, Jew, and then deny we said it," noting not only the American disavowal of antisemitism, but the ways in which the very Jewish tradition from which Espada writes will be evoked and also forgotten.[105] In the conclusion of the poem, the defeated tenant lawyer sees the Rosenbergs' son Robbie, now an old man, sitting on a bench. Comforting the narrator for his sense of failure, the dream-Robbie says the executioner intentionally demands the impossible. "Then all of us are killed, I say." Robbie responds, "Not yet . . . Not yet." In the move from "I" to "we" in the poem, the narrator, who is neither a member of the Communist Party nor on death row, includes himself in the collective targeted by the state. Robbie does not correct him, but offers instead a collective of struggle, a futuricity generated by the story of the poem itself.

In their blending of his own fate with the history of past Jewish radicals, Espada's biographies of working-class Jews call to mind another poet often included in progressive Passover Haggadot, Aurora Levins Morales. Her poem "Red Sea," which is included as often, if not more often, than Espada's "Imagine the Angels of Bread," is, like "Imagine . . .," a utopian redemption of history, in this case by refusing the nationalism implicit in the Exodus story.[106] Drawing on both images of climate change and migration, Levins Morales imagines an "Exodus" in which "this time . . . all of us must be chosen / This time it's all of us or none." As

Levins Morales, like Espada, describes herself as a Jewish Puerto Rican anti-colonial writer, she also fuses the working-class radicalism of both Jewish labor organizers and Puerto Rican anti-colonial activists into a diasporic reimagining of Jewish life. Evoking herself as the granddaughter of garment workers in New York City, she compares her own hands, which are now attempting to create a decolonized future for Puerto Rico, her "homeland," with the work-heavy hands of her union-activist grandparents.[107]

It seems like less a coincidence than an important affinity that the two living Jewish poets most often included in radical Haggadot and sermons are both of Puerto Rican descent and that both memorialize working-class Jewish life without irony or discomfort. Perhaps because their own anti-colonial struggle against the United States to liberate Puerto Rico does not fill them with the kind of disquiet that Israel evokes in many left-wing US Jews, their own Jewish radical histories—experienced or witnessed—seem less alien or distant. Perhaps it is their working-class backgrounds that place them at odds not only with Jewish literary culture, but American literary culture writ large. But their presence in American letters as radical Jewish writers and, more centrally, within the spiritual and communal traditions of Jewish life, suggests that there is a living and still-disruptive memory to Jewish radical history. Whether through Levins Morales's remembrances of Yiddish garment workers in New York or Espada's Jewish revolutionary activists or boxers, both seem to suggest that there is something vital about this history that can align with current revolutionary traditions, even if such history is not reducible to them. The question then remains: What if we were to make the history Espada and Levins Morales represent less implicit, and more explicit as textures of radical anti-Zionist practice; what worlds would we have to win?

This question of course arises at a moment of crisis for Palestine: the reemergence, always latent within Zionism, of a "second Nakba"—a post-1948 attempt to ethnically cleanse hundreds of thousands if not millions of Palestinians from their homes, by overwhelming military force, into refugee camps or mass graves. Yet despite predictions that the left will again split over Palestine as it has or has threatened to do in years past, this time around it appears that the opposite could happen: the left, even liberal-left, seems more united than ever in opposition to Israeli apartheid and Israeli militarism. From Politico to MSN, media

The Antinomies of Jewish Liberalism

outlets' characterizations of the left in rancorous debate over Palestine have been wildly overstated.[108] Indeed, the DSA and JVP have both *grown* by thousands of members since October 7, suggesting that JVP's and DSA's broad calls for a ceasefire and an end to US aid to Israel are uniting rather than dividing. As one Jewish DSA activist writes, protests against the Israeli assault on Gaza may "rebuild a new nationwide antiwar movement."[109] This sudden surge in Jewish left anti-Zionism does not mean that there is a wide agreement on what a new chapter of the Jewish left should look like, what role it should play in building a movement, and how it should relate to Jewish culture, Jewish history, even Jewish people.

If one could pinpoint three overlapping yet distinct anti-Zionist positions in our current conjuncture, one might say they are, loosely, classical liberalism, Marxism, and left religious Judaism. It has been my contention that these positions are often inseparable, and are conjoined by many shared assumptions about Jewish life and social justice, but also shared between families and institutions in ways that are, if not entirely new, at least creatively reconfigured. Religious Jewish leaders such as Brant Rosen are members of DSA; DSA members belong to the temple for which he is a rabbi; classical Jewish liberals such as Peter Beinart come closer to the left; JVP consists of both rabbinical students and very secular socialists; Old Left journals such as *Jewish Currents* increasingly embrace religious Judaism; and so on. Yet there are distinctions to be made in terms of how one conceives of the center of Jewish community and how one calls upon a Jewish history or tradition to anchor that community, both within a sense of time and a collective past. While religious and secular texts are not incompatible, they are distinct in terms of their epistemologies and their constitution of Jewish subjectivity. I would like to propose with this chapter that the memory of the American Jewish left is an integral part of keeping a broader anti-Zionist Jewish left alive, if the purpose is to live with a people, within many peoples, yet without a country to call home.

Acknowledgments

This book owes its stirrings, decades ago, to the many US social movements that have joined together in solidarity for a just, democratic future in Palestine. Social movements not only produce new subjects; they produce new forms of memory and history. The questions and stories the book poses arose among conversations with activists and intellectuals about a new formation of a Jewish left: what a new Jewish left might mean not only for global human rights and democracy, but also for Jewish identity, history, and our own sense of ourselves in community. In other words, my thanks begin with many people I do not know and do not know how to name or to thank.

I can, however, thank many friends, colleagues, and comrades who helped make this book possible. I would like to begin by thanking Linda Loew, who helped me to arrange many interviews with Jewish radicals from the 1960s and 1970s. As we joked, she played "yenta" between the Jewish Marxist New Left and me. I would like to further thank Myron Perlman (Z"L) who introduced me to memory of the Chutzpah Collective, whose friendship opened the doors and voices of many Chicago activists. And I would like to also thank Lane Silberstein, Javier Miranda, Jon Danforth-Appel, and Sharona Gordon, who connected me to many activists from DSA's Jewish Solidarity Caucus and who were generous with their time, stories, and personal archives. I am also extraordinarily grateful for the guidance, friendship, and inspiration of people who at one time or another read parts of the manuscript, offered help and suggestions, and were intelligent and gracious interlocutors: Rabab Abdulhadi, Scott Boehm, Aryeh Bernstein, Zackery Sholem Berger, Ari Bloomekatz, Rachel Ida-Buff, Rika Chandra, Tobi Erner, Martín Espada, José Fusté, Annie Sommer Kaufman, James Kim, Joo Ok Kim, Susan Klonsky, Ben Laurence, Vincent Lloyd, Brooke Lober, Ben Mabie, JW Mason, Jake Mattox, Nate Mills, Raffi Magarik, S. Ani Mukherji, Bill V. Mullen, Julie Oppenheimer, Chris Perreira, Robin Peterson, David Shulman, Laura Tanenbaum, Micah Uetricht, and Leslie Williams. Alan Wald has been a continual mentor and éminence grise through this process; we all come out from the shelves of his bookcase. I would especially like to thank Ben Lorber, who not only has been my bestie, comrade, and constant reader, but often reminds me why it is important to complete this work. And finally I would like to offer thanks in memory of Paul Chaim Mishler (Z"L), whose comradeship, friendship, and knowledge of all things Jewish left was an inspiration. His memory is a blessing and also the material substance of this book.

I am grateful for the support of Indiana University's New Frontiers Foundation and Faculty Research Grants, without which neither the travel nor the time would have been available to finish this project. I would also like to thank the librarians and archivists at the Labadie Collection, New York Public Library, Radcliff Institute, Interlibrary Loan, and Bolerium Books, as well as the personal pamphlet and newspaper collections of Mirriam Socoloff and Alan Wald. To my colleagues at Indiana University, I would especially like to thank (again) Jake Mattox, as well as the radical luminaries Darryl Heller and April Lidinsky, the AAUP crew, and especially my department chair, Elaine Roth, for her continued and ongoing support.

Casting a slightly wider institutional lens, I would like to thank Cindy Wu and Benjamin Robinson at IU Bloomington for their invitation to share my work with their colleagues; Shaul Magid for his kind invitation to speak to the Jewish Studies Program at Dartmouth College early in this research and his invitation to submit an article to a special edition of *Shofar* on critics of Zionism. I would also like to thank Atalia Omer for inviting me to contribute thoughts on the Jewish left for *Contending Modernities*, as well as Sai Englert and Alex de Jong for soliciting my work for a special issue of *Historical Materialism* on Marxism and antisemitism. I would especially like to

Acknowledgments

thank Mari Yoshihara, past editor of *American Quarterly*, for soliciting excellent external reviewers and for nominating my first scholarly essay on anti-Zionism and the Jewish left for the American Literature Society's 1921 Prize—it was quite a confidence boost. Vanessa Wills and Zach Levenson also deserve a shout-out for printing my thoughts on all things left-wing and Jewish at their wonderful journal, *Spectre*. And to Naomi Bennet, special thanks for making sure questions about the Jewish left and antisemitism from a Marxian perspective remain on the docket at the Socialism Conference, and for repeatedly inviting me to speak with you on the bimah. A big thanks to Mitch Jeserich for his invitation to let me speak on the Jewish left and anti-Zionism on my favorite radio show, KPFA's *Letters and Politics*. And lastly, to the activists at the University of Chicago Palestine Solidarity encampment, the Palestine, Arab, and Muslim Caucus of the California Faculty Association, Workman's Circle of Chicago, Civil Rights Heritage Center of South Bend, and Jewish Voice for Peace, your interest in my work and the sense that it might be useful to the movement have kept me going.

Of course, I also need to thank the good folks at Verso Books: Asher Dupuy-Spencer, for his editorial enthusiasm, political comradeship, and smarts about book publishing, and to Sebastian Bugden, for his early backing of the project, indefatigable labor for the press, and ongoing support of this project. And big thanks to Julie McCarroll, Chris Dodge, and Jeanne Tao for their labor, grit, and perseverance copyediting, indexing, and helping to produce this book.

I also need to thank Chicago Jewish Voice for Peace and Tzedek-Chicago for being my diasporic, anti-Zionist Jewish home: both communities have allowed me to find a meaningful Jewish life, a moral and political grounding in difficult times. Special thanks to Brant Rosen for bringing Tzedek-Chicago to life. And a distant shout-out over decades to Students for Justice in Palestine, UC San Diego, for inviting me to speak at a student divestment vote and for welcoming me in the organization in 2006—it was the beginning of a long journey.

And finally, I need to thank my family: my wonderful parents, Susan Mozenter-Balthasar and Lawrence Balthasar, whose support and (im)patience with my book writing have kept me going to the finish line. "Well, is it done yet?" has been the first line of nearly every phone call for the last eight years. And to my elder brother, Nicholas, for being smarter than me and more responsible—it takes the pressure off. And to my aunt Judith Tolchin, who always made sure books were in the Christmukah stockings and to whom I am always overdue a letter. And to my late grandparents, Hyman and Merriam Grossman-Mozenter, for my early education on the Jewish left.

Notes

Introduction

1. Robert Gessner, "The Volunteer," *George Amberg and Robert Gessner Papers*, New York Public Library Special Collections, "The Writings of Robert Gessner," Box 2.
2. Melanie Kaye/Kantrowitz, "Some Pieces of Jewish Left: 1987," *Bridges* 1, no. 1 (Spring 1990/5750), 7–22.
3. Podhoretz quoted in Keith Feldman, *Shadow over Palestine: The Imperial Life of Race in America* (Minneapolis: University of Minnesota Press, 2017), 109. See also Amy Kaplan, *Our American Israel: The Story of an Entangled Alliance* (Cambridge, MA: Harvard University Press), 104, 135; Melani McAlister, "The Good Fight: Israel after Vietnam," in *Epic Encounters: Culture, Media, and U.S. Interests in the Middle East since 1945* (Berkeley: University of California Press, 2005), 155–97; Marc Dollinger, *Black Power, Jewish Politics: Reinventing the Alliance in the 1960s* (Waltham, MA: Brandeis University Press, 2018), xii, 7, 9.
4. Michael Lind, "The Left's Campus Protest Scam," *Tablet*, May 15, 2024, tabletmag.com; Park MacDougald, "The People Setting America on Fire," *Tablet*, May 6, 2024, tabletmag.com.
5. Will Alden, "A New Jewishness Is Being Born before Our Eyes," *Nation*, May 10, 2024, thenation.com.
6. Abbie Hoffman, *The Autobiography of Abbie Hoffman* (New York: Four Walls Eight Windows, 1980), 139.
7. "Jewish Organizing at Columbia's Encampment," *On the Nose* (podcast), April 25, 2024, jewishcurrents.org.
8. David Duhalde, interview with author, March 2023. As a longtime DSA activist, Duhalde noted that up until the post-2016 "surge," one could make jokes in Yiddish and the room would laugh along with you. And while the influx of new members in states without a large Jewish population did lessen the ratio of Jewish to gentile members, this had little to do with the BDS vote in 2017.
9. Ronald Radosh, "Israel Boycott Backlash: 'This Is Not the DSA I Founded,'" *Daily Beast*, August 8, 2017, thedailybeast.com; Maurice Isserman, "Why I Quit the DSA," *Nation*,

October 23, 2023, thenation.com; Paul Berman, "Disgrace and the Democratic Socialists of America," *Tablet*, August 7, 2017, tabletmag.com; Michael Bernick, "America's Democratic Socialists Loved Israel," *Tablet*, October 24, 2023, tabletmag.com.
10. Michael R. Fischbach, *The Movement and the Middle East: How the Arab-Israeli Conflict Divided the American Left* (Palo Alto, CA: Stanford University Press, 2020), 201–3.
11. Jewish Solidarity Caucus, "About and Platform," *Jewish Socialism* (blog), August 9, 2017, medium.com.
12. Karen Brodkin, *How Jews Became White Folks and What That Says about Race in America* (New Brunswick, NJ: Rutgers University Press, 1998), 105.
13. Alan Fisher, "Realignment of the Jewish Vote?," *Political Science Quarterly* 94, no. 1 (Spring 1979), 97–116.
14. Tony Michels, *A Fire in Their Hearts: Yiddish Socialists in New York* (Cambridge, MA: Harvard University Press, 2005), 3–4.
15. Ibid., 74–5.
16. Michael Denning, *The Cultural Front: The Laboring of American Culture in the Twentieth Century* (New York: Verso, 1998), xv.
17. Brodkin, *How Jews Became White Folks*, 113.
18. Mathew B. Hoffman and Henry F. Srebrnik, eds., *A Vanished Ideology: Essays on the Jewish Communist Movement in the English-Speaking World in the Twentieth Century* (Binghamton: SUNY Press, 2016), 5.
19. Alexander Bittelman, *The Jewish People Face the Post-war World* (New York: Morning Freiheit Association, 1945).
20. Yuri Slezkine, *The Jewish Century* (Princeton, NJ: Princeton University Press, 2004), 204–372.
21. Amelia M. Glaser, *Songs in Dark Times: Yiddish Poetry of Struggle from Scottsboro to Palestine* (Cambridge, MA: Harvard University Press, 2020), 106–18.
22. Lisa Lowe, *Immigrant Acts: Asian American Cultural Politics* (Durham, NC: Duke University Press, 1996). Lowe argues that many immigrant novels feature a "teleology of assimilation" as either a shibboleth to observe or a dominant ideology to critique.
23. There is a long debate to be had about whether Marxism and intersectionality are identical, commensurate, analogous, and/or contradictory. I would suggest that Stuart Hall's "Race, Articulation, and Societies Structured in Dominance," Althusser's theory of overdetermination, and Omi and Winant's theory of racial formation are Marxist articulations of the complex manner racial identity is co-constitutive with formations of gender and class in ways that are contextual and historically specific. If there is a single difference between Marxism and Kimberlé Crenshaw's theory of intersectionality, it would be that capitalism as a political and economic system determines relations of class, race, and gender as structures required to secure conditions for future accumulation. It would seem Bittelman, like other Marxists of his era, including C. L. R. James and Claudia Jones, attempts such a formulation. Stuart Hall, "Race, Articulation, and Societies Structured in Dominance," in *Essential Essays*, vol. 1, ed. David Morley (Durham, NC: Duke University Press, 2019), 172–221; Louis Althusser, "Contradiction and Overdetermination," *New Left Review* 1, no. 41 (January/February 1967), newleftreview.org; Michael Omi and Howard Winant, *Racial Formation in the United States from the 1960s to the 1990s* (London: Routledge, 2014).
24. Alexander Bittelman, *Study Guide on the Jewish Question* (New York: National Jewish Commission of the Communist Party, 1946), 2.

25. Penny M. Von Eschen, *Race against Empire: Black Americans and Anticolonialism, 1937–1957* (Ithaca, NY: Cornell University Press, 1997); and Robin D. G. Kelley, *Freedom Dreams: The Black Radical Imagination* (Boston: Beacon Press, 2002).
26. Mark Naison, *Communists in Harlem during the Depression* (Urbana: University of Illinois Press, 2005), 39–41. Naison charts how, after the decline of the Garveyite movement, many Black radicals were actively recruited into the Communist Party, suggesting both the importance of Black self-determination for the Communist Party in the US as well as the fluidity of political discourse on the radical left.
27. Robin Kelley is dismissive of the importance of Communist Party's slogan "Self-determination in the Black Belt," citing the greater importance of the practical issues of racism, employment, and anti-lynching to Communist Party organizing strategy in the South in *Hammer and Hoe: Alabama Communists during the Great Depression* (Chapel Hill: University of North Carolina Press, 1990), 122, 225. However, Kelley argues in *Race Rebels* (New York: Free Press, 1996) that Black nationalism was a central part of the cultural literary production of Black CP activists. Mark Naison agrees that the doctrine was never a practical campaign issue, yet he argues formulating an answer to Black nationalism was theoretically crucial for focusing Communist Party leaders to take Black issues more seriously, organizing solidarity movements against the invasion of Ethiopia, and creating a revolutionary imaginary that could equal the Garveyites' visionary pull of militant nationalism.
28. Anthony Dawahare, *Nationalism, Marxism, and African American Literature between the Wars* (Jackson: University Press of Mississippi, 2003), 73–6; Robin D. G. Kelley, "'Africa's Sons with Banner Red': African American Communists and the Politics of Culture, 1919–1934," in *Race Rebels*, 103–22.
29. Abdul JanMohamed, "The Economy of Manichean Allegory: The Function of Racial Difference in Colonialist Literature," *Critical Inquiry* 12, no. 1 (Autumn 1985), 59–87.
30. Santiago Slabodsky, *Decolonial Judaism: Triumphal Failures of Barbaric Thinking* (New York: Palgrave MacMillan, 2014), 79.
31. Walter Benjamin, "Theses on a Philosophy of History," in *Illuminations*, ed. Hannah Arendt, trans. Harry Zohn (New York: Schocken Books, 1968), 256–7.
32. Theodor Adorno and Max Horkheimer, *Dialectic of Enlightenment: Philosophical Fragments*, ed. Gunzelin Schmid Noerr, trans. Edmund Jephcott (Palo Alto, CA: Stanford University Press, 2002), 1–34.
33. Slabodsky, *Decolonial Judaism*, 91.
34. Bittelman, *Study Guide*, 10.
35. Hannah Arendt, "Zionism Reconsidered," *Menorah Journal* 32, no. 2 (October–December 1945), 162–95.
36. Robert Gessner, "Brown Shirts in Zion: Jabotinsky—the Jewish Hitler," *New Masses*, February 1935, 12.
37. Stuart Hall, "Gramsci's Relevance for the Study of Race and Ethnicity," in *Essential Essays*, vol. 2, ed. David Morley (Durham, NC: Duke University Press, 2019), 43.
38. Susan Eanet-Klonsky, interview with author, June 2019.
39. Susan Eanet, "History of Middle East Liberation," *New Left Notes* 4, no. 11 (March 1969), 6.
40. Bittelman, *Study Guide*, 7–8.
41. "Breira Conference," *Chutzpah* 12 (n.d.), 3, 14.
42. Myron Perlman and Arden Handler, "Nazis Threaten Skokie and We Are Not Afraid," *Chutzpah* 13 (n.d.), 5.

43. Jewish Solidarity Caucus, "About and Platform."
44. Gabriel Winant, "You Don't Want to Know This," *n+1* 44 (Winter 2023), nplusonemag.com. As Winant summarizes, "Within SDS, opposed factions had squared off over the question of the class position of the students and young professionals who made up the group's base. Some argued that they were petit bourgeois and therefore had to commit a kind of social suicide in order to succeed in organizing the proletariat, the real potential force for revolution—cutting their hair, shaving their beards, quitting dope, and getting factory jobs. Others argued that this was far too narrow a definition of *proletarian*: Were students not in fact the leading edge of a new working class, since they would become the professionals who operated the giant firms that were the engines of American capitalism?"
45. David Gilbert, Robert Gottlieb, and Gerry Tenney, "Toward a Theory of Social Change: The 'Port Authority Statement,'" in Carl Davidson, ed., *Revolutionary Youth and the New Working Class: The Praxis Papers, the Port Authority Statement, the RYM Documents and Other Lost Writings of SDS* (Pittsburgh, PA: Changemaker Publications, 2011), 108.
46. Myron Perlman, conversation with author, July 8, 2014.
47. Claire Melissa Bergin, "We Were Made for These Times: Diasporism as an Emergent Jewish Movement" (master's thesis, Indiana University, 2021).
48. Molly Crabapple, "My Great-Grandfather the Bundist," *New York Review of Books*, October 6, 2018, nybooks.com; Diaspora Alliance, "Our Work," diasporaalliance.co; Melanie Kaye/Kantrowitz, *The Colors of Jews: Racial Politics and Radical Diasporaism* (Bloomington: Indiana University Press, 2007), xii; Judith Butler, *Parting Ways: Jewishness and the Critique of Zionism* (New York: Columbia University Press, 2012), 1–3; Jonathan and Daniel Boyarin, *The Powers of Diaspora: Two Essays on the Relevance of Jewish Culture* (Minneapolis: University of Minnesota Press, 2002), 4–6.
49. Butler, *Parting Ways*, 1; Daniel Boyarin, *The No-State Solution: A Jewish Manifesto* (New Haven, CT: Yale University Press, 2023), 1–6.
50. Atalia Omer, "Restorative Justice Pathways in Palestine/Israel: Undoing the Settler Colonial Captivity of Jewishness," *Shofar: An Interdisciplinary Journal of Jewish Studies* 41, no. 2 (Summer 2023), 154–85.
51. Chutzpah Collective, "Chutzpah Principles," 1979, personal collection of Miriam Socoloff.
52. Jacob Plitman, "On an Emerging Diasporism," *Jewish Currents*, April 16, 2018, jewishcurrents.org.
53. Peter Beinart, "I No Longer Believe in a Jewish State," *New York Times*, July 8, 2020; Peter Beinart, "Yavne: A Jewish Case for Equality in Israel-Palestine," *Jewish Currents*, July 7, 2020, jewishcurrents.org.
54. Philip Roth, *The Counterlife* (New York: Vintage International, 1986), 323–4.
55. James Bloom, *Roth's Wars: A Career in Conflict* (Lanham, MD: Lexington Books, 2022), 133.
56. Ben Burgis, "Left Identitarianism Is Also a Mirror World," *Damage*, July 30, 2024, damagemag.com.
57. Shaul Magid, *The Necessity of Exile: Essays from a Distance* (New York: Ayin Press, 2023), 13–20.
58. Herb Keinon and Greer Fay Cashman, "Netanyahu at Holocaust Memorial: 'The Strong Survive, the Weak Are Erased,'" *Jerusalem Post*, April 24, 2017, jpost.com.
59. Daniel Boyarin, *Unheroic Conduct: The Rise of Heterosexuality and the Invention of the Jewish Man* (Berkeley: University of California Press, 1997), xvii, 23–40; Hannah

Arendt, *The Origins of Totalitarianism* (New York: Harcourt Brace Jovanovich, 1973), xv.
60. Magid, *Necessity of Exile*, 22.
61. Edward Said, *Freud and the Non-European* (New York: Verso, 2014), 54, 41–3.
62. Butler, *Parting Ways*, 31.
63. Boyarin, *No-State Solution*, vii.
64. Ibid., x, 10.
65. Ibid., 27.
66. Ibid., x.
67. Ibid., 70, 54.
68. Brent Hayes Edwards, *The Practice of Diaspora: Literature, Translation, and the Rise of Black Internationalism* (Cambridge, MA: Harvard University Press, 2003), 11, 7.
69. Stuart Hall, "Thinking the Diaspora: Home Thoughts from Abroad," in *Essential Essays*, vol. 2, 209, 224.
70. Richard Wright and Edwin Rosskam, *12 Million Black Voices* (New York: Basic Books, 2008), 1–2, 16; Paul Gilroy, *The Black Atlantic: Modernity and Double Consciousness* (Cambridge, MA: Harvard University Press, 1993), 30.
71. Edward Said, "Reflections on Exile," in *Reflections on Exile and Other Essays* (Cambridge, MA: Harvard University Press, 2000), 184.
72. Hall, "Thinking the Diaspora," 208; Edwards, *Practice of Diaspora*, 8.
73. Gilroy, *Black Atlantic*, 55.
74. Tiffany Lethabo King, Jenell Navarro, and Andrea Smith, eds., *Otherwise Worlds: Against Settler Colonialism and Anti-Blackness* (Durham, NC: Duke University Press, 2020); Jared Sexton, "Afro-Pessimism: The Unclear Word," *Rhizomes* 29 (2016), rhizomes.net.
75. Hall, "Thinking the Diaspora," 216.
76. Glaser, *Songs in Dark Times*, 1–38.
77. Isaac Deutscher, "What Is a Jew," in *The Non-Jewish Jew and Other Essays* (New York: Verso, 2017), 52, 45, 51.
78. Mike Gold, *Jews without Money* (Philadelphia: Public Affairs, 2009), 87.
79. Josep Maria Antentas, "Daniel Bensaïd's Marrano Internationalism," *Historical Materialism: Research in Critical Marxist Theory* 30, no. 2 (2022), 135–68.
80. Ibid.
81. Daniel Bensaïd, *An Impatient Life: A Memoir*, trans. David Fernbach (New York: Verso, 2015), 271–3.
82. Ibid., 282.
83. See also writings on Middle Eastern and North African Communist Parties, often with outsized Jewish membership—and often, in Morocco, Egypt, and Iraq, with their own analogous if not identical construction of anti-Zionist Jewish and also national/international belonging: Alma Rachel Heckman, *The Sultan's Communists: Moroccan Jews and the Politics of Belonging* (Palo Alto, CA: Stanford University Press, 2021); Joel Beinin, *The Dispersion of Egyptian Jewry: Culture, Politics and the Formation of a Modern Diaspora* (Berkeley: University of California Press, 1998).
84. Alberto Moreau, "Appraising the Middle East War," *Political Affairs*, October 1967, marxists.org.
85. Max Kaiser, *Jewish Antifascism and the False Promise of Settler Colonialism* (Cham: Palgrave MacMillan, 2022), 6–8.
86. Howard Fast, "An Epitaph for Sidney," *Jewish Life* 1, no. 3 (January 1947), 10–13.
87. Morris Schappes, "Commentary on 'An Epitaph for Sidney,'" *Jewish Life* 1, no. 4 (February 1947).

88. Alexander Bittelman, "The Content of Jewish Culture," *Jewish Life* 1, no. 4 (February 1947), 21; Editors, "What Is Progressive Jewish Culture?," *Jewish Life* 1, no. 4 (February 1947), 25–7.
89. Milton Blau, "Right Ammunition—Wrong Target," *Jewish Life* 1, no. 5 (March 1947), 21–2; Moise Katz, "Who Is to Blame," *Jewish Life* 1, no. 5 (March 1947), 23–4.
90. Fast, "Epitaph for Sidney," 12.
91. Boyarin, *Unheroic Conduct*, xvii, 23–4.
92. Butler, *Parting Ways*, 42.
93. "The Palestinian Arabs," *Chutzpah* 9/10 (n.d.), 10.
94. Maralee Gordon, interview with author, July 30, 2021.
95. Theodor Adorno, *Minima Moralia: Reflections on a Damaged Life* (London: Verso, 2005), 38–9.
96. Terry Eagleton, "Irony and Commitment," in *Nationalism, Colonialism, and Literature* (Minneapolis: University of Minnesota Press, 1990).
97. Franklin Foer, "The Golden Age of American Jews Is Ending," *Atlantic*, March 4, 2024, theatlantic.com.
98. Dorothy Zellner, "What We Did: How the Jewish Left Failed the Palestinian Cause," *Jewish Currents*, May 12, 2021, jewishcurrents.org.
99. Shaul Magid, *Meir Kahane: The Public Life and Political Thought of an American Jewish Radical* (Princeton, NJ: Princeton University Press, 2021), 73–6.
100. Anna Elena Torres, *Horizons Blossom, Borders Vanish: Anarchism and Yiddish Literature* (New Haven, CT: Yale University Press, 2024), 4–6.
101. Caroline Chung Simpson, *An Absent Presence: Japanese Americans in Postwar American Culture, 1945–1960* (Durham, NC: Duke University Press, 2002). Simpson discusses the way Japanese internment shaped Cold War American culture, while it also remained the subject of a great disavowal, both in US culture and broader Japanese American culture. While it's not a precise analogy to the memory/forgetting of the US left, the Red Scare, the Rosenberg Trial, and the Holocaust refugee crisis, the way these events both structure Jewish American life and are disavowed seems similar. Also, Louis Althusser's structure of unconscious overdetermination in the "absent cause" of history might be another metaphor for this phenomenon, insofar as it is a dislocation of the historical subject within a conception of history. Louis Althusser and Étienne Balibar, *Reading Capital* (London: Gresham Press, 1977).
102. Eileen Jones, "The Coen Brothers and Their Big Socialist Losers," *Jacobin*, February 14, 2022, jacobin.com.
103. Gessner, "Brown Shirts in Zion," 11–13.
104. Robert Gessner, "The Volunteer," *George Amberg and Robert Gessner Papers*, New York Public Library Special Collections, "The Writings of Robert Gessner," Box 2.
105. Lazare quoted in Alain Brossat and Sylvia Klingberg, *Revolutionary Yiddishland: A History of Jewish Radicalism*, trans. David Fernbach (New York: Verso, 2016).
106. Hoffman and Srebrnik, *A Vanished Ideology*; Andrew Silverstein, "In the Story of Two Jewish Bunds, a Stark Generational Divide over Israel," *Forward*, February 21, 2024, forward.com.
107. Irving Howe, *World of Our Fathers: The Journey of the East European Jews to America and the Life They Found and Made* (New York: Schocken Books, 1976).
108. Lila Corwin Berman, *Speaking of Jews: Rabbis, Intellectuals, and the Creation of an American Public Identity* (Berkeley: University of California Press, 2009), 6; Cheryl Lynn Greenberg, *Troubling the Waters: Black-Jewish Relations in the American*

Century (Princeton, NJ: Princeton University Press, 2006), 8; Steven R. Weisman, "How America's Jews Learned to Be Liberal," *New York Times*, August 18, 2018, nytimes.com.
109. Michael Cholden-Brown et al., "Our World and the World of Our 'Fathers,'" *Chutzpah* 13 (n.d.), 10–13.
110. Dick Flacks, "The Liberated Generation: An Exploration of the Roots of Student Protest," *Journal of Social Issues* 23, no. 3 (1967), 52–75.
111. Michael Rogin, *Ronald Reagan, the Movie, and Other Episodes in Political Demonology* (Berkeley: University of California Press, 1987).
112. Ellen Schrecker, *Many Are the Crimes: McCarthyism in America* (New York: Little, Brown, 1998), x.
113. Yosef Hayim Yerushalmi, *Zakhor: Jewish History and Jewish Memory* (Seattle: University of Washington Press, 1989), 5.
114. Laurence A. Kotler-Berkowitz, "Ethnic Cohesion and Division among American Jews: The Role of Mass-Level and Organizational Politics," *Ethnic and Racial Studies* 20, no. 4 (October 1997), 797–829.
115. Jacob Savage, "The Vanishing: The Erasure of Jews from American Life," *Tablet*, February 28, 2023, tabletmag.com.
116. I use Louis Althusser's formulation of a historical conjuncture defined by a combination of social forces in a particular balance, "Contradiction and Overdetermination." Louis Althusser, *For Marx*, trans. Ben Brewster (New York: Verso, 2005), 87–128.
117. Michel-Rolph Trouillot, "Power in the Story," in *Silencing the Past: Power and the Production of History* (Boston: Beacon Press, 1995), 25–7.
118. Slavoj Žižek, *The Sublime Object of Ideology* (New York: Verso, 2009).
119. Stuart Hall, "Cultural Studies: Two Paradigms," in *Essential Essays*, vol. 1, 47–52.
120. Kaye/Kantrowitz, "Some Pieces of Jewish Left," 7–22.

1. When Anti-Zionism Was Jewish

1. Mike Gold, *Jews without Money* (Philadelphia: Public Affairs, 2009), 164.
2. Alan Wald, *Writing from the Left: New Essays on Political Culture and Politics* (New York: Verso, 1994), 2–3.
3. I use Michael Denning's formulation of the "Long Popular Front" from the late 1920s to the late 1940s, to mark the beginning and endpoint of the period under discussion. Denning defines the Long Popular Front as "a social democratic electoral politics; a politics of anti-fascist and anti-imperialist solidarity, and a civil liberties campaign against lynching and labor repression," Michael Denning, *The Cultural Front: The Laboring of American Culture in the Twentieth Century* (New York, Verso, 1998), 9–10.
4. Andrew Furman, *Israel through the Jewish-American Imagination: A Survey of Jewish-American Literature on Israel 1928–1995* (Albany: State University of New York Press, 1997), 21–38.
5. Yuri Slezkine, *The Jewish Century* (Princeton, NJ: Princeton University Press, 2004), 204–372.
6. Robert Gessner, "Brown Shirts in Zion: Jabotinsky—the Jewish Hitler," *New Masses*, February 1935, 11–13. See also Michael Letwin, with Suzanne Adely and Jaime Veve, "Labor for Palestine: Challenging US Labor Zionism," *American*

Quarterly 67, no. 4 (December 2015), 1047–55: "Through the 1930s, Jewish workers in the United States were adamantly anti-Zionist"; Sidney M. Bolkosky, *Harmony and Dissonance: Voices of Jewish Identity in Detroit, 1914–1967* (Detroit: Wayne State University Press, 1991), 166–9.

7. Originally a Yiddish folk song recorded by musicologist Moshe Beregovski in 1931 in Kiev: "Oy Ir Narishe Tsienistn" (O You Foolish Little Zionists), on Daniel Kahn, Psoy Korolenko, and Oy Division, *The Unternationale*, Auris Media Records, 2008.

8. See Karen Brodkin, *How Jews Became White Folks and What That Says about Race in America* (New Brunswick, NJ: Rutgers University Press, 1998); Mathew Frye Jacobson, *Whiteness of a Different Color: European Immigrants and the Alchemy of Race* (Cambridge, MA: Harvard University Press, 1999). See also David Roediger, *Working toward Whiteness: How America's Immigrants Became White: The Strange Journey from Ellis Island to the Suburbs* (New York: Basic Books, 2006); and George Lipsitz, *Possessive Investment in Whiteness* (Philadelphia: Temple University Press, 2006), which explore how working-class southern and eastern European immigrants "became white" through a mixture of state intervention, assimilation, housing segregation, and the cultural politics of racism.

9. Alain Brossat and Sylvia Klingberg, *Revolutionary Yiddishland: A History of Jewish Radicalism*, trans. David Fernbach (New York: Verso, 2016), 1.

10. David Randall Verbeeten, *The Politics of Nonassimilation: The Jewish Left in the Twentieth Century* (DeKalb: Northern Illinois University Press, 2017), 28; Cheryl Lynn Greenberg, *Troubling the Waters: Black Jewish Relations in the American Century* (Princeton, NJ: Princeton University Press, 2006), 42. Also of note, in recent years, the "Ashkenormativity" of US Jewish history has been under increased scrutiny. From available sources, Ashkenazi Jews formed the leadership of the US Jewish Communist left at this time; one could surmise many reasons for this both flattering and damning to all communities concerned, but they are beyond the scope of this project. For more on the Sephardic presence in the United States, see Aviva Ben-Ur, *Sephardic Jews in America: A Diasporic History* (New York: New York University Press, 2009).

11. Denning, *The Cultural Front*; Robin D. G. Kelley, *Hammer and Hoe: Alabama Communists during the Great Depression* (Chapel Hill: University of North Carolina Press, 1990); Bill V. Mullen, *Popular Fronts: Chicago and African American Cultural Politics, 1935–46*, 2nd ed. (Urbana: University of Illinois Press, 2015); Alan Wald, *Exiles from a Future Time: The Forging of a Mid-Twentieth Century Left* (Chapel Hill: University of North Carolina Press, 2002).

12. Denning, *The Cultural Front*, 239.

13. Joel Beinin, *Was the Red Flag Flying There? Marxist Politics and the Arab-Israeli Conflict in Egypt and Palestine* (Berkeley: University of California Press, 1990), 24. While Beinin draws a firm line before and after 1947, Yaacov Ro'i suggests that Stalin and the senior leadership in the Soviet Union quietly began shifting their position toward binationalism and even Zionism as early as 1943: Yaacov Ro'i, *Soviet Decision Making in Practice: The USSR and Israel 1947–1954* (London: Transaction Books, 1980), 13–42. Yet, "in the subsequent period [after 1945], only a few non-ruling Communist parties expressed support for the Jewish cause": ibid., 18.

14. Editor's note in Gessner, "Brown Shirts in Zion," 11.

15. Earl Browder, *Zionism: Address at the Hippodrome Meeting June 8, 1936* (New York: Yidburo Publishers, 1936). The CP and other left groups issued many pamphlets and study guides on the question of Palestine and "the Jewish question," including

Paul Novik, *Solution for Palestine: The Chamberlain-White Paper* (New York: National Council of Jewish Communists, 1939); Earl Browder and John Arnold, *The Meaning of the Palestine Partition* (New York: New York State Jewish Buro of the Communist Party, 1937); Alexander Bittelman, *The Jewish People Face the Postwar World* (New York: Morning Freiheit Association, 1945); James W. Ford, *Anti-Semitism and the Struggle for Democracy* (New York: National Council of Jewish Communists, 1938), and more. Before 1947–48, when the Soviet Union officially changed its policy, all defined themselves as anti-Zionist and split only on the question of whether Jewish emigration should be allowed to Palestine at all.

16. Browder, *Zionism*, 13.
17. Ibid., 31.
18. Enzo Traverso, *The Marxists and the Jewish Question: The History of a Debate, 1843–1943* (Atlantic Highlands, NJ: Humanities Press, 1994), 108.
19. Gessner, "Brown Shirts in Zion," 11.
20. Jack Ross, *Rabbi Outcast: Elmer Berger and American Jewish Anti-Zionism* (Lincoln: University of Nebraska Press, 2011).
21. Ibid., 59, 63.
22. Brossat and Klingman, *Revolutionary Yiddishland*, 20, 4.
23. Peter Buch, introduction to Leon Trotsky, *On the Jewish Question* (New York: Pathfinder Press, 1970), 6.
24. Verbeeten, *The Politics of Nonassimilation*, 1–10.
25. Ibid., 58.
26. Henry Felix Srebrnik, *Dreams of Nationhood: American Jewish Communists and the Soviet Birobidzhan Project, 1924–1951* (Newton, MA: Academic Studies Press, 2010). While the Soviet Birobidzhan project was complicated and ultimately undermined by the same Soviet authorities who promoted it, in the US it served as a socialist, cultural nationalist alternative to Zionism, with Yiddish as its language and not tied to the colonial predations of Great Britain or the United States.
27. Verbeeten's *Politics of Nonassimilation* devotes a chapter to Bittelman, 30, 54.
28. Noam Pianko, *Jewish Peoplehood: An American Innovation* (New Brunswick, NJ: Rutgers University Press, 2015), 2–15.
29. Alexander Bittelman, *Study Guide on the Jewish Question* (New York: National Jewish Commission of the Communist Party, 1946), 3.
30. Ibid., 4.
31. Ibid., 3.
32. Ibid., 1.
33. Ibid., 12.
34. Ibid., 10. Musa Budeiri, *The Palestine Communist Party 1919–1948: Arab and Jew in the Struggle for Internationalism* (Chicago: Haymarket Books, 1979), xiii, xv–xvi; see also James W. Ford's comment that Jews should be allowed to emigrate to Palestine only "with full consent of the Arab people" and Jewish rights "guaranteed as a national minority": James W. Ford, *Anti-Semitism, the Struggle for Democracy, and the Negro People* (New York: Workers Library Publishers, 1939), 16. Ford was the most prominent African American member in the upper echelons of the CPUSA.
35. SWP Jewish Committee, *Theses of Revolutionary Socialists on the Jewish Problem* (New York: Socialist Workers Party, 1944), 29, Alan Wald's personal collection.
36. Ibid., 30.
37. Hannah Arendt, "Zionism Reconsidered," *Menorah Journal* 32, no. 2 (October–December 1945), 162–95.

38. John Arnold, "The Partition of Palestine," in Browder and Arnold, *The Meaning of the Palestine Partition*, 10.
39. Brodkin, *How Jews Became White Folks*, 1.
40. Roger Daniels, *Not Like Us: Immigrants and Minorities in America: 1890–1924* (Chicago: Ivan R. Dee Publishers, 1998).
41. Jacobson, *Whiteness of a Different Color*, 171–82.
42. Mai M. Ngai, *Impossible Subjects: Illegal Aliens and the Making of Modern America* (Princeton, NJ: Princeton University Press, 2004), 21–54.
43. Ben-Ur, *Sephardic Jews*, 47.
44. Michael Omi and Howard Winant, *Racial Formation in the United States from the 1960s to the 1990s*, 2nd ed. (London: Routledge, 1994), 14–23, 96.
45. Jodie Melamed, *Represent and Destroy: Rationalizing Violence in the New Racial Capitalism* (Minneapolis: University of Minnesota Press, 2011), xii–xv.
46. Nathan Glazer, "Negroes and Jews: The New Challenge to Pluralism," in Norman Podhoretz, ed., *The Commentary Reader: Two Decades of Articles and Stories* (New York: Atheneum, 1967), 388–98.
47. Brodkin, *How Jews Became White Folks*, 147.
48. Michael Rogin, *Blackface, White Noise: Jewish Immigrants in the Hollywood Melting Pot* (Berkeley: University of California Press, 1998); V. P. Franklin, Nancy L. Grant, and Genna Rae McNeil, eds., *African Americans and Jews in the Twentieth Century: Studies in Convergence and Conflict* (Columbia: University of Missouri Press, 1999); Marshall Berman, "Broadway, Love, and Theft," in *Modernism in the Streets: A Life and Times in Essays*, ed. David Marcus and Shelley Sclan (New York: Verso, 2017), 286–309.
49. Henri Percikow, "Letter from Reader," *Jewish Life* 8, no. 1 (November 1947), 2.
50. Alexander Bittelman, "Palestine: What Is the Solution?," *Jewish Currents* 1, no. 1 (November 1946), 1, 4.
51. Samuel Barron, "The Policy of Discrimination in America," *Jewish Currents* 1, no. 1 (November 1946), 1, 11.
52. Greenberg, *Troubling the Waters*, 191–3. See also Gerald Horne's discussion of the Rosenberg trial and the NAACP, *Communist Front? The Civil Rights Congress, 1946–1956* (Rutherford, NJ: Fairleigh Dickinson University Press, 1988).
53. Bittelman, "Palestine: What Is the Solution?," 1, 26.
54. Greenberg, *Troubling the Waters*.
55. Hakim Adi, "The Negro Question: The Communist International and Black Liberation in the Interwar Years," in Michael O. West, William G. Martin, and Fanon Che Wilkins, eds., *From Toussaint to Tupac: The Black International since the Age of Revolution* (Chapel Hill: University of North Carolina Press, 2009), 155.
56. Eric Shickler, *Racial Realignment: The Transformation of American Liberalism* (Princeton, NJ: University of Princeton Press, 2016).
57. Horne, *Communist Front?*
58. "Despite the fact that Gold is recognized as the most representative polemicist of proletarian literature, few critics have realized that the ghetto or tenement pastoral that Gold helped invent in *Jews without Money* became one of the central forms of proletarian fiction," Denning, *Cultural Front*, 216–18.
59. Mike Gold, "Toward a Proletarian Art," in *Mike Gold: A Literary Anthology*, ed. Michael Folsom (New York: International Publishers, 1972), 65, 67.
60. Denning, *The Cultural Front*, 230–54.
61. Gold, *Jews without Money*, 44–5.
62. William Maxwell, "The Proletarian as New Negro: Mike Gold's Harlem

Renaissance," in Bill Mullen and Sherry Linkon, eds., *Radical Revisions: Rereading 1930s Culture* (Urbana: University of Illinois Press, 1996), 102.
63. Ngai, *Impossible Subjects*.
64. Howard Fast, "Where Are Your Guns," *Jewish Life* 2, no. 9 (July 1948), 15–16.
65. Also of note, Robert Gessner archly commented that the Zionists wished to "dispose of the Arabs as so many Indians" in his *New Masses* essay, "Brown Shirts of Zion," 13.
66. Budeiri, *The Palestine Communist Party*, 58–81.
67. David Roediger, "Making Solidarity Uneasy: Cautions on a Keyword from Black Lives Matter to the Past," *American Quarterly* 68, no. 2 (2016): 223–48.
68. Alexander Bittelman, "A New Fortress Is Rising," *Jewish Life* 1, no. 6 (April 1947), 14–16.
69. Alan Wald, *American Night: The Literary Left in the Era of the Cold War* (Chapel Hill: University of North Carolina Press, 2012), 1-21.
70. Morris Schappes, "Commentary on 'An Epitaph for Sidney,'" *Jewish Life* 1, no. 4 (February 1949).
71. Howard Fast, "Epitaph for Sidney," *Jewish Life*, January 1947, 10–13.
72. Judith Butler, *Parting Ways: Jewishness and the Critique of Zionism* (New York: Columbia University Press 2012), 1–3.
73. "Safeguard the Jewish State!," editorial, *Jewish Life* 2, no. 4 (February 1948), 1.
74. Alexander Bittelman performed one of the more dramatic about-faces, embracing Partition and writing, only a few years after authoring numerous anti-Zionist tracts, "the struggle for the independence and territorial integrity of the new Jewish state is part of the general struggle for peace, national independence, and democracy." "The New State of Israel," *Political Affairs* 17, no. 8 (August 1948), 720–30. See also Alexander Bittelman, "Demand America Grant Justice to Yishuv," *Jewish Life* 1, no. 9 (July 1947), cover. Howard Fast, soon after the commencement of the 1948 Arab-Israeli War, wrote a novel celebrating the Maccabees revolt against the Greek-Seleucids, a novel many interpreted as a celebration of the new Israeli state, *My Glorious Brothers* (Boston: Little, Brown and Company, 1948).
75. See Slezkine, *Jewish Century*, 206–7. According to Wald, "CP supporters' views of the Jewish Question/Palestine-Israel were also refracted through a belief that the true homeland of socialism, which must be protected at all costs, was the USSR. Soviet policy was never out of the picture. 'Defend the Soviet Union' was part of the definition of Communist identity, and that took the form of supporting whatever foreign policy the soviet leadership demanded or facing expulsion." Alan Wald, correspondence with author, July 23, 2018.
76. Mike Gold, "Warsaw Ghetto," Mike Gold (Irwin Granich) and Mike Folsom papers, Joseph A. Labadie Collection, University of Michigan Special Collections, Box 3, File 51.
77. Traverso, *Marxists and the Jewish Question*, 277.
78. Butler, *Parting Ways*, 1–3.

2. Not Your Good Germans

1. I define "New Left" rather broadly in this essay to mean left organizations and organizers who placed US imperialism, anti-racism, support of Black Power, anti-anti-Communism, the Cuban revolution, and a skepticism about the Soviet

Union at the center of their politics. As demonstrated by Maurice Isserman in *If I Had a Hammer: The Death of the Old Left and the Birth of the New Left* (Urbana: University of Illinois Press, 1993), James Miller in *Democracy in the Streets: From Port Huron to the Siege of Chicago* (Cambridge, MA: Harvard University Press, 1994), Dick Flacks and Mickey Flacks in *Making History/Making Blintzes: How Two Red Diaper Babies Found Each Other and Discovered America* (New Brunswick, NJ: Rutgers University Press, 2018), and Peter Camejo in *North Star: A Memoir* (Chicago: Haymarket Books, 2010), there was a great deal more overlap between Old Left organizers and organizations than is usually acknowledged. SDS itself emerged out the socialist League for Industrial Democracy (LID) and to a lesser extent, the Trotskyist followers of Max Shachtman. Ironically, what distinguished SDS from other socialist organizations was its refusal to red-bait former and current members of the Communist Party, and its tenuous willingness to bear with the Progressive Labor Party in its ranks. Alternatively, while many in SWP did not consider themselves to be part of the New Left formally, their willingness to work in coalitions around the New and Student Mobilizations against the war, support Black Power, and center opposition to the war in Vietnam meant they were very much a part of the 1960s left politically, if not necessarily culturally. More importantly for purposes of this essay, both SDS and SWP had large Jewish memberships, and much of the activist history of SDS and SWP members was very similar: attracted initially to the civil rights struggle in the north as well as the Freedom Rides, they were pulled into anti-war organizing by the US escalation in Vietnam.
2. Mark Rudd, *My Life with SDS and the Weathermen Underground* (New York: HarperCollins, 2009), 70–1.
3. Mark Rudd, "Why Were There So Many Jews in SDS? (Or, the Ordeal of Civility)," markrudd.com.
4. Rudd, *My Life with SDS*, 71–2.
5. Ibid., 77.
6. Amy Kaplan, *Our American Israel: The Story of an Entangled Alliance* (Cambridge, MA: Harvard University Press), 104, 135; Melani McAlister, "The Good Fight: Israel after Vietnam," in *Epic Encounters: Culture, Media, and U.S. Interests in the Middle East since 1945* (Berkeley: University of California Press, 2005), 155–97; Marc Dollinger, *Black Power, Jewish Politics: Reinventing the Alliance in the 1960s* (Waltham, MA: Brandeis University Press, 2018), xii, 7, 9.
7. Kaplan, *Our American Israel*, 104, 135.
8. Matt Berkman, "Coercive Consensus: Jewish Federations, Ethnic Representation, and the Roots of American Pro-Israel Politics" (PhD diss., University of Pennsylvania, 2018), 4–7.
9. Ibid., 12–16.
10. Michael R. Fischbach, *The Movement and the Middle East: How the Arab-Israeli Conflict Divided the Left* (Stanford, CA: Stanford University Press, 2020), 164.
11. Kaplan, *Our American Israel*, 77, 83.
12. Fischbach, *The Movement and the Middle East*, 163.
13. Keith Feldman, *Shadow over Palestine: The Imperial Life of Race in America* (Minneapolis: University of Minnesota Press, 2017), 110–11.
14. Eric Goldstein, *The Price of Whiteness: Jews, Race and American Identity* (Princeton, NJ: Princeton University Press, 2008), 215–17.
15. Myron Perlman, "The Better to Smell You with My Dear," in Steven Lubet and the Chutzpah Collective, eds., *Chutzpah: A Jewish Liberation Anthology* (San Francisco: New Glide Publications, 1977), 19–20.

16. Michael E. Staub, *Torn at the Roots: The Crisis of Jewish Liberalism* (New York: Columbia University Press, 2002), 214.
17. See note 8 in chapter 1 for a list of scholarship on Jewish whiteness.
18. Rudd, "Why Were There So Many Jews in SDS?"
19. Paul Berman, *A Tale of Two Utopias: The Political Journey of the Generation of 1968* (New York: W. W. Norton & Company, 1996), 44–5.
20. Rudd, *My Life with SDS*, 71.
21. Flacks and Flacks, *Making History/Making Blintzes*, 116.
22. Joyce Antler, *Jewish Radical Feminism: Voices from the Women's Liberation Movement* (New York: New York University Press, 2018), 113.
23. George Novack, "Isaac Deutscher and the Non-Jewish Jew," *Militant* 33, no. 6 (February 1969), 8–10.
24. Dick Flacks, interview with author, October 2020.
25. David R. Verbeeten, *The Politics of Nonassimilation: The Jewish Left in the Twentieth Century* (DeKalb: Northern Illinois University Press, 2017), 116–24.
26. Flacks and Flacks, *Making History/Making Blintzes*, 216–17.
27. Yuri Slezkine, *The Jewish Century* (Princeton, NJ: Princeton University Press, 2004), 204–372.
28. Camejo, *North Star*, 94–8.
29. Phil Passen, interview with author, August 2020.
30. Dollinger, *Black Power, Jewish Politics*, 6.
31. Ibid., 9, 25.
32. Leonard Fein, "The New Left and Israel," in Mordecai S. Chertoff, ed., *The New Left and the Jews* (New York: Pitman Publishing, 1971), 128.
33. Irving Howe, "Political Terrorism: Hysteria on the Left," in Chertoff, *The New Left and the Jews*, 45.
34. Ibid.
35. Seymour Lipset, "'The Socialism of Fools': The Left, the Jews, and Israel," in Chertoff, *The New Left and the Jews*, 103.
36. Walter Laqueur, "Reflections on Youth Movements," and Mordecai S. Chertoff, "The New Left and Newer Leftists," in Chertoff, *The New Left and the Jews*, 56, 175.
37. Nathan Glazer, "Jewish Interests and the New Left," in Chertoff, *The New Left and the Jews*, 159, 163.
38. Ibid., 157.
39. Gus Horowitz, "The Revolution in the Arab East since 1967: Draft Theses," in *Israel and the Arab Revolution: Fundamental Principles of Revolutionary Marxism* (Atlanta: Pathfinder Press, 1973), 32.
40. Meir Kahane's manifesto *Never Again!* (Hawthorn, CA: BN Publishing, 2009) is a diatribe against the internationalism of the New Left and a call for Jews to embrace Zionism, 115.
41. Staub, *Torn at the Roots*, 220–1.
42. Kahane, *Never Again!*, 87.
43. Ibid., 63.
44. Ibid., 166.
45. Joshua Bloom and Waldo E. Martin, *Black against Empire: The History and Politics of the Black Panther Party* (Berkeley: University of California Press, 2016), 3.
46. David Gilbert, *Love and Struggle: My Life in SDS, the Weather Underground, and Beyond* (Oakland, CA: PM Press, 2012), 126.
47. Ibid., 103.

48. David Gilbert and David Loud, *U.S. Imperialism* (Chicago: Students for a Democratic Society, 1968).
49. David Gilbert, Robert Gottlieb, and Gerry Tenney, "Toward a Theory of Social Change: The 'Port Authority Statement,'" in Carl Davidson, ed., *Revolutionary Youth and the New Working Class: The Praxis Papers, the Port Authority Statement, the RYM Documents and Other Lost Writings of SDS* (Pittsburgh, PA: Changemaker Publications, 2011), 52–127.
50. Richard Saks, interview with author, March 2021.
51. Rudd quoted by Michael R. Fischbach, "The New Left and the Arab-Israeli Conflict in the United States," *Journal of Palestine Studies* 49, no. 3 (Spring 2020), 11.
52. Susan Eanet-Klonsky, interview with author, August 2019.
53. Susan Eanet, "History of Middle East Liberation," *New Left Notes* 4, no. 11 (March 1969), 6.
54. Larry Hochman, *Zionism and the Israeli State: An Analysis in the June War* (Ann Arbor, MI: Radical Education Project, 1967), 4.
55. Gilbert, *Love and Struggle*, 101.
56. Susan Eanet, "Arab Women Fight," in special Women's Day issue, *New Left Notes* 4, no. 9 (March 1969), 4.
57. Michael R. Fischbach, *Black Power and Palestine: Transnational Countries of Color* (Palo Alto, CA: Stanford University Press, 2018), 26.
58. "The Palestine Problem: Test Your Knowledge," *SNCC Newsletter* 1, no. 2 (June–July 1967), 4; Carmichael as quoted by Fischbach, *Black Power and Palestine*, 47.
59. Fischbach, *Black Power and Palestine*, 42.
60. Ibid., 47.
61. Gilbert, *Love and Struggle*, 29.
62. Susan Eanet-Klonsky, interview with author, August 2019.
63. Suzanne Berliner Weiss, *Holocaust to Resistance, My Journey* (Black Point, Nova Scotia: Fernwood Publishing, 2019), 130–1.
64. Peter Buch, *Zionism and the Arab Revolution: The Myth of a Progressive Israel* (New York: Young Socialist Alliance, 1967), 6.
65. Ibid., 20.
66. Ibid., 28.
67. Ibid., 31.
68. Ibid., 3.
69. Horowitz, "The Revolution in the Arab East since 1967," 40.
70. Ibid., 7, 17, 13, 17–18.
71. Ibid., 18.
72. Steve Goldman, interview with author, November 2020; Richard Saks, interview with author, March 2021.
73. Linda Loew, interview with author, February 2021.
74. Richard Bernstein, interview with author, November 2019.
75. Daniel Boyarin and Jonathan Boyarin, *The Powers of Diaspora: Two Essays on the Relevance of Jewish Culture* (Minneapolis: University of Minnesota Press, 2002), 37–40.
76. Joel Beinin, interview with author, August 2020.
77. Dick Flacks, interview with author, October 2020.
78. Howe, "Political Terrorism," 45.
79. Michael Fischbach, "The New Left and the Arab-Israeli Conflict," 11–14.
80. Ibid.
81. Abbie Hoffman et al., "At the Chicago Conspiracy Trial," in Michael Staub, ed., *The

Jewish 1960s: An American Sourcebook (Lebanon, NH: Brandeis University Press, 2004), 245.
82. Joel Finkel, interview with author, July 2019.
83. Susan Eanet-Klonsky, interview with author, August 2019.
84. Rudd, *My Life with SDS*, 23.
85. Kathy Boudin, interviewed by Zayd Dohrn on "Chapter 9: Revolutionary Suicide," July 21, 2022, *Mother Country Radicals*, podcast.
86. Gilbert, *Love and Struggle*, 30, 15.
87. Rudd, *My Life with SDS*, 23.
88. Ibid.
89. Arlene Stein, *Reluctant Witnesses: Survivors, Their Children, and the Rise of Holocaust Consciousness* (Oxford: Oxford University Press, 2014), 15.
90. Hasia Diner, *We Remember with Reverence and Love: American Jews and the Myth of Silence after the Holocaust, 1942–1962* (New York: New York University Press, 2009), 2–6.
91. Philip Roth, "Defender of the Faith," in *Goodbye, Columbus* (New York: Vintage Books, 1959), 174.
92. Norman G. Finkelstein, *The Holocaust Industry: Reflections on the Exploitation of Jewish Suffering* (New York: Verso, 2003), 30.
93. Ibid., 48–50.
94. Enzo Traverso, *The End of Jewish Modernity*, trans. David Fernbach (London: Pluto Books, 2016), 57, 2.
95. Ibid., 58.
96. Paul Hanebrink, *A Specter Haunting Europe: The Myth of Judeo-Bolshevism* (Cambridge, MA: Harvard University Press, 2018), 210, 227.
97. Mark Tseng-Putterman, "Fear and Isolation in American Zion," *Protocols* 1 (2017), prtcls.com.
98. Finkelstein, *Holocaust Industry*, 37.
99. Michael Rothberg, *Multidirectional Memory: Remembering the Holocaust in the Age of Decolonization* (Stanford, CA: Stanford University Press, 2009), 34, 66–8.
100. Norm Fruchter, "Arendt's Eichmann and Jewish Identity," in James Weinstein and David W. Eakins, eds., *For a New America: Essays in History and Politics from Studies on the Left, 1959–1967* (New York: Random House, 1970), 22–3.
101. Isaac Deutscher, "Who Is a Jew?," in *The Non-Jewish Jew and Other Essays* (New York: Verso Books, 2017), 51.
102. *Auschwitz/My Lai*, Jewish Radical Community, pamphlet, 1968. From the personal collection of Sheryl Nestel.
103. "Genocide Then/Genocide Now," *Brooklyn Bridge* 1, no. 3 (May 1971), front cover.
104. "Israeli Hawks and Doves," *Chutzpah* 12, (n.d.), 8.
105. "Return of the Big Lie," *Chutzpah* 12, (n.d.), 9.
106. Weiss, *Holocaust to Resistance*, 263.
107. Ibid., 229.
108. Ibid., 94.
109. Ibid., 88.
110. Ibid., 99.
111. Ibid., 190–1.
112. Ibid., 189.
113. Dollinger, *Black Power, Jewish Politics*, 3.
114. Howard Fast, *Peekskill USA: Inside the Infamous Riots* (Mineola, NY: Dover Publications, 1951), 95.

115. Ibid., 33, 89, 118–19.
116. Ibid., 24–5.
117. Ibid., 61, 70.
118. Ibid., 88.
119. Kaplan, *Our American Israel*, 24–7.
120. Ibid., 23–4.
121. Flacks and Flacks, *Making History/Making Blintzes*, 60–5; Peter Seidman, interview with author, July 2020; Beinin, interview; Bernstein, interview.
122. Noami Allen, interview with author, June 2020.
123. Rudd, *My Life with SDS*, 108.
124. April Rosenblum, "Offers We Couldn't Refuse: The Decline of Actively Secular Jewish Identity in the 20th Century U.S.," aprilrosenblum.com, excerpt revised from *Jewish Currents*, May–June 2009, 8–28.
125. Cheryl Lynn Greenberg, *Troubling the Waters: Black-Jewish Relations in the American Century* (Princeton, NJ: Princeton University Press, 2006), 191–3.
126. Ibid.
127. Sid Resnick, interview with author, June 2005.
128. Flacks and Flacks, *Making History/Making Blintzes*, 49.
129. Mike Hecht, "Next to Godliness," *Jewish Life*, January 1947, 17.
130. Marianne Ware, "December 1947," in Judy Kaplan and Lynn Shapiro, eds., *Red Diapers: Growing Up in the Communist Left* (Urbana: University of Illinois Press, 1998), 63.
131. Chris Vials, *Haunted by Hitler: Liberals, the Left, and the Fight against Fascism in the United States* (Amherst: University of Massachusetts Press, 2014), 268.
132. Ibid., 274.
133. Ibid., 272.
134. Gilbert, *Love and Struggle*, 193.
135. Alberto Toscano, "The Long Shadow of Racial Fascism," *Boston Review*, October 28, 2020, bostonreview.net.
136. Herbert Marcuse, *Counterrevolution and Revolt* (Boston: Beacon Press, 1989), 1.
137. Ibid., 28.
138. Rudd, *My Life with SDS*, 194.
139. Gilbert, *Love and Struggle*, 143.
140. Benjamin Balthaser, *Anti-Imperialist Modernism: Race and Radical Transnational Culture from the Great Depression to the Cold War* (Ann Arbor: University of Michigan Press, 2016), 153.
141. Alexander Bittelman, *The Jewish People Face the Post-war World* (New York: Morning Freiheit Association, 1945), 14.
142. Samuel Barron, "The Policy of Discrimination in America," *Jewish Currents*, November 1946, 1, 11.
143. Gerald Horne, *A Communist Front? The Civil Rights Congress 1946–1956* (Rutherford, NJ: Fairleigh Dickinson University Press, 1988), 74–99.
144. Stanley Aronowitz, *Honor America: The Nature of Fascism, Historical Struggles against It, and a Strategy for Today* (New York: Times Change Press, 1970), 9.
145. Ibid., 23.
146. Hyman Lumer, "Zionism: Its Role in World Politics," in Daniel Rubins, ed., *Anti-Semitism and Zionism: Selected Marxist Writings* (New York: International Publishers, 1987), 135.
147. Ibid.
148. Ibid., 136.

149. Ibid.
150. Peter Seidman, *Socialists and the Fight against Anti-Semitism: An Answer to the B'nai B'rith Anti-Defamation League* (New York: Pathfinder Press, 1973), 24.
151. Ibid., 7.
152. Ibid., 19.
153. Ibid., 21.
154. Ibid., 10.
155. Novack, "Isaac Deutscher and the Non-Jewish Jew," 8–10.
156. Marcuse, *Counterrevolution and Revolt*, 1, 28.
157. Novack, "Isaac Deutscher and the Non-Jewish Jew," 9.
158. Gilbert, *Love and Struggle*, 21; Phil Passen, interview with author, September 2020; Linda Loew, interview with author, July 2020; Geoff Mirelowitz, interview with author, August 2020.

3. Exceptional Whites, Bad Jews

1. Grace Paley, "Enormous Changes at the Last Minute," in *Collected Stories* (New York: Farrar, Strauss, and Giroux, 1994), 207.
2. Leo Panitch and Sam Gindin, *The Making of Global Capitalism: The Political Economy of American Empire* (New York: Verso, 2012), 91–102.
3. Karen Brodkin, *How Jews Became White Folks and What That Says about Race in America* (New Brunswick, NJ: Rutgers University Press, 1998), 25–52.
4. Marc Dollinger, *Black Power, Jewish Politics: Reinventing the Alliance in the 1960s* (Waltham, MA: Brandeis University Press, 2018), 30.
5. Eric Goldstein, *The Price of Whiteness: Jews, Race and American Identity* (Princeton, NJ: Princeton University Press, 2008), 212.
6. Ibid., 195.
7. David R. Verbeeten, *The Politics of Nonassimilation: The Jewish Left in the Twentieth Century* (DeKalb: Northern Illinois University Press, 2017), 116–24.
8. "Poll Shows Whites in City Resent Civil Rights Drive; Majority Queried in Times Survey Say Negro Movement Has Gone Too Far, but Few Intend to Change Votes," *New York Times*, September 21, 1964, 1, 10.
9. Cheryl Lynn Greenberg, *Troubling the Waters: Black-Jewish Relations in the American Century* (Princeton, NJ: Princeton University Press, 2006), 118.
10. Dollinger, *Black Power, Jewish Politics*, 28.
11. Michael Rogin, *Blackface, White Noise: Jewish Immigrants in the Hollywood Melting Pot* (Berkeley: University of California Press, 1998), 73–120.
12. Brodkin, *How Jews Became White Folks*, 145–6.
13. Beryl Satter, *Family Properties: How the Struggle over Race and Real Estate Transformed Chicago and Urban America* (New York: Picador Press, 2005), 17–35.
14. Dollinger, *Black Power, Jewish Politics*, 12.
15. Seth Forman, *Blacks in the Jewish Mind: A Crisis of Liberalism* (New York: New York University Press, 1998), 196.
16. Abbie Hoffman, *The Autobiography of Abbie Hoffman* (New York: Four Walls/Eight Windows, 1980), 82.
17. Keith Feldman, *Shadow over Palestine: The Imperial Life of Race in America* (Minneapolis: University of Minnesota Press, 2017), 110.
18. Dollinger, *Black Power, Jewish Politics*, 87.

19. Ibid., 106–7.
20. Goldstein, *The Price of Whiteness*, 212–13.
21. Ibid., 214.
22. Dollinger, *Black Power, Jewish Politics*, 9, 56.
23. Mark Rudd, *My Life with SDS and the Weathermen Underground* (New York: HarperCollins, 2009), 132.
24. Ibid., 47.
25. Noel Ignatin, "White Blindspot, Letter to Progressive Labor," in Carl Davidson, ed., *Revolutionary Youth and the New Working Class: The Praxis Papers, the Port Authority Statement, the RYM Documents and Other Lost Writings of SDS* (Pittsburgh, PA: Changemaker Publications, 2011), 159.
26. Ibid., 149.
27. Ibid., 150.
28. David Gilbert, *Love and Struggle: My Life in SDS, the Weather Underground, and Beyond* (Oakland, CA: PM Press, 2012), 127.
29. Ibid., 147.
30. Ibid., 165.
31. Ibid.
32. Dollinger, *Black Power, Jewish Politics*, 104–6.
33. Nathan Glazer, "Negroes and Jews: The New Challenge to Pluralism," in Norman Podhoretz, ed., *The Commentary Reader: Two Decades of Articles and Stories* (New York: Atheneum, 1967), 388–98.
34. Brodkin, *How Jews Became White Folks*, 147.
35. Shaul Magid, *Meir Kahane: The Public Life and Political Thought of an American Jewish Radical* (Princeton, NJ: Princeton University Press, 2021), 26.
36. Ibid.
37. Myron Perlman, "Work, Study, Get Ahead," in Steven Lubet and the Chutzpah Collective, eds., *Chutzpah: A Jewish Liberation Anthology* (San Francisco: New Glide Publications, 1977), 75–7.
38. Ibid, 75.
39. "Philadelphia: Up against the Swastika Covered Wall," *Brooklyn Bridge* 1, no. 5 (Fall 1972), 14.
40. Georg Lukács, *History and Class Consciousness: Studies in Marxist Dialectics*, trans. Rodney Livingston (Cambridge, MA: MIT Press, 1972).
41. Myron Perlman, "The Rising New Right," *Chutzpah* 15 (n.d.), 1–2.
42. David Gilbert, Robert Gottlieb, and Gerry Tenney, "Toward a Theory of Social Change: The 'Port Authority Statement,'" in Carl Davidson, ed., *Revolutionary Youth and the New Working Class: The Praxis Papers, the Port Authority Statement, the RYM Documents and Other Lost Writings of SDS* (Pittsburgh, PA: Changemaker Publications, 2011), 100.
43. Ibid., 108.
44. Rachel Kranson, *Ambivalent Embrace: Jewish Upward Mobility in Postwar America* (Chapel Hill: University of North Carolina Press, 2017), 4–5.
45. Hoffman, *The Autobiography*, 86.
46. Ibid., 99.
47. E. L. Doctorow, *Book of Daniel* (New York: Random House, 2007), 105–7.
48. Hoffman, *The Autobiography*, 13.
49. Ibid., 14.
50. Ibid., 187.
51. Ibid., 201.

52. Ibid., 195.
53. Abbie Hoffman et al., "At the Chicago Conspiracy Trial," in Michael Staub, ed., *The Jewish 1960s: An American Sourcebook* (Lebanon, NH: Brandeis University Press, 2004), 245.
54. Hoffman, *The Autobiography*, 190.
55. Ibid., 28.
56. Ibid.
57. Ibid., 299–300.
58. Ibid., 14.
59. Ibid., 11.
60. Ibid., 139.
61. Rudd, *My Life with SDS*, 36–7.
62. Hoffman, "At the Chicago Conspiracy Trial," 244.
63. Ibid., 82.
64. Arnold Forster and Benjamin R. Epstein, *The New Anti-Semitism* (New York: McGraw-Hill, 1974), 140.
65. Joel Beinin, interview with author, August 2020.
66. Peter Seidman, interview with author, July 2020.
67. Linda Loew, second interview with author, January 2021.
68. Adam Shatz, "In Praise of Diasporism, or, Three Cheers for Irving Berlin," in Adam Shatz, ed., *Prophets Outcast: A Century of Dissident Jewish Writing about Zionism and Israel* (New York: Nation Books, 2004), xii; Roane Carey, "A 'Non-Jewish Jew,' Hitchens Welcomed Finding He Was Jewish—But Not Zionism," *Forward*, December 21, 2011, forward.com.
69. Susie Linfield, *The Lions' Den: Zionism and the Left from Hannah Arendt to Noam Chomsky* (New Haven, CT: Yale University Press, 2019), 144.
70. Mark Rudd, "Why Were There So Many Jews in SDS? (Or, the Ordeal of Civility)," markrudd.com.
71. Emily L. Quint Freeman, *Failure to Appear: A Memoir* (Bethel: Regal Crest Books, 2020), 3.
72. Isaac Deutscher, "The Non-Jewish Jew," in *The Non-Jewish Jew and Other Essays* (New York: Verso, 2017), 26–7.
73. Enzo Traverso, *The Marxists and the Jewish Question: The History of a Debate, 1843–1943*, trans. Bernard Gibbons (Atlantic Highlands, NJ: Humanities Press, 1994), 236.
74. Viren Murthy, "Beyond Particularity and Universality: Moishe Postone and the Possibilities of Jewish Marxism," *Jewish Social Studies* 25, no. 2 (Winter 2020), 127–67.
75. Deutscher, "The Non-Jewish Jew," 39.
76. Murthy, "Jewish Marxism," 158.
77. Theodor Adorno, *Negative Dialectics* (New York: Continuum International Publishers, 1966), 146–8.
78. Ibid., 363.
79. Max Horkheimer and Theodor W. Adorno, *Dialectic of Enlightenment: Philosophical Fragments*, trans. Edmund Jephcott (Stanford, CA: Stanford University Press, 2002), 137.
80. Walter Benjamin, "Theses on the Philosophy of History," in *Illuminations*, ed. Hannah Arendt, trans. Harry Zohn (New York: Schocken Books, 1968), 256.
81. Santiago Slabodsky, *Decolonial Judaism: Triumphal Failures of Barbaric Thinking* (New York: Palgrave-MacMillan, 2014), 86.

82. Daniel Bensaïd, *An Impatient Life: A Memoir*, trans. David Fernbach (New York: Verso, 2015), 272.
83. Ibid., 271.
84. Ibid., 273.
85. Ibid., 4.
86. Ibid., 282.
87. Daniel Bensaïd, "La question juive aujourd'hui—'La notion de people-classe: Un point de depart, non un point d'arrivée'" (1980), Europe Solidaire sans Frontières, europe-solidaire.org. My translation.
88. Bensaïd, *Impatient Life*, 283.
89. Josep Maria Antentas, "Daniel Bensaïd's Marrano Internationalism," *Historical Materialism: Research in Critical Marxist Theory* 30, no. 2 (2022), 135–68.
90. Hannah Arendt, *The Origins of Totalitarianism* (New York: Houghton, Mifflin & Harcourt, 1968), 290.
91. Bensaïd, *Impatient Life*, 284.
92. Antentas, "Marrano Internationalism," 152.

4. A Kesher with the Left

1. Dick Flacks, interview with author, October 12, 2022. Note: for this chapter, I relied primary on interviews with former members of the Chutzpah Collective, either conducted personally, and/or conducted by Aliza Becker for the American Jewish Peace Archive. Interviews with Chutzpah members included Rachel Abramson, Maralee Gordon, Myron Perlman, Miriam Socoloff, and Robbie Skeist. I also interviewed Rabbi Lynn Gottlieb for her perspective on the Jewish Renewal Movement, and Sheryl Nestel, who was a member of Jewish Radical Community. I (re)interviewed Dick Flacks for his perspective as a former member of SDS, on the "Jewish turn" of many former Jewish SDSers.
2. Mickey Flacks and Dick Flacks, *Making History/Making Blintzes: How Two Red Diaper Babies Found Each Other and Discovered America* (New Brunswick, NJ: Rutgers University Press, 2018), 116–17; Dick Flacks, interview with author, October 12, 2022.
3. Tariq Ali, correspondence with author, May 15, 2024. "Esther Singer . . . used to describe what it was like as a teenager listening to Rosa Luxemburg speak. Rosa Meyer-Levine (the widow of Eugene Levine who was executed after the Munich uprising and had said in the dock 'We communists are all dead men on leave') walked up to me after a very radical speech I had made and said: 'You remind me of my husband. Be careful, please.' These comrades were like gold dust, our link to 1917 and I referred to them more than once."
4. Michael Hardt, *The Subversive Seventies* (Oxford: Oxford University Press, 2023), 10.
5. The proceedings of this convention are recorded in Mordecai S. Chertoff, ed., *The New Left and the Jews* (New York: Pitman Publishing Corporation, 1971).
6. Arnold Forster and Benjamin R. Epstein, *The New Anti-Semitism* (New York: McGraw-Hill, 1974), 2–3.
7. Ibid., 4.
8. Stuart Hall, "Old and New Identities, Old and New Ethnicities," in *Essential Essays*, vol. 2, ed. David Morley (Durham, NC: Duke University Press, 2019), 67.

9. Mathew Frye Jacobson, *Roots Too: White Ethnic Revival in Post-Civil Rights America* (Cambridge, MA: Harvard University Press, 2006), 44–6.
10. Eric Goldstein, *The Price of Whiteness: Jews, Race and American Identity* (Princeton, NJ: Princeton University Press, 2008); Marc Dollinger, *Black Power, Jewish Politics: Reinventing the Alliance in the 1960s* (Waltham, MA: Brandeis University Press, 2018); Shaul Magid, *Meir Kahane: The Public Life and Political Thought of an American Jewish Radical* (Princeton, NJ: Princeton University Press, 2021).
11. Magid, *Meir Kahane*, 9.
12. Ibid., 8.
13. Ibid., 224–5.
14. Ibid., 113.
15. "Our Brothers and Sisters?," *Brooklyn Bridge* 1, no. 3 (May 1971), 16.
16. "The Jewish Defense League: Does Fascism Begin Where Nationalism Ends?," *Brooklyn Bridge* 1, no. 4 (June 1972), 3.
17. Michael E. Staub, *Torn at the Roots: The Crisis of Jewish Liberalism* (New York: Columbia University Press, 2002), 200–7.
18. Joyce Antler, *Jewish Radical Feminism: Voices from the Women's Liberation Movement* (New York: New York University Press, 2018), 326.
19. Ibid., 327.
20. Brooke Lober, "Narrow Bridges: Jewish Lesbian Feminism, Identity Politics, and the 'Hard Ground' of Alliance," *Journal of Lesbian Studies* 23, no. 1 (2019), 83–101.
21. Michael R. Fischbach, *The Movement and the Middle East: How the Arab-Israeli Conflict Divided the American Left* (Stanford, CA: Stanford University Press, 2020), 184–7.
22. Staub, *Torn at the Roots*, 217.
23. Ibid., 192.
24. Goldstein, *Price of Whiteness*, 219.
25. Hardt, *Subversive Seventies*, 6–9.
26. Amy Sonnie and James Tracy, *Hillbilly Nationalists, Urban Race Rebels, and Black Power: Community Organizing in Radical Times* (Hoboken, NJ: Melville House, 2001), 33–8.
27. Ibid., 36.
28. Keeanga-Yamahtta Taylor, *How We Get Free: Black Feminism and the Combahee River Collective* (Chicago: Haymarket Books, 2017), 22.
29. Ibid., 34.
30. Ibid., 38.
31. Miriam Socoloff, correspondence with author, October 17, 2022.
32. Magid, *Meir Kahane*, 26.
33. Sherry Nestel, interview with author, July 25, 2022.
34. Ibid.
35. Myron Perlman, interview conducted by Aliza Becker, American Jewish Peace Archive, June 29, 2016.
36. Lee Weiner, "Revolutionary Jewish Nationalism," *Brooklyn Bridge* 2, no. 4 (June 1972), 2, 14.
37. Ibid., 14.
38. Ibid.
39. Magid, *Meir Kahane*, 109.
40. Meir Kahane, *Never Again!* (Hawthorne, CA: BN Publishing, 2009), 85–9.
41. Magid, *Meir Kahane*, 87.
42. Myron Perlman, "The Jewish Stake in Vietnam," in Steven Lubet and the Chutzpah

Collective, eds., *Chutzpah: A Jewish Liberation Anthology* (San Francisco: New Glide Publications, 1977), 83–4.
43. Ibid., 84.
44. *Auschwitz/My Lai*, Jewish Radical Community, pamphlet. From the personal collection of Sheryl Nestel.
45. Myron Perlman, interviewed by Chutzpah Collective, "Anti-Semitism = Anti-Semitism?!?," special issue on anti-Semitism, *Chutzpah* 18 (n.d.), 10–11.
46. Miriam Socoloff, interview with author, July 3, 2021.
47. Arden Handler, "Bakke: Tsuris of a Jewish Leftist," *Chutzpah* 4 (n.d.), 4, 9.
48. Maralee Gordon, interview with author, July 30, 2021.
49. Lila Corwin Berman, *Speaking of Jews: Rabbis, Intellectuals, and the Creation of an American Public Identity* (Berkeley: University of California Press, 2009), 7–10.
50. Daniel Boyarin, *The No-State Solution: A Jewish Manifesto* (New Haven, CT: Yale University Press, 2023), 70–5; Judith Butler, *Parting Ways: Jewishness and the Critique of Zionism* (New York: Columbia University Press, 2013), 42.
51. To quote Hungarian Jewish theorist Georg Lukács, Chutzpah, BBC, and JRC's expression of diasporic identity also expressed their contradictory "standpoint" as Americans both inside and outside of the cultural and economic system they called home. Fredric Jameson refers to Lukács's Marxist theory of subjectivity as a prefiguration of "standpoint theory"—which poses that one's reality is produced materially through membership in a particular social and economic class; see *Valences of the Dialectic* (London: Verso, 2009), 204, 215–16.
52. *Brooklyn Bridge* 1, no. 1 (February 1971), front cover.
53. Walter Benjamin, "Theses on the Philosophy of History," in *Illuminations*, ed. Hannah Arendt, trans. Harry Zohn (New York: Schocken Books, 1968), 253–64.
54. Myron Perlman, "In the Ranks of Liberation: The Jewish Workers' Bund," in Lubet and Chutzpah Collective, *Chutzpah: A Jewish Liberation Anthology*, 167–71.
55. "Jewish Labor Bund," *Brooklyn Bridge* 1, no. 4 (June 1972), 8–9, 23.
56. Jeffry (Shaye) Mallow, "Politics of Language," in Lubet and Chutzpah Collective, *Chutzpah: A Jewish Liberation Anthology*, 143–6.
57. "Giving Up Assimilationist Privilege," *Brooklyn Bridge* 1, no. 4 (June 1972), 15, 23.
58. Perlman, "In the Ranks of Liberation," 169.
59. Ruth Balser, "Liberation of a Jewish Radical," in Lubet and Chutzpah Collective, *Chutzpah: A Jewish Liberation Anthology*, 15–18.
60. "A Nation without a State," *Brooklyn Bridge* 1, no. 4 (June 1972), 9–10.
61. Isaac Brosilow, "The Skokie March that Wasn't," *Jewish Currents*, November 7, 2018, jewishcurrents.org.
62. Ibid.
63. Myron Perlman and Arden Handler, "Nazis Threaten Skokie and We Are Not Afraid," *Chutzpah* 13 (n.d.), 5.
64. "Building a Coalition," *Chutzpah* 15 (n.d.), 8.
65. Les Friedman, "Nazism: Where the Personal Meets the Political," *Chutzpah* 14 (n.d.), 18–19.
66. Rachel Abramson, "Confronting the Nazis," *Chutzpah* 15 (n.d.), 8.
67. "To Fight Nazis, Jews and Blacks Join Together," *Chutzpah* 15 (n.d.), 9.
68. Jerry Herst, "Marquette Park: Confronting Racism and Anti-Semitism," *Chutzpah* 15 (n.d.), 4.
69. Daniel Boyarin and Jonathan Boyarin, *Powers of Diaspora: Two Essays on the Relevance of Jewish Culture* (Minneapolis: University of Minnesota Press, 2002), 5.
70. "Jewish Labor Bund," 8.

71. Myron Perlman, "The Rising New Right," *Chutzpah* 15 (n.d.), 1–2.
72. Robert Brenner, "The Economics of Global Turbulence," *New Left Review* 1, no. 229 (May–June 1998), newleftreview.org.
73. Perlman, "The Rising New Right," 2.
74. Ibid.
75. Boyarin and Boyarin, *Powers of Diaspora*, 5, 30.
76. Staub, *Torn at the Roots*, 233.
77. "The Jewish Defense League: Does Fascism Begin Where Nationalism Ends?," 3.
78. "Breira Conference," *Chutzpah* 12 (n.d.), 3, 14.
79. "To Fight Nazis, Jews and Blacks Join Together," 9.
80. Chutzpah seemed to adopt Antonio Gramsci's theory of fascism: that it arrives as a "passive revolution," tacitly or explicitly supported by layers of the bourgeoisie, even as its most populist elements take to the streets.
81. Stuart Hall, "Gramsci's Relevance for the Study of Race and Ethnicity," *Essential Essays*, vol. 2, ed. David Morley (Durham, NC: Duke University Press, 2019), 49–51.
82. Jefferson Cowie, *Stayin' Alive: The 1970s and the Last Days of the Working Class* (New York: New Press, 2012), 2–5.
83. Michael Denning, *The Cultural Front: The Laboring of American Culture in the 20th Century* (New York: Verso Books, 1998), 239.
84. Myron Perlman, conversation with author, July 8, 2014.
85. Myron Perlman, "Work, Study, Get Ahead," in Lubet and Chutzpah Collective, *Chutzpah: A Jewish Liberation Anthology*, 75–7.
86. Marian Neudel, "Temporary," *Chutzpah* 12 (n.d.), 20.
87. Miriam Socoloff et al., "The Joy of Socialism, the Heartbreak of Capitalism," in Lubet and Chutzpah Collective, *Chutzpah: A Jewish Liberation Anthology*, 72–4.
88. "Socialist Statement," *Chutzpah* 12 (n.d.), 3.
89. Ezra Berkley Nepon, *Justice, Justice You Shall Pursue: A History of the New Jewish Agenda* (Philadelphia: Thread Makes Blanket Press, 2012), 11.
90. "Philadelphia: Up against the Swastika Covered Wall," *Brooklyn Bridge* 1, no. 5 (Fall 1972), 14.
91. Myron Perlman, interview conducted by Aliza Becker, American Jewish Peace Archive, June 29, 2016.
92. "The Promised Land," *Brooklyn Bridge* 1 (January 1971), 6, 17.
93. Butler, *Parting Ways*, 42.
94. Keith Feldman, *A Shadow over Palestine: The Imperial Life of Race in America* (Minneapolis: University of Minnesota Press, 2015), 143; Steven Salaita, *Inter/Nationalism: Decolonizing Native America and Palestine* (Minneapolis: University of Minnesota Press, 2016).
95. Matt Berkman, "Coercive Consensus: Jewish Federations, Ethnic Representation, and the Roots of American Pro-Israel Politics" (PhD diss., University of Pennsylvania, 2018), 4–7.
96. "Henry Crown—Humanitarian?," *Chutzpah* 4 (February–March 1973), 3; Sai Englert, "The Rise and Fall of the Jewish Labour Bund," *International Socialism* 135 (Summer 2012), isj.org.uk.
97. Susan Schechter, "To My Real and Imagined Enemies: The Double-Binds of a Jewish Leftist," *Chutzpah* 12 (n.d.), 6–7, 13.
98. Staub, *Torn at the Roots*, 208.
99. Robbie (Sholem) Skeist, "The Way to Peace: Two Peoples, Two States," in Lubet and Chutzpah Collective, *Chutzpah: A Jewish Liberation Anthology*, 132–6; Simha

Flapan, "Zionism, Palestinians, and Peace," *Chutzpah* 16 (n.d.), 3, 12–13; Uri Avnery, "A Proposal for Peace in the Middle East," *Chutzpah* 4 (February–March 1973), 18.
100. "The Palestinian Arabs," *Chutzpah* 9/10 (n.d.), 10.
101. Jacylnn Ashly, "When Israel's Black Panther Party Found Common Cause with Palestinians," *Electronic Intifada*, March 7, 2019, electronicintifada.net.
102. "Sephardim: Bridge to Israel/Palestine Peace?," *Chutzpah* 11 (n.d.), 7.
103. "Moked: Israeli Doves," *Chutzpah* 12 (n.d.), 16.
104. Myron Perlman, interview with author, American Jewish Peace Archive.
105. "The Palestinian Revolution," *Chutzpah* 9 (n.d.), 3; "Arafat," *Chutzpah* 9 (n.d.), 3–4.
106. "About the Arab Guerrillas," *Chutzpah* 2 (1972), 12–13.
107. *Chutzpah Principles*, 1979, 9. From the personal collection of Miriam Socoloff.
108. Feldman, *A Shadow over Palestine*, 143.
109. Myron Perlman, interview with author, American Jewish Peace Archive; Perlman, "Anti-Semitism = Anti-Semitism?!?," 10–11.
110. "Israeli Hawks and Doves," *Chutzpah* 12 (n.d.), 8.
111. Ibid.
112. Miriam Socoloff, interview with author, July 3, 2021.
113. Grace Paley, *Collected Stories* (New York: Farrar, Strauss, and Giroux, 1994), 81–96.
114. Anthony Lerman, *Whatever Happened to Anti-Semitism: The Myth of the Collective Jew* (London: Pluto Press, 2022).
115. Benjamin Schreier, *The Rise and Fall of Jewish American Literature: Ethnic Studies and the Challenge of Identity* (Philadelphia: University of Pennsylvania Press), 5, 31, 50.
116. Mark Rudd, *My Life with SDS and the Weathermen Underground* (New York: HarperCollins, 2009), 70–1. Note that I discuss this scene in greater depth in chapter 2.
117. Philip Roth, *Portnoy's Complaint* (New York: Vintage International, 1994), 172.
118. Ibid., 234.
119. Daniel Boyarin, *Unheroic Conduct: The Rise of Heterosexuality and the Invention of the Jewish Man* (Berkeley: University of California Press, 1997), xvii, 23–4.
120. Roth, *Portnoy's Complaint*, 42, 45, 97.
121. Ibid., 41.
122. Boyarin, *Unheroic Conduct*, 28.
123. Roth, *Portnoy's Complaint*, 240.
124. Amy Kaplan, *Our American Israel: The Story of an Entangled Alliance* (Cambridge, MA: Harvard University Press, 2018), 74–6.
125. Ibid., 75.
126. Brooke Allen, "Philip Roth's Plot against Himself," *New Criterion* 19, no. 8 (April 2021), newcriterion.com.
127. Roth, *Portnoy's Complaint*, 254.
128. Ibid., 257, 264.
129. Ibid., 247.
130. Philip Roth, *The Counterlife* (New York: Vintage International, 1986), 132.
131. Ibid., 113.
132. Ibid., 115, 125.
133. Ibid., 54.
134. Ibid., 147.
135. Ibid., 73.
136. Ibid., 323–4.

137. Ibid., 146.
138. Cole Krawitz, "New Jewish Agenda Archive Online!," Jewschool, July 20, 2006, jewschool.com.
139. Melanie Kaye/Kantrowitz, "To Be a Radical Jew in the Late 20th Century," in Melanie Kaye/Kantrowitz and Irena Klepfisz, eds., *The Tribe of Dina: A Jewish Women's Anthology* (Boston: Beacon Press, 1986), 297–320.
140. Butler, *Parting Ways*, 43.
141. Kaye/Kantrowitz, "To Be a Radical Jew," 313.
142. Edward Said, *Freud and the Non-European* (New York: Verso, 2014), 34–5.

5. The Antinomies of Jewish Liberalism

1. Tony Kushner, *Angels in America: A Gay Fantasia on National Themes* (New York: Theater Communications Group, 2013), 289.
2. "Poll: 72% Support Humanitarian Pause; 20% Favor Unconditional Ceasefire," *FedBeat*, November 22, 2023, jewishfederations.org; see also the link in the same article to Jewish Federations of North America and Benenson Strategy Group, "Jewish Community Understanding Survey," November 7, 2023.
3. Dov Waxman, *Trouble in the Tribe: The American Jewish Conflict over Israel* (Princeton, NJ: Princeton University Press, 2016), 62–3.
4. Daniel Bensaïd, *An Impatient Life: A Memoir*, trans. David Fernbach (New York: Verso, 2015), 3.
5. Lila Corwin Berman, *Speaking of Jews: Rabbis, Intellectuals, and the Creation of an American Public Identity* (Berkeley: University of California Press, 2009), 6; Cheryl Lynn Greenberg, *Troubling the Waters: Black-Jewish Relations in the American Century* (Princeton, NJ: Princeton University Press, 2006), 8; Steven R. Weisman, "How America's Jews Learned to Be Liberal," *New York Times*, August 18, 2018, nytimes.com.
6. Laurence A. Kotler-Berkowitz, "Ethnic Cohesion and Division among American Jews: The Role of Mass-Level and Organizational Politics, *Ethnic and Racial Studies* 20, no. 4 (October 1997), 797–829.
7. Jacob Savage, "The Vanishing: The Erasure of Jews from American Life," *Tablet*, February 28, 2023, tabletmag.com.
8. Ezra Berkley Nepon, *Justice, Justice You Shall Pursue: A History of the New Jewish Agenda* (Philadelphia: Thread Makes Blanket Press, 2012), 29.
9. Shaul Magid, *Meir Kahane: The Public Life and Political Thought of an American Jewish Radical* (Princeton, NJ: Princeton University Press, 2021), 18.
10. Natan Sharansky and Gil Troy, "The Un-Jews: The Jewish Attempt to Cancel Israel and Jewish Peoplehood," *Tablet*, June 15, 2021, tabletmag.com; Joel K. Greenberg, "Jewish Voices for Hate: Understanding the Mistake We Made by Welcoming Anti-Israel Voices into the 'Jewish Tent,'" *Tablet*, December 18, 2023, tabletmag.com; Philip Weiss, "Anti-Zionist Jews Are 'Jews in Name Only' and 'More Dangerous than External Antisemitic Threat'—Chicago Reform Rabbi," *Mondoweiss*, November 26, 2021, mondoweiss.net3.
11. Antonio Gramsci, *The Antonio Gramsci Reader: Selected Writings 1916–1935*, ed. David Forgacs (New York: New York University Press, 2000), 217–20.
12. Emily King, "The Overlooked Jewish Identity of Roy Cohn in Kushner's 'Angels in America': American Schmucko," *Studies in American Jewish Literature* 27 (2008), 87–100.

13. Kushner, *Angels in America*, 69.
14. Ibid., 137.
15. Ibid., 138.
16. Ibid., 223.
17. Ibid., 96.
18. Ibid., 223.
19. Ibid., 265.
20. Shaul Magid, *American Post-Judaism: Identity and Renewal in a Postethnic Society* (Bloomington: University of Indiana Press, 2013), 3, 10; Mathew B. Hoffman and Henry F. Srebrnik, introduction to Mathew B. Hoffman and Henry F. Srebrnik, eds., *A Vanished Ideology: Essays on the Jewish Communist Movement in the English-Speaking World in the Twentieth Century* (Binghamton: SUNY Press, 2016), 11–16.
21. Bensaïd, *Impatient Life*, 267–85; Jacques Derrida, *Specters of Marx: The State of the Debt, the Work of Mourning and the New International*, trans. Peggy Kamuf (London: Routledge 1994), 106.
22. Kushner, *Angels in America*, 139.
23. Jacob Plitman, "On an Emerging Diasporism," *Jewish Currents*, April 16, 2018, jewishcurrents.org.
24. Daniel Kahn, "Yiddish Song Smuggling," *Smithsonian Folkways Magazine*, Winter 2016, folkways.si.edu.
25. Editors, "How Not to Fight Antisemitism," *Jewish Currents*, April 5, 2021, jewishcurrents.org.
26. Daniel Boyarin, *The No-State Solution: A Jewish Manifesto* (New Haven, CT: Yale University Press, 2023), 1–6.
27. Ibid., 98.
28. Michael Löwy, *Redemption and Utopia: Jewish Libertarian Thought in Central Europe*, trans. Hope Heaney (London: Verso, 1988), 12.
29. Noam Gil, "The Destruction of Israel and Other Fantasies in Jewish American Literature," *Studies in American Jewish Literature* 39, no. 2 (2020), 161–81.
30. Ibid., 162–3.
31. Joshua Cohen, *The Netanyahus: An Account of a Minor and Ultimately Even Negligible Episode in the History of a Very Famous Family* (New York: New York Review of Books, 2021), 31.
32. Ibid., 105.
33. Ibid., 33.
34. Ibid., 25.
35. Ibid., 126.
36. Ibid., 42, 81.
37. Ibid., 186, 189.
38. Ibid., 211–12.
39. Ibid., 218, 156.
40. Daniel Boyarin, *Unheroic Conduct: The Rise of Heterosexuality and the Invention of the Jewish Man* (Berkeley: University of California Press, 1997).
41. Cohen, *Netanyahus*, 35.
42. Nathan Goldman, "That Joke Isn't Funny Anymore," *Jewish Currents*, September 29, 2021, jewishcurrents.org.
43. Cohen, *Netanyahus*, 230.
44. Cohen's 2017 novel, *Moving Kings*, traverses a similar trajectory, if only to reverse the binary between diaspora and Zionist nation: two dopey Israeli teens come to

work for a blustery New York mover, and in part because of the Israelis' robotic, racist simplicity, things end badly. Joshua Cohen, *Moving Kings: A Novel* (New York: Random House, 2017).
45. Jess Row, *A New Earth* (New York: Ecco Press, 2023), i.
46. Ibid., 224.
47. Ibid., 367.
48. Ibid., 541.
49. Ibid., 422.
50. Nicole Krauss, *Great House* (New York: W. W. Norton, 2011).
51. Adam Mansbach, *The Golem of Brooklyn* (New York: Penguin Random House, 2023).
52. Lane Silberstein, "Gramsci, Yiddish, and Building Cultural Barricades," *Jewish Currents*, February 15, 2018, jewishcurrents.org.
53. Jewish Solidarity Caucus, "About and Platform," *Jewish Socialism* (blog), August 9, 2017, medium.com.
54. Michael R. Fischbach, *The Movement and the Middle East: How the Arab-Israeli Conflict Divided the American Left* (Stanford, CA: Stanford University Press, 2020), 201.
55. David Duhalde, interview with author, March 2023.
56. This "conversion" narrative has been documented by Atalia Omer, *Days of Awe: Reimagining Jewishness in Solidarity with Palestinians* (Chicago: University of Chicago Press, 2019), 71, 85. It also features heavily in the documentary film *Israelism*, directed by Erin Axelman and Sam Eilertsen, 2023.
57. Benjamin S., interview with author, April 2023.
58. Sharona Gordon, interview with author, March 2023.
59. Lane Silberstein, interview with author, December 2022.
60. Lane Silberstein, "The Dialectic of Assimilation," *Cosmonaut*, July 11, 2020, cosmonautmag.com; Silberstein, "Gramsci, Yiddish, and Building Cultural Barricades."
61. Javier Miranda, interview with author, December 2022.
62. Zac Goldstein, interview with author, December 2022.
63. Daniel Kahn, "The Jew in You," Jewish Voice for Labour, March 10, 2021, jewishvoiceforlabour.org.uk.
64. Kahn, "Yiddish Song Smuggling."
65. "Israel Nothing," on Daniel Kahn and Psoy Korolenko, *The Unternationale: The Fourth Unternationale*, Auris Media Records, September 11, 2020.
66. "JSC Notes," JSC digital Google drive.
67. Ella Shohat, "Sephardim in Israel: Zionism from the Standpoint of Its Jewish Victims," *Social Text* 19, no. 20 (Autumn 1988), 1–35.
68. Omer, *Days of Awe*, 2.
69. Ibid., 9.
70. Ibid., 26; Marc Ellis, *Toward a Jewish Theology of Liberation* (London: SCM Press, 2002).
71. Ariana Katz and Miriam Grossman, "Maggid: Telling the Story of How a People Gets Free," supplement, "Liberatory Passover Haggadah," Jewish Voice for Peace, jewishvoiceforpeace.org.
72. Dori Midnight and Joanna Kent Katz, "Tashlich T'zedek 2017/5778," available at "Tashlich," Jewish Voice for Peace, jewishvoiceforpeace.org.
73. Omer, *Days of Awe*, 57.
74. Ibid., 67–8.
75. Ernesto Laclau, *The Rhetorical Foundations of Society* (London: Verso, 2014).

76. Brant Rosen, "A Lamentation for Gaza on Tishah b'Av," Open Siddur Project, June 3, 2021, opensiddur.org.
77. Hansi Lo Wang, "The Complicated History behind BLM's Solidarity with the Pro-Palestinian Movement," NPR, June 12, 2021, npr.org.
78. Leslie Williams, "The Anti-Defamation League Kills the Black/Jewish Alliance," Jewish Voice for Peace, August 26, 2016, jewishvoiceforpeace.org.
79. Melanie Kaye/Kantrowitz, *The Colors of Jews: Racial Politics and Radical Diasporism* (Bloomington: Indiana University Press, 2007).
80. Arthur L. Waskow, *The Bush Is Burning! Radical Judaism Faces the Pharaohs of the Modern Superstate* (New York: Macmillan, 1971), 26.
81. Ibid., 70.
82. Ibid., 95, 133–5.
83. Michael E. Staub, *Torn at the Roots: The Crisis of Jewish Liberalism* (New York: Columbia University Press, 2002), 164–8.
84. Ibid.
85. Ibid.
86. Marita Sturken, *Tangled Memories: The Vietnam War, the AIDS Epidemic, and the Politics of Remembering* (Berkeley: University of California Press, 1997), 6–7.
87. Ilana Lerman and Aviva Cipilinski, *OUT! Zine*, QZAP Archive, last accessed April 2023, with thanks to Milo Miller, QZAP archivist.
88. "Not in Our Name! 350+ Jewish Socialists Say No to Apartheid and Genocide," October 2023, https://docs.google.com/document/d/1ixlxgxix1sxVv3Dj8uXckVk 6lYNbUvl30V_ra0if4G8/edit#heading=h.dk09k8dymgoj.
89. Dania Rajendra and Rebecca Vilkomerson, "Don't Let the Flailing Center Box Out the Left's Possibilities," *In These Times* 48, no. 1 (January/February 2024), inthese times.com.
90. Atalia Omer, "Restorative Justice: Pathways in Palestine/Israel: Undoing the Settler Colonial Captivity," in "Zionism and Its Jewish Critics," ed. Shaul Magid, special issue, *Shofar: An Interdisciplinary Journal of Jewish Studies* 41, no. 2 (2023), 154–85.
91. LilMissHotMess, "All of Us or None," Haggadah, LilMissHotMess.com; IJAN Network, "Legacies of Resistance: An Anti-Zionist Haggadah for a Liberation Seder," download, ijan.org; Brant Rosen, Category Archives: Passover, *Yedid Nefesh* (blog), ynefesh.com.
92. Martín Espada, interview with author, September 2023.
93. Walter Benjamin, "Theses on the Philosophy of History," in *Illuminations*, ed. Hannah Arendt, trans. Harry Zohn (New York: Schocken Books, 1968), 253–64.
94. Martín Espada, email correspondence with author, March 2023.
95. Bensaïd, *Impatient Life*, 282–5.
96. Martín Espada, email correspondence with author, March 2023.
97. Martín Espada, interview with author, September 2023.
98. Martín Espada, "How to Read Ezra Pound," in *The Trouble Ball: Poems* (New York: W. W. Norton, 2011), 49.
99. Espada, "Like a Word That Somersaults through the Air," in *The Trouble Ball*, 48.
100. Martín Espada, "The Carpenter Swam to Spain," in *A Mayan Astronomer in Hell's Kitchen: Poems* (New York: W. W. Norton, 2000), 53.
101. Benjamin, "The Task of the Translator," in *Illuminations*, 69–82.
102. Both Espada's poem and his comment about Jewish boxers were in the text of an email correspondence with the author, October 2023.
103. Janet Zandy, "The Making of Working-Class Literature," *Literature Compass* 5, no.

1 (January 2008), 42–57; Bill V. Mullen, "Proletarian Literature Reconsidered," *Oxford Research Encyclopedia of Literature*, June 28, 2017, oxfordre.com.
104. Martín Espada, "All the People Who Are Now Red Trees," in *Imagine the Angels of Bread: Poems* (New York: W. W. Norton, 1996), 78–9.
105. Martín Espada, "The Eleventh Reason," Rosenberg Fund for Children, rfc.org.
106. Aurora Levins Morales, "Red Sea," April 2002, auroralevinsmorales.com.
107. Aurora Levins Morales, *Cosecha and Other Stories* (Cambridge, MA: Palabrera Press, 2014), 14–15.
108. Ryu Spaeth, "Israel, Gaza, and the Fracturing of the Intellectual Left," MSN, November 30, 2023, msn.com; Emily Ngo and Nick Reisman, "'Unacceptably Devoid of Empathy': DSA Is Facing an Internal Reckoning on Israel," *Politico*, October 11, 2023, politico.com.
109. Daphna Thier, "Democratic Socialists of America Is Helping Rebuild the U.S. Antiwar Movement," *In These Times*, December 22, 2023, inthesetimes.com. Reports of JVP's membership growth were cited over JVP Chicago Slack, December 4, 2023.

Index

Abraham Lincoln Brigade, 61, 66, 267
ACJ. *See* American Council for Judaism (ACJ)
ACLU. *See* American Committee on Judaism; American Civil Liberties Union (ACLU)
Adi, Hakim, 62
ADL. *See* Anti-Defamation League (ADL)
Adorno, Theodor, 37
   Dialectic of Enlightenment, 10, 150
   Negative Dialectics, 149
   "non-identity," 155
African Americans, 8–10, 59–66, 74–6, 82, 110, 118–19, 127–35, 143
   Chicago, 182–5
   Combahee River Collective, 164–5
   Communist Party, 127, 279nn26–7, 285n34
   in fiction, 66
   Freedom Seder and, 257
   JDL attack on, 75, 130, 188
   JVP and, 255–6
   Moynihan, 60, 135
   Nation of Islam, 90, 163
   Ocean Hill–Brownsville teachers' strike, 135, 163
   in Port Authority Statement, 140
   Stein and, 100
   We Charge Genocide, 118
   in Yiddish poetry, 27–8
   See also Black Panther Party; Black Power movement

AIDS in drama. *See* HIV/AIDS in drama
AJC. *See* American Jewish Committee (AJC)
Albert, Judy Gumbo, 97
Alden, Will, 1–2
Aleichem, Sholem, *Tevye's Daughters*, 79
Ali, Tariq, 158, 296n3
Allen, Naomi, 113
Alter, Robert, 81, 163
Althusser, Louis, 39, 282n101
American Civil Liberties Union (ACLU), 110, 180
American Committee on Judaism, 197
American Council for Judaism (ACJ), 52, 54, 55, 62, 73
American Jewish Committee (AJC), 13, 16, 18, 42, 52, 54, 62, 197
   Bakke case, 163
   NAACP relations, 62, 127
   Rosenberg trial and, 113, 118–19
American Jewish Congress, 163
anarchists and anarchism, 39, 246
Angels in America (Kushner), 219–20, 223–7, 230, 232, 233, 264
Antentas, Josep Maria, 154
anti-Communism, 43, 110–14, 140
   in fiction, 225–6
   See also Second Red Scare
Anti-Defamation League (ADL), 13, 16, 52, 62, 159, 186–7, 197, 223
   Bakke case, 163
   Chicago and Skokie, 182, 185
   Greenberg, 42

Anti-Defamation League (ADL) (*continued*)
  JVP and, 255–6
  Rosenbergs' trial and, 113
  view of SWP, 121, 122
Antler, Joyce, 77, 162
Aptheker, Herbert, 117
Arab-Israeli War, 1967. *See* Six-Day War
Arafat, Yasser, 199–200
Arendt, Hannah, 120, 154
  Origins of Totalitarianism, 103
  "Zionism Reconsidered," 57–8
Aronowitz, Stanley, 119
Ashkenazi Jews, 14, 15, 34, 52–3, 58–60, 125, 136, 205, 230
  Abbie Hoffman, 140, 141
  "Ashkenormativity," 14, 15, 284n10
  Bittelman, 8
  Leon definition, 152–3
Avnery, Uri, 198

Bakke v. Regents of the University of California, 163, 170
Balfour Declaration, 40, 53
Balser, Ruth, 179
BDS movement and resolutions, 3, 243–5, 252, 255
Begin, Menachem, 21, 222
Beinart, Peter, 20, 271
Beinin, Joel, 53, 95–6, 112
Bellow, Saul, 205, 206
Bend the Arc (BtA), 20, 228, 230
Benjamin, Walter, 27, 38, 48, 150–1, 154, 175, 258–9, 264
  "Theses on the Philosophy of History," 10
  view of translation, 268
Bensaïd, Daniel, 14, 30–1, 151–6, 221, 264–5
  An Impatient Life, 152
  "The Jewish Question Today," 152–3
Berger, Elmer, 54
Berkman, Matt, 73
Berman, Lila Corwin, 172–3
Berman, Marshall, 133
Berman, Paul, 76
Bernstein, Dick, 94–5, 112
Bevin, Ernest, 112
Beyond the Melting Pot (Glazer), 128
Birobidzhan, 56, 285n26
Bittelman, Alexander, 7, 8–9, 11, 53–62, 66, 118, 287n74
  "Study Guide for the Jewish Question," 12–13

Black diaspora, 26, 27. *See also* African Americans
Black Face, White Noise (Rogin), 128
Black Liberation Army, 99, 130, 158
Black Lives Matter. *See* Movement for Black Lives
Black Panther Party (BPP), 84–5, 115–20, 129–34, 163, 169, 171
  James Forman, 84
  Maralee Gordon view of, 36
  Rainbow Coalition, 164
  SDS and, 76, 85, 115, 132, 134
  suppression of, 158
  United Front against Fascism conference, 116, 119
Black Panther Party (Israel). *See* Israeli Black Panther Party (IBPP)
Black Power movement, 74–6, 80–1, 129–31, 160–3
  Horowitz, 92
  Kahane and, 130, 169, 188
Blau, Milton, 33
Bolshevik Revolution. *See* Russian Revolution
The Book of Daniel (Doctorow), 141
Borowitz, Eugene, 23
Boudin, Kathy, 99
Boyarin, Daniel, 18, 23, 29, 34, 95, 156, 173, 217
  on Jewish gender norms, 209
  No-State Solution, 24–6, 231–2
Boyarin, Jonathan, 95
boycotts against Israel, 243, 246. *See also* BDS movement and resolutions
Breira, 13, 19, 188, 193–4
Britain, 26, 53, 88, 112
  Deutscher, 148
Brodkin, Karen, 5, 6–7, 58, 126–7, 134–5
Brooklyn Bridge, 105, *106*, 168, 175–9, *176*, 188
Brooklyn Bridge Collective (BBC), 74, 105, 130, 136–7, 165–79, 194–9, 217–18, 229
Browder, Earl, 53, 55
Brown, John, 132
BtA. *See* Bend the Arc (BtA)
Buch, Peter, 90–1, 92
Bund. *See* Jewish Workers' Bund
Burgis, Ben, 22
The Bush Is Burning! (Waskow), 257
Butler, Judith, 18, 67, 70, 156, 173, 216, 228, 259
  Parting Ways, 23–4

Index

Camejo, Peter, 79
Camp Wo-Chi-Ca, 112
Carmichael, Stokely, 88–9, 129, 145, 163
   Black Power, 160
CCP. *See* Community College of Philadelphia (CCP)
Césaire, Aimé, 118
   Discourse on Colonialism, 103
Chertoff, Mordecai, 81, 82
Chicago Eight (Chicago Seven) conspiracy trial, 97–8, 142
Chomsky, Noam, 81, 82, 85
Chutzpah, 18, 181–8, *181*, 202
Chutzpah Collective, 13, 17–19, 35–8, 42, 74–5, 130, 165–204, 217–18, 229
   class and, 136, 137, 177, 178, 186–95
Civil Rights Congress (CRC), 63, 110, 118, 119
Coen brothers' films, 39–40, 263
Cohen, Joshua
   The Moving Kings, 241, 302–3n44
   The Netanyahus, 233, 234–8
Collins, Frank, 180–1
The Colors of Jews (Kaye/Kantrowitz), 256
Columbia University, 2, 15, 71–2, 75, 87, 131, 146, 205–6
Combahee River Collective (CRC), 164–5
Communist Party of Israel. *See* Israeli Communist Party
Communist Party of Palestine, 65. *See also* Palestine Communist Party
Communist Party USA (CPUSA), 6–12, 32, 52–8, 62–6, 76, 91, 109, 117–20
   African Americans, 127, 2797nn26–7, 285n34
   Bittelman, 8
   Fast, 64
   in fiction, 32, 48
   Gold, 51
   Jewish Life and, 227
   Red Scare and, 43
   Weiner on, 168
Community College of Philadelphia (CCP) Jewish Student Union (JSU), 136–7, 194–5
The Counterlife (Roth), 21–2, 212–14, 238
Cowie, Jefferson, 190
Crabapple, Molly, 15, 18
CRC. *See* Civil Rights Congress (CRC); Combahee River Collective (CRC)
Cuba, 167, 195

David, Larry, 21, 263

Debray, Régis, *The Revolution in the Revolution*, 87
Debs, Eugene, 5
Democratic Socialist Organizing Committee, 245
Democratic Socialists of America (DSA), 3, 15, 20, 228, 243–6, 258–62, 271
   Jewish Solidarity Caucus (JSC), 3–4, 13, 243–52, 257–60
Denning, Michael, 6, 53, 63, 190
   on Gold, 286n58
   "Long Popular Front," 283n3
Derrida, Jacques, "hauntology," 154–5, 226
Deutscher, Isaac, 28–9, 85, 103–4, 122–3, 147–9, 155, 156
   "The Non-Jewish Jew," 14, 30, 72, 77, 145–6, 147
Dialectic of Enlightenment (Adorno and Horkheimer), 10, 150
diasporism, 17–39, 67, 173–4, 185, 196, 204–18, 227–33, 248
   Boyarin, 24, 95, 184, 187
   "peoplehood," 20–1, 55, 60, 217, 231
Di Cesare, Donatella, 30
Diner, Hasia, 100, 101
Discourse on Colonialism (Césaire), 103
Doctorow, E. L., *The Book of Daniel*, 141
Dohrn, Bernardine, 85, 206
Dollinger, Marc, 72–6, 81, 109, 115, 126, 129–34, 160
   "turn inward," 134, 170
Doppelganger (Klein), 22
DSA. *See* Democratic Socialists of America (DSA)
Duhalde, David, 15, 245–6, 277n8

Eagleton, Terry, 37
Eanet-Klonsky, Susan, 12, 82, 86–8, 90, 98–9, 103
Edwards, Brent Hayes, 25–6, 27
effeminacy, 34, 203, 209, 211
Eisenstein, Jethro, 253–4
Ellis, Marc, 253
Enlightenment (Protestant), 10, 24, 150
"Epitaph for Sidney" (Fast), 32–5, 37
Epstein, Benjamin, *The New Antisemitism*, 145, 159
Espada, Martín, 15, 262–70
exceptionalism, American, 104
exceptionalism, Jewish, 101, 119
exceptionalism, Holocaust, 104
"exceptional whites," 133–5

Exodus (Preminger), 73, 234
Exodus (Uris), 73, 210–11, 234, 254

Family Properties (Satter), 128
Fast, Howard, 287n74
   "Epitaph for Sidney," 32–5, 37, 66–7
   Freedom Road, 64–5
   Peekskill USA, 109–11
   "Where Are Your Guns," 65
Fatah, 82, 87–8
FBI, 117
Fein, Leonard, 81, 159
Feldman, Keith, 74, 76, 129, 197, 201
feminist movement. *See* women's movement
Finkel, Joel, 98
Finkelstein, Norm, 72, 101, 102, 103
Fischbach, Michael, 73, 88, 89, 97, 162, 245
Flacks, Dick, 42, 77, 78, 96, 112–14, 138–9, 157–8
Flacks, Mickey, 96, 112, 113, 114
Foer, Franklin, 37, 38
foquismo ("foco theory"), 87
Ford, James W., 285n34
Forman, James, 84, 161
Forman, Seth, 129
Forster, Arnold, *The New Antisemitism*, 145, 159
Fourth International, 30, 99, 151
Freedom Rides, 76, 123, 206
Freeman, Emily L. Quint, 147
French Revolution, 152
Freud, Sigmund, 23–4
Friedan, Betty, 162
Friedman, Benny, 143
Friedman, Les, 182–3
Fruchter, Norm, 103

Gaza, 1, 88, 89, 202, 220–1, 260, 271
General Jewish Labor Bund. *See* Jewish Workers' Bund
gender performance, 209. *See also* masculinity
gender relations and roles in Roth's fiction, 208–13. *See also* women's movement
Gessner, Robert, 11, 40–1, 52, 54
Gilbert, David, 78, 84–5, 87, 89, 99, 103–4, 116, 123
   on Black Power movement and race, 131–5
   on BPP, 117

"most wanted" poster, 206
Port Authority Statement, 14, 85, 138–40
Gilroy, Paul, 27, 155
Glaser, Amelia, 7–8, 27–8
Glazer, Nathan, 60, 74, 76, 81, 128, 134–5, 147, 159
Gold, Mike, 55, 117, 268–9, 286n58
   Jews without Money, 8, 29–30, 50–1, 63–4, 286n58
   "Warsaw Ghetto," 68–9
Goldman, Nathan, 237
Goldstein, Eric, 74–7, 127, 129–30, 133, 160
Goldstein, Zac, 247, 249
The Golem of Brooklyn (Mansbach), 233, 241–2
Goodbye, Columbus (Roth), 100
Gordon, Jerry, 79–80
Gordon, Maralee, 36, 171, 191
Gordon, Sharona, 246, 249–50
Gordon, Yehuda, 114
Gorz, André, 138
Gottlieb, Robert, Port Authority Statement, 14, 85, 138–40
Gramsci, Antonio, 11–12, 223, 262
Gray Panthers, 183, 184
Great Britain. *See* Britain
Great House (Krauss), 233, 240–1
Greenberg, Cheryl, 41–2, 113, 127
Grossman, Miriam, "Maggid," 254, 255
Gumbo, Judy. *See* Albert, Judy Gumbo
Gush Shalom, 171, 193

Hall, Stuart, 11–12, 26, 27, 47, 53, 135, 189
   "Old and New Identities," 160
Handler, Arden, 170
Hanebrink, Paul, 101
Hardt, Michael, 158, 164
Hashomer Hatzair USA, 91, 95, 145
Hecht, Mike, 114
Herst, Jerry, 184
Heschel, Abraham, 256, 259
Holocaust to Resistance, My Journey (Weiss), 105–9
Hillel International, 16, 18, 223
Hillel the Elder, 216–17
Hitchens, Christopher, 146
HIV/AIDS in drama, 219–20, 223–7
Hochman, Larry, 87
Hoffman, Abbie, 2, 43, 96–8, 129, 140–5

Index

Hoffman, Julius ("The Court"), 97–8, 142, 143
Hoffman, Matthew B., 7
Holocaust, Jewish. *See* Jewish Holocaust
Holocaust to Resistance (Weiss), 105–8
Hoover, J. Edgar, 117
Horkheimer, Max, *Dialectic of Enlightenment*, 10, 150
Horowitz, Gus, 82, 92–4
House Un-American Activities Committee (HUAC). *See* US Congress, HUAC
Howe, Irving, 41, 74, 81–2, 159, 206
   DSA, 245
   view of Roth, 207
   World of Our Fathers, 42, 176

identity politics, 164, 170, 178
IfNotNow (INN), 2, 15, 36
Ignatiev, Noel, 75, 131, 190
"Imagine the Angels of Bread" (Espada), 262, 263, 269
An Impatient Life (Bensaïd), 152
Industrial Workers of the World (IWW), 140, 168
INN. *See* IfNotNow (INN)
internationalism, 26, 40–1, 68, 118. *See also* Fourth International
International Labor Defense, 118
intersectionality, 8, 56, 63, 278n23
Israel Defense Forces (IDF), 81
   in fiction, 238, 239, 242
Israeli Black Panther Party (IBPP), 36, 168, 198–9
Israeli Communist Party, 171, 172
Isserman, Maurice, 3–4

Jabotinsky, Vladimir, 40
Jackson, George, 116, 117
Jacobson, Matthew Frye, 160, 178, 190
Japanese American internment, 116, 282n101
JDL. *See* Jewish Defense League (JDL)
"The Jew in You" (Kahn), 250–1
Jewish Anti-Fascist Committee, 32
Jewish Currents, 2, 19–20, 227–31, 237
Jewish Defense League (JDL), 81, 83, 137, 160–1, 168–9, 173, 187–91
   Black models for, 75, 130
   Breira and, 188, 194
Jewish Federation, 197, 223
   Chicago, 180, 182, 185, 187, 195
   Washington, DC, 206

Jewish Holocaust, 58, 68, 98–109, 118–21
   Bensaïd and, 151, 153, 154
   Chicago Seven trial, 142
   FDR and, 104, 121
   Pound and, 266
   See also Nuremberg Trials
Jewish Labor Bund. *See* Jewish Workers' Bund
Jewish Life, 55, 61, 66, 227, 229
"The Jewish Question Today" (Bensaïd), 152–3
Jewish Radical Community (JRC), 104, 165, 167, 169, 203
Jewish Renewal Movement, 74, 76, 129–30, 131, 133, 163, 166
Jewish Solidarity Caucus (JSC), Democratic Socialists of America. *See* Democratic Socialists of America (DSA) Jewish Solidarity Caucus (JSC)
Jewish Voice for Peace (JVP), 2, 12–14, 36, 166, 174, 204, 252–62, 271
   Finkel, 98
   intergenerational nature of, 15
   Jews of Color Caucus (BIJOCSM), 14, 256
Jewish Workers' Bund, 5, 19, 54, 69, 139, 177–80, 184–5
   "neo-Bundism," 195, 197
   slogan on democracy and socialism, 193
   songs and music, 250, 251
   Trotsky and, 153
   Waskow view, 257
Jews for Racial and Economic Justice (JFREJ), 14, 15, 20, 174, 215, 228, 230
   Kaye/Kantrowitz, 48, 229
   Rajendra, 261
Jews for Urban Justice (JUJ), 74, 75, 257
Jews without Money (Gold), 8, 29–30, 50–1, 63–4
JRC. *See* Jewish Radical Community (JRC)
JSC. *See* Democratic Socialists of America (DSA) Jewish Solidarity Caucus (JSC)
JVP. *See* Jewish Voice for Peace (JVP)

Kafka, Franz, 24
Kahane, Meir, 38, 82–4, 130, 135–6, 160–1, 169, 187–91, 222–3
Kahn, Daniel, 228, 250–1

Kaplan, Amy, 72–3, 112, 211
Katz, Ariana, "Maggid," 254, 255
Katz, Joanna Kent, "Tashlich T'zedek," 254
Katz, Moise, 33
Kaufman, Irving, 113
Kaye/Kantrowitz, Melanie, 15, 18, 208, 214–18, 229, 230
  The Colors of Jews, 256
  "Some Pieces of Jewish Left," 47–9
Kelley, Robin D. G., 9, 53, 279n27
kibbutzim
  Beinin experience with, 95–6
  Buch on, 90–1
  Eanet-Klonsky on, 87
  in fiction, 21, 211
  Gessner on, 40
King, Emily, 223–4
King, Martin Luther, Jr., 78, 84, 180
Kirk, Grayson, 71, 205–6
Klein, Naomi: *Doppelganger*, 22
Kotler-Berkowitz, Laurence, 43–4, 222
Krauss, Nicole, *Great House*, 233, 240–1
Ku Klux Klan, 59, 61, 64, 107, 118, 168–9
Kurshan, Nancy, 97
Kushner, Tony, 244
  Angels in America, 219–20, 223–7, 230, 232, 233, 264

labor unions. *See* unions
Laqueur, Walter, 82, 162, 163
Lazare, Bernard, 41
Lebanon, Israeli 1982 invasion of, 30, 204, 221, 222
Lemlich, Clara, 247, 259
Leon, Abram, 69, 152–3
Lester, Julius, 129, 145
Levin, Meyer, 51
Levins Morales, Aurora, 15, 269–70
Likud Party, 23, 70, 222
Lilith, 162
Linfield, Susie, 146
Lipset, Seymour, 81, 82, 159
Lipsitz, George, 132
Lober, Brooke, 162
Loew, Linda, 94, 123, 146
Long, Breckinridge, 121
Löwy, Michael, 232, 265
Lukács, Georg, 26, 137, 139, 298n51
Lumer, Hyman, 121

"Maggid" (Katz and Grossman), 254, 255

Magid, Shaul, 38, 135–6, 160–1, 166, 187–8, 222–3
  The Necessity of Exile, 22–3
Malcolm X, 90, 123
Mallow, Jeffrey, 178
Mansbach, Adam, *The Golem of Brooklyn*, 241–2
Marcuse, Herbert, 116, 122–3, 138
Marranos and Marranism, 14, 30, 151, 154–5, 156, 264–5
Marx, Karl, 138
  "On the Jewish Question," 10, 135, 150, 248
Marxists and Marxism, 55–6, 85, 119–20, 148–9, 155
  Bensaïd, 151
masculinity
  in fiction, 34, 208–14
  Israel and, 95, 203
  See also effeminacy
Max, Steve, 157–8
McAlister, Melani, 72
McCarthyism. *See* Second Red Scare
Meeropol, Michael, 262, 265
Meeropol, Robert, 262, 265, 269
Meir, Golda, 199
Michels, Tony, 5–6
Midnight, Dori, "Tashlich T'zedek," 254
Miranda, Javier, 249, 258
Mirelowitz, Geoff, 123, 146
Mizrahi Jews. *See* Sephardic and Mizrahi Jews
Moreau, Alberto, 31–2
Morgen Freiheit, 31, 55, 58, 60, 227
  publishing house, 117
Moses, 23–4, 217
Movement for Black Lives, 175, 255–6
The Moving Kings (Cohen), 241, 302–3n44
Moynihan, Daniel Patrick, 60, 135
Mullen, Bill, 53, 268
Murthy, Viren, 148

NAACP. *See* National Association for the Advancement of Colored People (NAACP)
Naison, Mark, 279nn26–7
Nakatsu, Penny, 116
National Association for the Advancement of Colored People (NAACP), 62, 118, 127
Nation of Islam, 90, 163
Native Americans, 65, 119
  genocide, 40, 120

Index

Nazi Party of America, 180–1
The Necessity of Exile (Magid), 22–3
Negative Dialectics (Adorno), 149
neo-Nazis, 180–6, 243
Nepon, Ezra, 194
Nestel, Sheryl, 166–7, 203
Netanyahu, Benjamin ("Bibi"), 23
   fictional family, 233, 234–8
The Netanyahus (Cohen), 233, 234–8
Neudel, Marian, 192–3
New America Movement, 245
The New Antisemitism (Forster and Epstein), 145, 159, 162
The New Earth (Row), 233, 238–40
New Jewish Agenda (NJA), 166, 174, 195, 204, 221, 222
New Masses, 51, 68
New Mobe, 79, 80
New Outlook, 105, 201
New Outlook movement, 36, 171, 198–203
New World Resource Center, Chicago, 182
Nixon, Richard, 120, 169
NJA. *See* New Jewish Agenda (NJA)
"The Non-Jewish Jew" (Deutscher), 14, 30, 72, 77, 145–6, 147
No-State Solution (Boyarin), 24–6, 231–2
Novack, George, 77, 122, 146
Nuremberg Trials, 101, 102

Ocean Hill–Brownsville teachers' strike, 135, 163
October Revolution. *See* Russian Revolution
Omar, Ilhan, 230, 250
Omer, Atalia, 18, 253, 254, 259, 261
Omi, Michael, *Racial Formation in the United States*, 59
"On the Jewish Question" (Marx), 10, 135, 150, 248
Operation Shylock (Roth), 21
Origins of Totalitarianism (Arendt), 103
Orwell, George, 148
Osheroff, Abe, 265, 266–7

Palestine and Palestinians, 11–16, 74, 86–97, 204, 270–1
   in *Angels in America*, 219–20, 225, 226
   Balfour Declaration, 40, 53
   Bensaïd, 153
   BPP, 171
   British mandate, 53
   Buch, 90–1
   Chutzpah, 18, 199–204
   CPUSA, 65
   DSA, 244–6
   Eanet-Klonsky, 12, 86–8, 99
   in fiction, 238–40
   First Intifada, 221, 222
   genocide, 2, 4, 70, 220–1, 260, 261
   Gessner, 40
   Gold, 68, 69
   IBPP, 199
   Israeli Communist Party, 171
   Israeli 2023 war, 1–2, 220–1, 260
   Jewish Currents, 230, 231
   JVP, 13–14, 254, 255
   Plitman, 20
   Said, 23, 26, 154, 216, 217
   SNCC, 88–9
   SWP, 57, 92–3
   "two-state solution," 172, 197, 201–2, 203, 218
   Weiss, 107
   Zellner, 38
   See also Gaza; Palestine Liberation Organization (PLO); West Bank (Palestine)
Palestine Communist Party, 57
Palestine Liberation Organization (PLO), 19, 36, 92, 174, 198
   Chutzpah and, 171, 172, 174, 194, 198, 199–200, 201
   IBPP and, 199
   SNCC support, 12
   SWP and, 91–2
Paley, Grace, 125
Parting Ways: Jewishness and the Critique of Zionism (Butler), 23–4
Passen, Phil, 79–80, 123
Patterson, William, 118
Peekskill riots, 1949, 109–11, 119
Peekskill USA (Fast), 109–11
Perlman, Myron, 17, 74, 136, 167–71, 177
   on Bund, 178
   class-related experience, 191–2
   on first meeting a Jewish Zionist, 195–6
   "a kesher with the left," 155–6, 170
   on trip to Israel and West Bank, 199
   on Weathermen, 195
Philadelphia Community College. *See* Community College of Philadelphia (CCP)
Pianko, Noam, 55–6, 60

PL. *See* Progressive Labor Party (PL)
Plitman, Jacob, 18, 19–20, 22, 227–30
Podhoretz, Norman, 1, 72, 128
Pogrebin, Letty, 162, 187
Poland
    Holocaust survivors, 108
    in plays, 69
    pogroms, 53
    Scherer, 179
    Weiss, 107, 10885
Port Authority Statement, 14, 85, 138–40
Port Huron Statement, 85, 138
Portnoy's Complaint (Roth), 207, 208–12
Postone, Moishe, 148, 155
Pound, Ezra, 266
Preminger, Otto, *Exodus*, 73, 234
Progressive Labor Party (PL), 79, 131–2, 139
Protocols, 20, 101, 228
Puerto Ricans, 56, 61
    Espada, 15, 262–70
    Levins Morales, 15, 269–70
    See also Young Lords Party

race and racialization, 9–14, 29, 53–64, 125–35, 160, 190–1
    in fiction, 239–40, 242
    JVP and, 255–6
    racism, 12, 56, 60, 86–7, 95, 176–7, 188
    white ethnic pride and populism, 160, 190
    See also white flight
Racial Formation in the United States (Omi and Winant), 59
Radical Zionist Alliance (RZA), 161, 197–8
Radosh, Ronald, 3
Rainbow Coalition (Chicago), 164
Rajendra, Dania, 261
Ratskoff, Ben, 102
Reagan, Ronald, 43
Red Scare (ca. 1947–57). *See* Second Red Scare
"Red Sea" (Levins Morales), 269–70
"Reflections on Exile" (Said), 26
refuseniks, 201, 204
Reich, Tova
    The Jewish War, 233
    My Holocaust, 242–3
Resnick, Sid, 113
The Revolution in the Revolution (Debray), 87

Robeson, Paul, Peekskill riots, 109, 110–11, 119
Rogan, Seth, 21
Rogin, Michael, *Black Face, White Noise*, 128
Ro'i, Yaacov, 284n13
Rolfe, Edwin, 265–6, 268
Roosevelt, Franklin, 104, 121
Rosenberg, Ethel, 112, 113, 118–19, 142, 269
    in *Angels in America*, 223–4
Rosenberg, Julius, 112, 113, 118–19, 142, 269
Rosenblum, April, 113, 115
Roth, Philip, 22, 39, 173, 205–14, 263–4
    The Counterlife, 21–2, 212–14, 238
    Goodbye, Columbus, 100
    I Married a Communist, 263
    Operation Shylock, 21
    Plot against America, 244
    Portnoy's Complaint, 207, 208–12, 263
Rothberg, Michael, 103
Row, Jess, *The New Earth*, 233, 238–40
Rubin, Jerry, 97, 98
Rudd, Mark, 2, 71–8, 82, 85, 99–104, 113–17, 124, 138
    on Black Power movement, 131
    family name, 71, 144
    in Grayson Kirk's office, 71–2, 76, 205–6
    on support for Palestinians, 86
    "we were peasant children," 146
Russian Revolution, 149, 152, 158, 179
RZA. *See* Radical Zionist Alliance (RZA)

Said, Edward, 23, 154, 216, 217
    "Reflections on Exile," 26
Saks, Richard, 86, 94
Salaita, Steven, 197
Salazar, Julia, 250
Sand, Shlomo, 24, 231
Satter, Beryl, *Family Properties*, 128
Schappes, Morris, 32, 33, 60, 66
Scherer, Emanuel, 179
Schrecker, Ellen, 43
Schreier, Benjamin, 205
SDS. *See* Students for a Democratic Society (SDS)
Second Red Scare, 112–17, 126
Seidman, Pete, 93, 112–13, 121–2, 145–6
Sephardic and Mizrahi Jews, 15, 30, 31–2, 198–9, 248
    in fiction, 64–5

Index

JVP and JREJ caucuses, 14, 20, 228, 256
Shacham, David, 201, 203
Sharansky, Natan, 253
Sharon, Ariel, 105–7, 109
Shatz, Adam, 146
Silberstein, Lane, 243–4, 246–7, 249
Six-Day War, 72, 74, 79–80, 83, 85, 101, 121–2, 205
Skeist, Robbie, 167, 191, 195
Skokie, Illinois, 180–3
Slabodsky, Santiago, 10–11, 27, 150–1, 256
Slezkine, Yuri, 7, 51–2, 68, 79, 135
Slotkin, Richard, 211
SNCC. *See* Student Nonviolent Coordinating Committee (SNCC)
Socialist Workers Party (SWP), 68, 76, 77, 89–95, 120, 287–8n1
    Allen, 113
    Horowitz, 82
    Loew, 94, 146
    Novack, 146
    Palestine and, 12, 57
    Passen, 79
    Seidman, 112–13, 121–2, 145–6
Socoloff, Miriam, 166, 191, 203
Sonnie, Amy, 163
South African apartheid, 10, 162, 182
Soviet Union, 9, 12, 16, 53, 67–8, 72, 90, 149
    Birobidzhan, 285n26
    JAC, 32
    Jewish emigration, 284–5n15
    Stalin, 90, 149, 284n13
    Wald on, 287n75
Spanish Civil War, 61. *See also* Abraham Lincoln Brigade
Srebrnik, Henry F., 7
Stalin, Joseph, 90, 149, 284n13
Staub, Michael, 74, 147
    Torn at the Roots, 169, 187, 188
Stein, Arlene, 100
strikes, 5, 158, 190
    Bund, 178
    students', 2, 71, 76, 131
    teachers', 135, 163
Student Mobilization Committee ("Mobe"), 79
Student Nonviolent Coordinating Committee (SNCC), 88–90, 129, 134
    James Forman, 161
    ouster of Jewish activists, 74, 129

"The Palestine Problem," 88–9
    Rudd, 99–100
    SDS and, 76
    support of PLO, 12
Students for a Democratic Society (SDS), 2, 12, 42, 76, 77, 84–97, 130–40, 287–8n1
    Black Panthers and, 76, 84, 115–16, 132, 134
    Dick Flacks, 42, 96, 113, 157–8
    Old Mole, 115
    Perlman, 17
    Port Authority Statement, 14, 85–6, 138–40
    Port Huron meeting (1962), 77, 157, 206
    Port Huron Statement, 85, 138
    reunion of 1977, 157–8
    RYM, 86
    socialist collectives and, 104, 165
Sturken, Marita, 258
SWP. *See* Socialist Workers Party (SWP)

"Tashlich T'zedek" (Midnight and Katz), 254
Tenney, Gene, Port Authority Statement, 14, 85–6, 138–40
Tevye's Daughters (Aleichem), 79
Thomas, Zellie, 255
Torn at the Roots (Staub), 187, 188
Torres, Anna Elena, 39
Toscano, Alberto, 116
Tracy, James, 163
Traverso, Enzo, 101, 148
The Tribe of Dina (Kaye/Kantrowitz), 214–15
Trotsky, Leon, 54, 148, 149, 153
Trouillot, Michel-Rolph, 45
Troy, Gil, 253
Trump, Donald, 228, 243, 248–9
Tseng-Putterman, Mark, 101–3
Ture, Kwame. *See* Carmichael, Stokely
"two-state solution," 172, 197, 201–2, 203, 218

unions, 5, 51, 139, 157, 168, 190
United Auto Workers (UAW), 139, 157, 190
United Kingdom. *See* Britain
United Nations
    We Charge Genocide petition, 118
    World Conference on Women (Mexico City, 1975), 162

Uris, Leon, 207
  Exodus, 73, 210–11, 234, 254
US Congress, HUAC, 112–13, 225
USSR. *See* Soviet Union

Valley, Eli, 251
Venceremos Brigade, 167, 195
Verbeeten, David, 77–8
Vials, Chris, 115
Vietnam War, 83–4, 85, 99, 105, *106*, 169, 287–8n1
  JDL, 75
  Jewish Holocaust compared, 104
  Kahane, 161, 169
  Rudd on, 116–17
  teach-ins, 145–6
Vilkomerson, Rebecca, 257, 261

Wald, Alan, 51, 66, 68, 287n75
Wallace, Henry, 210, 212
Ware, Marianne, 115
Warsaw Ghetto Uprising, 68–9, 257
Warsaw Ghetto Uprising Coalition (WGUC), 35, 180–5
Waskow, Arthur, 38, 191, 201
  The Bush Is Burning!, 257
  Freedom Seder (1969), 2, 15, 49, 74, 257
Waxman, Dov, 220–1, 254
Weathermen/Weather Underground Organization (WUO), 76, 99, 116, 117, 131
Weiner, Lee, 167–8
Weinglass, Leonard ("Lenny"), 142
Weiss, Suzanne, 90
  Holocaust to Resistance, 105–9
West Bank (Palestine), 152, 223, 252, 259
  in fiction, 21, 213, 238–42
  Perlman visit, 199
white flight, 128, 175, 180

"whiteness theory," 14
white skin privilege, 62, 75, 93, 132, 133
Williams, Lesley, 256
Williams, Raymond, 47
Winant, Gabriel, 280n44
Winant, Howard, *Racial Formation in the United States*, 59
women's movement, 162
  Combahee River Collective, 164–5
World War II, 126, 177
  Japanese American internment, 116, 282n101
  Warsaw Ghetto Uprising, 68–9
  See also Jewish Holocaust
Wright, Richard, 26
WUO. *See* Weathermen/Weather Underground Organization (WUO)

X, Malcolm. *See* Malcolm X

Yerushalmi, Yosef, *Zakhor*, 43
Yiddish, 41, 56, 177, 277n8
  in *Angels in America*, 224
  Deutscher view, 28
  Kahn, 228, 250–1
  poetry, 8, 19, 27
  songs, 52, 228, 250–1
Yiddish newspaper *Morgen Freiheit*, 31, 55, 58, 60, 227
"Yiddish Song Smuggling" (Kahn), 228
Yippies, 96–7, 130, 140–1, 145, 256
Yishuv, 11, 56–7
Young Lords Party, 137, 161, 164, 168–9, 171, 172, 194
Young Patriots, 164

Zakhor (Yerushalmi), 43
Zandy, Janet, 268
Zellner, Dorothy, 37–8